Missions
in Contexts of
Violence

WILLIAM CAREY
LIBRARY

OTHER TITLES IN THE EMS SERIES:

Missions
in Contexts of
Violence

Keith E. Eitel, ed.

Evangelical Missiological Society Series

Number 15

Cover Design: Elumin Creative

Published by William Carey Library
1605 E. Elizabeth Street
Pasadena, CA 91104
www.WCLBooks.com

William Carey Library is a ministry of the
U.S. Center for World Mission, Pasadena, CA
www.uscwm.org

Printed in the United States of America

Library of Congress Cataloging-in-Publication Data

Missions in contexts of violence / edited by Keith E. Eitel.
    p. cm. – (Evangelical Missiological Society series ; no. 15)
    ISBN 978-0-87808-389-3
    1. Missions. 2. Violence--Religious aspects–Christianity. I. Eitel,
Keith Eugene, 1954-
    BV2063.M567 2007
    266--dc22

                                    2007032174

BV
2063
.M567
2007

"God is our refuge and strength, an ever-present help in trouble. Therefore we will not fear, though the earth give way and the mountains fall into the heart of the sea, though its waters roar and foam and the mountains quake with their surging."

Psalm 46:1-3 NIV

Contents

Missions in Contexts of Violence

General Reflections on Missions in Contexts of Violence

Biblical and Theological Foundations for Engaging in Contexts of Violence

Lifestyles, Strategies, and Practices in Contexts of Violence

Area or Thematic Specific Studies of Contexts of Violence

Editorial Note: The reader is advised that each article is comprised of the individual author's work. Some authors used pseudonyms for security reasons. Each writer documents the facts and details of their line of argumentation using their individual research technique. It has been reviewed for clarity, consistency, and completeness but the substance, content, and documentation have been generally left intact. The opinions reflected herein are those of the writers of each article.

Foreword

Missions in Contexts of Violence

Keith E. Eitel

It was a simple letter that Karen Watson wrote about a year before it was needed. She handed it to her pastor in Bakersfield, California just prior to departing for Iraq to serve as an international missionary for the Southern Baptist Convention. Her statement to him at that time was, "I hope you'll never need this but put it in a safe place in the event that I don't return." The pastor placed it in the church safe and promptly forgot about it until that day months later. That day did come; it was March 15, 2004 in the city of Mosul. Five SBC missionaries were ambushed while driving in the city. A nefarious person murdered four of them. Karen was one of those that died.

The letter she left behind is profoundly illustrative of the motivations and convictions that many like her down through the centuries have possessed. They each have wished to follow Christ, even if it means paying the ultimate price. While terrorists strike the world with fear that others may die; Karen and her colleagues were willing to die that others might know Christ and through Him have life abundant. The letter described Karen's understanding of the heart of a missionary, one that is resigned to God's will whatever it may be:

The Missionary Heart
Cares more than some think is wise.
Risks more than some think is safe.
Dreams more than some think is practical.
Expects more than some think is possible.

She continued with a summary of her sentiments: "I was called not to comfort or success but to obedience."

So God called her home that day. The life she lived seems cut short from an earthly point of view. It was just at the perfect time from a heavenly vantage point. Perhaps that is how to explain those like Karen who are called to demonstrate their faith so poignantly. They have resolved to live this life solely in view of the next.

This volume deals with the contexts of violence. In an age of increasing concern for this type of missionary work, the missions community needs to hear from those that have reflected on the multifaceted elements involved in understanding the phenomenon of martyrdom-persecution-violence as it relates to telling the age old Gospel story. The place to begin is with Biblical and theological analyses followed by the grounding provided by constructing consequent lifestyles, strategies, and practices in physically risky settings. Finally, insights from the live settings of violence are warranted.

Special thanks are due numerous people for the production of this volume. First and foremost those who have lived the lives and suffered the deaths described herein are to be thank for living so well. Next, there are several staff members at Southwestern Baptist Theological Seminary that deserve special recognition: Jennifer Wiese, Arthur B. Savage, Mandy M. Moots, and two others whose names I cannot use due to the simple fact that they live now or will return to work in sensitive zones. To those unnamed, and to thousands of others like them, a special thanks is due because they serve with unrecognized honor. May the joy of the Lord Jesus Christ be evident in and through their lives, and verbal witness, wherever they serve.

Keith E. Eitel is the Dean of the Roy Fish School of Evangelism and Missions at Southwestern Baptist Theological Seminary in Fort Worth, TX.

Author Profiles

E. Paul Balisky and Lila W. Balisky serve in Ethiopia with an emphasis on theological education. Paul teaches at both the Evangelical Theological College (ETC) and the Ethiopian Graduate School of Theology (EGST) in the areas of Ethiopian and African church history. Lila works with women's ministries and teaches informally. Both are presently involved in the Dictionary of African Christian Biography (DACB) project.

James Butare-Kiyovu is the associate professor of applied linguistics at William Carey International University (WCIU). He was born in Tutsi, Rwanda in 1947, but in 1959 fled with his family to Uganda as refugees. In 1992 he began working as the director of the Rwandese Patriotic Front (RPF) in Brussels, Belgium. Before WCIU, he served in the Global Research Institute at Fuller.

How Chuang Chua has served as a missionary with his wife since 1998 with OMF International. They served as church planters in the city of Sapporo, Japan for four years until 2002 and will resume missionary service in Japan in 2007.

Stephen M. Clinton is the president of the Orlando Institute, where he also serves as a professor of religion and philosophy. He is also the director of the International Leadership Council, serves on the board of directors (interim director) for Vision Orlando, and is the program director of the doctor of education program for the Universidad Ibero-Americana de Liderazo. He and his wife served thirty-five years with Campus Crusade.

Karen Fancher is the dean of students at Multnomah Bible College and Seminary. She served as a missionary in Resistencia, Argentina, where she helped establish a Christian school, working as the Bible teacher and counselor in the school, as well as participating in local church ministries. She holds masters degrees in Bible and counseling.

D.M. Kinoti is a Ph.D. student at Fuller Theological Seminary, where he is researching how churches in Los Angeles are teaching peace-building skills among interethnic youth groups. His passion is to help the Church be more involved in peace-building efforts among people groups.

Chris Lindley is an instructor in intercultural studies at the William Carey International University.

J. D. Payne is the assistant professor of church planting and evangelism and the director of the Church Planting Center at Southern Baptist Theological Seminary. Prior to joining the Southern faculty, he was an assistant professor at Crossroads Bible College in Indianapolis.

J. Nelson Jennings is the associate professor of world mission at Covenant Theological Seminary. He served in Japan with the PCA's Mission to the World as a church planter and assistant professor of international Christian studies at Tokyo Christian University. He is currently president of Presbyterian Mission International (PMI).

Tony Maalouf is the associate professor of missions and assistant dean at Southwestern Baptist Theological Seminary in Fort Worth. He has served as assistant academic dean and professor of biblical studies at Jordan Evangelical Theological Seminary in Amman, Jordan, and as an adjunct professor at the Arab Baptist Theological Seminary in Beirut, Lebanon. He teaches and speaks throughout the Middle East and works on developing theological literature for Christians in the Arab world.

John Moldovan is the associate dean for doctoral programs, associate professor of evangelism and intercultural studies and George W. Bottoms chair of missions at Southwestern Baptist Theological Seminary in Fort Worth. He is a native of Romania, where he served in various ministries from 1969-1980—years of heightened persecution—and survived Communist imprisonment..

Robert Reese is the director of the World Mission Resource Centre, World Mission Associates, Lancaster, PA. He and his family served as missionaries with Zimbabwe Christian Mission in Central Africa from 1981 to 2002.

Nik Ripken (pseudonym) is a missionary, speaker and writer who has focused on persecuted regions of the globe and has been involved with ministry to Muslims for many years.

David W. Shenk was raised in a Christian missionary home in Tanzania. For ten years he was involved in educational work in Islamic Somalia and lectured in comparative religion and church history at Kenyatta University, Nairobi. Since 1980, Shenk has been based at Eastern Mennonite Missions (EMM) headquarters, Salunga, PA, where he helps coordinate interfaith commitments.

Marti Smith is the managing editor and resource reviews editor for Caleb Project, where she trains and supports the various research teams. She co-authored *Praying Through the Window III - The Unreached People*s and has contributed to many of Caleb Project's resources and publications. She is also author of *Through Her Eyes*, a book about the lives of missionary women in the Muslim world.

Barry Stricker is currently pastor of Huron Shores Fellowship in Michigan. For the past thirteen years, Barry served as pastor of Tiburon Baptist Church in California. During that time, he traveled extensively and prepared and led a number of mission teams.

David K. Strong is a professor of missiology and Bible at Simpson College and Graduate School.

Charles L. Tieszen is a Ph.D. candidate at the University of Birmingham, U.K. He and his wife currently live in the United Kingdom and spend most of their time doing research at the Center for the Study of Islam and Christian-Muslim Relations at the University of Birmingham.

Molly M. Wall is the assistant professor of education at William Carey International University.

Enoch Wan is a professor of intercultural studies and the chairman of the division of intercultural studies at Western Seminary. He has served on the faculty of the Canadian Theological Seminary and Reformed Theological Seminary. He is currently serving as a board member of Great Commission International, Message Inc., and China Academic Consortium. He is the executive vice president of the Evangelical Missiological Society.

Ralph Winter is founder of the U.S. Center for World Mission, William Carey International University, the American Society of Missiology, International Society for Frontier Missions and other mission organizations. In 1979, he founded and continues to edit *Mission Frontiers*, the bulletin of the U.S. Center for World Mission.

Dale Wolyniak has served the past several years in the area of member care with Morningstar Star Development, an agency committed to helping the people of Afghanistan rebuild their country and their lives by offering practical hope and resources.

General Reflections on

Missions in Contexts of Violence

Chapter One

Three Journeys:
Jesus—Constantine—Muhammad

David W. Shenk

I am editing this presentation in Chisinau, Moldova, at the conclusion of two weeks teaching courses on Islam and the Christian faith; most of the students are from Central Asia, and most from Muslim background. In discussions with these students I hear comments like this:

> Some of our Muslim neighbors in Central Asia are disturbed about the recent wars in our regions. These wars seem to them to be Christian wars against Muslims. Furthermore, some American Christian leaders have said some unkind and critical things about Islam. These statements are broadly publicized in our countries. Sometimes the anger of our Muslim neighbors about these matters turns into hate against our churches.

Shortly after 9/11, I asked Mark Oxbrow, a missions director with the Church Missions Society of the Church of England, "What do you say in churches in the United Kingdom when you are asked to speak on the Christian faith and Islam?" Mark responded, "I speak about three different journeys for peace: Jesus, Constantine, and Muhammad. Those different journeys are options for each of us, and each of us needs to choose which one we will take."

Just as is true of British Christians, followers of Jesus in North America and around the world are faced with the option of these three different journeys for peace. Bishop Kenneth Cragg, who has invested many years in the Middle East and is a reputable scholar of Islam, occasionally reminds both Muslims and Christians of the theological significance of two journeys: Jesus from Galilee to Jerusalem and Muhammad from Mecca to Medina. Mark Oxbrow reminds his audiences of a third journey as well, that of Constantine to Rome that laid the foundations for Christendom. [1]

The Journey of Jesus to Jerusalem

Jesus was at the height of his popularity in Galilee after feeding the five thousand men plus women and children by blessing and breaking five loaves of bread and two fish. The Galileans were impressed, and attempted to make him their king "by force" (John 6:15). Surely an army of Zealot independence fighters would have joined forces with Jesus to gain independence from the Romans, and then from the Galilee beachhead they could expand the Kingdom of God throughout Israel and eventually throughout the earth. Jesus resisted that invitation and from that time onward he "resolutely set out for Jerusalem" (Luke 9:51). In the following weeks Jesus tried to make his disciples aware that in Jerusalem the authorities will arrest the Son of Man and ". . . mock him, insult him, spit on him, and kill him. On the third day he will rise again" (Matthew 18:32–3).

By this time the disciples were convinced that Jesus was the promised Messiah. They could not fathom that an arrest and death were possibilities for the Messiah. Peter, representing the convictions of all the disciples, rebuked Jesus for such notions, and Jesus responded very sharply, "Get behind me Satan! You are a stumbling block to me; you do not have in mind the things of God, but the things of men" (Matthew 16:23).

Finally, as Jesus approached Jerusalem, he mounted a colt. Jubilant children singing hosannas accompanied him. Yet as he came over the crest of the Mount of Olives and saw the city before him, he stopped his colt and wept, because Jerusalem would not receive "what would bring you peace" (Luke 19:41). Then with the children still singing, he and the youngsters entered the temple and cleansed it of the merchants who were corrupting the whole system with their exploitative practices.

All of this is tremendously significant as it relates to the mission of Jesus and the nature of the Kingdom of God. In that colt ride he was proclaiming the fulfillment of two biblical prophesies in regard to the messianic kingdom.

First, he was fulfilling Zechariah's prophecy of five centuries earlier. Most frequently we read only the introduction to the prophecy and miss the universal, peacemaking, nonviolent, and voluntary messianic rule that Jesus was announcing when he rode that colt into Jerusalem.

> Rejoice greatly, O Daughter of Zion! Shout, Daughter of Jerusalem! See your king comes to you, righteous and having salvation, gentle and riding on a donkey, on a colt the foal of a donkey. I will take away the chariots from Ephraim and the war-horses from Jerusalem, and the battle bow will be broken. He will proclaim peace to the nations. His rule will extend from sea to sea and from the River to the ends of the earth (Zechariah 9:9–10).

A second observation is that Jesus was announcing that he was fulfilling Ezekiel's prophecy that the radiant glory of God would enter Jerusalem from the East, fill the temple with the glory of God, and cleanse the temple of all corruption forever (Ezekiel 43:1–9). The contemporary British theologian, N. T. Wright, develops this theme. In regards to Jesus' entrance into Jerusalem and his encounter in the temple, Wright comments:

> Jesus of Nazareth was conscious of a vocation, given him by the one he knew as, "father," to enact in himself what in Israel's scriptures, God had promised to accomplish all by himself. He would be the pillar of cloud and fire for the people of the new exodus. He would embody in himself the returning and redeeming action of the covenant God.[2]

How, then, does Jesus establish the kingdom that he is inaugurating? First, he went into the temple and drove those who exploited the poor from the temple precincts. In the confrontation he also made it known that the temple of stone was needed no more. He was the new temple; later the apostles proclaimed that the church as the body of

Christ was the temple. "Place" was not necessary in the kingdom Jesus was establishing. The "place" of the kingdom was wherever Christ was welcomed.

Second, during his last meal with his disciples, Christ washed the feet of his betrayer! Consider the significance of the moment. The One who is the radiant glory of God who created the fifty billion galaxies in space washes the feet of his betrayer!

Third, as Jesus the Christ is dying on the cross he cries out in forgiveness of those who have crucified him. This is God in Christ seeking to embrace the world in his reconciling invitation. In that suffering embrace, we are reconciled to God and to one another and with all of creation; in that embrace the kingdom of God breaks into human experience.

Fourth, after his resurrection he appeared to the disciples several times. John described an appearance where Jesus showed the disciples the nail prints in his hands and the wound from the spear thrust into his side. Then he said to them, "Peace be with you! As the Father has sent me, I am sending you. . . . Receive the Holy Spirit" (John 20:21–22). In that same commissioning he proclaimed the forgiveness of sins!

Within several weeks the Holy Spirit came upon the gathering of disciples, and from that time onward the apostolic church believed that the journey of Jesus from Galilee to the cross in Jerusalem is the way of the kingdom of God. These first Christians believed that in Jesus crucified the God of all creation suffers for us and because of us. He identified fully with the suffering of all humanity, and especially with the outcasts and powerless; he was crucified between two thieves. He suffered a "cursed death "hung on a tree" (Galatians 3:13) outside the centers of power; he died in disgrace at Golgotha "outside the camp" (Hebrews 13:13). This one who is crucified with the outcastes stripped of all earthly power is in fact the full in history presence and revelation of the power of God. Christ crucified and risen is the power center of the universe; he is the Lamb slain who stands in the center of the throne of God (Revelation 5:6)! In his redemptive sacrifice Christ forgives and redeems people from "every tribe and language and people and nation" (Revelation 5: 9). Christ crucified—the power of God (1 Corinthians 1:23, 24)!

For the apostolic church, all kingdom ethics were grounded in the reality that in Christ crucified, God revealed himself as our Suffering Servant. Jesus proclaimed, "A new command I give you: Love one another. As I have loved you, so you must love one another." (John 13:34) The Apostle Paul wrote, "Your attitude should be the same as that of Christ Jesus. . . who. . . made himself nothing, taking the very nature of a servant. . . he humbled himself and became obedient to death—even death on a cross" (Philippians 2:5, 8).

With remarkable consistency, for the next three centuries the church insisted that a cross-centered ethic meant that the Christian as a disciple of Jesus could not take arms. This was a costly commitment, for the church was a minority movement often persecuted for refusing to venerate the emperor. Yet the church confessed that Jesus is Lord—therefore, disciples of Jesus could not venerate the emperor or participate in practices that were in variance with the way of the Lord Jesus Christ. This meant that Christians would not participate in sacrifices to the spirit of the emperor and they would not participate in the imperial military. Origen, who was one of the early pioneers in developing the Alexandrian Catechetical School, was a forceful yet typical voice insisting that Christians desist from any participation in warfare and informing the governing authorities on the commitments of the church.

Origen wrote, "No longer do we take the sword against any nation, nor do we learn war any more, since we have become sons of peace through Jesus who is our author. . . "[3]

Celsus was a scathing critic of the church and accused the church of abandoning the responsibilities of patriotic citizenship. To this charge Origen responded, 'Even more do we fight on behalf of the emperor. And though we do not become fellow-soldiers with him, even if he presses for this, yet we are fighting of him and composing a special army of piety through our intercessions to God."[4]

Remarkably, the early church thrived without the benefit of political support. It was a minority movement on the margins; yet the crucified and risen Christ it proclaimed was powerfully attractive.

The Journey of Constantine to Rome

However, the church's commitment to a cross-centered kingdom commitment began to undergo a dramatic transformation when Constantine gained the Roman imperial throne. For months, Constantine had been engaged in a long march from Britain south to Rome, where he knew he would meet in battle his rival to imperial power and his enemy, Maxentius. Constantine commanded only 40,000 troops. Maxentius had the full force of the garrison in Rome at his command. Where could Constantine acquire adequate power for the military engagement ahead? Perhaps the divine sun? So Constantine turned to the sun in worship, a commitment that he never fully abandoned.

Then on the eve of battle on the outskirts of Rome, Constantine allegedly saw the sign of the cross in the sky with the words beneath that cross: *In hoc signo vinces* (under this sign conquer). He took that as an omen and painted the *chi rho* sign of Christ crucified on his weapons of war.[5] The next day the battle with Maxentius was joined, and Constantine won a decisive victory. He went on to become emperor of the Western empire and Licinius emperor of the Eastern empire. Licinius in his wars in the East also reported on a message from God. Every night an angel appeared instructing him to pray to the Summus Deus.[6] He encouraged his troops to do likewise.

Within a year of Constantine's victory, he and Licinius issued the Edict of Milan (313 A.D.), which assured religious freedom throughout the Roman Empire, not only for Christians, but for all religions. Letters were sent throughout the empire proclaiming, "Everyone who has a common desire to observe the Christian worship may now freely and unconditionally endeavor to do so without let or hindrance. . . . To others also freedom of their own worship is likewise left open and freely granted."[7]

The churches rejoiced in the new freedom. Yet the vision quickly developed into far more than that of a pluralist society with benevolent government assuring the freedom of worship to all. Constantine tilted the western empire towards favoring the church. The church historian, Eusebius, was ecstatic when Constantine ordered Bibles to be made available for leaders in his seat of government in Constantinople. Eusebius believed that a Christian civilization was now a possibility. This civilization would unite political and ecclesial authority and power.

Eusebius wrote, "There were a multitude of rulers before the coming of Christ. All nations were governed by different tyrannies and democracies and men had no intercourse with each other. . . nation rose against nations and city against city. . . "[8] However, in the mind of Eusebius, Christ and Augustus were co-rulers whose mission was to bring order, as well as peace. W. H. C. Frend observes, "Mankind was moving forward towards a universal monarch under one Church, and Constantine was God's chosen instrument, the reflection of his divine power."[9]

The Constantinian cross used as a weapon for violence against the enemy is not the cross of the one who proclaimed forgiveness for his enemies as he died absorbing their taunting violence. The cross within a theology of Caesaropapism (the coming together of papal authority and the power of Caesar) was a symbol of sacramentally effectuated grace, not a revelation of normative Christian ethics or the cross of the God who is our Suffering Servant, of the God who reaches out to us in forgiveness and redemptive love even as our sins crash upon his broken body, the cross of the One who has taken our place and in whom we are forgiven.

The implications were astounding and transformational for the church that had experienced three centuries of intermittent persecution, and which was always on the periphery of social and political norms. With astounding rapidity the church was seated with empire at the centers of power. Nowhere was that more evident than in the Council of Nicea (325 A.D.), where the unbaptized Constantine presided over a council of bishops to determine Christological and Trinitarian doctrine. Not only did Constantine preside at the opening sessions, but he also implemented instruments of force to impose the decisions made at Nicea on recalcitrant churches, as for example the Donatists of North Africa.

For the ecclesial authorities, the preservation of the truth of the Gospel required temporal power. It is not surprising that before long the church joined hands with the political order to use "fire and steel"[10] to confront evil, such as the pagans who were outside the reach of the church. The imperial sword and the mission of Christ were merged.

To help the individual Christian as well as the Christian political authorities discern how to live in a world of conflict and war, Augustine developed a just war ethic. If a Christian nation had to fight, the bottom line was that the war had to be just and that there were no other alternatives. These principles of just war have been further refined, but Augustine borrowing from the wisdom of some of the Greek political philosophers has had significant influence on Western Christian understandings of just war.

The implications of this kind of politico-ethical transformation were devastating for the churches in the East. For the first three centuries of the Christian era, it was mostly the churches in the West that were persecuted. However, with the emergence of caesaropapacy in the West, it was the churches in the East that began to experience the wrath of the persecutors. Under Constantine, Christianity in the West had become transformed into the religion of western empire. Peace had come to the western church, as Bishop Mar Jacob of Edessa wrote, ". . . Constantine, the chief of victors, reigns and now the Cross the emperor's diadem surmounts." [11] This legacy provided the paradigm for what became known as the Holy Roman Empire, and later as Western Christendom.

For the church in Persia developments in the Western church became the sentence of death. The Roman Empire and Persia had engaged in several centuries of conflict. Another war was pending when Constantine wrote to the Shah of Persia, Shapur II, "I rejoice to hear that the fairest provinces of Persia are adorned with. . . Christians. . . Since you are so powerful and pious, I commend them to your care, and leave them in your protection."[12]

For the Shah, this letter meant only one thing; the Christians were a fifth column representing Rome by sabotaging Zoroastrian Persia from within. Twenty years later, Constantine massed his troops for war against Persia with bishops accompanying his armies. According to Eusebius, they accompanied Constantine "to battle with him and for him by the prayers to God from whom all victory proceeds."[13]

The rage of the Persians against the Christians knew no boundaries. For more than twenty years the Christians were systematically hunted from one end of the empire to the other, tortured and killed. The Persian Church was nearly eradicated by this, "The Great Persecution." It has never recovered from that blow. Ever since Constantine, the church in the East has sought to make it clear that it is not beholden to the church in the West. Constantine and the development of the "Holy Roman Empire" and later "Christendom" have made it necessary for churches of the East to become alternatives to the Western church. Sometimes this need to preserve some distance from the Western church has pushed the Eastern church into directions that the Western church considered to be "heretical," e.g., Nestorianism.[14]

These alternative definitions were also expressed in a thousand years of Eastern missionary outreach across Central Asia into China; it is a remarkable story how these minority churches that had no imperial support reached out in mission across Asia.[15] This was quite different than the church in the West where the mission of the church was expressed in concert with imperial and military conquest.

The Constantinian transformation in the Western church contributed to the opening for Islam in the East. This is because the persecutions in Persia decimated the church. It also meant that the churches of the East had to distance themselves from the churches of the West. One way they did this was by defining their theology as an alternative to that of the West. The Dutch historian of religion, Arend Theodoor van Leeuwen, insists that this redefinition has been most persuasively expressed by Islam for "Islamic power... offered to anti-Byzantine sentiment a far more effective ideology than anything that heretical Christianity was able to provide."[16]

We should ponder. Are there themes within the American church today that are similar to those of the Constantinian era? How does the perceived alliance of the American evangelical churches with the American international agenda affect the vulnerable churches in Muslim lands?

These questions confronted me profoundly when I was engaged in several days of dialogue with a Muslim theologian in Germany, after I had presented the journey of Jesus to the cross as the way of peace. She turned to me and with anger exclaimed, "This is the first time I have ever heard that the cross has anything to do with peace. Our Muslim perception is that the cross is a symbol of violence and that the Christian movement is a violent religion. I found myself weeping as I asked her forgiveness for the sins of the church in distorting the cross and the Gospel so tragically.

After a break she took the floor and thanked me for my tears of repentance. Then she said, "I have never before experienced a Christian asking forgiveness for the sins of the Church against us Muslims. Your confession has opened my eyes to a Jesus I never knew was there, and I have been transformed."

We now explore another journey that birthed an alternative vision of religion and territoriality, that of the Muslims.

The Journey of Muhammad to Medina

Six centuries after Christ, and three centuries after Constantine, the unlettered Muhammad began preaching in Mecca in Arabia, among a people who were on the periphery of civilization and power. For twelve years he proclaimed portions of the Qur'an as they came to him. He warned the Meccans to leave their polytheistic worship and evil practices. He preached a message of hope for the poor and compassion for the dispossessed.

Very few Meccans accepted Muhammad's message, for he challenged the entrenched networks of polytheism that supported the political and economic structures of Arabian society. However, hope for the Muslim movement came from Medina; emissaries invited him to come to their city and become their prophet and statesman—the same invitation that Jesus had received from the Galileans six centuries earlier. Muhammad accepted the invitation believing that this was a sign of favor from God.

This migration to Medina is the *hijrah*, which took place in 622 A.D. It is significant that this event is the beginning of the Muslim era—not the birth of Muhammad in 570 or the advent of revelations in 610. The *hijrah* is most significant theologically for this event enabled Muhammad to gain political and military control of a region. With those instruments of power he and his followers established the *dar al Islam*, the region under Muslim political control. This accomplishment was evidence indeed that Muhammad was a prophet of God and the thriving Muslim community had God's favor.

In Medina a constitution was developed that in later centuries formed the nucleus for full fledged Muslim systems of law known as the *Shari' a*. The goal of the Medina constitution was to include all minorities within a covenant of cooperation with the Muslims. The Muslims were tremendously disappointed when some minority communities resisted inclusion in the Muslim led covenant. Subsequently, these dissidents, who were perceived to be a threat to the Muslim community, were dealt with as traitors. Judgment included banishment or death.

Battles ensued between the Meccans and the Muslim armies; the Muslims were victorious, and within ten years a triumphant army of ten thousand Muslim soldiers were peacefully received by the Meccans who had been defeated on the battle field. The Muslims then cleansed the Ka'bah of its idolatries, and Mecca became a Muslim city.

As Muhammad led the Muslim forces into the city of Mecca he exclaimed, "Truth had come, and falsehood hath vanished away" (Qur'an 17:81).
In Medina, Muhammad became both prophet and statesman. With the mechanisms of political power he established the embryonic *dar al Islam*. Wherever *dar al Islam* was established, Christian, Jewish, or Zoroastrian communities were circumscribed a *dhimmi*, protected

communities. They were assured peace providing they functioned within the parameters established by the Muslim state. This included paying a special tax. Regions outside the *dar al Islam* were the *dar al harb*, or regions of war not yet brought under the control of Muslim authorities.

Kenneth Cragg observes, *"Dar Al-Islam* and *Dar Al-Harb* is a fundamental distinction running through all humanity; the household of submission to God and the household of non-Islam still to be brought into such submission."* [17]

Muhammad left the suffering of Mecca for Medina, and later returned to Mecca as victor. This pattern is normative. Defeat for the faithful Muslim *ummah* is a theological anomaly, for God is all powerful and sovereign. Tactical retreat might be necessary, but in time the *dar al Islam* of the Muslims must prevail.

Although Muslims are not to initiate aggression, if the *ummah* is under threat, then the defense of the *ummah* is mandated by any means necessary. This is *jihad,* a three dimensional striving in the defense of Islam (1) within ones soul, (2) with the pen, and (3) with the sword when necessary.

The Qur'an commands, "Fight in the way of Allah against those who fight against you. . . . And fight them until persecution is no more, and religion is for Allah. But if they desist, then let there be no hostility except against wrongdoers" (Qur'an 2:190–193).

The *ummah* will persuade and even seek to induce non Muslims to convert, but are prohibited from using coercion to convert anyone. The Qur'an declares, "There is no compulsion in religion. The right direction is henceforth distinct from error" (Qur'an 2:256).

Within a century of the *hijrah*, the *dar al Islam* had extended its political authority from the Indus River, throughout the Middle East, across North Africa, and into Spain. On the western European front the advance was stopped in the Battle of Tours (732 A.D.), just over a century after the *hijrah*. Half of the Christian population on earth had come under the authority of the Muslim *dar al Islam*. These churches across North Africa and the Middle East were circumscribed as *dhimmi*. Within all these regions within the *dar al Islam* the primary function of the political system was protection of the integrity of the Muslim *ummah*.[18] Ideally, the churches and Jewish communities were protected as long as they did not threaten the integrity of the *ummah*. Of course, this meant that Muslim political, community and family systems cooperated to assure that conversions could go only one direction—toward the *ummah* and never away from Islam.

In modern times, the *dar al Islam* vision of Muslim territoriality *vis a vis* the *dar al harb* persists with considerable resiliency. This is the reason that American military bases in Saudi Arabia in the wake of the Gulf War of 1991 became so tendentious, apparently contributing to the decisions by militant *jihadists* to initiate the tragedy of 9/11. For the *jihadists* it is self evident that for regions of the *dar al harb* to place military forces within the soul of the territoriality of the *dar al Islam* is theologically untenable and must be rectified by any means necessary.

However, there are also significant countervailing forces. It is exceedingly significant that at the beginning of the twenty-first century one fourth of all Muslims live in regions that are not within the suzerainty of Muslim authority. This is a tremendous transformation—even a century ago is was exceptional for non Muslims to reside outside the parameters of Muslim authority. Even the western colonial powers generally respected the authority of the Muslim jurists in regions under western colonial administration. However, there are now 300 million Muslims living outside the parameters of Muslim authority and whose neighbors are Hindus, Christians, atheists, or Buddhists. Notions of a monolithic idealized *dar al Islam* is diluted by the realities of modern mobility and globalization. The vision for a *dar al Islam* and Muslim diaspora are often in tension.

Christendom and the *Dar al Islam*

There are parallels between the theologies of territoriality within a Christendom world view and that of the *dar al Islam*. In

Christendom the world is divided into two regions—the civilized regions that are ruled by Christianized governments and the uncivilized regions that are ruled by other kinds of governments. In the *dar al Islam* the world is also divided into two—the regions of peace under Muslim rule and those regions of war not yet brought under Muslim rule.

Christendom fights just wars; the *dar al Islam* fights jihads. Christendom seeks to extend territory—in modern times the United States has frequently taken up a secularized version of this agenda through it vision of manifest destiny—extending the gift of democracy and free enterprise into regions not yet democratized. The *dar al Islam* likewise from time to time has fought wars to extend the blessings of Islam into non-Islamized societies. Both movements have occasionally merged their missionary impulse with imperialist nationalist goals. Both movements have sometimes viewed war as a means to extend territorial influence and to provide opportunities to extend the faith.

These themes suggest convergences between the political theology of the Muslim *dar al Islam* and the Constantinian Western church. Both systems viewed their faith communities and the kingdom of God as identical to political control of territory. These convergences have provided ample grist for territorial conflict right from the beginning of the Muslim movement. Today the conflict is intensifying in the clash between Islamic theocratic systems and the secular democratic systems of the West. Samuel Huttington's *Clash of Civilizations* is remarkably relevant.

So What?

The confrontation between Islam and the West is not trivial. Both movements are moving to the edge of the precipice. In these times the West is largely incapable of engaging Islam at the spiritual level, for Islam is a profoundly spiritual and scriptural movement. Too often, the church has also squandered its spiritual birthright and is incapable of addressing the conflict at a spiritual and scriptural basis. Yet, a New Testament vision of the church as a community committed to the way of the cross that Jesus reveals, is healing for the nations, and healing for our times. This was my profound impression when participating in a Muslim Shi'ite-Anabaptist dialogue with Iranian theologians, a dialogue sanctioned by the Guardian Council in Iran.

A significant dimension of these conversations took place in Toronto in the fall of 2003 with a follow-up in Qom, Iran, February, 2004. Anabaptists have miniscule political power. Yet the Islamic theological establishment in Qom, Iran, invited the conversation.[19] However, the journey in dialogue and witness is fraught with challenges. "Do not humiliate us," a mullah in Qom, Iran, advised me when I asked what his counsel is to North American Christians.

Another observed that Jesus would also have taken the same path that Muhammad took in Medina, if he had an opportunity. His public ministry lasted only three years! Given more time, Jesus would also have commanded an army! "But thanks be to God," the mullah exclaimed, "Constantine brought to conclusion what Jesus could not do, for Constantine, like Muhammed, united the political and religious order."

Indeed, the New Testament vision of the Kingdom of God is radically different than the understandings of these Shi'ite Muslim clerics! Yet they listened! They engaged. We based our dialogue on the Scriptures—supremely the New Testament for us—a Christ-centered dialogue.

Others commented that never before have they spoken with Christians about faith in serious open dialogue. This is significant.
Yet, even more significant are the hundreds and thousands of friendships that Christians meeting Muslims are developing in neighbor-to-neighbor relationships, whether in North America or regions around the world.

Surely all followers of Jesus are called of God to transcend territorial divisions and in the spirit of Christ serve in ways that enable wider and wider circles of Christians and Muslims to meet one another. Every Christian needs a Muslim friend! I also wish that every Muslim had a Christian friend. And friends never kill each other!

Notes

1. I presented the main themes of this paper in a dialogue in Indonesia. The theme was peacemaking in Islam and the Christian faith. The Muslim presenter was Rahmawati Hussein from the Universitas Muhamadiah Yogyakarta. The venue of the dialogue was at the Universitas Hristen Satya Wacana, Salatiga. The sponsors decided to have the presentation published in the *Journal WASKITA, A Journal on Religion and Society*. By permission of the Journal WASKITA, I adapted that presentation for an essay in a compendium, *Anabaptists Meeting Muslims*, Herald Press. This essay is an abbreviation and adaptation of those two presentations. This essay is presented with permission from Herald Press.

2. N. T. Wright, *The Challenge of Jesus, Rediscovering Who Jesus Was and Is* (Downers Grove: Intervarsity Press, 1999), 123.

3. Jean-Michel Hornus, It is not Lawful for me to Fight: Early Christian Attitudes toward War, Violence, and the State (Revised Edition) (Scottdale: Herald Press, 1980), 86–7, from Origen, Contra Celsum, V., 33.

4. Hornus, 160, from Origen, *Contra Celsum*, 8:73.

5. W. H. C. Frend, *The Early Church* (London: Hodder and Stoughton, 1971), 136–7.

6. Ibid., 313.

7. J. W. C. Wand, *A Hhistory of the Early Church to A. D. 500* (London: Methuen & Co. Ltd., 1965), 128.

8. *Demonstratio Evangelica* vii, 2 as quoted in Frend, 138.

9. Frend, 138.

10. Firmicus Maternus, *The Error of the Pagan Religions* (New York: Newman Press, 1970), 77–8.

11. "Oration on Habib the Martyr," in *Cureton, Ancient Syriac Documents, 95* as quoted in Samuel Hugh Moffett, *A History of Christianity in Asia*, Volume 1 (Maryknoll: Orbis Books, 1988), 138.

12. Theodoret, *Ecclesiastical History* 1, 24, quoted in Moffett, 144.

13. Eusebius, *Life of Constantine*, 4:56, quoted in Moffett, 138.

14. Arend Theodoor van Leeuwen, *Christianity in World History, The Meeting of Faiths East and West* (New York: Charles Scribner's Sons, 1964), 210.

15. Moffett, 288–323.

16. Ibid., 211.

17. Kenneth Cragg, *The Call of the Minaret* (Maryknoll: Orbis Books, 1985), 189.
18. Bernard Lewis, *The Political Language of Islam* (Chicago: Chicago University Press, 1988), 29.
19. "The Challenge of Modernity: Shi'ah Muslim—Mennonite Christian Dialogue," *The Conrad Grebel Review,* Volume 21, Number 3, Fall 2003 (Waterloo: Conrad Grebel University College), 2–111.

Chapter Two

Christian Mission and "Glocal" Violence in 2006 A.D. / 1427 H.

J. Nelson Jennings

Violence, suffering, and death did not originate in the twenty-first century. For proof of that we need look no further than the collective testimony of the Bible from Genesis 3 forward, all of human history, and our own personal experiences. Led by our deceived first parents, all of creation fell under the promised resulting curse of struggle and death. That actual, historical, theological reality under girds the world's ongoing violence, suffering, and death, despite our best and manifold attempts to alleviate them.

Not only are violence, suffering, and death not new, they obviously have not yet ceased. As Christians, we look to the Second Coming of Jesus as the ultimate remedy to all the world's problems, while trusting the currently exalted Son of God further to usher in his kingdom of goodness, justice, and peace. We even on occasion catch glimpses of relief and apparent solutions, although we realize such situations are temporary and imperfect. This is especially true when considering the thorny area of suffering and violence related to Muslim-Christian relations, the subject of this particular paper.

On the one hand, then, for many Christians there is a seeming futility of dealing satisfactorily and permanently in the present age with violence and suffering. Political and humanitarian efforts may heal certain symptoms, but they cannot cure the underlying disease of sin and its just curse. It is thus easy for an evangelical compassion for people and their eternal destinies to embrace D.L. Moody's image of seeking to pull into the heavenly lifeboat as many souls as possible away from the sinking ship of this world, including the leaky vessel of Islam.

Carl Henry et al (including a host of non-Western Evangelicals), however, have called for a wider scope of gospel ministry in this world. More than just word-focused evangelism, and more than the twin foci of evangelism and church planting, the importance of holistic gospel ministry has increasingly been embraced by Evangelicals around the world. To be sure, there are still many discussion points: How should we prioritize "word" and "deed" ministries? Are the categories "word and deed" themselves too bifurcated for ministering in what is actually a more seamless creation? Should we focus only on social "relief" ("mercy ministry")? What about socio-economic development? What about social "action" that seeks to change social, economic, and political structures? We Evangelicals continue to differ among ourselves about such questions, and some choose to remain focused on a more narrow, spiritualized gospel.

Such differences should give us pause in our deliberations about violence, suffering, and death. In our efforts to be distinctively Christian in this whole matter, we have to realize that even as Evangelicals, we are not unified. In any case, at the very least, ordinary human concern means that Christians, not to mention most human beings, are saddened and struggle to respond when we directly experience the horrors of various forms of violence throughout our sin-wracked world. Specifically for our purposes here, Christians in Nigeria, Mindanao (Southern Philippines), Iran, and elsewhere have suffered violence at the hands of Muslims, and, perhaps even more sadly, *vice versa*. Our objective in this paper is to reconcile our distinctively Christian, missiological concerns with a common humanitarian compassion about these matters.

Approaching Violence, Suffering, and Death in Muslim-Christian Relations

I do not pretend to think that my own views on all of these issues will satisfy every other Evangelical. I would, however, like to offer here at the outset three areas of a distinctively Christian missiological concern about suffering and violence in relations between Muslims and Christians that I hope can be embraced across a wide Evangelical spectrum. The first area is our inherently Christian trait, now more extensively the actual case than ever before, of being an *international Church*. That is, while we Christians share in the corporate solidarity of the entire human race, by faith we belong even more fundamentally to a different and heavenly kingdom that stretches across all ethnic and national boundaries. We are a new international "third race," [1] whose citizenship is in heaven (Philippians 3:20). As those who belong to each other in Christ all around the world, we suffer and rejoice together (Romans 12:15). Our international, corporate, Christian self-identity should thus compel those of us who live in peace and comfort to *co*-suffer out of *com*-passion with those of us who suffer and even die in violent situations.

The worldwide Islamic *umma* in many ways mirrors the worldwide Church. The distinctively *Christian* missiological reality of the Church, however, is the unifying presence of Christ's Holy Spirit with his followers, who are both united to the risen and reigning Jesus by faith as well as sent into his world to serve him and others.

Second, is the divine calling Christians have to *witness*. Muslims as well are to spread Islam. But for our part Christians are assured that God the Holy Spirit is with us as we go and witness "to the end of the earth" (Acts 1:8). In beginning to fulfill his prediction that Christians would indeed be his worldwide witnesses, Jesus used persecution and suffering to move his followers to Judea, Samaria, and beyond (Acts 8:1–5, 11:19–21). Even as we might be scattered against our wishes, it is to be said of all Christians that they "went about preaching the word" (Acts 8:4).

Including with respect to Muslims, then, "As Evangelicals, we refuse to confine our mission to the development of better Christian-Muslim relations or to involvement in social service on their behalf. Jesus Christ has defined our agenda, and because we love him we are constrained to embrace as well the mandate he has given the Church to evangelize the Muslim world"[2] Evangelism and witness to Jesus

Christ is one distinctively Christian way of dealing with violence and suffering connected with Muslim-Christian relationships.

In addition to the worldwide Church and Christians' responsibility to witness-evangelize, a third area upon which all Evangelicals can agree regarding how to approach Christian-Muslim relations that involve violence and suffering is that *Jesus reigns* over the entire cosmos. All that exists and happens in this world ultimately is under King Jesus' control and supervision. Christians can thus approach Muslim-Christian relations, as well as violence, suffering, and death, with the confidence that our heavenly ruler is aware, concerned, and involved.

On the one hand, Evangelicals have different eschatological schemes that are intertwined with how we see Jesus exercising his present rule. Those schemes also relate (or, as the case may be, do not relate) in a special way to Middle Eastern political realities, particularly those involving the modern state of Israel. At the same time, all Christians believe that God requires us "to do justice, and to love kindness, and to walk humbly with your God" (Micah 6:8). We are not to be selective as to which areas of life this all-encompassing requirement is applicable. Our king reigns over the entire world and over all of life, be it political, social, economic, interpersonal, ethnic, moral, emotional, or whatever other area we can imagine.

As we proceed in this paper to examine Christian-Muslim interactions in light of the violence, suffering, and death that is sometimes associated with those relations, Christian distinctives, such as the international Church, Christian witness, and Jesus' cosmic reign, should deeply shape, and indeed strengthen, our humanitarian compassion about these matters. To make our analysis both more manageable, as well as anchored in concrete reality, we will focus on particular situations involving Muslims and Christians living together. Many of these situations will be those I have personally and recently visited. By following this more "on-the-ground" route, I hope we can avoid the kind of meaningless platitudes that can say whatever one simply wants to assert by way of empty generalities. Our goal is an accurate understanding that will support constructive Christian understanding and action.

"Glocal" Particularities

One can attempt to grasp "Muslim-Christian relations" on a macro scale, but in doing so one cannot ignore concrete, local situations. Similarly, in examining particular neighborhoods and communities, one cannot escape the reality that wider, global political-economic dynamics are at work. Labeling situations as "glocal" seeks to encapsulate their dual macro-micro feature, while (here at least) giving weight and precedence to their local particularity.

Take, for example, Muslim-Christian relations in West Africa. That is a huge region with multiple examples of different sorts of interactions. For example, relations are mostly peaceful in Ghana and often violent in Nigeria. Upon zooming in on two cities, for example Kumasi, Ghana and Jos, Nigeria, their particular histories, economic developments, political structures, religious communities, ethnic makeups, and myriad of other peculiar features become evident. When one zooms in further, say to Kumasi's eastern community of Adukrom, the businesses, languages spoken, neighborhood mosques, family dynamics, people's national origins and predominantly Muslim religious affiliations, road conditions, eating patterns, and other realities come into sharper focus. Hence, as I walked Adukrom's main street this past November, making various observations and talking with residents, the wide international connections of that small community came to light. People had moved there from all over West Africa, through the economic and political push and pull so often associated with urbanization. Somehow, despite linguistic and other challenges they face every day, the people of Adukrom get along with each other, as well as with others throughout the religiously pluralistic, albeit predominantly Christian, Kumasi metropolitan area.

By way of contrast, the Islamic City of Marawi, situated in north-central Mindanao, is in many ways quite isolated. Few outsiders want to go there, either out of fear or lack of any positive reason for visiting. Almost all of the city's 130,000-plus inhabitants are ethnically Maranao as well as Muslim. Indeed, those two identities are inseparably intertwined in the eyes of Maranao-Muslims themselves, as well as others in the general vicinity, including Marawi City's miniscule non-Maranao Christian community.

Mindanao State University was created in Marawi City in 1961 as a means of creating socio-economic uplift and wider connections for Maranaoans, but economic development continues to lag behind most other parts of the Philippines.

At the same time, this socially and religiously conservative town has been shaped in large part by external, international forces. The Americans made Marawi City their Mindanaoan administrative headquarters during the U.S. occupation of the Philippines. The national "Christian" government's policy of encouraging other Filipinos (from Visayas and Luzon) to settle on the "frontier" of Mindanao helped to press in on traditional Muslim communities like Marawi. Such inroads of the global economy, coupled with the Marcos government's actions of the late 1960s and early 1970s that culminated in the imposition of martial law, sparked the beginning in Marawi City of the Mindanaoan war. The insurgent-secessionists were led by intellectuals who had been educated both within and outside of Mindanao, including in the Middle East. Subsequent educational, financial, cultural, and religious connections developed with leaders and institutions in Libya, Egypt, and elsewhere.

When I met some Maranao-Chinese Christians who had fled Marawi City in the 1970s, they represented to me glocal realities in which they had lived as children. I could not understand them in all of their peculiar individuality without seeing them against the backdrop of the wider Chinese diaspora, Islamic expansion throughout Southeast Asia, Spanish colonization up through the nineteenth century, American missionary (and military) efforts, economic development (and lack thereof) in Mindanao, ethnic rivalries, as well as Muslim-Christian religious differences in their former neighborhood located in the southern sector of Marawi.

In sum, it is crucial to remember that glocal particularities are a central characteristic of these and other examples of situations involving Muslims and Christians interacting with each other.

.620138

(signature)

b203928

9203928

Multifaceted Complexities

Besides exhibiting particular glocal traits, each situation involving Muslim-Christian interaction is multifaceted and complex. Hence, while the struggles throughout Mindanao since the early 1970s, as well as the violence in northern Nigeria since the early 1980s, have often been characterized as Muslim-Christian violence, each incident cannot be justifiably reduced to such an oversimplification.

Cities

Jos, Nigeria, is a classic example of this multifaceted complexity. Largely spared the type of rioting that had broken out in cities throughout northern Nigeria over the previous two decades, Jos' peaceful atmosphere was shattered by an almost unthinkable scale of mayhem and death as hundreds were killed in September, 2001. Some outside reporting characterized the debacle as "religious violence" that also had an "ethnic dimension."[3] Many Christians have seen the outbreak as part of an Islamic master plan for ruling all of northern Nigeria and ultimately the entire country.[4] Other analyses have pointed primarily to the local issue of political control of the city.[5] For comparison's sake, it is interesting to note how similar alternative frameworks have been used for understanding the commonly viewed Muslim-Christian conflict in Mindanao as essentially a political and economic struggle.[6]

I contend that the situation in Jos, as well as elsewhere, is much more complicated than any mono or bi-causal explanation suggests. No doubt, the Muslim-Christian religious divide was, and continues to be, of basic importance to the 2001 violence and continuing tension in Jos. Religious affiliation usually stands out as crucial because of the peculiarly strong way that, in northern Nigeria, "Religion is used to consolidate existing identities and to forge new ones."[7] Corresponding ethnic differences—Hausa-Fulani Muslims versus Indigene-and-Other Christians—help to stoke trouble. Who is really in decision-making control is a central problem as well. But in reality, these and other contributing factors stem from Jos' unique, colorful, and complex historical development.

Various groups inhabited the area during the countless generations leading up to the twentieth century. By the early 1900s more recently arrived Hausa-Fulani people—who carried with them the Muslim faith that had been perpetrated across a wide region north and west of Jos by the Sokoto Jihad of a century earlier—had also established themselves enough to have set up a governing structure over what was becoming the town of Jos. Soon the British colonial presence entered Jos and its environs, as did a steady flock of newcomers from all directions (on newly constructed train lines) in light of the developing tin-mining industry there.

Christian missionaries were among these latest arrivals. They came to preach the gospel and to minister to those plagued by the 1918–1919 influenza epidemic. They were allowed to enter the area because of Jos' unusual location within British colonial zones. Northern Nigeria was governed by Islamic emirates through the British system of indirect rule. Southern Nigeria, on the other hand, was more Christianized. Lying on the crooked border between the two, Jos was geographically within the north and thus practically surrounded by Hausa-Fulani governed areas. The colonial borders, however, were drawn such that Jos was within a "pagan" district and was thus open to Christian missionary work in ways that more Muslim territories were not.[8]

Across all of northern Nigeria, the British colonial era had further subordinated non-Muslim groups socio-politically to Hausa-Fulani rulers.[9] With national independence in 1960 came the politicization of religious groups due to the activities of regionally based political parties.[10] National discussions in the late 1970s and again in the late 1980s over the northern-proposed implementation of Islamic law or *shari'ah* were intense and inconclusive. The actual institutionalization of *shari'ah* by certain northern states starting in 1999 increased unease among non-Muslims, in some cases sparking further violence.[11] All of this occurred on the social, economic, ethnic, and urbanized historical backdrop of Jos at the turn of twenty-first century. Clearly no single factor, religious or otherwise, adequately explains what happened in September, 2001.

The same could be said (and we will say it more briefly in this case) for a city in a totally different situation, Cagayan de Oro, Mindanao. Cagayan is a bustling port city on the north central coast of the second largest Philippine island. Unlike Jos, and unlike the Islamic City of Marawi two and one-half hours inland and to the southeast, Cagayan has not seen outbreaks of violence, or so-called sectarian strife, in recent years. In fact, the only fighting of any note that the city has experienced occurred either during World War II, during the earliest years of the early twentieth-century American occupation, or in the early 1600s, when the sultan under whose self-proclaimed jurisdiction Cagayan fell unsuccessfully tried to subdue the inhabitants and the newly arrived Jesuit missionarie s.

The relative prosperity of Cagayan is one aspect of the city's stability. So is the strong political leadership of the current mayor, the Hon. Vicente Emano.[12] Under his leadership new businesses are regularly recruited, crime is not tolerated, and all groups are included in the political process—particularly including Muslims. Also, there is significant religious and ethnic diversity, although the Muslim population is quite small (approximately 5%) and basically mono-ethnic (Maranao).

Why have cities like Cagayan de Oro and Kumasi, Ghana, been at peace? Why have Marawi City and Jos seen intense periods of violence? A common answer is respectively to credit or blame religious affiliation. Hence despite the richness and complexity of the situation in Jos and all of northern Nigeria, religion stands out as the perceived cause of conflict: "Religion divides Nigerians, accentuates ethnic differences among them, and reinforces the North-South polarity". [13] That sort of religious division was accentuated in the reports about the recent February, 2006 rioting in both northern and southern Nigeria; those riots occurred in the midst of the worldwide protests over the cartoons about Muhammad. With respect to Christian witness towards Muslims in the midst of that violence, reports from the southern Christian city of Onitsha were not encouraging: "Ifeanyi Ese, 34, a Christian, said as he stood Thursday amid the concrete rubble of a mosque: 'We don't want these mosques here anymore. These people are causing all the problems all over the world because they don't fear God.' He used a burned stick to scrawl a message on a shattered wall: 'Mohammed is a man, but Jesus is from above.'"[14]

"Religion" indeed "divides Nigerians," both in their self-understandings and in analyses about them. As we have seen, however, more multifaceted explanations clearly are required. How we in the worldwide body of Christ, who are concerned about effective witness to Muslims and who believe in Jesus' worldwide reign, can understand such glocal, complex situations, and act constructively as a result, is what we are attempting to facilitate within this paper.

Countries

On a more macro scale, one can look at the mutually demonizing relationship between Iran and the United States. Direct, violent confrontation between the two countries has been relatively minimal: the CIA helped to overthrow Iranian Prime Minister Muhammad Musaddiq in 1953, and—as any American alive at the time starkly remembers—sixty-six U.S. Embassy personnel in Tehran were held captive during the 1979–1981 hostage crisis. What is the basic problem between the "Great Satan" and a centerpiece of the "Axis of Evil?"

Religious difference is a convenient analysis to employ. An overlapping "civilization clash" type of framework is also easy to use. One quickly realizes, however, that these religio-cultural categories alone cannot do full justice to a situation that also involves colonial and Cold War political residues, political alliances, oil and other economic realities, basic interpersonal mistrust, linguistic gaps, the current political leaders themselves, and a host of other factors.

Add to the mix the precarious and often dangerous circumstances under which many branches of the Christian Church face in Iran on a daily basis, and the following complicated question inevitably arises: How should we Christians express our international, worldwide unity that includes the Church in Iran, plus work towards the evangelization of Iranians in general (most all of whom are

Muslims), as well as recognize Jesus' reign over all things American, Iranian, and otherwise—all with respect to Christian-Muslim interactions as they overlap with U.S.-Iranian relations? The question's missiological thrust has international-ecclesiological, evangelistic, confessional, political, and interreligious aspects. In asking such a question, our challenge is to do justice to the complexity of our missiological approach, as well as to the complexity of this and every other situation we must deal with.

Legitimacy of Authority

Mention of relations between Iran and the United States has taken us from a glocal, community-based focus into a more macro, international level of our consideration. To boldly press ahead on this track: How might we missiologically view—particularly in light of Jesus' worldwide reign—the verbal sparring between these two countries that do not have official diplomatic relations with each other? The question is especially urgent at the present time, given the increased international tension over Iran's nuclear development program. The United States has led the chorus of warnings and threats of any and all options, including military ones. Iran has been responding with virulent declarations of pressing ahead with its nuclear program, plus it has promised retaliation against any hostile external deterrents, threats backed up with recent successful tests of new and improved military hardware.

An important component of understanding this tense, political dynamic is to consider the legitimacy of authorities involved. The litany of concerns for Evangelicals we will consider in the end boil down to the following two intertwined questions: Are nation-state governments to be trusted and supported more than insurgents and rebel movements? What relative value do Christian and Islamic assertions—including their intertwined character with governments or rebel movements—have regarding the same socio-economic-political situations?

The world of the early twenty-first century largely recognizes the political sovereignty of nation-states. For its part, the United Nations "is based on the principle of the sovereign equality of all its

Members" as it seeks to achieve its first purpose "To maintain international peace and security." The U.N. Security Council has been given particular responsibility for encouraging the peaceful resolution of international disputes, or for employing such punitive actions as sanctions or military measures.[15] Evangelicals (including American Evangelicals, reflecting their government's basic posture) have a bent towards recognizing the God-given legitimacy of nation-states, or "duly elected" and "recognized" governments, along with the post-World War II United Nations structure. Even so, how does a Christian missiological understanding of these recognized authorities jive with a recognition of the kingship of Jesus?

Romans 13:1 is certainly an important word on the matter: "Let every person be subject to the governing authorities. For there is no authority except from God, and those that exist have been instituted for God." So is Peter and John's reply, when warned by them not to preach in Jesus' name, to the rulers, elders, scribes, and high priestly family of their day: "Whether it is right in the sight of God to listen to you rather than to God, you must judge, for we cannot but speak of what we have seen and heard" (Acts 4:19–20). Jesus' monumental "render to Caesar the things that are Caesar's, and to God the things that are God's" (Matthew 22:21) might even steer us clear of this political arena altogether.

The Christian confession that "Jesus is *Kurios*" does not afford us this last option, however. That confession is a comprehensive declaration that the God-Man Jesus of Nazareth rules over everything, everyone, and every aspect of his world, including political matters. In the New Testament Greco-Roman world, Christians countered the absolutist claims of Caesar by claiming that Jesus must be the one who ultimately is acknowledged and followed. As Christians then and now we stand in the biblical tradition of acknowledging God's sovereign rule over "the nations [that] are like a drop from a bucket, and are accounted as the dust on the scales" (Isaiah 40:15), knowing that "He who sits in the heavens laughs [and] holds [arrogant kings and rulers] in derision" (Psalm 2:4).

With respect to the New Testament passages just cited, the basic Christian confession that "Jesus is *Kurios*" thus counters any absolutist or ungodly claim of any governing authority. The seeds of a critical prophetic distance, as well as proper civil disobedience, are thus effectively sown for Christians. And while Jesus' "render to Caesar" teaching has been used as a foundational teaching for church-state separation, an autonomy of the state from Jesus' rule, that some have thus tried to conclude, is untenable. Whatever Jesus meant by those words, he pointed out the triviality of his challengers' attempt to trap him in light of the overarching kingdom of God over all matters, political and otherwise.

An anthropologically informed missiological view of U.S.-Iran relations can step back and see that, "The source of much misunderstanding in international relations lies in the failure of nations to understand the symbolic bases for both the actions and the discourse used to describe those actions by other nations. Iran and the United States are at loggerheads over just these symbolic matters." In particular, "Iranians have, since the beginning of the revolution been engaged in symbolic discourse which emphasizes *resistance* as a means of establishing and maintaining revolutionary credentials and a correct moral posture on the international scene. The United States maintains discourse which emphasizes *accommodation* to achieve the same goals."[16] Such a perceptive analysis dovetails with an international-ecclesiological perspective that will check an arrogant nationalistic viewpoint that only has self-interest in view—as is the case with many American analyses of Iran and of U.S.-Iran relations.[17] Similarly, missiological concern for gospel progress will seek to understand people—in this case Iranians and Americans—in all of their fascinating complexity, not simply view them en bloc for strategic political purposes.

In other words, devotion to Jesus, his international people, and the worldwide movement of his gospel will temper blind nationalistic-patriotic devotion to select nation-states on the one hand and whole scale condemnation of other states on the other hand.[18] In the present case, American and Iranian Christians ought to be able to see at least some measure of legitimacy in either state's derived authority, as well as imperfections in both governments and their policies.

Nation-State Governments or Rebel Movements?

We have already been flirting with this first main question in the present section about legitimate authority. To pursue it further, we can think about current events in the Middle East.

Perhaps no single Middle Eastern issue is as crucial as that of the relationship between Palestinians and Israel. Recent outbreaks of violence in southern Lebanon and in Gaza have been a painful reminder of this tenuous and politically charged relationship. The intricacies of the issue prevent us from seeking any definitive solution here; so do the varying Christian viewpoints concerning the modern state of Israel and its relationship, or lack thereof, to biblical prophecy. Worthy of special note is the fact that for some Arab Christians, the very existence of the state of Israel presents poignant theological challenges, the deepest of which is the identity of God.[19] What Christians can say across the board is that the legitimate authority of the modern state of Israel, like that of any state, is derived and imperfect. Moreover, Micah 6:8 and other biblical constraints mean that Christians must be concerned about justice and peace in the region, including what that means for Israelis and Palestinians alike. Part of what that means for Evangelicals is that we do the hard work to be as familiar with "the Palestine actually inhabited by millions of contemporary Palestinian Arabs" as with the Palestine of the Bible.[20]

Even though some Evangelicals will disagree with the first part of the statement below, David Bosch's words in connection with "The Pauline Missionary Paradigm" are pertinent:

> Any theological dialogue with and discussion about Israel should distinguish between Israel's place in the covenant of God and the empirical modern state or nation of Israel. It is a dangerous theological misconception to lay a direct connection between the unique position of Israel as a theological entity and the survival of Jews in a separate nation-state—quite apart from the fact that events in recent years have shown that Israel behaves no differently from any other nation.[21]

Our Christian missiological insistence on the reign of Jesus should hold all contemporary states to the same standards of justice.

As for Iraq, once again there is a spectrum of viewpoints on the U.S.-led coalition's invasion and continuing occupation, plus the current state of affairs. Certainly Christians can at least critically discuss the legitimacy of the competing authorities there (e.g., U.S.-initiated political process, neighborhood imams) and thus question how such terms as "insurgency" have been used from early on after the invasion. We must not fall prey to baptizing existing rulers simply because of their greater military backing—something that has in some sense occurred through the Western media.

On a worldwide scale, Christians will gravitate towards order and stability—for which we are to pray in I Timothy 2:1–2. At the same time, there will be times to make difficult judgments in light of Jesus' guidance regarding what is just and right in particular and complex situations. Modern nation-states may be the assumed order of the day, but they are not ultimate and beyond challenge.

Next, we need to step back from a strictly macro view of international relations and merge our concern with how we missiologically consider more glocal situations. In Jos, Nigeria, how should Christians view the competing indigene and Hausa-Fulani claims of original jurisdiction? The U.N.-recognized Nigerian state took shape once it became independent from the British colonial state, which had institutionalized non-Muslim peoples' subordinate socio-political position to Hausa-Fulani rulers.[22] How, then, should Nigerian and other Christians unravel Nigeria's complicated political history and appeal to "legitimate" authority for peace, order, and fairness with respect to religious affiliation?

Similar questions arise in Mindanao, Philippines. At the same time, those questions take on different hues, depending on which side of the religious fault line Christians live. Christians (and others) in the Islamic City of Marawi might more easily recognize the "legitimacy" of MILF-type claims for Mindanaoan independence. Citizens of Cagayan de Oro, on the other hand, would in the main advocate the legitimate sovereignty of the Philippine central government over all of the territory recognized by the U.N. as "the Philippines." Which is more just—taking into account the federal government's initiative to allow for Autonomous Regions of Muslim Mindanao (AARM), per those regions' public vote?

Through all of these questions, how Christians understand the different aspects of human identity is important. U.N.-recognized nationality is only one of those aspects, and under no Christian scheme must that aspect be ultimate or isolated. Take, for example, the killing of Christian Peacemaker Teams activist Tom Fox in early March, 2006. He was subsequently and variously described by the press under such labels as American, Virginian, Christian, and Peace Activist. Which was most important and fundamental? Moreover, it was worthy of note that it was the U.S. military that identified his body, announced the finding, transported his body to America, etc. Is the "American" identity in such instances the default, ultimate identity? Christians must be missiologically savvy enough not to allow that to be the case.

Christian Versus Islamic Political Viewpoints

From a Christian missiological point of view, should U.S. foreign policy trump Iranian foreign policy because the former allegedly has more of a Christian background? Similarly, should the Philippine federal government and its military be backed over Mindanaoan paramilitary movements because of the former's more traditional Christian affiliation? The situation in Nigeria is more complicated, since it is often difficult to filter out federal government officials' religious motivations for political positions. Even so, should Christians stand for the federal government over Northern leaders because the latter are almost always explicitly Muslim – even though the federal government leaders often are also Muslims?

And what about the Palestinian-Israeli issue? Again, an array of different Christian interpretations of biblical teaching on the contemporary political matters surrounding this issue make this particular discussion extremely difficult to approach. Nevertheless, we can at least ask questions as to what kind of criteria should be important for thinking through evaluations of political leadership:

Are Israeli political and military decisions always right, simply because they are Israeli? Are Palestinian political and military decisions always wrong, simply because they are affiliated somehow with Islam? How do the categories of "justice" and "rightness" relate to our Christian missiological analyses?

Related is who is considered a "terrorist," including so-called terrorist states. The U.S. Council on Foreign Relations lists six states that support terrorism: Libya, North Korea, Sudan, Syria, Cuba, and Iran.[23] Curiously, two are communist, and four are (of varying types) Muslim. Similarly, a basic American framework of what constitutes terrorist acts and what is legitimate use of force is reflected in events labeled as terrorist by CBS News, including those in Iraq in the wake of "the U.S.-led invasion." [24] By contrast, along with the fiery Venezuelan President Hugo Chavez, analysts such as Noam Chomsky label the U.S. as a "leading terrorist state," citing, for example, the World Court's condemnation of U.S. actions in Nicaragua in the 1980s "for what it called 'unlawful use of force,' which means international terrorism."[25]

Of course, even defining "terrorist" or "terrorism" is part of the discussion.[26] Depending on one's perspective, Samson, for example, could be considered a religious terrorist (at least from the Philistines' perspective), similar to contemporary suicide bombers.[27] In all such discussions about "terror," Christians are faced with the challenge of following Jesus in his universal reign, while not falling prey either to nationalistic blindness or to politically correct neutrality.

I believe that our complicated missiological questioning of such issues can actually simplify our focus here. As stated above, our Christian concern is for devotion to Jesus, his international people, and the worldwide movement of his gospel. Missiologically speaking, specifically political policies should be viewed in light of this triad, not solely in relation to its traditional religious origin per se. Issues of justice, peace, and gospel progress trump any particular political posture. Paul's words in I Timothy 2:1–2 are to be indiscriminately and universally applied here for Christians' prayerful involvement and understanding: "I urge that supplications, prayers, intercessions, and thanksgivings be made for *all* people, for kings and *all* who are in high positions, that we may lead a peaceful and quiet life, godly and dignified in every way" (emphases mine).

God's people walk before God and within the world by faith, not cultural, ethnic, or political badges. We are free as the international Church to realize a measure of distinction from our respective national identities and speak and live prophetically within those settings into which our King Jesus has sent us. Our posture vis-à-vis socio-political matters will not always be clear. Judging which authorities are legitimate and to be followed takes great Spirit-led care before the Scriptures. What we can say with confidence is that our place in this world as aliens and strangers comes out in such socio-political arenas as starkly and uncomfortably as it does in any other.

Spiritual Forces

Of course, we Christians do not analyze situations in which we live and serve only with sanctified social science tools, as vital as they are. Besides looking at situations in their particularity, their complexity, and as governed by various socio-political authorities, Christians are aware of unseen powers that are at work. We pray for God to work, and we understand how angels and demons wage war in the heavenlies over this world's events. Where does this whole arena of unseen reality fit into approaching Christian-Muslim relations involving violence, suffering, and death?

The matter of so-called 'territorial spirits" is one subject that we must consider here. In general, Christians who recognize and give focused attention to such forces cite biblical precedent and numerous examples of demonic powers working in specific locations. Partly in connection with many Evangelicals' sense that the 10/40 Window, in which Islamic areas are prominent, is a satanic stronghold,[28] Islamic countries, regions, cities, villages, families, and individuals can be seen as demonically controlled. Basic to this view, then, is that Christian ministry on behalf of Muslims involves the waging of "Strategic-Level Spiritual Warfare" to release them from Satan's grip and overarching influence.[29]

I do not want to go into greater detail here into the discussion about territorial spirits per se. For those interested in pursuing the matter further, please refer to the helpful Lausanne "Deliver Us from Evil Consultation Statement."[30] My greater concern here in this matter is threefold: First, I fear that Evangelicals—especially including American Evangelicals—can too easily and unwittingly view Muslims and Islamic areas, countries, and regions through the lenses of spiritual forces in a way that masks more basic, and often intertwined, underlying racist, nationalistic, and political attitudes. It is not hard to imagine, for example, how an American Evangelical's view of Iran's nuclear development program can be couched in a framework of seeing it demonically motivated (to destroy Israel, for example), whereas that view more fundamentally could be due to an unwillingness to acknowledge a socio-economic political legitimacy to what their program entails. Similarly, a preference for a U.S.-established Philippine government versus a Mindanaoan secessionist position could help more fully to explain the why and what of prayers for unreached Islamic peoples in Mindanao, alongside a specifically spiritual concern.

Second (and not unrelated to the first concern), Christians need a biblically balanced view of other religions, not a reductionist view that focuses exclusively or even primarily on demonic deception. To be sure, the Bible speaks of Satan's deception and rule over "the whole world" (I John 5:19). At the same time, the Bible also speaks of how sinners "suppress the truth" in their sin (Romans 1:18), as well as how unbelievers are genuinely seeking after God and the truth (Acts 17:23ff.). This three-legged stool of Satan, sin, and searching together help to explain how non-Christians, including Muslims, stand before God. To focus on only one aspect, in this case satanic bondage, skews how constructively to relate to and pray for Muslims and Islamic entities.

A third area to note in connection with the notion of "territorial spirits" vis-à-vis Christian-Muslim relations is the danger of bracketing off where and how evil forces work and don't work. Perhaps due to racist-nationalist-political concerns, and perhaps due to a skewed view of Muslims, Christians might limit the influence of demonic powers to non-Christians and non-Christian entities or areas. To assume, however, that Satan and his hosts do not, will not, or cannot work in relation to Christians or Christian entities (geographic, political, or otherwise) is biblically and otherwise fallacious and dangerous. As Christians, we must heed Peter's warning to "Be sober-minded; be watchful. Your adversary the devil prowls around like a roaring lion, seeking someone to devour. Resist him, firm in your faith, knowing that the same kinds of suffering are being experienced by your brotherhood throughout the world" (I Peter 5:8-9).

There are spiritual powers at work in this world. They influence, with careful and seasoned discernment, relations between Muslims and Christians. Violence, suffering, and death are connected to how unseen forces move about. We must be wise, which includes being not overly simplistic, as well as not overly skeptical about how angels and demons influence the matters of this world.

Instructions from I Peter

Christians, to whom the Apostle Peter wrote the letter we call I Peter, lived in circumstances not unlike those of Christians and Muslims today who know firsthand violence, suffering, and death. Insofar as those first-century believers were a socio-religious minority within their religion-infused Greco-Roman environment, their situation resembled that of Christians today in primarily Muslim northern Nigeria, and certainly within overwhelmingly Muslim Iran. Those situations resemble as well that of Mindanaoan Muslims within the predominantly "Christian" Philippines, and to a less severe extent within the majority-Christian city of Kumasi and country of Ghana.

Curiously, I Peter has not been used as a mission paradigm to the same extent that the gospel accounts, the Book of Acts, or Paul's letters have. For example, Bosch's *Transforming Mission* devotes sections of its "New Testament Models of Mission" only to Matthew, Luke-Acts, and Paul.[31] As for Christian-Muslim relations, Peter's first letter seems to provide particularly relevant instruction, imagery, and encouragement, so that letter is what we are going to consider here.

For Muslims

The main point of this final section is to tie together the entire paper with some helps that I Peter gives to Christians today regarding how to deal with violence, suffering, and death, particularly with regards to relations with Muslims. Before turning our attention there, however, I would like to consider briefly how Peter's (and the whole Bible's) instructions might be applied by Muslims and Islamic communities. Clearly, they would disregard the explicit references to Christ's death and resurrection (1:2, 3, 11, 19, 21, 2:24, 3:18, 4:1, 13), but how might they otherwise appreciate Peter's encouragements and admonitions?

Perhaps the easiest swath of Muslim peoples we could consider would be the one-third of the world's Muslims "who live in non-Muslim societies."

> Muslim minority communities, as in the case of all minorities, are at the forefront of external challenges and are involved in a constant struggle for the recognition and maintenance of identity that constitutes the driving force in all living communities. Among minorities, the issues of cultural or group identity are not just theoretical or esoteric questions but matters of grave practical implication. Minorities face, on a constant basis, challenges to their own identity and hence, to their survival.[32]

As a minority people, they could draw great encouragement from Peter's admonitions to anticipate a future deliverance in the midst of suffering, to live in unity, to submit to civic authorities, and to live sober and sanctified lives. Their worldwide identity as part of the Muslim *umma* would resonate with Peter's reference to his Christian readers' identity with "your brotherhood throughout the world." One can imagine Mindanaoan Muslims, as well as those in Onitsha, southern Nigeria, somehow drawing strength from Peter's words to the minority Christians of the first century.

For Christians

As for Christians, the centrality of Jesus Christ in I Peter and in our lives of course makes this letter pertinent in ways that no Muslim could ever appreciate. Jesus has suffered and died, "leaving you an example, so that you might follow in his steps" (2:21). In terms of how he has dealt with our guilt and helplessness before God, "He himself bore our sins in his body and on the tree, that we might die to sin and live to righteousness. By his wounds you have been healed" (2:24). Peter goes on: "For Christ also suffered once for sins, the righteous for the unrighteous, that he might bring us to God" (3:18). Indeed it is the triune God who has acted decisively in the life, death, and resurrection of Jesus Christ, insofar as Christians are elect "according to the foreknowledge of God the Father, in the sanctification of the Spirit, for obedience to Jesus Christ and for sprinkling with his blood" (1:2).

Christians thus have our central focus on our Savior, Jesus Christ, the one whom we love and in whom we believe and rejoice, even though we have not yet seen him (1:7). It is through his death that we are forgiven, by his resurrection that we have been born again to a living hope, and for his final revelation that we wait with anticipation. Moreover, he is the cornerstone for the new temple of God of which we are all together the various parts. In Christ we are "a chosen race, a royal priesthood, a holy nation, a people for his own possession, that [we] may proclaim the excellencies of him who called you out of darkness into his marvelous light" (2:9). "Here the church is not the sender but the one sent."[33] As such, it is as his temple and body that we Christians "keep loving one another earnestly. . . , show hospitality to one another without grumbling. As each has received a gift, use it to serve one another. . ." (4:8–10).

Built together on Christ, the Christian "brotherhood throughout the world" is called and equipped to serve in this world "as sojourners and exiles" (2:11). It is this Christ-centered, international-corporate, and pilgrim posture that thrusts us into the present world of violence, suffering, and death. In such situations, and with respect to Muslims and all others, we are to heed Peter's admonition to "Keep your conduct among the Gentiles honorable, so that when they speak against you as evildoers, they may see your good deeds and glorify God on the day of visitation" (2:12). We thus can proactively participate in civic-political structures (2:13–17), socio-economic entities (2:18), and families (3:1–7), ever regarding Jesus as *Kurios* and "always being prepared to make a defense to anyone who asks you for a reason for the hope that is in you" (3:15).

Jesus' followers in Kumasi, Jos, Cagayan do Oro, the Islamic City of Marawi, as well as Iran and the United States can all approach their/our situations humbly, full of confidence and hope: "Humble yourselves, therefore, under the mighty hand of God so that at the proper time he may exalt you, casting all your anxieties on him, because he cares for you" (5:6-7). Some of us live in Christian-majority situations, some not. All of us live in a globalized world in which the United States and other non-Muslim countries interact with Iran and other Islamic states. Wherever we live in particular, we are to be "sober-minded" and "watchful," mindful of our connection with the worldwide fellowship of faith (5:8-9). "And after you have suffered a little while, the God of all grace, who has called you to his eternal glory in Christ, will himself restore, confirm, strengthen, and establish you. To him be the dominion forever and ever. Amen" (5:10-11).

Should Christians in Nigeria "Turn the Other Cheek"?

One vexing issue for Nigerian Christians concerns whether or not they should defend themselves against Muslim attacks on their homes, businesses, and churches. Recently, the President of the influential Christian Association of Nigeria announced to "our Muslim brothers that they do not have the monopoly of violence in this nation." He also demanded protection and compensation for church structures that have been destroyed.[34] As noted earlier, certain residents of the southern city of Onitsha attacked, self-consciously *as Christians*, Muslims as payback for earlier violent attacks in the north. Other Christians take a less retaliatory position, claiming that Jesus' followers should not seek reprisals for churches being burned down or other acts of violence.[35]

Interesting in this regard is an Islamic posture that "strikes a mean between the two" options of pacifism or war. Such a view regards Christian pacifism as impractical, pointing out that "throughout their long history, no Christian people have ever hesitated to make war."[36] Certainly the varying positions of Christians are a puzzle to

Muslims, as well as a continuing difficult struggle for Christians in such situations as the present one in Nigeria.

Some might ask whether Christians who are neither Nigerian nor personally involved with the Nigerian situation should even venture to speak to the matter. Undoubtedly those of us who are cultural and national outsiders should be cautious about what we should offer. At the same time, we as the international Church are bound together, even though we live and serve in a variety of contexts. Moreover, outsiders' etic views complement insiders' emic understandings. Both are needed to approach situations from a proper critical distance as well as with impassioned vested interest.

Hence in I Peter we read the Apostle's instruction to follow Christ's example and suffer for doing good: "When he was reviled, he did not revile in return; when he suffered, he did not threaten, but continued entrusting himself to him who judges justly" (2:23). Later Peter encourages his Christian readers to "rejoice insofar as you share Christ's sufferings, that you may also rejoice and be glad when his glory is revealed. If you are insulted for the name of Christ, you are blessed, because the Spirit of glory and of God rests upon you.... Therefore let those who suffer according to God's will entrust their souls to a faithful Creator while doing good" (4:13-19). These verses very much lean in the direction of Christians accepting any attacks in a posture of non-violent acceptance of God's protection and providence, and it is entirely proper for both emic and etic Christians to bring such scriptural admonitions into the discussion.

However, the plot thickens when we recall the multifaceted complexity of such situations, including what has been happening in Nigeria. "Muslim-Christian" violence is not as simple as "Christians" deciding whether or not actively to defend themselves and retaliate against "Muslims." As noted earlier, ethnic differences are perhaps the most obvious complicating factor to see. But interrelated political, economic, and other historically-based aspects enter into the picture of why certain people are angry, frustrated, desperate, or just warped thrill-seekers and resort to violence. One can also suggest that multiple factors besides religious affiliation are involved in the Anglican Archbishop's role as President of C.A.N.

How will people's responses to violence contribute to its escalation or reduction? How will the response to violence and suffering of people who consider themselves Christian, and are viewed by others similarly, hinder or contribute to the progress of the gospel among those people who consider themselves to be Muslim? What does Jesus' reign over Nigeria, West Africa, and the whole world have to say about people's actions and reactions?

What about the "Christian" United States?

For many Muslims, the United States is spearheading a war against Islam. The recent cartoons of Muhammad are seen as part of that same assault.[37] Whether Christians like it or not, or whether it is accurate or not, that is the widespread perception.

As Christians, including those of us who are Americans, we need to have the tri-fold missiological perspective of being an international Church, of striving for evangelistic witness to Muslims worldwide, and of the reign of Jesus over all countries and peoples. As such we will long for justice and Christian service more than any nation's prerogatives or "national interests," including those of the United States of America. American Christians thus need to be able to distance themselves and their own sympathies enough from the United States as a world economic, political, cultural, and military superpower in order to interact constructively and sympathetically with other sorts of people, be they Christian, Muslim, or otherwise. Furthermore, all Christians need to live in the tension of having both earthly and heavenly citizenships as "sojourners and exiles" in this world.

In a related way, American missionary ventures need to be evaluated with respect to how they are perceived by others in terms of connection to the United States' international interests and policies. Such ventures also need to be considered in light of their actual facilitation and reinforcement of American presence and influence. Thankfully the international reality of the Christian Church can counteract Islamic perceptions of the alleged Western character of the Christian faith. The increasingly multi-directional and multi-origin character of missionary flow is also conducive to the three missiological objectives we have been discussing.

This study has raised more questions than it has answered. More than solving problems per se between Christians and Muslims, we have focused on pointing to more constructive approaches to those problems. The projected takeaway here is to see Muslim-Christian relations in their particularity and complexity, as well as in relation to socio-political authorities and spiritual forces. Instructions in I Peter for Christians who lived in the volatile and violent Greco-Roman world of the first century have served as a particular guide for us to consider here.

Muslim-Christian relations are a central part of the Christian mission throughout the world today and for the foreseeable future. Approaching these relations is a matter of utmost importance, both for now and for eternity. May God grant his people wisdom as we serve him in a world of violence, suffering, and death—all of which will be done away with when the risen and conquering Jesus returns in full glory.

Notes

1. Bediako K. 1992, Theology & Identity: The impact of culture upon Christian thought in the second century and modern Africa, Regnum Books, Oxford. 34–41.
2. Lausanne Committee for World Evangelization (LCOWE) 1978, Lausanne Occasional Papers: No.4 The Glen Eyrie Report – Muslim Evangelization, 5.
3. 'Dozens killed in Nigeria violence' 2001, BBC News, [Online]. Available at: http://news.bbc.co.uk/1/hi/world/africa/1534404.stm
4. Jos, Nigeria: October 19–27, 2005, various interviews.
5. Bagudu, N. (ed.) 2004, Recrudescent Civil Disturbances and Human Rights: The Jos and State-Wide Crises, League for Human Rights, Jos. xi.

6. Saber M. 1975, 'Majority-Minority Situation in the Philippines' *Mindanao Journal*, vol. II, no. 1, 20–38.
7. Falola T. 1998, Violence in Nigeria: The Crisis of Religious Politics and Secular Ideologies, University of Rochester Press, Rochester. 44.
8. Crampton E.P.T. 1976, *Christianity in Northern Nigeria.* 2nd edn, Gaskiya Corporation Zaria, Nigeria. Davidson L. 2005, 'Christian Zionism as a Representation of American Manifest Destiny', *Critique: Critical Middle Eastern Studies* vol. 14, no. 2, 72–75, 157–169.
9. Turaki Y. 1982, 'The Institutionalization of the Inferior Status and Socio-Political Role of the Non-Muslim Groups in the Colonial Hierarchical Structure of the Northern Region of Nigeria: A Socio-Ethical Analysis of the Colonial Legacy', Unpublished PhD dissertation, Boston University.
10. Kastfelt N. 1994, Religion and Politics in Nigeria: A Study in Middle Belt Christianity, British Academic Press, London – New York. ix.
11. Ostien P., Nasir J. M. & Kogelmann F. (eds) 2005, *Comparative Perspectives on Shari'ah in Nigeria*, Spectrum Books Limited, Ibadan. AND Gaiya M. A. B. 2004, 'The Complexity of the Shari'ah Debate in Nigeria', in *T.C.N.N. Research Bulletin*, no. 42, 26–43.
12. Cagayan de Oro, Mindanao, Philippines: September 1, 2005, Hon. Vicente Y. Emano (Mayor); September 2, 2005, Chinese-Maranao; Christian woman; September 3, 2005, Christian teenager; September 5, 2005, Maranao-Muslim medical doctor; September 7, 2005, Sultan M.C. Macagungun and Imam Aleem: September 8, 2005, Chinese-Maranao Christian man.
13. Falola 1998, 46.
14. 'Christian-Muslim battles continue across Nigeria' 2006, Associated Press, [Online]. Available at: http://www.stltoday.com/stltoday/ news/stories.nsf/world/story/A22D53D3CC89D4D486257123000ABB 14?OpenDocument&highlight=2%2C%22nigeria%22.
15. *Charter of the United Nations*, Chapter I, Articles 1.1, 2.1; Chapters V–VII, [Online]. Available at: http://www.un.org/aboutun/charter/ index.html.
16. Beeman W.O. 2005, The 'Great Satan' vs. the 'Mad Mullahs': How the United States and Iran Demonize Each Other, Praeger, Westport, Connecticut. 190.
17. Pollack K. M. 2004, The Persian Puzzle: The Conflict Between Iran and America, Random House, New York. AND Timmerman K. R. 2005, Countdown to Crisis: The Coming Nuclear Showdown with Iran, Crown Forum, New York.

18. Lausanne Committee for World Evangelization (LCOWE) 2004, *Lausanne Occasional Papers: No.50 The Impact on Global Mission of Religious Nationalism and 9/11 Realities*, [Online]. Available at: http://community.gospelcom.net/lcwe/assets/LOP50_IG21.pdf. 11.

19. Reitsma B. J. G. 2002, 'Who is our God? The Theological Challenges of the State of Israel for Christian Arabs – Faith and Ethnicity in the Middle East', in Eddy A. J. G. et al, eds., *Faith and Ethnicity Volume 1*, Meinema, Zoetermeer.

20. Davidson 2005, 158.

21. Bosch D. J. 1991, Transforming Mission: Paradigm Shifts in Theology of Mission, Orbis Books, Maryknoll. 173.

22. Turaki 1982.

23. Council on Foreign Relations 2006, 'State Sponsors of Terrorism', [Online] Available at: http://www.cfr.org/issue/458/.

24. 'Terror Strikes' 2005, *CBSNEWS.com*, [Online]. Available at: http://www.cbsnews.com/htdocs/terror/framesource_map.html.

25. Barsamian D. 2001, 'The United States is a Leading Terrorist State: An Interview with Noam Chomsky by David Barsamian', *Monthly Review*, vol. 53, no. 6, [Online]. Available at: http://www.monthly review. org/ 1101chomsky.htm.

26. 'Terrorist' 2006, *Wikipedia*, [Online] Available at: http://en. wikipedia.org/ wiki/Terrorist.

27. Ateek N. 2002, SUICIDE BOMBERS: What is theologically and morally wrong with suicide bombings? A Palestinian Christian perspective', *Cornerstone*, Issue 25, [Online] Available at: http://www.sabeel.org/old/news/cstone25/suicidebombers.htm. 2.

28. Bush L. 1995, 'What is the 10/40 Window?' in Wagner C. P., Peters S., and Wilson M., eds., *Praying Through the 100 Gateway Cities of the 10/40 Window*, YWAM Publishing, Seattle. 15.

29. Arnold C. E. 1997, *3 Crucial Questions about Spiritual Warfare*, Baker Books, Grand Rapids. 146–150.

30. Lausanne Committee for World Evangelization (LCOWE) 2000, 'Deliver Us from Evil: Consultation Statement', [Online]. Available at: http://www.lausanne.org/Brix?pageID=13860.

31. Bosch 1991, 15–178.

32. Mahmood S. S. 2004, 'A Word About Ourselves' *Journal of Muslim Minority Affairs*, vol. 24, no. 1, 5–7.

33. Bosch 1991, 372.

34. Akinola P. J. 2006, 'Archbishop Akinola on the recent Violence in Nigeria', *titusonenine*, [Online]. Available at: http://titusonenine. classical anglican. net /?p=11515.

35. McCain D. 2005, Tough Tests for Top Leaders: God's Strategy for Preparing Africans to Lead Global Christianity, MoreBooks, Jos. pp. 24–35.

36. Ahmad H. 1990, 'Comparative Religious Teachings on WAR AND PEACE', *Al Islam*, [Online] Available at: http://www.alislam.org/jihad/warandpeace.html.

37. 'Muslim scholars in cartoon talks' 2006, *BBC News*, [Online]. Available at: http://news.bbc.co.uk/1/hi/world/middle_east/4838286.stm.

Biblical and Theological Foundations for

Engaging in Contexts of Violence

Chapter Three

The Biblical Contexts of Violence and Responses

Stephen M. Clinton

Violence goes on in every culture and in many relationships. Some violence is physical, some is emotional, some is spiritual. All violence hurts someone. The American Heritage Dictionary gives six definitions of violence which are related in some ways, but each one focuses on the element of purpose:

> 1. Physical force exerted for the purpose of violating, damaging, or abusing: *crimes of violence.* 2. The act or an instance of violent action or behavior. 3. Intensity or severity, as in natural phenomena; untamed force: *the violence of a tornado.* 4. Abusive or unjust exercise of power. 5. Abuse or injury to meaning, content, or intent: *do violence to a text.* 6. Vehemence of feeling or expression; fervor.[1]

Thus violence in definitions 1, 4, 5, 6 most often has a purpose: to damage or abuse someone. These four kinds of violence are human violence, and can happen any time, any place. Thus violence is diametrically opposed to the values of the Kingdom of God.

For this paper I am going to focus on violence as persecution for being Christian,[2] offense against the gospel translated into hostile actions toward Christians.[3] Further, I will focus on biblical data both as to the kinds of violence which occur and the response from Christians to the violence. As Bishop Njoroge says, "As Christians, we are invited to dismantle the conspiracy of silence and the culture of death, and to create a culture of life."[4]

Reports of violence are increasing,

> A new militancy among non-Christian religions in the 1990s has meant that in some parts of the world Christian efforts at conversion are being resisted with *violence*. In September, a Roman Catholic priest was killed in India for his 'illegal' attempts to convert Hindus. And Muslim gangs in Java have ransacked hundreds of churches.[5]

The theme of this paper is to identify in the scripture the contexts of violence when the gospel is preached and show the biblical responses. There are eight forms of the English word "violence" which occur 113 times in the Bible, with 13 of these in the New Testament. There are seven forms of the English word "force", 11 in the New Testament. Three Greek words are used which are translated force: *pornia* (Eph. 6:12); *anagkazo* (Acts 26:11; 28:19); and *arpazein* (Matt. 11:12; John 6:15). In a more comprehensive summary, biblically the main types of violence are:

Table 1

Violence	biazo	Mt. 11:12; Acts 2:2; Rev. 18:21
Force	pornia	Eph. 6:12
Torture	tumpanizo	Heb. 11:35
Persecution	dioko	Mt. 5:10-11;44; Jn. 15:20; I Tim. 1:13; 2 Cor. 12:10
Insult	hubris	Mt. 5:11; 2 Cor. 12:10;
Speak evil	eiposin poneron	Mt 5:11;
Scourge	mastigo	Mt. 23:34;
Kill	apoktenete	Mt. 23:34
Betray	prodotes	Acts 7:52
Destroy	protheo	Gal. 1:13
Distress	anagkais	2 Cor. 12:10

The Bible gives examples of and responses to these contexts. The examples of the biblical responses to violence are:

Table 2

Bless	eulogeite	Rom. 12:14;
Be Content	eudoko	2 Cor. 12:10;
Endure / faith	anechometha	1 Cor. 4:12; 2 Thess. 1:4
Persevere	upenegka	2 Tim. 3:11;

By looking at the context of the uses of force and violence and discerning when there are parallels to present contexts the appropriate response can be discerned. This does not offer a complete set of responses to present situations but it does present the main biblical patterns. Some of the instances of violence are done by God; most are done by humans. The context shows the difference, but the use of violence is not just against believers, the plagues for example.[6]

There are three types of material which can be applied to contemporary problems with violence. First, there is the example of Jesus experiencing and confronting violence. Second, there is the example of the disciples experiencing and confronting violence. Third, there is teaching in the gospels and the epistles about responding to violence. Since the early experience of the Jesus and the disciples created the patterns of response, this paper will focus on these three contexts, with two of the teaching passages from the gospels and one from the epistles.

Biblical Teaching

In Matthew 23:34 Jesus said, "Therefore, behold, I am sending you prophets and wise men and scribes; some of them you will kill and crucify, and some of them you will scourge in your synagogues, and persecute from city to city." The context is Jesus' admonition to the Jews and Jewish leaders. Jesus' testimony is they have always persecuted the prophets God sent. Jesus is going to send more witnesses, knowing that the Jewish leaders will persecute them also. This future event of sending and persecution will fulfill the violence of the city and then God will judge the city and the leaders. There are two issues here which pertain to our limited study. First, what kinds of persecution will occur? Second, how can God send his children into situations in which He knows they will be persecuted? Jesus uses four words to describe persecution:

Kill	(Apoktneite)
Crucify	(Starriest)
Scourge	(Mastigosete)
Persecute	(Diosete)

All these words occur here in the indicative future active second person plural. There is one sense of progression from the specific action of the first three to the general statement of the fourth. There is also a progression from murder in the first two actions, to scourging, to persecution. There is no difference in the judgment against these actions—they are all examples of wrongful actions against God's prophets. There will be violence suffered just for being a Christian, a follower of Jesus, in a fallen world.

The second issue concerns the ethics of sending people into danger with expectation, even knowledge, that they will be persecuted or killed. We justify this in time of war when our own lives, or our fellows' lives, are at risk. Some lives are risked, with the knowledge that some will die, in order to save others and a way of life. Verse 40 says that God does this so that the full amount of blood may be spilt to justify the final destruction of Jerusalem and the Jewish leaders. God does not cause the violence; He hates it. But He allows it for a purpose. This reminds us of the definition which takes into account the purpose of violence. The prophets who are called and experience violence simply have to recognize that their life is in God's hands and if it is spent, it is for a purpose. There are already lives at risk, the lives and souls of the ones to whom the prophet speaks; often these are the ones who perpetrate the violence.

Jesus speaks directly to His disciples in a similar way. This teaching occurs at the last supper. "Remember the word that I said to you, 'A slave is not greater than his master.' If they persecuted Me, they will also persecute you; if they kept My word, they will keep yours also" (John 15:20). The word for persecute is the general word used in many other passages. The change is from the aorist tense to the future tense. What they did to Jesus they will do to his followers. Here in the United States we have freedom of speech and persecution takes less obvious forms.[7] In other countries missionaries, brothers and sisters, do not share these rights. Whether the persecution takes more or less violent form, there will be persecution. This passage also includes a contrary result. Some people will listen to our word and receive it, as some listened to and received Jesus' word.

Based on these two passages we can say that our witness is necessary even at risk of persecution (1) so some can turn to obey Christ and (2) so full justification is present for the just judgment of God against sin. Jesus does not suggest that most people will simply ignore the gospel and the speakers of the word. As we reach people with the gospel we see new converts and we see new opposition. In effect, when we preach we create new family and new enemies.

World population divides into the following categories, which show our potential missions, friends, and future sources of persecution.

Table 3
Chinese (1.2 billion)
Hindu (0.9 billion)
Muslim (1.2 billion)
Christian (2 billion)
All others (1.1 billion)

As we more effectively preach to non-Christian audiences (people groups) we will see increasing church growth and increasing opposition. World population will double; each city will double by 2050.[8] The next half-century of missions will focus on Chinese, Hindu, and Muslim peoples.

The Bible also talks about how we should respond to violence. The most general passage in the epistles is II Cor. 12:10 "Therefore I am well content with weaknesses, with insults, with distresses, with persecutions, with difficulties, for Christ's sake; for when I am weak, then I am strong." Paul includes five forms of weakness. Three (weakness, distress, difficulties) could be caused by life in general or by others. Two (insults and persecutions) are specifically caused by other people. All these things take away from our person, they make us weak. But when we are weak in ourselves then Christ comes to help us and we become strong (dunatos) or powerful.

If we respond in faith to the situation, and expect God to be strong through us, then how do we respond outwardly? Table 2 gave us four responses: bless the ones doing violence to us, be content that this is of God, endure the pain with faith, persevere in being faithful to the gospel. May God help us to respond this way rather than to use force/violence in return, lose our value base, and become part of the problem. Where we have legal rights of freedom we can use these; where we do not have this freedom, we still have the call to preach the gospel, entrusting our souls to God.

Notes

1. American Heritage Dictionary. (2000). Violence.
2. Njoroge, Nyambura J. (July, 2005). "An Ecumenical Commitment: Transforming Theological Education in Mission," Ministerial Formation, Vol. 105. AND Lyon, Alyanna. (Sept, 2002). "International Influences on the Mobilisation of Violence in Kosovo and Macedonia," Journal of International Relations & Development, Vol. 5 Issue 3, pp.275–295.
3. Aragon, Lorraine. (2003). "Missions and Omission of the Supernatural," Anthropological Forum, Vol. 13, No. 2.
4. Njoroge, 2005.
5. Report. (Dec., 1999). "Ye Shall be Hated of All Men," Newsmagazine, Vol. 26, Issue 44.
6. Marshall, Lucinda. (March, 2004). "Reclaiming the Paradigm," Off Our Backs, Vol. 34 Issue 3/4, pp. 55–56.
7. Fetzer, 2001.
8. Clinton, Stephen. (April, 2005). "Populations Factors in the 21st Century and Leadership of Spiritual Movements," Evangelical Missions Quarterly.

Chapter Four

Missions in the Context of Violence:
A New Testament Response

J. D. Payne

As the Church continues her missionary work in the twenty-first century, the issue of violence will continue to be both a present and a growing reality. Immediately following the Apostle Paul's reminder that "all who desire to live godly in Christ Jesus will be persecuted" (2 Tim 3:12),[1] Paul quickly notes that evil men will proceed from bad to worse, leaving readers to assume that as such men digress more and more, persecution will increase. The purpose of this paper is to develop a theological response to guide the Church during times of persecution.

John S. Pobee notes that, "Since theology emerges from the experience of a people, it would be a surprise if the experience of attack, indeed persecution, did not leave its mark and did not influence the documents of the Church. . . . It could even be argued that experiences of persecution provided the language and imagery suitable for describing Christian experience."[2] The New Testament reveals that there were at least three ways in which Jesus and Apostolic Church responded to persecution. A simple reading of the biblical text reveals that there were times when the Church responded by 1) flight; 2) avoidance; or 3) engagement. In this paper, I will trace these themes throughout the New Testament. Second, I will conclude with an attempt to develop a New Testament response for the Church in light of twenty-first century persecution.

Before examining the Scriptures, it is necessary to define the three themes. First, whenever the Scriptures portray Jesus or the Apostolic Church intentionally leaving an area or people because of opposition, here is an example of flight. Second, in passages where the biblical characters knew of possible persecution and avoided such areas, here is an example of avoidance. Finally, the most common response of the Church to persecution is engagement. Whenever the biblical text portrays the Church interacting with Her opponents through proclamation in the face of persecution, here is an example of engagement.

Synoptic Gospels

Each of the three themes is evident in the Synoptics. Even prior to the birth of Jesus, His family found themselves under persecution. This pattern would continue throughout His adult life resulting in His crucifixion.

Flight. A chronology of events reveals that the first synoptic example of persecution is located in Matthew's gospel. Following the departure of the Magi, Joseph is warned in a dream to flee to Egypt from the persecution "for Herod is going to search for the Child to destroy Him" (Matt 2:13).[3] The theme of flight is also witnessed in the "shake off the dust" passages in Matthew and Luke (Matt 10:14; Luke 9:5; 10:11). Jesus offers the Twelve instructions regarding their missionary work followed by a text predicting persecution (Matt 10:16–23) and thus the need for flight (Matt 10:23).

Avoidance. Mark's first record of persecution is related to the imprisoning of John the Baptist (Mark 1:14). Though he notes that after John's arrest that "Jesus came into Galilee preaching" (Matt 1:14), Matthew leads one to believe that it was appropriate for Jesus at this time to avoid tension to fulfill prophecy (Matt 4:13–14), specifically noting that He "withdrew" to Galilee (Matt 4:12).

Engagement. Though Jesus engages his opponents throughout Mark's writings (e.g., 3:6), halfway through the work He begins to teach his disciples that the Son of Man "must suffer" and "be killed" (Mark 8:31; cf. 9:12, 31). Possibly the clearest example of an attitude of engagement is Mark 10:33, "Behold, we are going up to Jerusalem, and the Son of Man will be delivered to the chief priests and the scribes; and they will condemn Him to death, and will deliver Him to the Gentiles. And they will mock Him and spit upon Him, and scourge Him, and kill *Him,* and three days later He will rise again" (Mark 10:33–34).

Ironically, in the same text advocating flight (Matt 10), Matthew and Luke record that Jesus *intentionally* sent his disciples out as "sheep in the midst of wolves" (Matt 10:16; Luke 10:3) with the warning that they should "beware of men; for they will deliver you up to *the* courts, and scourge you in their synagogues; and you shall even be brought before governors and kings for My sake, as a testimony to them and to the Gentiles" (Matt 10:17–18).

Fourth Gospel

Within John's Gospel, all three themes are present. Though John omits the childhood persecution narratives from his writing, he does include other passages showing persecution. Several times throughout this work, Jesus is significantly engaged in conflict with the religious leaders.

Flight. Following Jesus' heated debate with the Pharisees when He revealed his eternality with the Father (John 8:58), His opponents attempted to stone Him, "but Jesus hid Himself, and went out of the temple" (John 8:59). Later, while walking in Solomon's Colonnade, the Jews confronted Jesus. Following another tense debate, they again attempted to seize Him. It is during this encounter John simply writes, "and He eluded their grasp. And He went away again beyond the Jordan to the place where John was first baptizing, and He was staying there" (John 10:39–40).

After the significant meeting between the chief priests and Pharisees that resulted with Caiaphas unknowingly prophesying that Jesus would die for the nation and the scattered children of God, a conspiracy was made to kill Jesus (John 11:47–53). John then notes that, "Jesus therefore no longer continued to walk publicly among the Jews, but went away from there to the country near the wilderness, into a city called Ephraim; and there He stayed with the disciples" (John 11:54).

Avoidance. John notes that the Jews began persecuting Jesus for healing a man on the Sabbath (John 5:16). The first example of avoidance in his Gospel is in chapter seven. Here John notes that Jesus "was walking in Galilee; for He was unwilling to walk in Judea, because the Jews were seeking to kill Him" (John 7:1). Though He later went into Jerusalem, He informs His brothers that He would not go to the city on their desired timetable for His time "has not yet fully come" (John 7:8).

Engagement. When Jesus does arrive in Jerusalem, He boldly engages the people, and though they try to seize Him (John 7:30; 8:20), their attempts are in vain. Upon entering Jerusalem Jesus begins to physically engage those buying and selling in the temple complex (Mark 11:15–18), but the priests and scribes did not harm him because they feared Him since the people were astonished by His teaching (Mark 11:18). Later, John records that Jesus declares that His hour to be glorified has arrived (John 12:23; 13:1). Following this time, He quickly approaches His crucifixion (John 19:16).

Acts

The concept of persecution is found throughout Luke's second volume. What begins as opposition toward Jesus in the Gospel concludes with opposition toward the Church in Acts. All three themes are found in this work.

Flight. The first clear picture of this theme in Acts occurs in conjunction with the martyrdom of Steven in Jerusalem. On the same day of his death, a severe persecution breaks out against the Church. Luke records that the disciples, except the apostles, scatter throughout Judea and Samaria (Acts 8:1–4). The result of this scattering was at least that Philip ends up in Samaria preaching the gospel and that some anonymous believers end up preaching the gospel in Antioch (Acts 11:19–21).

Soon after Saul's conversion, a conspiracy is developed to kill him. The opposition is so strong that he has to escape Damascus by night through an opening in the wall of the city (Acts 9:25). Later, in Jerusalem, the Hellenistic Jews attempt to kill him. Luke notes, "But when the brethren learned *of it*, they brought him down to Caesarea and sent him away to Tarsus" (Acts 9:30).

On the night before Herod was to bring Peter out for execution, an angel releases him from prison. Though this was a miraculous escape, the angel's words (e.g., "Get up, quickly") emphasize the flight theme (Acts 12:7–10). Upon arrival at the prayer meeting of the Church, Peter explains the work of the Lord and then Luke notes, "And he departed and went to another place" (Acts 12:17).

Immediately, following his stoning in Lystra, Paul departs for Derbe (Acts 14:19–20). The day after his prison time in Philippi, he departs the city (Acts 16:40). Following an uprising in Thessalonica including the attack on Jason, as soon as it was night, the believers send Paul and Silas to Berea (Acts 17: 5–10). When the persecutors in Thessalonica eventually arrive in Berea causing a disturbance, again the believers "immediately" send Paul "out to go as far as the sea" (Acts 17:14). During the riot in Ephesus, some of the believers keep Paul from going into the amphitheater. Following the uproar, Paul then meets with the church and immediately departs for Macedonia (Acts 19:30; 20:1).

Avoidance. Though Paul confesses that he was willing to go to Jerusalem and die for the Lord Jesus, the Church in Caesarea admonishes him to avoid Jerusalem. Luke records the details of the situation after Agabus' arrival from Judea.

> And coming to us, he [Agabus] took Paul's belt and bound his own feet and hands, and said, "This is what the Holy Spirit says: 'In this way the Jews at Jerusalem will bind the man who owns this belt and deliver him into the hands of the Gentiles.'" [12] And when we had heard this, we as well as the local residents *began* begging him not to go up to Jerusalem. (Acts 21:11–12)

The Church finally agrees, however, to allow Paul to go. Since he would not be persuaded, they end their conversation stating that the Lord's will be done.

Engagement. Clearly in Acts, engagement is the most popular theme regarding the Church's response to persecution. It is within this book that the Church engages the culture with the gospel in Jerusalem, Judea and Samaria, and the ends of the earth (Acts 1:8). For the most part, the Church engages the people around them, even in light of persecution. There are numerous passages that reveal the disciples confronting others to take responsibility for their actions (2:22–23; 36; 3:12–18; 4:8–11; 4:25–28; 5:27–30; 7:52).

Having been ordered not to preach or teach in the name of Jesus, Peter and John declared, "for we cannot stop speaking what we have seen and heard" (Acts 4:20). Upon returning to meet with the other believers, rather than avoidance or flight, they petition God for boldness to speak the gospel clearly (Acts 4:29). Steven engages the religious leaders though it costs him his life (Acts 7). Luke foreshadows the fact that Paul will engage the unbelievers *and* will suffer. Recording the Lord's words to Ananias, Luke writes, "But the Lord said to him, 'Go, for he is a chosen instrument of Mine, to bear My name before the Gentiles and kings and the sons of Israel; for I will show him how much he must suffer for My name's sake'" (Acts 9:15–16).

Pauline Literature

There are numerous references to persecution throughout the Pauline writings. In defense of his apostleship, Paul is even quick to note that he has suffered much persecution (2 Cor 11:23–25). Only one of the three themes is found in his writings.

Flight. This theme is not found in the Pauline literature. The closest one comes to locating this theme is in his first letter to the Thessalonians. Following the persecution, Paul attributed his departure from Thessalonica as something forced upon himself (1 Thess 2:17).

Avoidance. Avoidance as a legitimate option for the Church is not shown in Paul's writings. He does speak of avoidance, but with a negative connotation. In his letter to the Galatians, Paul states that there are some people arguing in favor of circumcision. These people are "those who desire to make a good showing in the flesh and try to compel you to be circumcised, simply that they may not be persecuted for the cross of Christ" (Gal 6:12). They try to avoid persecution, but sacrifice the call of Christ in the process.

Engagement. Paul did not have a martyr complex whereby suffering was something he sought. He clearly petitions the Thessalonians to pray, "that we may be delivered from perverse and evil men; for not all have faith" (2 Thess 3:2). Paul realizes that his boldness for engagement comes from the Lord. He was not hesitant to request that the Ephesians pray for him for boldness to speak the mysteries of God (Eph 6:19–20). He writes to the Corinthians noting both he and Apollos endure persecution when faced with it (1 Cor 4:12).

This endurance manifests itself in Ephesus. For Paul was willing to remain in the city until Pentecost because of a great door of opportunity for ministry had opened, in spite of much opposition (1 Cor 16:9). Paul was most definitely someone who could speak about persecution from experience (2 Cor 11:24–26). Clearly, God provides comfort for those who engage the unbelievers and experience suffering (2 Cor 1:4). Along with suffering for Christ comes comfort through Christ (2 Cor 1:5). When engagement results in persecution, the Church can know that God has not and will not abandon Her (2 Cor 4:9). Paul was able to maintain the engagement theme in his life; for it was through personal persecutions that Christ's power was perfected (2 Cor 12:9–10).

Sometimes persecution has an indirect effect on the assumed outcome of engagement. Rather than be a hindrance to the spread of the Gospel, persecution can be beneficial For example, Paul notes that many brothers, upon hearing of his imprisonment, are "trusting in the Lord because of my imprisonment, [and] have far more courage to speak the word of God without fear" (Phil 1:14). Rather than the persecution in Philippi stifling his witness, Paul writes, "we had the boldness in our God to speak to you the gospel of God amid much opposition" (1 Thess 2:2). Though the Thessalonian believers suffered much from their own people (1 Thess 2:14), the Lord's message rang out in Macedonia, Achaia, and a multitude of other places (1 Thess 1:6–10).

General Epistles

There is nothing in the General Epistles that seem to advocate the themes of flight or avoidance. Engagement, however, is clearly present. The author of Hebrews and Peter address persecution in several passages.

Engagement. The writer of Hebrews notes that there was a divine intentionality to the suffering of Christ (Heb 29–10). Moses was intentional about the engagement with Pharaoh and "choosing rather to endure ill-treatment with the people of God, than to enjoy the passing pleasures of sin; considering the reproach of Christ greater riches than the treasures of Egypt; for he was looking to the reward" (Heb 11:25–26).

Peter seems to advocate that the Church should not go looking for persecution but be prepared to engage it when it arrives. While discussing suffering for righteousness, he reminds his readers that they should always be prepared to give a defense for the Lord, but to do so with gentleness and respect (1 Pet 3:15). He notes that believers should not be surprised by suffering (1 Pet 4:12), should not be ashamed (1 Peter 4:16), and should entrust themselves to God (1 Pet 4:19).

Apocalypse

The notion of suffering and persecution is woven throughout Revelation. Not only is suffering at times expected of believers, but also death (Rev 6:11). While discussing martyrdom in Judaism, Pobee writes, "Persecutions and martyrdom are part of the evil that goes to complete that full sum of sins necessary for the arrival of the Day of the Lord."[4] At least two of the three themes are found in Revelation.

Flight. Soon after the woman gives birth to her son, she flees into the wilderness to escape the great fiery red dragon. It is here the Lord cares for her (Rev 12:6; 13–14). Instead of her son being devoured by the dragon (Rev 12:4), he is caught up to God and His throne (Rev 12:5).

Avoidance. The theme of avoidance is not found in Revelation.

Engagement. The two witnesses of the Lord engage unbelievers and bring judgment upon the earth (Rev 11:6). John notes that he saw the souls of many who had engaged unbelievers and had been killed because of their testimony, their refusal to worship the beast or his image, and their refusal to accept the mark of the beast (Rev 20:4).

Theological Significance of Persecution

Before concluding with a theology of response, it is necessary to ask what is the theological significance of persecution? For the sake of brevity, I am not able to discuss this issue in great detail. An entire paper could be developed on this topic alone. In this section, however, I will offer a few brief statements by scholars noting the theological significance of persecution particularly in the theologies of Luke and Paul.

Persecution is never to be taken lightly, according to Joel F. Williams in general its effects are destructive, yet the Church should remember that the Lord is able to work through such acts of evil:

> Persecution is intended to be damaging to the church and it sometimes is. Persecution may impede growth, rob the church of its leaders, and leave the faithful with the difficult task of restoring those who have denied their commitment. Yet God is able to make even persecution work out for good, by producing a stronger, more sincere community of believers. Although persecution may be difficult, faithfulness to Christ is necessary regardless of the cost. Ultimately, Christians maintain their conviction concerning the truth of the gospel not to gain power or prestige but to preserve for themselves the opportunity, if necessary, to suffer for the sake of Christ. Then in our weakness, God displays his power. Jesus himself came not to be served but to serve and to give his life, and Christianity functions best when it follows its master. Believers fulfill their mission most effectively when they go the way of the cross and live with sacrificial love toward others.[5]

Luke clearly understands that the persecution of the Church is equivalent to the persecution of Christ (Acts 9:5). Scott Cunningham, in his work, *'Through Many Tribulations:' The Theology of Persecution in Luke-Acts* writes, "Persecution is an undeniable significant element in the author's development of plot in Luke-Acts. It is the frequent and sometimes climactic manifestation of conflict between the characters and is particularly directed against Jesus (in the Gospel) and his disciples (primarily in Acts)."[6] According to Cunningham, there are at least six theological functions of persecution in the writings of Luke:[7]

Persecution is Part of the Plan of God. Commenting on the differing persecutors found in the Scriptures, Beverly Roberts Gaventa wrote, "While both groups act against God's people and are responsible for their actions, both serve to fulfill God's will. Even the resistance to the gospel stems from God's plan and eventually leads to the church's growth."[8] Throughout Luke's writings, persecution does not happen by chance nor is it understood as a surprise to God. What happens to the Messiah is included in God's sovereign plan. Numerous times the English word "must" is used in conjunction with suffering to communicate necessity (Luke 2:49; 4:43; 9:22; 13:33; 17:25; 19:5; 22:37; 24:7, 26, 44, 46). In Acts, Paul is one who "must suffer" for Christ (Acts 9:16). Later, Paul informs the Lycaonians "Through many tribulations we must enter the kingdom of God" (Acts 14:22).

Persecution is the Rejection of God's Agents by Those Who are Supposedly God's People. Throughout Luke's writings, the Jews are the primary source of opposition toward Jesus and the Church. In both the Gospel and Acts, those who persecute the believers begin by displaying personal frustration toward God's agents but soon that frustration becomes hostility and finally climaxes in destructive acts. Cunningham commented:

> In the Gospel the only Gentile participation is at the trial of Jesus, where Pilate and Herod are involved by the Jewish leadership. In Acts, there are only three incidents of purely Gentile persecution: at Philippi, Athens and Ephesus. In all other cases of Gentile persecution it is in conjunction with and at the instigation of the Jews. Remarkably, even as the mission moves into Gentile areas, it is not the Gentiles, but still primarily the Jews who reject the message and persecute the missionaries.[9]

Following most Jewish uprisings, the missionaries turn more and more of their attentions toward the more receptive Gentiles (Acts 13:46–47; 18:6; 28:25–28).

The Persecuted People of God Stand in Continuity with God's Prophets. A reading of the New Testament quickly brings to mind the infamous Old Testament Jewish legacy that God's chosen people are those who persecute God's messengers. According to Luke-Acts, those who continue in the ways of the Lord will also continue in the ways of persecution that came upon the Lord's prophets (Matt 23:31). Cunningham writes, "Thus, the persecution of Jesus and his disciples are clearly presented by the narrative in terms of a continuation of the pattern of the rejection of God's messengers typical of Israel's salvation-history."[10]

Persecution is an Integral Consequence of Following Jesus. Acts continues the theme of persecution that Luke established in the life of Jesus in his Gospel. Since Jesus experienced persecution, his followers will continue in the pattern. Numerous parallels exist between the opposition experienced by Jesus in the Gospels and the Church in Acts.[11] Persecution comes to the followers of the Way because they *are* followers of the Way.

Persecution is the Occasion of the Christian's Perseverance. Not only will true believers experience persecution, but they will also persevere under such persecution (Luke 12:1–9). Paul is described as admonishing and encouraging the believers to continue in the faith despite their present opposition (Acts 14:22). He sets forth his own life as an example of perseverance while under persecution (Acts 20:22–24). Cunningham writes, "But even in the case of martyrdom, Luke reassures the Christian community that this is not the end, that there is an eternal reward for the one who confesses Jesus."[12]

Persecution is the Occasion of Divine Triumph. Nothing stops the growth of the Church. In fact, according to Cunningham, persecution "is used in the providence of God actually to stimulate the spread of the message of salvation."[13] Luke clearly portrays the Sovereign Lord as triumphant. Following the death of Stephen (Acts 7), the gospel spreads to Samaria and Antioch (Acts 8; 11). Though in prison, the missionaries are able to see the gospel spread to the jailer and his household (Acts 16:25–34). Even under house arrest, Paul continues to preach and teach "with all openness, unhindered" (Acts 28:31).

Other scholars have commented on the theological significance of persecution in the writings of Paul. For example, in his work, *Persecution and Martyrdom in the Theology of Paul,* Pobee suggests several issues of theological significance for sufferings and persecution.[14] According to him,

> Persecution and sufferings were a *sine qua non* of Paul's apostolic ministry. Indeed, it could be said that the more he was persecuted the more he demonstrated his zeal for the Lord and through that authenticated his apostolic authority. For that same reason he became an example to other Christians. Moreover, his own sufferings constitute a part of the cosmic battle between the forces of God and the forces of Satan. Finally, his sufferings are put in an eschatological frame of reference; for not only is his endurance of persecution rooted in the eschatological hope but also his persecution is seen as part of the filling up of the full score of sins predestined to precede the coming of the Parousia. One striking point is the absence of any ideas of vicarious atoning efficacy attaching to his sufferings because that had been achieved once for all by the martyrdom of Christ. Paul is a confessor and may yet be a martyr. But Christ is the martyr *par excellence* and whatever Paul experiences is in imitation of Christ.[15]

While addressing the theology of 1 Thessalonians, Karl Paul Donfried states, "for Paul, suffering is part of the cosmic struggle which is leading to God's triumphant victory. . . .Thus, on the one hand, accepting persecution is a sign of obedience to the gospel; on the other hand, accepting it with joy is a gift of God given through the Holy Spirit."[16]

A Theology of Response

In view of the themes of flight, avoidance, and engagement, along with the theological significance of persecution, how should the twenty-first century Church respond to its Commission in an age of violence? During a discussion of such themes, questions arise such as, when should missionaries flee, avoid, or engage their persecutors? Is there ever a time when flight or avoidance actually becomes sinful acts? Is there ever a time when engagement is foolish? What is the relationship of flight or avoidance to Christ's command for His disciples to take up their crosses and follow Him (Matt 16:24)?

It is a great conundrum that some believers are severely persecuted while others are not. For example, Johnny V. Miller observes this tension in the book of Revelation when he writes, "Some witnesses are protected throughout their mission, while others die for their boldness (Rev. 6:9–11; 12:11)."[17] God only knows why James was killed and Peter was set free (Acts 12:1–17). The mystery has not been revealed to us in the detail that we may desire.

Whether one lives or dies, it is clear that the believer will not be separated from the Lord (Rom 8:35–39). Reflecting on Luke 21:16–19, Cunningham states, "There is a promise that God will physically protect, but in his providence, if the disciple endures to death, he has assurance that he is eternally secure."[18] Continuing on, he notes that in Luke-Acts, "Although the divine protection and aid given to the messengers of God illustrates the inability of persecution to stop the message they proclaim, ultimately it is not the *messengers* who cannot be defeated . . . but the *Word of God* that is triumphant."[19]

Is Flight Still an Option? Though there were times in the Scriptures when Jesus and the Apostolic Church could have engaged their oppressors, there are examples of them taking advantage of the flight option. With Jesus, many times we read that He is in flight to fulfill prophecies and because it was not time for Him to die. The Apostolic Church is seen taking to flight following an outbreak of persecution (Acts 8) and as an option for Paul as desired by the believers (Acts 21:12).

The Scriptures allow for times of flight from persecution. As the Church makes disciples, She is a part of the fulfillment of prophecy. She is given wisdom to discern Her present situations. If the heart of the missionary is right before the Lord, then it seems likely that when faced with persecution, he or she can prayerfully discern if flight is an option. At times Paul chose the flight option (Acts 9:25); however, on other occasions, he refused the same option (Acts 21:13–14).

Is there ever a time when flight or avoidance becomes sinful? The immediate answer is that there are times when flight or avoidance are sinful acts. It is difficult, however, to answer at what time these options become ungodly acts. Much of the answer to this question is found within the hearts of believers. Clearly, there were times in the New Testament when flight was an option to save one from harm. Again, the missionary must keep his or her heart in fellowship with the Lord. If self-preservation, rather than God's glory, is the desire behind flight or avoidance, then this would be a sinful situation. Sometimes the flight option allows a person to walk by sight and not by faith.

Is there ever a time when engagement becomes foolish? Nowhere does the New Testament encourage a martyr complex, nor does it advocate that the Church should go into the world looking for persecution or even attempt to cause persecution for Herself. Engagement becomes a foolish option when it is an outcome of a martyr complex. Both Jesus and the Church never intentionally sought persecution. As they continued on their mission, whenever they encountered such opposition, they dealt with it and continued on their mission or died.

As already mentioned, the most prominent of the three New Testament themes is engagement. Despite opposition and even the possible reality of martyrdom, the Church continued to take the gospel to the world. There were times, however, when the Apostle Paul refrained from engagement at the urging of other believers (e.g. in Ephesus).

What is the relationship between flight or avoidance and Matthew 16:24? All believers are called to die physically for the sake of the Gospel if necessary. One is required to take up his or her cross and follow God's will. Some missionaries will die for the spread of the gospel; other missionaries will avoid such persecution. Though

Stephen was killed, others fled the city and planted the Church in Antioch.

For example, though the Apostle Paul was not looking for imprisonment, he was arrested. He was no longer allowed to travel freely (his area for missionary activity changed), but continued to engage his persecutors with the gospel. By the time he writes to the Philippian Church, the gospel has already entered into Caesar's household (Phil 4:22). Paul would also attribute the further the spread of the gospel to his arrest (Phil 1:12–13).

For the missionary who is walking in the light, when persecution comes, (if time and circumstances allow) wisdom and counsel are needed before the next step is taken. In certain situations for some missionaries, flight may be appropriate and consistent with Matthew 16:24, but given the same situation, for other missionaries it is not an option. For the latter, flight or avoidance may be disobedience to Matthew 16:24.

Divine sovereignty and the complexity of persecution, along with the three themes in the New Testament, do not allow for a single simple answer to the aforementioned question. What may be a perfectly legitimate response to persecution for one person may not be appropriate for another person because much depends on the Spirit's leading and the present fellowship with the Lord.

Conclusion

Though there is no simple New Testament response to persecution in every situation, the Scriptures do offer at least three acceptable practices: flight, avoidance, and engagement. These practices are not always equally appropriate for any given situation; hence, the missionary must remain prayerful and if possible, seek the council of other believers to determine the best response. Flight or avoidance (and engagement) is sin to those not walking by faith. Individuals not directly involved in the persecution, however, should not be quick to judge the hearts of those who are forced to make life and death decisions during such opposition.

Though there are several passages that support flight or avoidance, by far the majority of the persecution passages portray Jesus and the Church in engagement. Flight or avoidance were never understood to be a failure on the part of the believers, but rather resulted in a change of their missionary contexts. If they were prevented from preaching in one area, then they would travel to another location to fulfill the Great Commission.

Notes

1. Unless otherwise noted, all Scripture references are taken from the New American Standard Bible (1977).
2. John S. Pobee, *Persecution and Martyrdom in the Theology of Paul* (Sheffield, England: JSOT Press, 1985), 13.
3. Matthew clearly notes that this flight was so that prophecy could be fulfilled (Matt 2:15).
4. Pobee, 39.
5. Joel F. Williams, "Conclusion," in *Mission in the New Testament: An Evangelical Approach* (William J. Larkin, Jr. and Joel F. Williams, eds., (Maryknoll, NY: Orbis Books, 1998), 2246.
6. Scott Cunningham, *'Through Many Tribulations:' The Theology of Persecution in Luke-Acts* (Sheffield, England: Sheffield Academic Press, 1997), 337.
7. See Cunningham, pages 296–327 for a more extensive treatment of these functions.
8. Beverly Roberts Gaventa, "To Speak Thy Word with All Boldness Acts 4:23–31," in *Faith and Mission* 3 (Spring 1986): 80. 76–82.
9. Cunningham, 303.
10. Ibid., 311.
11. For example, compare the Passion narrative with the account of the martyrdom of Steven.
12. Cunningham, 341.
13. Ibid., 321.
14. See Pobee, for a detailed examination of these issues.
15. Pobee, 106. Though Pobee's comments provide insight into Paul's theology, I disagree with Pobee that the Apostolic Church saw Jesus as a martyr. Unfortunately, space will not permit me to address this concern.

16. Karl Paul Donfried, *Paul, Thessalonica, and Early Christianity* (Grand Rapids, MI and Cambridge, U.K.: William B. Eerdmans Publishing Company, 2002), 244.
17. Johnny V. Miller, "Mission in Revelation," in *Mission in the New Testament: An Evangelical Approach*, William J. Larkin, Jr. and Joel F. Williams, eds., (Maryknoll, NY: Orbis Books, 1998), 235.
18. Cunningham, 323.
19. Ibid., 325.

Chapter Five

Mission in Contexts of Violence: Forging Theologies of Persecution and Martyrdom[1]

Charles L. Tieszen

The present study serves as a call to theological reflection on both persecution and martyrdom. Despite the growing, global presence of persecution and martyrdom, theological reflection on the two events remains all but completely absent in the Church. Thus, forging theologies of these events will support Christians in their efforts to carry out the mission of God in contexts of violence.

The purpose of this paper is to examine the role of persecution and martyrdom in contexts where violence and mission may occur congruently. Statistics show that since the Church's inception nearly 70 million Christians have been killed for their faith.[2] Even more startling is the fact that sixty-five percent of these martyrs died in the twentieth century alone.[3] Including victims of persecution which do not die for their faith, but rather live daily with threats, ridicule, torture, and/or imprisonment would further affect these numbers. These facts are startling indeed, but they are not met with the theological reflection that their frequency and significance demand.

This lack of theological reflection is illustrated by Christian groups who react to persecution and martyrdom with their own brands of violence.[4] Such ungodly responses to persecution and martyrdom effectively blur a theological understanding of the events and mar Christ's intended purposes behind them. With this in mind, the present study stresses the importance of forging theologies of persecution and martyrdom, especially in contexts of violence. In so doing, we will examine the role of persecution and martyrdom as an expression of present-day Christian spirituality and mission. Secondly, we will explore the importance of adequately defining persecution and how this might foster subsequent theological reflection. Finally, we will illustrate these two aspects at work in the Coptic Church of Egypt and their struggle to forge a theology of persecution and martyrdom in a context where mission must face violence.

Persecution and Martyrdom as an Expression of Spirituality and Mission

The statistics mentioned above should shape our qualitative view of persecution and martyrdom. Accordingly, the presence and consistency of persecution and martyrdom is widespread and frequent, more so than at any other point in human history. These facts should also affect our theological perspective. With this in mind, the significance and growing presence of persecution and martyrdom should compel the Church to give these events a greater role in its expression of spirituality and mission. This means that the global Church must freshly acknowledge Christ's claim that those who follow him will be persecuted, the experience of which may end, like Christ, in martyrdom.[5] Taken seriously, this promise should affect how we view our experience of persecution and martyrdom and their relationship to Christian spirituality. In the same light, we must acknowledge that persecution and martyrdom are used by God to spread and glorify his name in mission. In these ways, persecution and martyrdom are rightly understood as an expression of both Christian spirituality and mission.

If such acknowledgements are to occur, we must overcome the build-up of misconceptions and misguided thinking that often characterize our views of persecution and martyrdom. To begin with, we must acknowledge the present-day experience of persecution and martyrdom by re-focusing our views of them away from the future and on the here-and-now. In this way, our perspective on persecution and martyrdom must include more than just the experience of them that may be an eschatological event.[6] Hal Lindsay's *The Late Great Planet Earth* and the more recent *Left Behind* series of Tim LaHaye and Jerry Jenkins have popularized the view that a time is coming when intense persecution will begin to occur or significantly increase.[7] While elements of this perspective may be true depending on one's eschatology, such a view cannot be emphasized at the expense of present experiences. Doing so effectively demeans our perspective of the persecution and martyrdom that occur presently. If persecution and martyrdom are to receive the place in spirituality and mission that they deserve, we must acknowledge our present day experience of them regardless of the place they have in future events.

Building from this, we must also re-focus theological reflection away from the past and the view that persecution and martyrdom are isolated historical events. Dan Kyanda refers to this view as the "historical exemption" in light of the opinion that persecution and martyrdom ". . . [do not] happen anymore."[8] Such a view mitigates the present-day experience of an event that is much more frequent and wide-spread then the early Church's experience of it. For instance, although the reign of Constantine brought wider recognition and greater peace for Christianity, it did not quell the presence of violence against the Church. This was especially true in areas lying on the fringes or outside of the Roman Empire. With this in mind, Samuel Moffett labels the intense persecution endured by Persian believers beginning in 339 A.D., after the rise of Constantine, as ". . . the most massive persecution of Christians in history. . . ."[9] In effect, intense persecution moved east while Christendom rose in the west. As western, intense persecution and martyrdom decreased, so did western awareness and theological reflection on the events. A similar situation exists in the West today where theological reflection on persecution and martyrdom is often misguided and truncated if not altogether absent.[10] Giving persecution and martyrdom their proper place in spirituality and mission means applying the lessons of history to events that still occur in the present.

While isolated historical and eschatological views of persecution and martyrdom form the bookends of misguided thinking, there also exists the view that all types of suffering can be thought of as persecution. In this way, natural disasters, sickness, or even becoming a victim of theft is equated with religious persecution.[11]

As Glenn Penner points out, "Because the biblical texts on persecution cannot be readily applied to a setting where there is little [less apparent] . . . persecution, the tendency seems to be . . . to misapply these passages to situations of general physical, psychological, and spiritual suffering."[12] While natural disasters and sickness are serious issues that demand a response from the Church, they cannot be equated with the experience of persecution and martyrdom. When they are, it is most often the former which garner the full attention of the Church leaving victims of religious violence without the advocacy they need and without a strong ability to theologically reflect or respond to their experience. In addition, persecution and martyrdom are left without the place they deserve in Christian spirituality and mission. Distinctions must be made between general suffering and persecution and martyrdom so that neither experience is mitigated nor is one emphasized over the other.

Other pitfalls may exist, especially in areas where violence in general is less predominant.[13] The three areas outlined above, however, suggest that current theological treatments of persecution and martyrdom are inadequate and do not allow for the two events to hold a proper place in Christian spirituality and mission. If we understand persecution and martyrdom rightly, we acknowledge that these events are a part of Christian living in the here-and-now, for every member of the Church. This involves recognition of the fact that all who seek to follow Christ *will be* persecuted (2 Tim. 3:12). Thinking this way means carefully identifying cases where persecution and martyrdom do exist and making sure that converts, especially those in contexts of violence, understand the central role of these events in Christian spirituality. In the same manner, the Church must renew its understanding of persecution and martyrdom as an expression of the *Missio Dei*. On one hand, God will at times use persecution and martyrdom to spread his church geographically and grow it numerically. We see this in the case of the early Church of Acts where believers spread geographically and their numbers grew in connection with widespread persecution (Acts 11:19ff). Christians in China are a contemporary example. In the mid-twentieth century, their numbers swelled to 50 million strong in the presence of a communist, persecuting state and the absence of Western missionaries.[14] In this, God's name is glorified and extended. The churches of South-central Asia, Western Asia, or Northern Africa on the other hand, caution any formulaic assumption whereby the 'blood of martyrs' must always be the 'seed of the Church.'[15] For Christians here, persecution and martyrdom have not equaled numerical growth. In fact, they have met the opposite effect. Since the spread of Islam and the invasions of Genghis Khan and Tamerlane, Christian numbers have dwindled and their areas of influence have shrunk. This does not however, signal the defeat of God's mission. On the contrary, God will continue to use persecution and martyrdom to glorify his name. In addition, churches in these circumstances can begin or continue to experience revival and the strengthening of their bodies. In these ways, persecution and martyrdom can be understood as an expression of spirituality and mission. This recognition will provide strength for the journey, when signs of life are seen quicker as in China, and when the road may seem longer as in Northern Africa.

Defining Persecution and Fostering Reflection

Underlying the myths outlined above is a tendency to inadequately define religious persecution.[16] Such inadequacies begin with poor or completely absent definitions of the term. Accordingly, Peter Kuzmic aptly states, "Contemporary reference works on religion move remarkably easily from 'Perfectionism' to 'Perseverance.'"[17] Penner agrees, remarking, "There is, unfortunately, no universally accepted legal or theological definition of the word."[18] Indeed, even where attempts are made, current definitions all too commonly focus on only certain manifestations of persecution or only its presence in a certain period of time. Inadequacies continue where understandings of persecution among those who experience it most are truncated. In this light, many note the tendency of persecuted Christians to deny their experience because they do not see specific manifestations of the event, such as brutality or systematic oppression. For instance, a pastor in former Czechoslovakia denied the presence of religious persecution because he saw no cases of physical brutality even though his church, under a religiously oppressive government, was forced to worship in secret. Additionally, worshippers traveled to church using complex and hard-to-follow streets in order to ensure secrecy.[19] Similar responses come from Christians in areas such as

Palestine and India[20] or in areas where religious freedom may be granted in theory, but in practice Christians are still subject to a wide range in types of persecution, including acts resulting in martyrdom. Overcoming the obstacles of poor definitions will further bolster the Church's ability to add theological reflection to a growing, Christian experience. This can happen when a clear theological definition is put in place.

When defining persecution, i must be understood from the outset that persecution is neither exclusively directed towards Christians, nor is it solely a religious issue.[21] Persecution can be perpetrated on the basis of ethnicity, political persuasion, nationality, or any number of other factors. When religion is involved, adherents of any religion or belief can be targets. In this light, Baha'i communities are persecuted in Iran; Muslims are persecuted in India and Nigeria; and Tibetan Buddhists are persecuted in China. Similar examples are numerous. With this in mind, it is important to identify religion's role in persecution. If its role is primary, then it is likely religious persecution. Further, when Christians are targeted for their Christianity, we can understand this as the religious persecution of Christians. The present study understands an expanded theological definition of the religious persecution of Christians to be:

> Any unjust action of varying levels of hostility perpetrated primarily on the basis of religion and directed at Christians, resulting in varying levels of harm as it is considered from the victim's perspective.[22]

This definition has five essential elements which can be further elucidated as follows:

1. Unjust action. One cannot merely have anti-Christian attitudes and be qualified as a persecutor. Instead, they must *act* on these attitudes.[23] Further, these actions must be unjust. For instance, one can reject a gospel presentation given to him or her by a Christian simply by stating that they do not want to hear it. Such an action is not unjust, for it is this person's right to do so. Thus, rejection, in this case, may not necessarily be unjust, and therefore every action may not necessarily be persecution.

2. Varying levels of hostility/Varying levels of harm. Persecution manifests itself within a broad spectrum ranging from mildly hostile to intensely hostile actions. Mildly hostile actions are less intense, not violent, and can be carried out psychologically or socially. These actions could include ridicule, restriction, certain kinds of harassment, or discrimination. Intensely hostile actions lie at the opposite end of the spectrum and can also be carried out psychologically or socially, as well as physically. Such actions could include torture, imprisonment, or ostracism. In this light, we cannot define persecution based on the level of harm it might cause or the level of hostility in which it occurs. On the contrary, it must be understood to encompass actions spanning the full range of hostility whether they are violent, physical, psychological, or social.

3. Perpetrated primarily on the basis of religion. As stated earlier, persecution rarely has a single impetus. Instead, there is usually an overlap of motivations. In this light, Paul Marshall offers a helpful demarcation: ". . . if the persons had other religious beliefs, they [*sic*] would still be treated in the same way. If the answer is yes, we probably should not call it specifically religious persecution, though not for a second should we forget that it is real persecution and that it is real people who suffer it."[24]

4. Christians. The commitment level of a Christian may affect the extent to which they are persecuted. For instance, 'Great Commission Christians', by virtue of their high-level of commitment to Christianity and its propagation are often more at risk than 'affiliated Christians' whose religious affiliation may be traditional and nominal.

5. Victim's Perspective. Perhaps most important, this element acknowledges the fact that persecutors cannot be the judges of their actions. The significance of this is best seen in cases of nationalism. For nineteenth and early twentieth-century Turks, their nationalistic slogan, 'Turkey for the Turks', provided a basis for the expulsion of Armenians. While the situation was complex, the deportation, genocide, and other horrific events that followed were justified for many Turks in terms of nationalism. They were protecting or ridding their country of what to them were foreign and evil influences. For

Turks, their actions were just and their results were positive. For Armenians however, this was a clear case of persecution. It was an unjust action perpetrated on the basis of, in this case, religion, ethnicity, and politics. The results were in fact negative and persecutory. As Marshall states, "The *motive* is not, per se, the issue; the key question is, what is the result?" (emphasis in original).[25]

Finally, it is important to understand this definition theologically and distinguish it from socio-political definitions. Socio-political definitions in general understand religious persecution to be any systematic violation of religious freedom.[26] For example, Saudi Arabia maintains severe restrictions upon non-Islamic expressions of religion. Within Saudi Arabia, these restrictions are widespread and consistent and are therefore understood as religious persecution. To such systematic violations, Marshall adds the elements of religious harassment (non-systematic or arbitrary violations) and religious discrimination (consistent, non-violations).[27] Definitions like these are helpful, for they give specific, measurable parameters in which persecution can be analyzed and areas of the world in which persecution occurs can be ranked. This process aids both the Church and the international community in their efforts to act as advocates for those who are persecuted. Such definitions, however, do not account for other types of persecution that come as a consequence of following Christ such as ridicule or ostracism. These actions may not be a part of systematic violations, nor may they be a part of arbitrary actions like harassment or discrimination. Yet, theologically, they are still persecution.[28] A theological definition such as this must be acknowledged and used by the Church in tandem with socio-political definitions. In this way, the Church can account for the full spectrum in which persecution occurs. It can act as an advocate for those who endure systematic violations of religious freedoms in the same way as it might for those who endure forms of persecution which may not be illegal, but are nonetheless a consequence of following Christ. Recognition of this definition will bolster further theological reflection on persecution and will begin to solidify the place that persecution and martyrdom receive in spirituality and mission.

Forging Theologies of Persecution and Martyrdom –
A Coptic Case-Study

The Coptic Church of Egypt is remarkable in its use of persecution and martyrdom as an expression of its spirituality and mission. Similarly, the Coptic understanding of persecution and martyrdom helps them to foster theological reflection. For these reasons, Egyptian Copts are forging theologies of persecution and martyrdom in a context where mission must face violence.

Although Egypt grants the Coptic Church legal status and the right to worship in theory and in law, in practice Copts are still subject to a wide range of types of persecution, some of which end in martyrdom.[29] In general, much of the persecution perpetrated against the modern Coptic Church is done so at the hands of Islamist militants. From such sources, "Actions include spreading false rumors, extortion, and violence up to and including murder, sometimes carried out with the tacit approval of local officials."[30] Of course, Copts are not the only victims of such militants who target even moderate Muslims choosing to go against the grain of Islamist ideals. In this light, violence by militants is kept in check, but done so for the threat they pose to state powers as opposed to providing protection for Copts.[31] Even so, despite weak and veiled attempts at protection, it is the Christianity of Copts that is targeted and thus such actions are indeed religious persecution.

Despite the relatively recent development of extremism directed towards Copts, these Christians have long been the targets of persecution simply because they are non-Muslims living in an Islamic state. In this light, they are victims of a myriad of discriminations, not only from Islamist militants, but from the whole of Egyptian society as well.[32] In the government and military they are severely underrepresented.[33] Once the recipient of prized positions in the workplace (many are highly educated), they are now more frequently the targets of discrimination in the job market. In fact, some Copts have been known to convert to Islam merely for the economic advantages.[34] In addition to disadvantages in economy, Copts are also the victims of educational discrimination whereby federal aid is often denied to them.[35] Other actions remain the leftovers of centuries of restriction under the *dhimma*.[36] Accordingly, Coptic churches must first seek government approval to build or repair their churches provided they are not too close to mosques.[37] As Marshall cites, "One church, having failed to obtain such permission after a year of trying, went ahead and repaired its toilet. For this 'offense' they were fined heavily, and the repaired toilet was demolished."[38] While current Egyptian president Hosni Mubarak has been more generous in granting permits for such construction, others, often Islamist militants, insist on disturbing, interrupting, and halting these endeavors. Other examples of persecution exist including the restriction of Christian broadcasting, public speech, holiday celebration, and certain Coptic institutions.[39] These actions exist among more intensely hostile types of persecution such as beatings and threats of death in addition to cases of martyrdom.

In light of this consistent religious persecution, theological reflection has become a necessity for Copts. While the government feigns toleration, persecution from militant and non-militant sources alike is clearly present in light of a context which makes no pretense about hiding religious identity. Copts, most of whom have tattooed a cross on their wrist, almost literally wear their identity on their sleeves.[40] Even those without the Coptic 'mark' are easily identified by their Christian name.[41] Easily distinguished from a Muslim name, such labels make Copts easy targets. This, even the Copts do not deny and consequently, they have developed a centuries-old tradition that informs their theology of persecution and martyrdom. In this way, Copts recognize persecution and martyrdom to be an intimate part of their history and identity.

To be a Copt is to be a part of a persecuted Church. Such an identity is further rooted in suffering for Christ's sake.[42] In fact, they have in place a mythical history which celebrates those in their past who, like Christ, have been martyred and persecuted.[43] These histories are celebrated in order to instill perseverance in the course of persecution. In like manner, ". . . stories of miracles are rewritten apocryphally to give encouragement in dark times."[44] In addition to a close connection with their history and tradition of persecution and martyrdom, they have stressed the education of their church. In the mid-twentieth century, Pope Shenuda III[45] initiated a reform movement known as the Sunday School Movement. This initiative sought to strengthen the church in general, but it also brought stability to a body that might easily be corrupted and weakened amid the pressures of militancy.[46]

This understanding of persecution and martyrdom forms the basis of the Coptic response to violence. The celebration of historic martyrs and miracles gives them strength to endure persecution, not in such a way as to glorify the experience, but to recognize it as a part of their spirituality. They also resist persecution as is seen in their opposition of legal discrimination, their cries for ethnic and national recognition, and their labeling of injustices.[47] They are not opposed to making their complaints known to authorities even if it means further persecution.[48] Perhaps most importantly, Copts recognize the importance of community and solidarity within their church. Such ideals are instilled from birth: "Priests make the sign of the cross thirty-six times on the bodies of baptized infants, signaling the uneasy lot of each newborn Copt and the protection of his group identity."[49] With such a theology in place, many Copts are able to see God's sovereignty and ultimate control of their situation. In this way, persecution is used to further the glory of God. Accordingly, Copts ". . . have spiritual resources and are able to see sunlight on an overcast day. Persecution becomes an asset. A priest explains: 'As persecution increases, we will be more in power, in heart.' . . . They feel they are counted as Christians and must act as Christians."[50] With this in mind, the Coptic Church serves as a helpful example of the hope found in forging theologies of persecution and martyrdom.[51]

Conclusion

The consistency in which persecution and martyrdom occur demands that the Church strive to forge theologies of the two events. If this is to occur, we must adjust the misguided thinking of past theological reflection. In this light, persecution and martyrdom must not be thought of as solely eschatological or isolated historical events. Similarly, we cannot reflect theologically upon persecution and martyrdom in the same way in which we reflect upon suffering in general. Modifying this type of reflection will give persecution and martyrdom a greater role as an expression of spirituality and mission. Christians must also seek to agree upon an adequate, theological definition of persecution. A definition such as the one offered above will account for the full spectrum in which persecution occurs. This will in turn foster further theological reflection and allow the Church to appropriately act as advocates. When the Church forges ahead in this process of reflection, mission in contexts of violence will perhaps take on new meaning and significance.

Notes

1. The following is based, in part, on the author's thesis: Charles L. Tieszen, "A Theological Framework for Understanding Persecution" (master's thesis, Gordon-Conwell Theological Seminary, 2005).

2. David B. Barrett and Todd M. Johnson, *World Christian Trends: AD 30 – AD 2200* (Pasadena, California: William Carey Library, 2001), 227.

3. Ibid., 229. 45,400,000 of the Church's 69,420,000 martyrs died in the twentieth century. Given this rise in martyrs, and their rate of constant presence (0.8 percent), we can project a similar rate of presence and increase upon persecutions which do not end in death.

4. This occurred recently in northern Nigeria when Muslims demanded passersby to recite the *Shahada*. If they could not, they were beaten and killed. Christians responded in like manner by demanding that passersby quote John 3:16. When they could not, as was the case for Muslims, they too were beaten and killed. Similar events continue to occur in Nigeria. Ida Glaser, interview by author, 7 August 2005, email, South Hamilton, MA. See also, Obed Minchakpu, "Eye for an Eye: Christians Avenge February Murders, Spark Muslim Retaliation," *Christianity Today* 48, no. 7 (July 2004): 17; "Rioting in Southern Nigerian City," BBC News [on-line]; accessed 22 February 2006; available from http://news.bbc.co.uk/ go/pr/fr/-2/hi/africa/4739726.stm Internet.

5. Matt. 5:11-12; cf. Paul's 'theological expectation' in 2 Tim. 3:12: "In fact, everyone who wants to live a godly life in Christ Jesus *will be persecuted*" (emphasis added).

6. This does not imply that we neglect the connection of persecution and martyrdom with the glorious hope found in Christ's future return. Rather, we cannot neglect present experiences and their significance by focusing on the role of persecution and martyrdom in the future.

7. See also Hal Lindsey, *Planet Earth – 2000 A.D.* (Palos Verdes, California: Western Front, Ltd., 1994); Larry W. Poland, *The Coming Persecution* (San Bernadino, CA: Here's Life Publishers, 1990); Dave Hunt, *Global Peace and the Rise of Antichrist* (Eugene, OR: Harvest House Publishers, 1990); John F. Walvoord, *Armageddon, Oil and the Middle East Crisis* (Grand Rapids, MI: Zondervan Publishing House, 1979; revised, 1990); Billy Graham, *Approaching Hoofbeats* (Minneapolis, MN: Grason, 1983).

8. Dan Kyanda, "The Attitude of the Prepared Christian," in Brother Andrew, ed., *Destined to Suffer?* (Orange, CA: Open Doors With Brother Andrew, Inc., 1979), 98.

9. Samuel Hugh Moffett, *A History of Christianity in Asia*, vol. 1, *Beginnings to 1500* (San Francisco: Harper Collins, 1992), 142. These persecutions would be far exceeded by events in later centuries, most notably by the twentieth century.

10. Nina Shea, *In the Lion's Den* (Nashville, Tennessee: Broadman and Holman Publishers, 1997), 5; Paul Marshall, *Their Blood Cries Out* (Dallas: Word Publishing, 1997), xxii, 98, 151-152.

11. See Aída Besançon Spencer and William David Spencer, *Joy through the Night: Biblical Resources for Suffering People* (Downers Grove, Illinois: InterVarsity Press, 1994), 76, 119. Here, the author's claim that the death of a family member is persecution given the fact that both share evil as their origin. The authors go on to distinguish between 'life-threatening' persecution, which they attribute to the early Church, and 'everyday' persecution. This, the authors connect with such experiences as losing one's car to theft or being harassed by motorists on the street. For these authors, there seems to be no major distinction between intense religious persecution and unfortunate circumstances, other than the level of threat it imposes. See ibid., 77-78. Cf. Paul Marshall, "Persecution of Christians in the Contemporary World," *International Bulletin of Missionary Research* 22, no. 1 (January 1998) : 4.

12. Glenn M. Penner, *In the Shadow of the Cross: A Biblical Theology of Persecution and Discipleship* (Bartlesville, OK: Living Sacrifice Books, 2004), 8-9. He also cites a ". . . misunderstanding or neglect of the scriptural link between persecution and discipleship." See, ibid., 9.

13. For instance, considered globally, there is a tendency to view persecution and martyrdom as the experiences of only Majority World (areas not including Northern America, Western Europe, and Australia) Christians. Violence in these regions often far surpasses that of the West which is generally tolerant of religion. Thus, due to the absence

of this much more apparent type of persecution, it is said that this is not the experience of Western Christians. This view stems from an inadequate theological definition of religious persecution, one which does not acknowledge mildly hostile forms of persecution such as ridicule even though such forms exist both in the Majority World and in the West and are a consequence of following Christ. For proponents of such a view see Herbert Schlossberg, *Called to Suffer, Called to Triumph* (Portland, OR: Multnomah Press, 1990); Brother Andrew, ed., *Destined to Suffer?* (Orange, CA: Open Doors with Brother Andrew, Inc. 1979), 4, 17, 51-52; and Scott Cunningham, *'Through Many Tribulations': The Theology of Persecution in Luke-Acts* (Sheffield, England: Sheffield Academic Press, 1997), 340-342.

14.   John Piper, *Let the Nations be Glad! The Supremacy of God in Missions* (Grand Rapids, Michigan: Baker Books, 1993), 65, 71-112.

15.   See Tertullian's famous statement, "The oftener we are mown down by you, the more in number we grow; *the blood of martyrs is seed*" (emphasis in original translation). See Tertullian *Apology L.*

16.   There has been much less difficulty in defining 'martyr' and 'martyrdom'. Someone who dies for their faith takes part in an event which has a clearly recognized end. Religious persecution has much broader manifestations without, necessarily, any clear culmination or result such as death. For a definition of 'martyr' see Barrett and Johnson, *World Christian Trends*, 225, 229, 231, and 234.

17.   Peter Kuzmic, "To Suffer with Our Lord: Christian Responses to Religious Persecution," *The Brandywine Review of Faith and International Affairs* 2, no. 3 (Winter 2004-2005): 35.

18.   Penner, 163.

19.   Schlossberg, 17.

20.   Mitri Raheb, "Sailing Through Troubled Waters: Palestinian Christians in the Holy Land," *Dialog: A Journal of Theology*, 41, no. 2 (Summer 2002): 100. Responding to the question of whether or not Arab, Palestinian Christians are persecuted Raheb remarks, "If persecution means a systematic policy of discrimination because of beliefs, then the answer is definitely, 'No'." See also, Monica Melanchthon, "Persecution of Indian Christians," *Dialog: A Journal of Theology* 41, no. 2 (Summer 2002): 109. Melanchthon is hesitant to describe the situation of Indian Christians as persecution due their own hesitancy to do so. Cf. Herbert Hoefer, "Why are Christians Persecuted in India? Roots, Reasons, Responses," *International Journal of Frontier Missions* 18, no. 1 (Spring 2001): 7-13.

21. Paul Marshall, "Persecution of Christians in the Contemporary World," *International Bulletin of Missionary Research* 22, no. 1 (January 1998) : 2. Cf. Paul Marshall, "Patterns and Contexts of Religious Freedom and Persecution" *The Brandywine Review of Faith and International Affairs* 2, no. 3 (Winter 2004-2005): 27.

22. For a full treatment of persecution's definition including an 'expanded' and 'standard' theological definition, see Tieszen, 28-42.

23. Clearly, the line between attitude and action is thin. It seems rare that one with persecutory attitudes would not act upon these attitudes. Nonetheless, such a line does exist and must be crossed in order for persecution to occur.

24. Marshall, "Persecution of Christians in the Contemporary World," 5. The recent genocide in Rwanda is a helpful example here. Extremist Hutus annihilated Tutsis on the basis of tribal affiliation, not religion. Although there were certainly Christians persecuted and killed in this horrible event, religion was not a primary motivation, and thus cannot be identified as religious persecution.

25. Paul Marshall, ed., *Religious Freedom in the World: A Global Report on Freedom and Persecution* (Nashville, Tennessee: Broadman and Holman Publishers, 2000), 17. Cf. Marshall, "Persecution of Christians in the Contemporary World," 7.

26. This would include the systematic denial of any of the rights of religious freedom understood by United Nation's 'Declaration on the Elimination of All Forms of Intolerance and of Discrimination Based on Religion or Belief, 1981'. Here, individuals must be free to worship in accordance with the fundamentals of their faith and appropriately propagate their faith. See, Paul Marshall, "Present Day Persecution of Christians," *Evangelical Review of Theology* 24, no. 1 (January 2000): 20-21.

27. Religious harassment refers to a ". . . situation where people, although perhaps not systematically imprisoned or denied the basic possibility of following their faith, nevertheless suffer from legal impediments and are interfered with by the authorities or others and face arbitrary arrest and possible physical assault." Religious discrimination refers to a ". . . situation where people, although perhaps being guaranteed basic freedom of worship and other forms of religious freedom, nevertheless suffer consistent civil and economic disadvantage under the law for exercising such freedoms." See Marshall, "Persecution of Christians in the Contemporary World," 4-5.

28. To illustrate this, consider a child of Muslim parents who converts to Christianity. Upon converting the child's parents disinherit and

ostracize him/her from the family and entire community. Doing so does not violate any religious freedom (unless the child is subsequently attacked). However, considered theologically, this action is persecution and demands a response from the Church, perhaps not to the family, but in support of the child. See Marshall, ed., *Religious Freedom in the World*, 16.

29.   See Jonathan Fox, "The Copts in Egypt: A Christian Minority in an Islamic Society," in *Peoples versus States: Minorities at Risk in the New Century*, ed. Ted Robert Gurr (Washington, D.C.: United States Institute for Peace Press, 2000), 140; cf. Edward Wakin, *A Lonely Minority: the Modern Story of Egypt's Copts* (William Morrow, 1963; reprint, Lincoln, NE: iUniverse.com, Inc., 2000), 176 (page citations are to the reprint edition).

30.   Fox, 141. See also S. S. Hasan, *Christians versus Muslims in Modern Egypt: The Century-long Struggle for Coptic Equality* (Oxford: Oxford University Press, 2003), 175-182; Timothy C. Morgan, "Church of the Martyrs: Copts Thrive in the Face of Bloody Carnage, Legal Restraint, and Discrimination," *Christianity Today* 41, no. 9 (August 11, 1997): 44-47, 57; Warren Cofsky, "Copts Bear Brunt of Islamic Extremism," *Christianity Today* 37, no. 3 (March 8, 1993): 46-47; R. N. S., "Egyptian Christian Killed in Ongoing Strife," *Christian Century* 114, no. 16 (May 14, 1997): 474; "Extremists Kill Christian Copt," *Christianity Today* 41, no. 5 (April 28, 1997): 78; Joseph Assad, *Testimony on the US State Department Annual Report on International Religious Freedom for 2000* [manuscript on-line]; accessed 11 October 2005;   available   from http://www.freedomhouse.org/religion/news/bn2000/bn-2000-09-07.htm; Internet.

31.   Fox, 141-142.

32.   Ibid., 140; cf. Wakin, 176.

33.   Fox, 139.

34.   Ibid.

35.   Ibid; Hasan, 170-172.

36.   The Muslim 'contract' allowing certain groups like Christians, to maintain their faith and live under Islam.

37.   In this light, it is not entirely uncommon for Muslims to build a mosque near the proposed cite of a Coptic church, thus prohibiting the completion of the church. See Fox, 140.

38.   Marshall, "Persecution of Christians in the Contemporary World," 4.

39.   Fox, 140.

40. Hasan, 140; Wakin, 43. In like manner, many Coptic priests carry a cross with them at all times.

41. Wakin, 43.

42. Such an identity is captured in the symbol of the cross. "The cross suits this cruel culture of poverty and persecution, both an identification and an outlet for the Copts. It is their brand and their balm; it gives a meaning to life when there are only blind nature and inexplicable misfortune. If Western Christianity gives prime glory to Easter - the day of Resurrection, deliverance and confirmation of Christ's divinity - Good Friday is more appropriate psychologically to the Copts." See ibid., 136.

43. Hasan, 21. According to Hasan, this history is mythical not because it is something which did not really happen, but because it has reached mythical stature over time. She further notes that, "To this day the two main Coptic traditions remain monasticism and martyrdom." See ibid., 22.

44. Ibid., 22. Hasan continues, "Recently, with the upsurge of bloody attacks by Islamic militants, such stories have been put to good use by the church leadership."

45. From 1971 to the present, Shenuda III has been the Pope of the Coptic Orthodox Church. Ibid., 4.

46. Ibid., 3, 58.

47. See Wakin, 176; Youssef M. Ibrhaim, "Egypt Copts Protest Alleged Moslem Harassment," *New York Times*, 31 March 1980. As to their fight for recognition as Arabs and Egyptians see Wakin, 75-76.

48. It is in such resistance that an interesting cycle occurs. As Wakin notes, "The Moslems have imposed a self-fulfilling prophecy on the Copts by regarding them as fanatics. Feeling cornered, the Copts struggle to protect themselves, intensifying clannishness and increasing their unrest and dissatisfaction. A chicken-and-egg cycle goes on uninterrupted: the Copts feel persecuted, the Moslems cite Coptic sensitivity, the Copts strain to overcome discrimination, the Moslems indict Coptic aggressiveness." See ibid., 169-170. Despite this cyclical struggle, theological responses to persecution continue.

49. Ibid., 5.

50. Ibid., 36.

51. See Menes Abdul Noor's comments in Morgan, 57: "We think of the Christian in Egypt as the burning bush . . . The more it burns – the more it becomes green. The more we feel we need Christ. I think there is a lack of hope in this part of the world. I see hope. The big hope." Such an attitude is interesting in light of the fact that Copts have been a

consistent minority for eleven centuries. In other words, persecution has not been a seed for numeric growth up to this point, but for many it may be a seed for growth in spiritual maturity, perseverance, and potential vitality. It should be noted that cases of numerical growth do exist as in the large cave churches in Cairo's garbage dumps where congregations numbering in the thousands meet regularly. See, for instance, Kees Hulsman, "Trash-Collector Church Salvages Cairo Village," *Christianity Today* 41, no. 9 (August 11, 1997): 46. It should also be noted that not all Coptic responses to persecution are positive or biblical. Cases exist where Coptic militant groups such as the *Umma Coptya* have formed in response to Islamic militancy. See Wakin, 95-98.

Chapter Six

Divine Suffering and Divine Grace: A Missiological Interpretation of Kitamori Kazo's Pain of God Theology

How Chuang Chua

The story of the rapid recession of Christianity in the West and its unprecedented advance in other parts of the world in the twentieth century has given rise to what Andrew Walls calls "a post-Christian West and a post-Western Christianity."[1] As Christianity comes into increasing contact with non-Western world cultures and societies, the need for theology to be relevant to local, particular contexts has never been more urgent. At the same time, the global spread of Christianity has increased our awareness of the emergence of what Lamin Sanneh and others refer to as "world Christianity." The missiological dialectic between local and global carries an important theological implication: authentic, biblically sound theology must not only be locally relevant, but also globally significant in advancing the church's knowledge of God and His work in the world. If David Bosch, following Martin Kähler, is right in his assertion that mission is the "mother of theology,"[2] then serious theological reflection becomes a missiological imperative. As we deliberate on the theme "Mission in the Context of Violence" in its different aspects, I propose in relation to this that we consider an original theological construction that seeks a voice on the global theological stage.

This paper highlights a couple of pertinent points from the groundbreaking work of the late Japanese theologian-pastor, Kitamori Kazo,[3] and offers a tentative missiological interpretation of his theology, especially in relation to the preaching of the gospel in a world increasingly wracked by violence, suffering, and death. Kitamori, arguably the most famous Japanese theologian outside his native country, is most well-known for his pain of God theology. Through his particular explication of the Atonement, Kitamori offers us an enlarged and enriched understanding of the character of God beyond what is conveyed through the classical Atonement theories of Western theology. The thesis of Kitamori's theology is this: *Divine pain is constitutive of divine grace.* The pain of God in Kitamori's writings refers not only to the suffering of the Son of God on the cross, as we commonly understand it, but also to the deep anguish of the Father who has lost His only Son.[4] And it is this aspect of the Father's pain that we will turn our attention to. But before proceeding further, let us first sketch a brief biography of Kitamori's life.

Biography of Kitamori Kazo (1916–1998)

Kitamori Kazo was born in Kumamoto on the southern island of Kyushu in 1916. While at high school he encountered the witness of Lutheran missionaries, which led to his conversion and baptism. Kitamori, like all Lutherans of his day, read *Young Luther*, an extremely popular book written by the Japanese Lutheran scholar, Sato Shigehiko (1887–1935). Sato had actually taught at the Lutheran seminary in Kitamori's native Kumamoto for two years before pursuing further Lutheran studies in Germany under Karl Holl from 1922 to 1924. In any case, the young Kitamori was so impressed by Sato's work that he decided to pursue studies on Luther himself. As Sato was at that time teaching at the Japan Lutheran Theological Seminary in Tokyo, Kitamori decided to enroll in that seminary upon completion of high school in 1935. It was unfortunate that Kitamori was not able to study under Sato as the latter died that same year. Still, Kitamori received a solid education in Lutheran theology, and graduated from the seminary in 1938. In his first year at seminary, Kitamori read the book of Jeremiah, and wrote a theological essay on the pain of God.[5] After seminary, Kitamori entered the philosophy department of the prestigious Kyoto Imperial University where he did graduate studies under Tanabe

Hajime. Kitamori graduated in 1941, and remained at the university over the next two years working as a teaching assistant.

In 1943, Kitamori received an appointment to teach Systematic Theology at the Tokyo Union Theological Seminary, which he did so until his retirement in 1984. Throughout most of his years as seminary professor, Kitamori also pastored Chitose Funabashi Church, a church that he founded in 1950 under the United Church of Christ in Japan (UCCJ) denomination. The whole denomination was in moral shambles because of its uncritical support for the war, and Kitamori helped reorganize it and even drafted its confession of faith. Although he remained within the UCCJ for the rest of his life, Kitamori was unwaveringly Lutheran in his theology. He refers to Luther as "our pioneer and guide in matters of faith."[6] In particular, following Luther's *theologia crucis*, Kitamori insists that "to understand everything one must proceed from the Christ of the cross."[7] For Kitamori, the actuality of the cross is the foundation of all theological thought.[8]

Exegesis of the Pain of God

It was through the Old Testament prophet Jeremiah that Kitamori was led "to see the heart of God most deeply."[9] He draws an interesting parallel between Jeremiah and Paul, calling Jeremiah "the Paul of the Old Testament," and conversely, Paul "the Jeremiah of the New Testament."[10] Moreover, "'God on the cross' as revealed to Paul is for Jeremiah 'God in pain.'"[11]

The verse that ignited Kitamori's thought on divine pain is Jeremiah 31:20. In the King James Version,[12] the verse reads:

> Is Ephraim my dear son? Is he a pleasant child? For since I spake against him, I do earnestly remember him still; therefore my bowels are troubled for him; I will surely have mercy upon him, saith the Lord.

In this verse, the expression "my bowels are troubled" is translated from the Hebrew *hamû me'ay* comprising two lexical items: the verb *hamah*, and the noun *me'eh*. The latter refers literally to one's intestines or inward parts. In this context, it is used figuratively to refer to the seat of emotions, and is appropriately translated into English as "heart." According to the *Theological Workbook of the Old Testament*, the verb *hamah* means to 'cry aloud, mourn, rage, roar, sound; make noise, tumult; be clamorous, disquieted, loud, moved, troubled, in an uproar." [13] In the context of this verse, Kitamori sees this verb as describing the heart of God in an emotional state of turmoil, anguish and restlessness. [14] Kitamori's interpretation can be validated from the way *hamû me'ay* is rendered as *bricht mir mein Herz* (literally, "my heart is broken") in Luther's Version, or as "my heart bursts with longing" in Eugene Peterson's paraphrase *The Message*. In the Japanese Literary Version, the translated expression is *waga harawata itamu* (literally, "my insides are in pain").

Kitamori did a further word study on *hamah* from Jeremiah 4:19, Jeremiah 48:36, Psalm 39:6, Psalm 55:17, Psalm 77:3, and Isaiah 16:11, and concluded that the very heart of God can be apprehended analogically from human emotions. Indeed there is no way to understand the pain of God other than through the Thomist "analogy of existence." [15] In other words, human experience of pain is the only means by which we understand the pain of God. Kitamori gives the example of the parable of the Prodigal Son, a story told by Jesus so that "we are permitted to know the heart of God by means of events that happen in the world of men." [16]

Concerning Jeremiah 31:20, Kitamori exclaims, "Jeremiah must have seen in God the same condition of the heart which the prophets and psalmists themselves experienced. What kind of condition? The pain! The pain of God!" [17] In other words, Jeremiah saw the severest compassion of God's love toward sinners, and appropriately used the word "pain" to describe it. Kitamori justifies his interpretation of Jeremiah by citing John Calvin's commentary on this verse:

> God enhances the reconciling grace further by saying, 'therefore my bowels are troubled for him; I will surely have mercy upon him.' Here God attributes human feelings to himself; for our bowels are shaken and roar under extraordinary 'pain' (dolor), and we sigh and groan deeply under the pressure of great sorrow. God, therefore, expresses his feelings as an affectionate father: 'my

bowels are troubled' [literally "roar"] in accepting his people back in his grace. . . . God's nature is to feel this way.[18]

To strengthen his case, Kitamori quotes a whole host of other commentators, including C. F. Keil's comment that "God suffers pain on account of Ephraim his son."[19] In sum, Kitamori's exegesis led him to the insight that the pain of God is engendered when God refuses to stop loving those who turn against him. Kitamori is quick to point out that divine pain is therefore not to be understood in the substantive sense (*jittai gainen*), but only in the relational sense (*kankei gainen*).[20]

Next, Kitamori observes that the word *hamah* is also used in Isaiah 63:15, but in this context, it refers not to divine pain but to divine love.[21] He concludes that the Hebrew word *hamah* carries the semantic content of pain and love simultaneously.[22] This linguistic fact is "not simply a mystery of language, but also a mystery of grace."[23] If Kitamori is right, the question to ask then is this: How should we understand the relationship between love and pain? Here is where Kitamori's theological creativity becomes most evident.

The Nature of God's Love: Three Orders of Love

Using Augustine's concept of *ordo amoris*, Kitamori suggests that the love of God can be understood as comprising three orders: (1) the immediate love of God, (2) the pain of God, and (3) the intent love rooted in the pain of God.[24]

The immediate love of God. The object of the immediate love of God is the person who is completely worthy of receiving it. Such a person is loved directly by God without mediation. This is the love that exists ontologically within the Godhead. The Father loves His completely obedient Son with a full and immediate love. God's love for Adam and Eve in their pre-Fall state was also an immediate love. Sin, however, betrayed that love. Because sin has come in between God and humans, God is no longer able to love human beings with an immediate love. Moreover, mediated by sin, divine love can only turn into divine wrath.[25] And as a result of the universal effects of sin on humankind, all humans have now become objects of His wrath.

The pain of God. According to Kitamori, the righteousness of God demands that sin should *never* be forgiven. In fact, Kitamori defines forgiveness as the act of forgiving the unforgivable.[26] Yet the scandal of the gospel is that God has acted in an "ungodlike" and "improper" way.[27] Instead of repulsing those who must be repulsed, God desires to forgive sin, and enfold (*tsutsumu*) and embrace (*daku*) the sinner.[28] The gospel is indeed hard to believe, but it is true: God *still* loves the sinner who has lost all claims to be loved (cf. Jer 31:20). However, as Kitamori points out, divine love is not a smooth and easy love, for it is "the love for the enemy" (Rom 5:10).[29] And this love for the enemy creates a real conflict within God Himself, between His love and His wrath. And that conflict engenders pain: "God who must sentence sinners to death fought with God who wishes to love them. The fact that this fighting God is not two different gods but the same God causes his pain. Here heart is opposed to heart within God."[30] The pain of God is most fully manifested at Golgotha, the site where "God fought with God."[31] For on the cross, not only was the love of God supremely revealed, but so was the wrath of God. Citing Theodosius Harnack's interpretation of Luther, Kitamori argues that divine pain is the "tertiary" (*tertium*) that unites the wrath of God and the love of God.[32] Kitamori elaborates,

> The Lord [Jesus] wants to heal our wounds, which were caused by God's wrath; this Lord suffers wounds, himself receiving his wrath. ". . . with his stripes we are healed" (Isa. 53: 5). . . The Lord was unable to resolve our death without putting himself to death. God himself was broken, was wounded, and suffered, because he embraced those who should not be embraced. By embracing our reality, God grants us absolute peace. But the peace has been completely taken away from the Lord who grants us absolute peace. "My God, my God, why hast thou forsaken me?"[33]

In other words, in order to secure atonement for humankind, it was necessary for God the Father to experience the searing pain of abandoning His beloved Son and giving Him over to a most violent and unjust death. Only then would divine wrath be placated and divine love realized—but at the expense of divine sorrow. Conversely stated, by divine grace, the violence that we, as God's enemies, ought to have suffered was borne for us by our Savior. In sum, the divine hospitality extended to us comes at the cost of divine violence suffered on our behalf.

The intent love rooted in the pain of God. Herein lies a deep divine mystery. The death of Christ results in *mors mortis*, the death of death (so John Owen). For the resurrection of Christ vindicates His death, and demonstrates the victory of the pain of God: divine love has conquered divine wrath! Forgiveness of sin is now not only a possibility; it has become an actuality. God is now able to welcome sinners back as His reconciled children, in the same way the waiting father welcomes the prodigal son home. Our wounds have been healed by Christ's wounds, and our pain saved by God's pain. The victory of divine pain is "the intent love rooted in the pain of God."[34] Yet, argues Kitamori, while God is now able to love us freely, He is still not able to love us immediately.[35] For God's love for us will always be mediated by divine pain. The reason is that the intent love of God is "constantly being shipwrecked" by sin.[36] By this Kitamori seems to mean that even though we who are forgiven are delivered from the penalty and power of sin, we are still not delivered from the presence of sin. The reality of sin's presence continues to pose a constant threat to our faith, seeking to drive a wedge between us and the love of God. For this reason, it is important for Christians to live a crucified life (Gal 2:20), remembering always "Jesus Christ and him crucified" (1 Cor 2:2).

Translating the knowledge of "Jesus Christ and him crucified" into the language of divine pain, Kitamori stresses that it is only within the pain of God that we are sheltered and protected from the wrath of God.[37] "God's pain is truly our peaceful abode. . . [for it] results from the love of the one who intercepts and blocks divine wrath from us."[38] Kitamori tells this fascinating parable to illustrate his point:

A traveler is walking across a field in summer, when suddenly a thunderstorm breaks out above him. There is neither tree nor habitation; the traveler must walk on alone, in danger of being struck by lightning at any moment. Around him the lightning is striking here and there; in a minute it may strike him dead. But

> look! A mysterious hand is stretched over the traveler, covering
> and protecting him. Guarded by this loving hand, he can safely
> walk on through the thunderstorm. Because of that wonderful hand
> the lightning will not touch him. But look further. Like a linen
> cloth pierced by countless bullets, the hand which protects the
> traveler is being repeatedly struck by the lightning. This protecting
> hand is catching and intercepting the thunderbolts, which should
> fall on the traveler.[39]

In other words, the forgiven and reconciled sinner is called to trust
and fear God at the same time. When a person puts his wholehearted
trust in God's intent love, a love rooted in His pain, he can be fully
assured of God's love protection to the point of knowing that "even
the very hairs of [his] head are all numbered" (Lk 12:7). Yet it is this
same God that one needs to fear. Outside of God there is power that
is capable of destroying us, but it can never destroy us completely
the way that only God, by virtue of His wrath, can (Lk 12:4–5). It is
hence imperative that those who have been forgiven as a result of the
pain of God lives their lives in such a way that they are always
within the protection of His intent love.

Kitamori does not say if the intent love rooted in the pain of God
ever becomes an immediate love. He does mention the theological
reality of an incomplete and unfulfilled sanctification as long as we
are in this world.[40] The fact is that as long as sin is present, the love
of God will remain in an unresolved condition. But that is not a
critical problem, for we do have an eschatological hope in a glorious
End, when the suffering of the world, corresponding to the pain of
God, is completely diffused.[41] Presumably, then and only then will
the pain of God be fully resolved, the expected consequence of
which is that humans will once again become the objects of God's
immediate love.

Two Scripture Passages

According to Kitamori, there are numerous passages in Scripture that
offer us a glimpse into the pain of God. Let me cite two of these
passages. The first relates to Herod's slaughter of the Innocents in
Matthew 2:16–18. This text is set in the context of the Christmas
story, but is almost never read during Christmas. Because of the

violence inherent in this episode, it has become somewhat of a taboo to the Christmas spirit. The question is often asked as to why God, in His power, did not prevent such senseless bloodshed. Indeed why such suffering was not prevented, we do not know, but Kitamori suggests that in this instance, the untold suffering as echoed in the haunting cry of Rachel reveals to us the suffering heart of God.[42] The extreme contrast between the irenic scene of the Nativity and the following scene of the Slaughter of the Innocents is indicative of the unparalleled significance of the birth of Jesus. For the birth of Jesus is related to His death. The goal of Christmas is nothing less than the Passion. For all human beings, death is the final *result* of birth, but in the case of Jesus, death was the very *purpose* of His birth. And so, along with the blessed news of the birth of Jesus, Matthew foretold His violent death, through the Slaughter of the Innocents. More than this, Kitamori suggests that the Slaughter of the Innocents expresses the unrelieved pain and grief of the Father who refuses to be comforted, like Jacob at the loss of his son Joseph.[43] And the lament of the mothers in Bethlehem over the senseless slaughter of their sons points to the lament of the Father who would similarly witness the cruel slaughter of His own Son on the cross. For this reason, insists Kitamori, without the pain of God, the Christmas story becomes meaningless sentimentalism.[44]

A similar observation can be made of Luke 2:28–35. The words that Simeon pronounced to Mary about a sword piercing her soul were difficult words, to say the least. And indeed Mary would experience the full import of these words when she saw her son, Jesus, brutally beaten up and crucified. At the foot of the cross, Mary must have felt utterly lonely, that no one understood the hellish pain that she was going through. For who could empathize with her unique situation of losing a perfect son, a son who was miraculously conceived, the promised Savior, and who was now being subject to the greatest injustice in history? This is where Kitamori's genius comes in. Kitamori points out that Jesus was not only the son of Mary, but He was also the Son of God, and therefore the very same sword that pierced Mary's soul would also pierce the soul of the Father.[45] For Jesus died on the cross not only as the son of Mary, but as the Son of God. And so, just as Mary suffered the indescribable pain of losing her son on the cross, God the Father too underwent intense pain and suffering when He saw His Son being cruelly put to death. Both Mary and God the Father lost the same son on Calvary. And so in this sense, Mary's pain was not unique. Simeon's prophetic words hence were not only for Mary, but they were intended to give a glimpse of what God would experience at the Crucifixion.

For Kitamori, buried in these two biblical passages that we have just considered is a theological pearl of great price. The pain of God is an inherent and essential part of His salvation plan, a point that is often neglected or forgotten in our gospel proclamation.

Missiological Implications

It remains for us to reflect on how we can appropriate Kitamori's pain of God theology in our missiological thinking and practice. Here I propose four preliminary points for consideration. First, we must acknowledge that suffering is an inescapable part of human experience. While Christians should work to alleviate pain and suffering, we must realize that suffering can never be fully eliminated this side of heaven. But it can be illuminated, so that we can experience more deeply and participate more fully in the work of divine grace through our suffering. For suffering is not a uniquely human experience; it is also a divine experience. One of the wondrous implications of the Incarnation is that in the person of the God-man Jesus we see the unity of divine pain and human pain.[46] This means that God knows our pain and suffering. For not only is the Son the object of God's pain, but through the Son all human beings have become objects of God's pain as well.[47] Kitamori would even go so far as to say that since God is the Father of humankind, He also experiences pain when we suffer.[48] And this is the precisely why we can receive the very real comfort of God, because on Calvary, God not only suffered for us, but He suffered *like* us.

To illustrate this point, Kitamori tells the following true story of Origuchi Nobuo (1883–1953), a well-known folklorist and Shinto scholar. Origuchi never married but adopted a son. However, his son died fighting in the Battle of Iwo Jima during the Second World War. Overcome with grief, Origuchi wrote this poem:

ningen wo fukaku aisuru kami arite
moshi mono iwaba ware no kotokemu [49]

This poem is translated as such, "If indeed there is a god who loves humanity profoundly, and f indeed such a god speaks, he would speak like me." In essence, Origuchi was lamenting that there is no divine being among the eight million Shinto gods who could ever understand the excruciating pain of losing a son. Kitamori comments that while this may be true of the Shinto pantheon, the God and Father of Jesus Christ *did* suffer profoundly when His only Son died on the cross.[50] Kitamori adds that it is only through the suffering of God that our suffering can be truly redeemed and our wounds healed. Such is the "wondrous truth" of the gospel.[51]

Second, suffering is not only an inescapable part of human experience; it is a necessary component in missionary service. We learn from Kitamori the missiological purpose of the pain that God experienced in embracing the world, the enemy of God, in love. In the same way when missionaries live incarnationally among a people who have no knowledge of God, or worse, who are overtly antagonistic to the gospel, they should not be surprised when they encounter pain and suffering as if something strange were happening. Indeed if God had to suffer in order to save the world, it would be presumptuous of us to think that we can be exempt from suffering when we preach the gospel. Moreover, missionaries share in the common sufferings of humankind. How missionaries understand suffering theologically and respond spiritually, in identification with the sufferings of their fellow human beings, becomes an essential part of the gospel witness. Indeed the pain of God provides us with a divine warrant to embrace suffering for the sake of the world and the church, rather than suppressing or denying it. This is an important point because the people whom we preach the gospel to will model us in our attitude to pain and suffering.

Third, Kitamori suggests that one way in which we can deal with our pain is to let our pain testify to the pain of God.[52] There are two ways to render service to divine pain. The first is "to let our *loved ones* suffer and die."[53] In so doing, we are witnessing to the pain of God, since we experience the pain of God the Father who let His beloved

Son suffer and die. The thought here is that because God knows precisely the pain involved, we need to trust Him when our loved ones suffer and die, and not demand healing as if it were our intrinsic right. This is a powerful theological counterpoint to the health and healing industry so rampant in the modern church today. The second means by which to render service to the pain of God is "for *us* to suffer and die."[54] When we allow ourselves to suffer, we are witnessing to the pain of God because we identify with God the Son entering pain and dying. In sum, to serve the pain of God with our pain is, in biblical jargon, to deny ourselves, take up our cross and follow Jesus (Mt 16:24). The central message of the gospel is not salvation from suffering. That would be Buddhism. Rather, the gospel is about salvation from sin, and that involves suffering. In the words of Dietrich Bonhoeffer, "When Christ calls a man, he bids him come and die."[55] Indeed, suffering is "the fruit of an exclusive allegiance to Jesus Christ."[56] If missionaries do not understand this elementary principle, neither will the people to whom they preach the gospel.

The final point relates to the ministry of the church. Earlier we mentioned that it is in the person of Jesus that we see the unity of divine pain and human pain. Kitamori sees the church, being the extension of the life and ministry of Jesus Christ, as now tasked with the responsibility of bearing the pain of God in the world and relating human reality to divine pain.[57] In other words, a theology of pain must service an ecclesiological appropriation of pain and suffering that is so vital in the mission of the church. In practical terms, it means that in order to relieve the suffering of the world, the church must be involved in its suffering. The task of preaching the gospel must therefore include an active engagement with the existential human realities of pain and suffering, violence and death.

Coda

Because of the brevity of this paper, I recognize I could do no meaningful justice to Kitamori's theology. Rather, this paper has likely raised all sorts of questions relating to theological content and methodology that certainly need to be addressed. However, it is hoped that through this presentation of a non-Western theologian, we can be reminded that the mystery of who God is and what He has done for us is far deeper than we can ever fathom. Here is a God who not only loves us passionately, but also who shares profoundly in our pain and suffering.

It is fitting to conclude with an anecdote from Kitamori relating to Japanese Buddhism More than half of Japanese Buddhists belong to the True Pure Land Buddhist Sect. Like Christianity, True Pure Land Buddhism teaches salvation by grace through faith. Only the object of faith is different. In Pure Land, one is saved by the grace of the Amida Buddha, by putting one's faith in Him. Kitamori observes that while the doctrinal structure of salvation between Christianity and Pure Land is similar, the fundamental difference is that in Pure Land there is no cross.[58] In other words, the Buddha knows and feels no pain. Enlightenment for the Buddha is freedom from pain, but for the Christian God, the existential reality is one of pain. For that reason, ultimately, only the suffering God, not the passionless Buddha, is able to save a world wracked by violence, pain, and suffering.

Notes

1. Andrew F. Walls, The Cross-Cultural Process in Christian History: Studies in the Transmission and Appropriation of Faith (Maryknoll, NY: Orbis, 2002), 65.
2. David J. Bosch, Transforming Mission: Paradigm Shifts in Theology of Mission (Maryknoll, NY: Orbis), 489.
3. Following Japanese convention, Japanese personal names are written with the surname first followed by the given name. The romanization of Japanese words follows the modified Hepburn system.
4. Paul's injunction not to grieve the Holy Spirit in Ephesians 4:30 implies that the Holy Spirit can be inflicted on. The posited possibility of the suffering of the Father, the Son, and the Spirit, opens the way for a construction of a trinitarian theology of suffering. This may well be a worthy theological project.
5. It is easy to attribute the theme of Kitamori's theology to the suffering of the Japanese as a result of the country's defeat in the Second World War. The fact is that Kitamori reflected on the pain of God fully ten years before the end of the war. It is true that the circumstances

surrounding the war gave greater relevance to Kitamori's ideas and brought them into sharp focus. That notwithstanding, Kitamori insists that divine pain is a fundamental biblical theme and constitutes "the very heart of the gospel." Kitamori Kazo, *Kami no itami no shingaku* (*Theology of the Pain of God*), 7th ed. (Tokyo: Kodansha, 1986), 24.

6. Kitamori, *Kami no itami*, 164.
7. Ibid., 74.
8. Ibid.
9. Ibid., 24.
10. Ibid.
11. Ibid.
12. The King James Version is the closest to the Japanese Literary Version, the version that Kitamori used. Both versions are similar in linguistic style.
13. R. Laird Harris, Gleason L. Archer, Jr., and Bruce K. Waltke, *Theological Workbook of the Old Testament*, in Bible Works 6.0.
14. Kitamori, *Kami no itami*, 259.
15. Kazoh Kitamori, *Theology of the Pain of God* (Eugene, OR: Wipf and Stock, 2005), p. 153. This is the English translation of Kitamori's *Kami no itami no shingaku*. It was first published in 1965. For the purposes of this paper, I use the original text alongside this excellent translation.
16. Kitamori, *Pain of God*, 152.
17. Ibid., 153.
18. Ibid., 154.
19. Ibid., 155.
20. Kitamori, *Kami no itami*, 11.
21. Kitamori, *Pain of God*, 156–57.
22. Ibid., 157.
23. Ibid. At this point, it is important to note that, contrary to what some have supposed, Kitamori did not construct his whole theology on a single verse, namely Jeremiah 31:20. See, for instance, William A. Dyrness, *Learning about Theology from the Third World* (Grand Rapids, MI: Zondervan, 1990), 143. While it is true that Jeremiah 31:20 pivotal to Kitamori's thought, he was careful to interpret that verse in the context of the whole Scripture. Throughout Kitamori's book, a total of 327 different Scriptural texts from 30 biblical books were cited.
24. Kitamori, *Pain of God*, 117.
25. Ibid., 118.
26. Kitamori, *Zetsumyo no shinri* (*Wondrous Truth*) (Tokyo: Kyobunkan, 2000), 38.

27. Kitamori, *Pain of God*, 119.
28. Kitamori, *Kami no itami*, 204–205
29. Ibid., 155.
30. Kitamori, *Pain of God*, 21.
31. Kitamori, *Kami no itami*, 28.
32. Ibid.
33. Kitamori, *Pain of God*, 22. Emphasis in the original.
34. Ibid., 94.
35. Ibid., 123.
36. Ibid.
37. Ibid., 123–24.
38. Ibid.
39. Ibid., 126.
40. Ibid., 143.
41. Here Kitamori draws an interesting correlation between the diffusion of the gospel throughout the world and the diffusion of the world's suffering and divine pain. The global spread of the gospel is an eschatological sign pointing to the end of the world's suffering. It is not clear though how the suffering of the world is related to divine pain. Kitamori, *Kami no itami*, 240–41.
42. Kitamori, *Zetsumyo no shinri*, 22–30.
43. Ibid., 26–27.
44. Ibid., 22.
45. Ibid., 53.
46. Kitamori, *Pain of God*, 56.
47. Ibid., 57.
48. Ibid.
49. Kitamori, Zetsumyo no shinri, 29.
50. Ibid.
51. Ibid.
52. Kitamori, *Pain of God*, 54.
53. Ibid., 81. Emphasis in the original.
54. Ibid. Emphasis in the original.
55. Dietrich Bonhoeffer, *The Cost of Discipleship* (New York: Touchstone, 1995), 89.
56. Ibid., 58.
57. Kitamori, *Pain of God*, 104.
58. Ibid., 26–27.

Lifestyles, Strategies, and Practices

in Contexts of Violence

Chapter Seven

Choosing How to Live in a Muslim Context: Case Studies From Missionary Women

Marti Smith

The Significant Presence of Women in Missions

Is the mission field any place for a woman? In spite of the challenges women in many times and places have faced by following God's call in missions, they have followed him in numbers. By 1910 more women than men were serving in missions.[1] In the coming years, the numbers of women would continue to climb until women in some areas outnumbered men by two to one.[2] Statistical studies on the topic are few, but one in the late 1980s, a survey of nineteen mission agencies representing 20,333 missionaries, showed that fifty-six percent of them were women, with unmarried women outnumbering unmarried men six to one.[3] A more recent report, from 2002, found that some fifty-four percent of Southern Baptists' 5,241 missionaries were women, about a fourth of them single.[4]

In short-term missions, as well as in situations that are considered too dangerous to send families, including many areas with a Muslim majority, the foreign mission force is composed largely of workers who are single, and a majority of them are women. Representatives of Frontiers, which works solely in the Muslim world, report that they are seeing women respond to the call in great numbers. In 2002 women comprised seventy-five percent of their short-term team applicants.[5]

Anecdotal evidence produces similar numbers. In a 2002 personal interview, a woman working with Operation Mobilization reported that of the 100 people working with her agency in one Asian country, sixty were women and forty were men; and in ratios that seem fairly typical, these included thirty-five married couples, twenty-five single women, and five single men. Friends currently studying in Yemen say the expatriate community in their city includes twenty-six couples, two single men, and twenty-one single women. We must conclude that women have a significant presence in the mission force: not that of a minority, but a majority.

Yet many report receiving less training, encouragement, and support than their husbands, male teammates, or other missionaries. Mothers of young children seem to be at a particular disadvantage. When, as is often the case, they choose to stay behind the scenes to tend to family matters, they have fewer opportunities to tell their stories, build relationships with others who share their experiences, ask questions, pool insights, or seek feedback on their thoughts, experiences, and approaches to life.[6]

Purpose

What challenges and opportunities do these missionary women face? What are their lives like? What concerns do married women, most of them raising children, have? What concerns do single women have? What obstacles to effectiveness might they face? What advantages might they have? What about women working in areas where their movements may be restricted by cultural mores or personal safety concerns? How do they cope?

The purpose of this paper is to explore some of the struggles that seem most common and how various women respond to them. It is based on qualitative research: several dozen face-to-face interviews with missionary women, primarily in 2002 and 2003. Some of the women were interviewed just once, though none of the interviews lasted less than two hours. Others were interviewed multiple times over several months. Four of them were members of a church-planting team with whom I served, in order to experience their way of life, for a period of ten months in 2001 and 2002. The project was

conceived as part of a one-year educational sabbatical from my regular responsibilities with the ministry of Caleb Project, supporting ethnographic research projects and mobilization efforts. Among other things this sabbatical resulted in a book, published in 2005 by Authentic Media and describing, as much as possible in their own words, the lives of missionary women in the Muslim world.[7] While the book is designed to raise questions and present models from women who have a variety of different perspectives,[8] this paper presents just a few case studies and draws out the principles they illustrate. Some of its contents (where noted) have been previously published and are used with permission from the publishers.
Focus: Lifestyle Choices

Among the things research revealed was the fact that lifestyle choices—those having to do with choosing where and how to live; how much to interact with or cut oneself off from local culture and values; and how to dress, eat, keep house, and behave at home and in the neighborhood—often seem to weigh more heavily on women than they do on men. In traditional Muslim societies, in particular, the honor of a family may be wrapped up in the appearance and behavior of the women. This puts missionary women in a position where their choices significantly affect the effectiveness of their family's ministry. It also makes the lifestyle questions many missionary women deal with every day more important and more complicated than they may at first appear. With lifestyle issues, in particular, they have to learn to balance becoming the servant of all (as described in 1 Corinthians 9.22) with modeling a gospel that brings freedom from conformity to the ways of the world (as described in Romans 12:1–2).[9]

What follows are a few scenarios in the lives of different women. Each of the stories below is true and illustrates principles I found common to many woman. The women's names have been changed at their request.

Case Studies in Identification: Isabelle and Vivian

Isabelle: Cultural Immersion—Until a few years ago Isabelle, a single woman, had not spent much time overseas. Then four years ago she moved to Central Asia to join a church-planting team. From the beginning, Isabelle's team was committed to helping her adjust to cross-cultural living. In keeping with team policy, they arranged for her to live with a local family and spend time building relationships and learning language during her first months on the field.

> So on my second day there, I moved out to a village on the outskirts of the city. Our house had no phone to connect to the city, and no running water. There was an outhouse that was just a hole in the dirt floor, and I had to take bucket baths. That wasn't such a big deal, but the fact that they were Muslims and did not speak any English was.

Isabelle came into the city regularly, but she lived in the village. She would have to learn to adapt. Living with the family felt quite confining at first.

> I'd been an introverted girl living on her own, and now I was in a community-minded family that seemed to think things like, "Why *wouldn't* the brothers go through your stuff and steal your deodorant?" I was being dragged to parties all the time, and my "mom" Olivia was always watching over me and trying to protect me. I'd catch her looking at me all the time . . .

Although it was sometimes hard for Isabelle to be patient and give up the freedoms to which she was accustomed, in time she came to realize she was not the only one making sacrifices. After all, this family had taken her into their home and patiently tried to communicate with her and understand her ways.

> I realized *they* were the ones who took in this incompetent American girl. They were so patient with my crying fits. They got used to me! "Oh Isabelle, she just cries." Here was this family that took me in as their own. We were connected.

Although she is usually fairly flexible and amenable, Isabelle found herself chafing against the restrictions she had to follow, not just as a foreigner in a new culture but as a single woman, in order to avoid raising eyebrows in her traditional community. She had to have a chaperone to spend time with the other singles on her team (who were men), and she had to be home before dark; at times her life seemed too confining. How was she going to have her needs met?

> I felt like I needed more interaction for encouragement, to keep going, and I couldn't find it. It was hard to find with Central Asians because I didn't have enough language, and besides I needed to be this different person with them, a person I wasn't comfortable with yet. I didn't know what to do. "Well, you could die to yourself," God said to me. It sounds harsh, but it was true. I feel like I had a need and was going to have to let it die, and trust God. Obviously God doesn't think I "needed" it or he'd make a way. So I learned that if I don't have something I think I need, I have to trust that I'm going to be okay.

After four years, the things Isabelle learned from the local culture made her more capable and competent in dealing with practical challenges as they come along. Was it worth the emotional pain of immersion to get to that point? While the route she chose was difficult, Isabelle believes the pain of never becoming capable in her new community would be worse.

> Immersion is going to sap you. Everything is unfamiliar. You have to let go of a lot of yourself, and that's going to wear you out. . . On the other hand I cannot imagine *not* doing it. You reap benefits as time goes on. Immersion is not sapping me now. It's energizing me and giving me the coping skills to do it well and even thrive here. It's become much more natural. . . . You think immersion gets you wet on the outside and you can get out and dry off, but it's more like ink than water. It soaks into you and becomes part of who you are.

Another of the chief benefits Isabelle enjoyed from her immersion experience was the opportunity to learn the local language to the point where she could be more fully part of the local community than those without this advantage. Many other women who have been able to experience high degrees of immersion report similar results—especially single women.

Vivian: Houseguests and Hospitality[10]—In more than ten years as a church-planter in Central Asia, Vivian has found that being available or abandoned to God's will, rather than protective about her own time and space, is one of the best ways to secure contentment in ministry and motherhood. While there is a time for saying no, Vivian explains,

> It's too stressful to live protectively. When I can make myself come to a place of saying, "Okay, Lord, I am here for you," it turns out to be mu ch more pleasant and fruitful.

One of the chief ways Vivian has learned to abandon herself to God is in the area of hospitality. After sowing broadly in her relationship building, Vivian found herself acting as hostess much more than she ever would have in her home country, and more than she might have chosen. In her fourth year on the field, when things were at their busiest, Vivian counted how many guests she fed and entertained during a three-week period. The figures were above 150.

> When we averaged it out, we realized we had people spending the night five nights out of seven. These were not people we had invited or planned on; almost all of them were drop-ins!

Sometimes Vivian would cook, serve, and clean up after guests three times a day before falling into bed exhausted. Vivian had to balance serving, cooking, and answering the door with frequent emergency breaks to get her kids, often sick in those days, to the toilet.

> It was a very busy time of life. I knew it was not always going to be this way. I was a mother of three young children, all under four years old.

In addition, a local man, who was the first believer in the area, was starting to see his ministry and relationships take off as he was living at Trent and Vivian's house. While he was a great help and blessing, she was also entertaining his guests, as well as her own.

Time to set boundaries, you might think. But Vivian disagrees. She and her husband would lie in bed and think about it.

> We would say, "We need to pace our lives," then wonder, "How?" We couldn't figure out how to do it. In this culture, you just don't send anyone away when they come to your door, especially if they come from far away! So when, at two or three in the morning, we would have people coming in from the capital and knocking on our door; we'd get up, get everything out, feed them, and take care of them.

It was not long before Vivian realized this was not a healthy way to live. The problem was not having too many guests or having the wrong things on her list, she realized as much as it was that she had personal expectations for herself and her life which could not be met.

> It's so stressful to live like that, and it wears me out. God just spoke to my heart and showed me the need every day to just offer my list to him, saying, "If this is what you want me to get done today, great. If you bring someone else, I want to trust that you brought them." Every time the phone rang or there was a knock at the door, I would say, "Here I am, Lord, I'm your handmaid." I'd say that inside, and go. It so changed me on those days. It liberated me to go with the flow and be more like Jesus. Jesus wasn't upset and frustrated that people were crowding in and changing his plans!

> I do feel we were stretched beyond what we thought we could handle. The pace went on and on and on. But if we had tried to stick to our own schedule and protect our lives and all that, we really would have burned out.

Living according to the local style also relieved much of Vivian's stress and anxiety. Figuring out how to cook western food and set up a western household would have been a huge challenge. Learning to cook local food and enjoy local ways of life—and teaching her kids to enjoy them as well—was much less stressful. Local food requires a few simple ingredients that are always on hand, and entertaining guests overnight requires only stacks of quilts and big open rooms. This made it easier for Vivian to respond graciously when guests came.

Principles of Identification

What can we learn from Isabelle and Vivian? These women and others like them are discovering the value of identification, the personal side of contextualization. Women who can make lifestyle choices that help them press into the local culture will experience great rewards. Those who choose to embrace a new identity, die to self, become learners, and take advantage of the opportunities they have to be insiders may struggle with personal identity and setting boundaries, but they will usually get closer to those they wish to serve—and that is a key factor in being content and able to "make it" overseas. While there is no one perfect model for identification, the following principles stand out.

Choosing Cultural Immersion

Many women face the loss of their identity and personal freedom that they are used to taking for granted, as Isabelle did in living with a Central Asian family. Among the strategies she learned were to look for things she could enjoy about her new culture—like dancing, wearing frilly clothes, enjoying hospitality, and learning to bargain. She discovered the benefits of having local friends who could be like family to her, even though they seemed at times intrusive. She also experienced the great benefits of becoming culturally fluent. Jumping in with both feet may be the best way to do this. Certainly, the sooner and the more deeply workers can get to the place where their new culture becomes "home," the happier they will be to stay there.

Of course, zeal to do things in the local way may lead to embarrassing mistakes, so it is best to stay open to correction and be ready to adjust when you misinterpret or misapply some local practice. Another woman, Connie (whose insights are discussed further below) discovered this firsthand in working with the poor:

I really like the little cups they drink from here. We hunted and found these tiny little clay ones—they were great! But then I realized when we went out to visit people in the refugee camp, they would sit us down and go dig through boxes and find us nice china cups and saucers. They served us tea in the best they had to offer. And here we had gone out and tried to find these cheap little clay pottery ones to make them feel at home![11]

Every missionary woman has experienced what it is like to go to great effort to dress in a local way or prepare a local meal, only to realize she has been blind to some key aspect. This can be very humbling, but is sometimes the only way to learn.

Dying to Self

Like Isabelle, Vivian learned to see that what she thought she needed might not be so essential after all. In getting up to entertain guests who arrive in the middle of the night, she found that what saved her from burnout was to let go of the internal resistance and resentment she felt. Instead, she chose to look for the hand of God in the situation. She had to let go of her assumptions about the way her life was supposed to be and accept whatever God brought her instead. She also learned that trying to keep a foot in both camps—following both local patterns and expectations and those of her home country—making her home into a little America—would have a significant social and emotional cost. She and her family took vacations, furloughs, and weekend trips to the capital city, but when she was in her own home it was easier to live like the locals did as much as she could. Because she was living as they did, she could have more compassion for their struggles and say with greater integrity, "Follow me as I follow Christ."

God spoke to my heart and showed me he had not sent me to call these women to a more comfortable life; he had sent me to demonstrate a joyful and abundant life in the midst of circumstances like theirs.[12]

Living according to the local patterns is often more difficult for women with families than it would be for single women; those living and working with the very poor might never be able to bridge the gap very much. But Vivian feels it is very important to do what she can. She puts aside her foreign ways and "rights" as much as she can.

Letting Others Teach You

Isabelle, in living with a local family, and Vivian, in hosting so many guests, opened themselves up let their local friends become their teachers and sometimes judges, teaching them the right way to dress, cook, do chores, and set up house. This can be humbling but it is also the invitation to become a cultural insider, an important part of the path to both contentment and effectiveness in another culture. The only way to understand why things are the way they are may be to participate in the culture at a fairly deep level. As Paul Hiebert says,

> Whenever a culture "makes no sense" to us, we must assume that the problem is ours, because people's behavior makes sense to them.[13]

The solution is to become a learner. It means giving up one's rights and assumptions about how things are done, withholding judgment on what one does not understand, and asking others to help you understand.

Isabelle admits she gets frustrated and discouraged, sometimes, when local friends lecture her about the things she is doing wrong or tease her over language and culture mistakes.

However, as she explains, cultural knowledge is the one thing her Central Asian friends know they have that she does not. From their perspective she seems to have everything else: wealth, freedom, and opportunities, but there is one way in which they have the upper hand.

> They are fluent in the culture, and I am not, and I shouldn't take it away from them. It's good that I should be the one who has something to receive.

Exposing herself to the correction of others may be just the thing to help her gain their love and respect, and it helps her better understand the people she is serving.

Developing "Real Life" Relationships

Isabelle is an unmarried woman, and Vivian is still quite busy raising her children; each might envy others who do not face the restrictions each of them faces. Would it not be easier to be a man in these settings? Women may start off in a traditional society with some significant challenges or disadvantages, but they also have some great advantages. It helps to recognize and capitalize on these advantages rather than grieving over the struggles that accompany them.

Generally missionary women have more opportunities to get involved in people's "real" lives, because they are less likely to interact with people in an office or a sterile environment. Instead, they will spend more time with other women in the home and other less-formal social settings, where it is easier to develop the life-on-life relationships that constitute true friendship. Depending on their family situation, they may have more freedom and flexibility to spend the extended time with friends that it takes to build a ministry. Language learning may be more natural as well; they may not be in the classroom as much but they are interacting with hired housekeepers and buying goods on the street. They interact more with everyday culture and language. In many cases they can become more a part of the local culture and build closer relationships than a man can. Attending parties, drinking tea with one's neighbors, and cooking and shopping together may be wonderful ways to draw close to local families at a heart level.

Case Studies in Maintaining Health and Balance: Donna and Angela

Several other principles must be held in tension with the principles of identification. These "balancing principles" involve accepting oneself and one's limitations. No one can do it all. Women who can "pick their battles" in lifestyle choices, knowing they will never fit in entirely and that they do not have to, will last longer and be happier on the field. So will those who dare to be different, who can accept themselves and that they do not have to be just like everybody else. Having high expectations for oneself can lead to debilitating disappointments that take workers out of the field or prevent them from being able to accept and respond appropriately to the realities of life on the field. Those who are trapped in guilt or shame over lifestyle choices lose their joy and may have a negative witness instead of a positive one.

Donna: Chores and Childrearing[14]—In the Central Asian country where Donna and her family live, good housewives rise before dawn, take up their brooms, and sweep their yards, sidewalks, and even the street in front of their houses. It is a culture where women pride themselves on their hard, physical labor. Faithfulness in sweeping not only demonstrates their diligence and keeps down the dust, it also welcomes and honors any guests who may come.

> I should sweep. I did not mean to blow this off, but when we came I had a seven-month old baby. Then it was winter and so cold and dark. Then I was pregnant with the twins. When we came back after they were born, I was up all night with them! So there was no getting up and sweeping.

> What's really funny is that my husband loves to sweep. Kevin is something of a perfectionist, and loves to bring order out of disorder.

This is a bit of a problem though. While getting the sweeping done matters, it is supposed to be work for a woman, not a man. One night Kevin went out at eleven to sweep, hoping nobody would see him.

> But at the next neighborhood gathering one of the women brought it up; she said she had seen him! ...And actually, they thought it was wonderful, even though they were sure their husbands would never do it.

Nobody has ever said anything to Donna about neglecting her sweeping, but she wonders what the older women are thinking. In spite of a commitment to relationship building, respecting the local culture, and contextualization, she has to face the humbling reality that she will never get it all "right" in the eyes of her neighbors. "We are going to end up making choices that make us look bad to locals," she says.

> Something that really affects women here is that the values and choices we as believers and Christian families have are opposed to local values. I don't think the men are going to experience as much as we do. They may feel it, but they are more often looked up to than we as foreign women are. As missionaries, we enculturate on lots of things in order to be accepted, but we may have different priorities behind those decisions. And we make these decisions as a family, but it is the women who live it out.

> Some of the things we, as believers, ought to do fly in the face of local values. The biggest one for me is how much time I spend with my children. They don't do that here.

Missionary women like Donna also add to their roles as wives and mothers a commitment to spiritual disciplines, language learning, ministry, and team life, as well as trying to stay in touch with family, friends, and supporters back home. These aspects of their lives may be invisible to local friends.

> I wonder, do they think I'm lazy? They don't see all the things we do, so they may not understand how I can say I "don't have time" to teach their kids English.

Women who don't have sympathetic friends around them to help them navigate their decision-making—and pick their battles—are the ones who struggle most with guilt and uncertainty.

> My goal is not to be a local, because I'm not. Jesus did not enculturate, he incarnated. It's different. But I ask, "What are the things that will help them feel I came close?"

In addition to talking at greater length about the counter-cultural decisions she made in raising her children, Donna also mentioned in these interviews a decision to plant a lawn inside her courtyard (something that seemed very foreign to her neighbors, but brought no criticism).

Angela: Blue Jeans and Washing Machines[15]—"I just love it when Michelle wears her blue jeans," says Angela, an American missionary and mother of four in Central Asia. She is talking about a fellow worker in her city.

> Our agency is more conservative, and so are the people we work with. When I first came I wore the local clothing styles everywhere, and I still do around the house, like my neighbors do.

After four years, while she still does not wear blue jeans, Angela has discovered subtleties that loosened her standards.

> The locals put on Western clothes to "dress up" when they go places, and now I do the same. When we go outside the city to villages, I put my traditional dresses back on.

Deciding how to dress, what kind of food to serve, what to buy or own, and how to set up a home are questions every family living cross culturally deals with. These questions are part of identification, living like the people you serve so you can better understand them, and contextualization, living life in ways the people you serve respect and understand so you can share your faith and model godliness. In many cases, the day-to-day impact of these decisions falls on the women more than the men. This can be a heavy weight to carry, as Angela has found.

> Your first term, you are likely to come at i from one extreme or another, either making little effort to accommodate the local culture for fear it isn't godly or that you won't be able to survive, or giving up everything you know and becoming a slave to local expectations.

Making these initial decisions is only half the battle, she has discovered. The rest is fighting off the guilt that you are doing it wrong, staying open to change, and holding back from comparing yourself to others.

Sometimes the people you compare yourself to are local friends and neighbors. Angela's Central Asian neighbors may envy her relative wealth, but if she chose to live at the simplest level she could, she fears they would be suspicious of her. What is she trying to hide?

> They have no concept of simple living. That's one of *our* ideals. If we didn't have more than they do, they would wonder what was wrong with us. I don't want to use that as an excuse to have everything we'd want, but there's a tension: they would have what we have if they could.

Many missionary women in Angela's region go back and forth between one way of life and another, sometimes simply by setting up part of the house in a more western style and another part according to the local ways. Angela's house is not big enough for that.

For her first few years on the field, embarrassed that her way of life was different from that of her neighbors, she kept a cover over her washing machine. Washing machines are considered something of a luxury, and maybe a sign that a woman was too lazy to do the hard work of washing clothes. Angela decided this did not matter, and stopped hiding hers. "It began to seem silly, a matter of false pride and a hindrance more than anything."

Allowing room for other people to make their own decisions may help.

> When we set team rules we have to be careful to allow for individualization. In the same town, even on the same team, something might work for one that won't work for another. One woman may be able to have an expensive house, and because of her love for local friends, it's not a hindrance. It would be with me, I think. But on the other hand, if I lived totally like my neighbors,

who are poorer than I am, I would only last a year and that wouldn't be good.

Angela found some of the greatest struggles missionary women in her city faced were the insecurities that came from doing something they had never done before and, comparing their situation, family, or personal needs to other expatriates, fearing their own decisions were wrong.

Principles for Maintaining Heath and Balance

Picking One's Battles—While learning from and identifying with the local culture are important principles, they may not be the bottom line. Many women struggle with what they think they should do and what they want to do. They fear they are being lazy or compromising some sacred principle if they do what they want to do when it is not what may be expected. Finding a way of life they can live with for the long term requires working through these fears to get to a place of peace. Donna, for example, was afraid that because she did not get up at 5:00 am to sweep her section of the street she would be judged. When it came down to it, living up to those expectations would mean pushing too hard and probably neglecting her children. She had to come to the point where she realized she simply did not have the same values as her neighbors did and was not willing to sacrifice certain things in order to look good to them. Somewhat to her surprise, they understood. She found, as many other women do, that getting feedback from a good local friend allowed her to choose when to be different and when to try harder to fit in. Another foreign woman working in the same region, Linda, says that she looks to her trusted house-helper to help her evaluate household decisions.

> As I see her reaction and hear her comments about what I buy and the way I behave and keep house, I can know how things are perceived. Then I'll know what to do differently. I'll see what things I should put away.[16]

Linda also tries to look below the surface behavior to the values these behaviors represent, and then try to find common ground, rather than rejecting what does not make sense to her or assuming that others can see the motives behind the choices she makes. She also discusses these choices with trusted local friends and adjusts when she sees her decisions getting in the way of building relationships.

Daring to Be Different—Angela came to recognize how easy it is to let one's insecurities about choices fester into self-condemnation, guilt, and shame, or self-righteous attitudes towards others. It is too easy to fall into the trap of comparing oneself to others, when there may not be one right choice to make in any given situation. For example, it was important to Angela to live in an ordinary neighborhood, but she could accept that some of her teammates lived in the nicer part of town. She would wear local clothes and cover her hair to go visit a traditional village but still respect another worker who wore blue jeans around town. Angela recognized that a way of life that was good for someone else might not work for her, and might not be a matter of right and wrong.

One of the most important factors in making these lifestyle decisions, says Angela, is to avoid the kind of stress that makes it impossible to be content and joyful. Living in a nicer house or spending money on imported foods might not be ideal, but that did not mean those choices were going to destroy someone's witness either.

> You can only live under great stress for so long; you have to make decisions to take away that stress. . . If survival is all we're doing, we're not doing what God wants us to do We know several families in town who are doing what they have come to do, and doing it well, but they have no joy! God doesn't want us to live that way. Our first years here, there was no joy, so we've struggled with that ourselves.[17]

Case Studies in Living in Isolation

In some conservative societies, missionary women find identifying with and getting close to local women very difficult. Practicing the principles of identification may still be possible, but having close, trusting relationships may be a long time in coming. Women in these situations may also have more trouble making those lifestyle decisions because they are not sure with whom they should identify or have fewer models. What issues do women in these toughest places face? What strategies will help them find contentment and effectiveness in time?

Ginny: Life in Seclusion[18]—While people in many parts of the Muslim world are religiously moderate, Ginny has been living in one of the cities in South Asia where many of the stereotypes about uneducated, impoverished, fundamentalist Muslims tend to prevail.

> I remember in 1998 when we first came to scout it out. My first impression was, "Golly, where are all the women?" You scarcely see women outside. It's such a male-dominated society; the women are kept in seclusion, uneducated, and under male control. That is what the conservative movement wants to implement in the whole country. That was quite an awakening, especially living in it.

> Our first house was surrounded by a twelve-foot wall. Here I was with a small child, a year old, and trying to live a contextualized life. That meant I never went out to purchase groceries; we decided Jack would do that, because the men usually do it. So I was stuck in the house. For the first few weeks I was quite miserable, wondering, "What am I doing here?"

> I couldn't go out and practice my language with everyone, the vegetable seller, the butcher, and baker—like you can in some places. I could go out to get materials for clothes, bangles, or something, with another expatriate lady. But none of my close neighbors would go. Many women are not allowed to go out at all.

At first Ginny seemed to have no friends, and wondered what it would take to change this. But she was patient.

> They had to check me out, first: Is she a good woman? Then they came to my house. I didn't take that for granted. It means something for people from a conservative family to show up at a

foreigner's house. They trusted me, and they were comfortable in my house.

They also knew we were honoring their values and traditions. It is not allowed for men to see women who are not in their family. So at first Jack would leave the house completely if the women came; later he would just spend time in another part of the house, but they knew he would never come in where we were. If we visited another family, I would be ushered in with the women and he would sit with the men. They live quite a separate life. There's no interaction.

Ginny has also faced some personal struggles that left their mark.

I thought I had it all figured out. . . As a woman you don't go out by yourself, unless you are with another woman and/or have your kids with you. Then they know you are a woman of good repute. If you break those rules they can think whatever. So, I have gone to the bazaar with my expatriate friends. It's a bit tense, it's not like going to the mall, but it's okay.

Then, one day I went out our door and just down the street, alone, to return a book to a neighbor. This guy rides by on a bike and grabs my breast! I screamed at him; I was so angry, devastated. Jack was with a neighbor, and I called to both of them over the wall. They came out and went off to try to find this guy, but of course he was long gone.

After that I was afraid that I was now considered a bad person in the neighborhood. My close neighbors came to my house and comforted me, though. "That was a bad man who did this to you. It was not your fault. It can happen to anyone, not just to you because you are a foreigner. There are bad men in every place. It can happen in any society. It can happen to anyone, not just to you." That comforted me. But, they would add, "You see why we can't go to the bazaar."

Ginny appreciates the modesty and quiet family life valued in her new culture, even though the isolation and restrictions she faces can be trying. To some extent she still lives a double life, one way when she and Jack are alone and another when local friends are around. The room where she entertains guests is set up according to the local style, but her kitchen, where no one goes, is modern. She has learned to be content in her host culture, but she continues to pray and long for the day when the women around her have greater freedom.

Connie: Loneliness and Expectations[19]—Connie and her husband helped pioneer new work in a Muslim country in South Asia more than a dozen years ago. They were reaching out to a specific population within the refugee community in their host country—a minority within a minority. The challenges were great. Her expectations were simple:

> I expected to learn language, build relationships with Muslims, and investigate ways to reach the people we were interested in.

However, to reach people like that, she would need to leave behind the world she had known. "Loneliness was my biggest concern and my biggest fear," says Connie. Whatever she was most afraid of, she believed, would be her area of greatest vulnerability. So Connie and her husband both felt they needed to name their fears and turn them into prayer requests.

> I asked people at home to pray for another foreigner to be my friend, for a national Christian friend, and for a friend in the unreached community we were focusing on.

> Well, my fear was accurate. I was very lonely. I knew the facts of the situation when I was going into it, but I didn't really know the magnitude of the loneliness. Nobody prepared me for that. No one could! It's the kind of thing that has to be experienced. We went in not knowing a soul and not knowing who could help us. The only two people we knew in the whole country were two single guys with our organization.

Early on, one of the single men on their team was able to introduce Connie and her husband to a local Christian family who had children. It was not quite the same as having a friend from her home culture, but the wife took Connie around to get clothes and taught her how to dress and behave, and their children kept each other entertained. "They would play camping together and builds tents in the living room," says Connie. Soon Connie and her husband found other Christian friends, both foreigners and locals, and became part of an international church.

Making friends in the broader community was more challenging. In the society Connie lived in, most significant relationships are within the family. It was almost impossible for an outsider to get in. Connie's next-door neighbors were also her landlords, though, and the wife became one of her first friends. But as a member of the city's upper-class Muslim community, this woman never left her house.

> We were actually in the same "compound," but she only came to visit me twice; I always had to go to her.

Making friends in the refugee community they were interested in serving was another challenge. Connie remembers the first day they went to visit a refugee camp.

> We met a refugee woman that day. It was like the Lord had given us a supernatural understanding and knit our hearts together when our eyes met. "Come to my house," she said. You have to seize these moments! We went to her tent in the camp and had tea together. "This relationship gave me a reason to care, a reason to try."

In her language study, as well as in overcoming loneliness, building relationships, and beginning a ministry, Connie learned an important truth: her reality might not measure up to her ideals.

> You have to learn to merge your idealism with your reality! It's good to be idealistic, but what motivates us also creates high expectations within us, expectations for ourselves. Then we feel our failure very keenly. . . . I've seen this with women all over the world.

Now Connie provides training, counsel, and care for other missionary women in her organization, sharing the lessons about prayer and perseverance she learned in those early years.

Principles for Women Living in Isolation

Staying Open to Change—As many women interviewed mentioned, one thing that helps a great deal is not to feel one's decisions must be made in advance or be set in stone. As a woman learns more about herself and her situation, as she learns more about the culture and becomes comfortable with it, she may make some mid-course corrections. Often these have to do with schooling her children. ("What's best for this child, this year?") She may make lifestyle choices that bring her closer to the traditional people she wants to reach or she may realize she has been making a sacrifice that is misunderstood or unnecessary.

While some choices (such as which language to learn in a multilingual situation) might be best made in advance, others (like how to set up your house) can be delayed until one has had a chance to explore the options. Others can be experiments, like working with a certain language helper or dressing a certain way; try things out and make changes if they do not work.

Connie recommends, for example, not arranging housing before coming to the field, or making it one's first priority on arriving:

> Some families might only be able to manage it for a month, but I recommend that people get some kind of temporary place. During that time, get into as many homes as you can, foreign and local, and see how people use their resources. I think people who come here with kids are in such a hurry to get settled. That should not be such a high value. Don't lock yourself in too soon.[20]

Accepting Challenging Realities—What about those women who are working in highly traditional societies where they are likely to live in isolation and where their own safety may be in question? These situations are relatively rare, but women like Connie and Ginny do face some additional struggles with personal safety. Ginny's family lives in a volatile part of the world and has had to leave more than once when violence escalated, visas were denied, or all the other families with children left the region. She was even injured in a terrorist attack and medically evacuated. After all these struggles, she sees the importance of giving those who consider joining her team a realistic view of the situation.

> When you come for a visit, have your eyes open. Look for what might not be great about coming back long-term. Then, be honest about it. People who have a somewhat realistic picture of what it's like when they come seem to do much better than those who just come to change the world. It may take a lifetime, and you may not be here to see it.[21]

Ginny has struggled to get far in learning language and building relationships because she is on and off the field and busy with her children, but her challenges have forced her to see that God is merciful and will continue to use her even if she fails or is unable to follow her dreams. Connie says much the same thing; if a woman is trying to prove something to God or herself she will get too discouraged by the realities of these hard places. It may be necessary for God to "break" her so that she can accept long periods of ambiguity or a lack of success without thinking he is not pleased with her or cannot use her. Finding someone or something to help restore her perspective and bring balance to her life is critical.

Special Concerns for Single Women[22]

Many of the women God calls to missions are unmarried. What specific challenge and opportunities do they have, in lifestyle choices and in other areas? In this research four things rose to the surface.

Embracing a New Identity—While some missionaries are able to do the same work abroad as they did at home, it is not a "given." Many women, both married and single, face the prospect of fewer outlets for their professional abilities and may find themselves obsolete in their professions on returning home. Ann, in her thirties, shares after seven years in Southeast Asia, how her career was something she would have to lay down.

> I thought I'd use my skills overseas. But as time passed I realized I had to ask myself, "Am I here to use my skills or am I willing to sacrifice them for the ministry?"

Even her ministry became a quiet, behind-the-scenes one, and she had to learn to find her identity in Christ and not in her achievements. Similarly, Isabelle shares,

> As an economist-turned-teacher working in Central Asia, I experienced an identity shift not only with my career, but at every level. A few months into my first term overseas it dawned on me, everything about me had changed. Before, I was a carefree, independent single woman who had a good job and was competent in many areas. Now I was "Miss Isabelle" the teacher, just learning to operate in my new language and culture.

> With time, however, I began to develop a new, broader concept of who I was. I had thought the American "me" was set in stone—gifts, personality, and all. But I came to realize that while God was indeed "chipping away" at the initial "me," he was doing so only to build on something new.

Being Dependent on Others—Giving up personal independence can be a challenge for many single women missionaries. In some cultures, this may mean not walking home after sunset. In others, it may mean going everywhere with an escort, or spending the night somewhere if you find yourself out visiting too late. Ann had to always think about how the neighbors would view her actions, and she learned to enjoy doing things in groups. Isabelle knew she could not spend time with the single men on her team without a married couple present as chaperones.

Dealing with government officials and traveling throughout the country may be some of the areas single women find most stressful; they may envy married women who rely on their husbands to take care of these situations. Women, married or single, may have to guard themselves against harassment. This makes it a challenge to strike up casual conversations with men they meet. Both older and younger singles may face the pressure of local matchmaking efforts and frequent questions about their singleness.

Discovering and respecting the host culture's rules for single women is important. Detailed discussions with teammates about what to expect and how to respond are also helpful. To what extent can or should they rely on help from teammates? When is it better to work things out on their own or with the help of local friends? Isabelle says,

> I came to see that while being dependent on others can be incredibly inconvenient at times, it strengthened my sense of what community really means. Is it really the best thing for us to be as independent as we can be? I hear of Christians in the US longing for a sense of community, where everything is designed to make people as free from needing others as possible. I myself struggle with being indebted to a neighbor, or inconveniencing her by asking for her help, but in this culture, I can see that debt means friendship.

Immersion: The Greatest Tool—Singles, and especially single women, may find it easier than other people do to join everyday life in the community. They are more likely to be "adopted" by national families and be looked after by their neighbors. While at times this can feel invasive, it allows the single woman access to the greatest tool for becoming at home in the new culture: immersion.

Often singles have an easier time than married missionaries do with learning language and culture. They do not have to spend time and energy caring for the needs of a family, and often have greater opportunity to spend extended time with local friends. On the other hand, they usually have no help shopping, cooking, keeping house, and maintaining communication with supporters and friends back home. If it is possible and appropriate for the single woman to live with a local family at least for a season, she can avoid some of these burdens and have more freedom to invest in other things. Single women who can immerse themselves in local life will also adjust and find their place in the community much more quickly than those who—by choice or necessity—are only able to dabble in local culture and language.

Weathering Periods of Loneliness—Loneliness seems to be part of the human condition. Ironically, many feel the most alone when surrounded by other people. Many women on the field have experienced the emotional exhaustion of forcing themselves out on the streets day after day, visiting and attending social events, submitting to being misunderstood or even laughed at.

When a woman is single, there may not be anybody else bearing these burdens with her. Sharing her pain with family and friends at home may cause them needless concern. Knowing she is missing out on life back home, as nephews and nieces grow up and friends get married, may increase her struggle. From a distance, other Christian workers may seem to "have it all together." Who can understand what she is going through?

For single women and married women alike, finding sympathetic local friends is crucial. Well-adjusted Christian workers make friends with people they enjoy, not just those who seem "strategic" in some way. In addition to building relationships with nationals, workers should take initiative in building relationships with other expatriates, even those in other cities. This will lessen the sense of social isolation many missionaries often feel. "Reach out to whoever is available," says Ann, "even if you never find the mentor or soulmate you pray for."

Conclusion

Many years ago historian Steven Neill wrote,

> Christian missionary work is the most difficult thing in the world. It is surprising that it should ever have been attempted. It is surprising that it should have been attended by such a measure of success. It is not surprising at all that an immense number of mistakes should have been made.[23]

In conducting research among missionary women, I came away with the conclusion that the challenges they face are indeed great and can be very perplexing. Yet as the women I interviewed attested, it is certainly possible to have a healthy life and effective ministry even in the most challenging situations. Furthermore, there is no formula, no ideal role model, and no one right way to do things. For married women, raising their children cross-culturally without the kind of support network they would like may seem a huge challenge. For single women, the greatest challenge may be the prospect of never being able to marry and have a family. Yet these and other concerns and vulnerabilities can be turned into advantages, or bridges into relationships with local friends.

In the same way, both married and single women face many questions when it comes to choosing how they are going to live: how to set up house, build relationships, and conduct their lives in ways others will recognize as godly and find appealing. It is not possible to figure out a formula that will work for all women and all situations, even all Western women in traditional Muslim societies. It is possible, however, to think through the possibilities and look for models that will work for you, with who you are, in your situation. Discerning which of these principles to apply and how is difficult. In listening to the stories of our friends overseas, our prayer may be the same as Paul's for the Philippians:

> And this is my prayer: that your love may abound more and more in knowledge and depth of insight, so that you may be able to discern what is best and may be pure and blameless until the day of Christ, filled with the fruit of righteousness that comes through Jesus Christ—to the glory and praise of God. (Philippians 1:9–11, NIV)

Notes

1. Ruth Tucker, *From Jerusalem to Irian Jaya* (Grand Rapids: MI, 1983), 232.
2. Tucker, 232.

3. Howard Erickson, "Single Missionary Survey," *Fundamentalist Journal,* January 1989, 27, cited in John Piper's *Recovering Biblical Manhood and Womanhood* (Wheaton, IL: Crossway Books, 1991), 23. The foreword to this book, which addresses single men and women, includes some very helpful thinking on the topic of singleness and includes thoughts from a number of single missionaries throughout history.

4. Mary Jane Welch, "Obedient and Faithful," *The Commission* 65:5 (July-August 2002), 8. Also available at http://www.archives.tconline.org/Stories/JulyAug02/obedient.htm. *The Commission* is the magazine of the International Missions Board, the mission of the Southern Baptist Convention. Most of the articles in this issue deal with missionary women serving in challenging mission fields.

5. Frontiers, http://www.frontiers.org, accessed March 15, 2004.

6. Based on personal observation and interviews conducted by the author, illustrated at length in: Marti Smith, *Through Her Eyes: Life and Ministry of Women in the Muslim World* (Waynesboro, GA: Authentic Media, 2005).

7. During the time I conducted most of the interviews I was living in a fairly conservative part of Central Asia under the care of a frontier church-planting team, living with a local Muslim family, studying the language and culture, and experiencing many of the things workers typically experience in their first year in a new field. One of my primary purposes was to document this particular team's experiences. Their opinions had a strong effect on coloring my own and affecting whom I chose to interview or what I chose to emphasize, although I also conducted interviews with those who saw things quite differently.

8. A large percentage of these women were Americans (including several Asian-Americans) and Canadians, but women interviewed also included Britons, Swiss, South Africans, and Australians, and represented ten mission agencies. More than half were living in former Soviet Central Asia, although several spoke at length about their pervious experiences in Pakistan and Afghanistan.

9. A thoughtful analysis of this question by John Piper can be found in his June 27, 2004 sermon, "Do Not Be Conformed to This World." See http://www.desiringgod.org/library/sermons/04/062704.html.

10. Adapted from "Available in the Busiest Season," in *Through Her Eyes,* 109–113. For more about Vivian's team, see *Pioneer Church-Planting: A Rookie Team-Leader's Handbook* (Littleton, CO: Caleb Project, 2001).

11. Through Her Eyes, 160.

12. Through Her Eyes, 11.
13. Paul Hiebert, "Cultural Differences and the Communication of the Gospel," in Arthur F. Glasser, et al, *Crucial Dimensions in World Evangelization* (1976). Quoted in Winter, Ralph, and Steven Hawthorne, *Perspectives on the World Christian Movement* (Pasadena, CA: William Carey Library, 1999), 273.
14. Adapted from "What Will People Think?" in *Through Her Eyes*, 165–169.
15. Adapted from "The Comparison Trap," in *Through Her Eyes*, 170–173.
16. Through Her Eyes, 156.
17. Through Her Eyes, 173.
18. Adapted from "Life in Seclusion," in *Through Her Eyes*, 151–154.
19. Adapted from "Loneliness and Adjustment," in *Through Her Eyes*, 18–21.
20. Through Her Eyes, 161.
21. Through Her Eyes, 29.
22. The entire section on single women is adapted from Marti Smith, "Life Alone on the Mission Field: Issues Single Women Face in Missions." *Mission Maker Magazine* 2005, 52–53. *Mission Maker* is a relatively new, annual publication. Quotations are from personal interviews.
23. Stephen Neill, Call to Mission (Philadelphia, Fortress Press, 1970), p. 24. Quoted in J. Herbert Kane, Life and Work on the Mission Field (Grand Rapids, MI: Baker Book House, 1980), ix.

Chapter Eight

Member Care Perspectives for Working in a Context of Violence

Dale M. Wolyniak

This paper's primary task is to identify a few key concepts to ensure the health and safety of those committed to mission activity within a context of violence. This is the role of member care for the workers on the foreign and hostile fields. A larger discussion should examine, discover, and understand the role of Missions within a context of violence and antagonism. A third and future discussion would attempt to establish a biblical perspective on suffering for the emerging church.

Introduction

When is the last time you heard a message in the American Church that discussed the issue of suffering as a believer for the sake of fulfilling the Great Commission? Not many of us have been discipled within the context of sharing our faith to an antagonistic audience, let alone one in which physical violence and bodily harm may be the norm for expressing ones faith in Christ. Yet, that is exactly what needs to take place for the Church Universal to establish itself in the context of violent and oppressive cultures, worldwide. A timid and powerless ministry, based more on comfort and results, that commitment and obedience, will not reach the lost in these forgotten lands. Forgotten not to God, but at times to a church occupied with self-interest, comfort, prosperity, and ethnocentric attitudes. Matthew 24:14 says, "and this gospel shall be preached in every nation, and then the end shall come." The Church needs to find its way by the Spirit of God and the spirit of obedience even to these lands, peoples, ethnic groups, who oppose the gospel of Christ.

The challenge before us is to identify ways to assist those living in violent cultures to stay healthy and strong for the long haul. There are many cultures which are intolerant, oppressive, and violent to those who bring the Christian message of hope and love. Missions outreach must adapt to existing real life conditions on the field and then clarify the methodology we will use to reach into that community. We need to mobilize the church body, and its ambassadors, to the task of working and living among such people groups, proclaiming Christ Jesus as Savior and Lord. Such a challenge has been taken up by various denominations, sending agencies and individuals, who have risen to the challenge of establishing beachheads in these difficult sectors of our world.

There are a number of questions that need an answer. How did the church deal with persecution and violence in the New Testament? What strategy did the church develop to expand its mission? How is the present day mission of the church dealing and working in a context of violence? What are some of the prevailing issues and antagonistic forces that the Church is facing in fulfilling its mission of preaching and establishing churches? Are there any specific trends, or main obstructions, forces, and ideologies, that need to be identified for the church to be successful in its missiological approach? If so what are they? Is the Church finding Spirit directed strategies to overcome these challenges of violence? Is the Church thriving or merely surviving in the midst of violence and oppression? Who is God raising up to press on, in the midst of a violent response to Christianity and Christian mission? How and what should member care personnel be doing to assist those called to work in violent and often militant cultures?

What is Needed in Our Strategy?

What is needed to accomplish world missions in this arena where Christianity and culture conflict? There are three areas that need our focus: The raising up of courageous believers to go to the field; the

Church to be committed to the mission task; and the sensitivity to the Spirit for working in hostile and violent cultures.

Courageous Believers. Timidity and caution are two words not found in the vocabulary of today's intrepid ministers for Christ. This new generation is willing to take risks, surrender comfort, and forge into difficult situations in obedience to the call of God. When the Commission of Christ is obeyed by courageous believers we will see open doors into violent cultures. God always blesses faith and faithfulness. As God told Joshua to be very courageous in the face of a new opportunity, the church today needs that same message to solidify its resolve to press on in difficult and seemingly unreceptive audiences.

The Church needs to recognize these individuals, assist in their preparation and training, and get behind them. YWAM is just one example, with over 200,000 in its ranks around the world. They do have a mission, they do have a role. Many are short-term, but others are career workers in the Lord's harvest fields. Adequate pre-field preparation and an understanding of the call of God are essential. The areas of character, competency and commitment all need special attention prior to sending out workers.[1]

Where are the Daniel's, the Nehemiah's, the Paul's, who in the face of great opposition and threat, remained faithful to God and accomplished much for the Kingdom. This is not a time for retreat, but a time to press on in the worldwide witness of Christ. There is a price to be paid for the Gospel message to be proclaimed, lived out, and contextualized in individual cultures and ethnic groups.

Mission Agencies and Churches Committed to Pray, Give and Go. The Church and sending agencies need a strong commitment to the task of world evangelism. Within the context of strategy and philosophical understandings of each agency there must be a commitment to the prayerful support and focused attention on the people involved in establishing churches in violent cultures. To give responsibility without authority and accountability to ones missionary force without a proper commitment is not only unprofessional but irresponsible. Those that strategize for working in hard places with a view to long term commitment are in a better place to manage the constant setbacks and issues of their personnel. The mission of the church is not a secondary effort, it is the primary task. The church is mission.

What do people need who are living in a context of violence?

Support Group. One of the primary functions of the sending church is that of support, both financially and relationally. The sending church must see itself as the lifeline for its advocates stationed in tough places and must strengthen its prayer initiatives. There is no substitute for Spirit inspired prayer on behalf of those on the frontlines. Also, the missionary needs relationships with individuals and congregations over the long haul. Distant though they may be from daily personal interaction, the missionary needs to know and experience the ongoing relational aspects of friendships, support and love. Support groups must be more than merely financial support giving agencies, they must become a part of the team of each missionary. This writer always felt that of his 120 supporting churches that he was on staff of each individual church congregation, representing them on the field.

Creating a large support group involves maintaining contact via adequate communication. Prayer cards, newsletters, email updates, and regular reporting all contribute to the health of the relationship between the sent and the senders. Those missionaries who do not maintain adequate contact with their sending agencies and friends will find their financial support weakening and their prayer base eroded. Maintaining contact does take time but the rewards are great. When the missionary gives an accounting for the funds received and their time on the field to their constituents there is a healthy environment of lasting value for both.

A few items that deal with supportive roles for maintaining healthy people on the field need some attention here. Expectations and demands of those living in war-zones or high risk fields are only inflated. Job descriptions and well defined expectations can eliminate undue stress and keep individuals focused on priorities and objectives. Without good job descriptions, workers tend to become confused, frustrated, and often lose momentum and purpose.

Time off the field at regular intervals is a primary tool for maintaining the mental and emotional health of individuals and teams. One agency, World Vision, requires their workers to leave the country every eight weeks for two weeks, at the expense of the agency. Protocol here has assisted this agency in maintaining healthy workers in violent cultures. Member care or human resources offices must be innovative and intentional in their management and support for those stationed in harms way. Policies and plans must be written and adhered to for the safety of all associated with missions to violent and aggressive cultures. Regular visits by stateside team members, member care personnel and supporting churches and teams can give an added element of encouragement.

Identity with Christ and the Early Church Pioneers. Some missionaries resolve to stay strong and represent a stand-alone model of Christianity. These are not weak people. They are tough-minded, experienced, and willing to trust God alone. They work and minister to an audience of one. These people are typically more driven by obedience, adventure, than comfort, status, or results.

Focused Living. Living and working in a context of violence requires those that are truly called to focus on the Lord and the work before them. Recall the story of Nehemiah (6:3), where Sanballat and his friends were scheming to harm Nehemiah by trying to get them to meet together to discuss the work. Nehemiah's reply was, " I am carrying on a great work, that I cannot go down (Neh. 6:3)." This great leader realized that the taunt of the enemy was a distraction away from the work at hand. Violence was in the thoughts of his enemy, but Nehemiah stayed focused. The enemy of the missionary will try and intimidate by words, violence, or any other tool crafted to stop the work of the Lord. Elsewhere in Nehemiah 6:11 when it was suggested that Nehemiah go into the temple itself and lock the doors, he said, "Should a man like me run away? Or should one like me go into the temple to save his life? I will not go!"

The courage and tenacious spirit of Nehemiah is needed today if the work of evangelism, discipleship and church planting are to occur in the difficult places. Without focus one can be distracted, discouraged, and eventually defeated in the primary tasks to which one was called. When individuals and teams, along with their sending agencies, maintain their focus, and give of themselves to that task, then by their obedience can they say they have achieved success.

Success for those working in closed countries, or in violent cultures may mean accepting the fact that there will be only limited numbers of converts or disciples. A spiritual toughness is required as individuals deal, not with hundreds seeking the life-giving spirit of Christ, but perhaps the few who are simply finding their way in this new pilgrim's journey of life. There is a price to pay for obedience to Christ, and it is often the limited results of hard work, weary circumstances and downright hostile neighbors.

The environment of aggressive response to the Gospel, antagonism, violent cultures, and open hostility does create such tension that unless one stays focused on the primary objectives of ones mission and call, it is easy to become defensive or pack up and leave ones posting. God needs individuals who are more than purpose driven. They need to be power supplied, in touch with a living Lord, who enables them to achieve His purpose in the midst of difficult circumstances. That power is none other than the Holy Spirit of God, who equips, directs, and leads into all truth. The early church moved forward amidst a hostile populace due to its sense of empowerment by the Spirit of God. We today can do no better than to be a Spirit filled people who fulfill our Lord's purposes.

Identify with the Local Believers. Recently in Afghanistan, the newly formed government had a situation where the traditional Islamic courts and Sharia law were ruling on the case of a man, Abdul Rahman, who had converted to Christianity from Islam nineteen years ago. The local courts were pressing for his execution, but the international community voiced their concerns about maintaining the rights and regulations of the Constitution. There was great conflict within the Constitution in that at one point there was agreement to abide by the UN human rights to religious freedom, and at another, that no law shall supersede Sharia Islamic law. President Karzai was in a tight spot. All eyes were on him. Eventually, Mr. Rahman was released and spirited away to Italy. The case was not decided, nor is the issue resolved. Mr. Rahman did not want to flee his country, as he felt that if he ran for his life, his country had not changed.

A violent response to conversion to Christianity still exists within Afghanistan. Those working in this particular country and culture need to listen to their Afghan brothers, and be supportive at a time like this. The international workers, nearly all of who are identified as non-government workers (NGO's), are clearly in need of identifying with the tension amidst the violent tendencies of those within Islam. Many of the NGO's have clearly identified themselves as Christian aide agencies, and thus live in the same world of potential harm and loss.

To be truly Spirit led in the relationships and discipleship of new believers takes on a new dimension. No longer the ones leading the way, foreign workers for Christ must now follow those who have the most to lose. There is a tension, a certain fear, that clouds everyday conversations. One must use caution in how one relates to those who have the watchful eye of every person on them. Learning to trust that God will protect and lead amidst the ambiguity of living for Christ in a war-torn area, where suspicion is a lifestyle, will help the missionary avoid undue stress and tension. Foreigners who come in the name of the Lord must do more than survive, they must learn to thrive. The circumstances may not be conducive to open evangelism but the creativity and sensitivity of believers to their national counterparts can bring about the growth of individuals and a strengthening of the resolve of Christian leaders in the midst of public opinion and traditional views.

To continually do good to those who hate you will be a constant challenge for workers for Christ in Muslim nations and other closed societies. Sometimes just listening to our afflicted brothers and sisters in Christ is all we need to do. Standing beside them in hard times can give strength and support. Praying for the lives of friends, and praying with them in the midst of troubles are two different things. One is supportive, the other can be sacrificial and costly.

Church is a Relational Organism. It is not above ground, but is one of relationships that are fluid, not rigid. The living Church is Spirit directed rather than directed by mandates from home, the sending agency, or supervisors. Because of this fluidity, many westerners face frustration and tension, in that they are unable to establish viable church structures in the place of their calling. Jesus said he would build His church and the gates of hell would not prevail against it. We are reminded that it is His Church, not ours, not our agencies. We have the example of Paul planting, Apollos watering, but God giving the increase (I Cor. 3:6). The church belongs to God Almighty, and He is bringing resources of people and funding to the task of world evangelism and witness.

In cultures of violence, we are to be reminded that what the church body looks like may be quite different than what we in the west are accustomed to seeing. Relationships must take priority over organizational structures. This concept can be quite freeing for those who will accept the ambiguity of a loose group of individuals who in their networking locally have the essence of a church body. Missionaries to the 10/40 window countries and to closed access countries would do well to recognize that God can grow, maintain, and direct His people. The task of the missionary working in violent cultures will soon realize that they must work more in the shadows, more in a partnership and supportive role, rather than as an expert church planter, or a visible leader.

Access and Platforms for Ministry. In today's world of unreached peoples, many if not most are hostile, opposed or closed to traditional ways of Christian missions. New entry strategies are being developed and launched to enter these often violent and hostile cultures. These non-typical mission enterprises are linking up with other humanitarian and business-as-mission concepts. Limited access nations require that those coming must serve as tent-makers, students, or as career people in government or business serving as bi-vocational Christian workers. Flexibility is the name of the game to have access to closed countries.

Those going to serve their Lord in violent cultures would do well to find out what is being done currently by other sending agencies, and what is working in their particular culture and field of service. Having a strategy for the long haul is needed to ensure that the worker has an adequate culturally appropriate platform from which to work.

The Task Ahead for the Church

The task that lies ahead for the Church is one of great effort, great love, and great expense. There is no easy way. Our message is one of reconciliation, transformation. It is a kingdom not of this world. It challenges all other faith religions, social, economic, and political ideologies, and relational approaches to life. It is narrow in that it claims to be the only way to eternal life. Acts 4:12 says "there is no other name given among men whereby we must be saved."

The message of the Church is focused on two days: Friday and Sunday; the cross and the resurrection of Christ. Both events challenge the pride of man, the intellectual approach of a postmodern world, where pluralism reigns supreme. Christianity is adamant that only it has a God who involved Himself, who in fact stated that He is the way, the truth and the life. Only in Christ do we have a message of God reaching down to mankind, offering Himself as supreme sacrifice for our sins. Timothy George, in *Is the Father of Jesus the God of Muhammad?* wrote, " there is no Christianity without this event [the cross].[1] There can be no Islam with it." Jesus gave himself as a ransom for many. Logically, if all religions are right, then none of them are, as the differences on their approach to truth collide and do not agree. The Christian worldview claims it has the answers right from a loving Father in Scripture. Within this intolerant Islamic context and its resulting animosity, hatred and violence there is the opposite position of the Christian who comes in a spirit of love and humble service. What a difference a few days make.

A suffering church does not appear to be glorious, successful, or to have the blessing of God, at least to a western view of progress. Yet, as we examine history we find so many that held to their faith in God, who paid the ultimate price by their obedience to Christ, rather than to man. The will of God may indeed cost a follower of Christ even their own life. Serving Christ in a cross-cultural context does not guarantee immunity to the deeds of darkness, to the consequences of people who live in sin, or to the life choices of those who are deceived to believe a lie of Satan. Philippians 3:10 expresses the attitude of a pioneer spirited person, "I want to know Christ and the power of his resurrection and the fellowship of sharing in his sufferings, becoming like him in his death, and so, somehow, to attain the resurrection from the dead." The victory of Christ is found in the resurrection, which gives courage and strength for the suffering that is to be the lot of the believers, knowing that we too have the hope of heaven and the security of a firm and eternal future in Christ if we have suffered with Him in this life for the cause of our calling.

Understanding the dynamics of doing missions in a context of violence needs our attention today, if we are to fulfill the great commission. Our Lord's last command should be our first priority, regardless of the price to be paid. So many other religions and their adherents are willing to die for their faith beliefs, yet so many Christians appear to be little moved to live for theirs. May the Spirit of God raise up a new generation of believers, who like Christ, and his early followers, choose the cross, not as an emblem of adornment, but as a way of life and ministry. Their symbol is the towel and the basin of service (John 13). To die with Christ, Paul said, is gain. Eternal life meant more to him than his earthly life, yet he worked, and suffered as an apostle of Christ to his generation, suffering rejection, ridicule, the whip, and at times the sentence of death. Apostle Paul would eventually die a martyr's death, in the will of God.

Conclusion

Missions, the clarion call to the Church to expand its base of influence within cultures, is a living enterprise which requires its emissaries to be grounded in the faith, the scriptures, and led by the Spirit of the living God, Jesus Christ. When faced with violence, opposition, aggression and open hostility, the church needs to rethink its purpose and objectives in such a way that the message goes out through loving hands, and kind deeds, not in retaliation or retreat. A theology of suffering, of living in the midst of stressful cultural and political issues, needs to be developed and understood by those who would go as missionaries to a hostile environment. These are people, and nations, for whom Christ died. They are still loved by the Father, and the Church was told to "go into the world", and not retreat into a zone of comfort, or a monastic isolated life of contemplation. We are to be engaged in the world and the forces of darkness at local levels, if people are to find the way out of darkness and into His marvelous light.

Today, more than ever we need leaders in the Church, in mission, who have the spirit of the men of Issachar. It is said that they, "Understood the times and knew what Israel should do" (I Chronicles 12:32). Our times are changing quickly. The open door of ministry is open in many violent cultures, but for how long? Mission leaders, missionaries and those supporting them must ask the Lord of the Harvest for insight, understanding and courage to move forward.

The message to the church today must include a concept of the suffering church and its would-be ambassadors. Bill Musk writes of the conflict and suffering that is inherently a part of doing ministry in our world:

> Christ's call to Saul of Tarsus is to conflict and suffering. He confides to Ananias that the transformed Pharisee is 'my chosen instrument to carry my name before the Gentiles and their kings and before the people of Israel. I will show him how much he must suffer for may name' (Acts 9:15-1). In turn, the apostle passes on the same message. He writes from prison to the believers whom he has founded in the faith: 'For it has been granted to you on behalf of Christ not only to believe on him, but also to suffer for him, since you are going through the same struggle you saw I had, and now hear that I still have' (Phil: 1:29-30).[2]

The Church cannot content itself that there are 99 in the fold, when there is one still missing from the flock. The ministry of reconciliation and transformation by the power of Jesus Christ, through his obedient church, is resulting in pockets of believers, underground churches, house churches, and of souls being saved, even in the midst of intolerant governments, restrictive religious and cultural values and societies, and those fundamentally opposed to the message of redemption. God is having his say, in fulfillment of Matthew 16:18 "You are Peter, and on this rock I will build my church and the gates of hell will not prevail against it." God is still building His Church. He is still using people. May we be that people who join Him.

Notes

George, Timothy. Is the Father of Jesus the God of Muhammad? 2002. 97.
Musk, Bill; *The Unseen Face of Islam.*, Grand Rapids, MI: Monarch Books, 2003. 232.

Bibliography

Blackaby, Henry. *The Power of the Call.* Nashville, TN: Broadman & Holman, 1997.

Clowney, Edmund P. *The Church.* Downers Grove, IL: Intervarsity Press, 1995.

Donovan, Kathleen. *Growing Through Stress.* Berrien Springs, MI: Institute of World Mission, 2002.

Farber, Barry A. Stress and Burnout in the Human Services Professions. Pergamon Press, 1983. (Pergamon General Psychology Series).

George, Timothy. Is the Father of Jesus the God of Muhammad? 2002.

Headley, Anthony J. *Achieving Balance in Ministry.* Kansas City, KA: Beacon Hill Press, 1999.

Inlander, Charles B. and Moran, Cynthia K. *Stress: 63 Ways to Relieve Tension and Stay Healthy.* New York City, NY: Walker Publishing Company, 1996.

Livingstone, Greg. Planting Churches in Muslim Cities, A Team Approach, Grand Rapids, MI: Baker Book House, 1993.

Musk, Bill; *The Unseen Face of Islam.*, Grand Rapids, MI: Monarch Books, 2003.

New International Version. *The Bible*. Nashville, TN: Broadman & Holman Publishers, 1996.

O'Donnell, Kelly. Doing Member Care Well. Perspectives and Practices *from Around the World*. Pasadena, CA: World Evangelical Alliance Missions Commission, 2002.

Oswald, Roy M. *How to Build a Support System*. Bethesda, MD: Alban Institute, 1991.

Taylor, William D., ed. Too Valuable to Lose. Exploring the Causes and *Cures of Missionary Attrition*. Pasadena, CA: William Carey Library, 1997.

Wolyniak, Dale. Finishing Well; Focusing on the Essentials . Unpublished Doctoral Thesis. New Geneva Theological Seminary, Colorado Springs, CO. May 2005.

Chapter Nine

Muslim Background Believers and Baptism in Cultures of Persecution and Violence

Barry Stricker and Nik Ripken

Introduction: Context and Parameters

In 1991 there were approximately 150 Muslim Background Believers (MBBs) in Somalia, a country classified as 99.9% Muslim. Seven years later, only four of those MBBs were alive and still in Somalia. Historically, persecution had always been severe in Somalia, but this level of persecution was something new. As civil society deteriorated, a more fundamentalist Islam emerged, which led to the persecution of local believers even beyond the historical norm.

Without question, those who were martyred were followers of Jesus Christ. Even so, the timing of most of these "martyrdoms" was not directly linked to an individual's relationship with Jesus. Typically (and tragically), the martyrdom was more closely related to the individual's relationship with Christian workers from the West than to any focused attempt by these MBBs to be positive witnesses to their families and neighbors. In depth, on-site interviews with both believers and persecutors indicate that the "trigger" or antecedent for many of these deaths was related to secondary issues. Several types of examples illustrate the point:

- In some cases, MBBs were murdered specifically because they worked for Christian relief agencies headquartered in the West. Mistakenly, some Muslims believed that the removal of local believers would lead to greater access to relief funds and

155

commodities. Therefore, removing the MBB from the scene was a prerequisite to acquiring these goods, monies, and opportunities for themselves.

- In other cases, MBBs were killed for worshipping regularly, and sometimes openly, with outsiders. Simply being seen with westerners or spending significant time with westerners often invited the hostility of the host community.

- Other MBBs were persecuted when they were found in the possession of written discipleship materials, often materials written at a level significantly beyond their own ability or educational background.

- Finally, those MBBs who were employed by westerners specifically to evangelize their friends and neighbors (often in culturally inappropriate ways) found themselves subject to even more intense and immediate persecution.

There is, of course, no way to establish a direct connection between a particular event or relationship and the martyrdom of an MBB. No single event or relationship can be identified as "the cause" for martyrdom. It is clear, however, that western missionary involvement and leadership created a mission culture that inadvertently placed local believers at risk. What is perhaps most significant is that this risk was typically *not* the direct result of a positive witness for Jesus.

Martyrdom remains a possibility for all who follow Christ. The road to resurrection traveled through a gruesome crucifixion. God the Father has used, and continues to use, the sacrificial deaths of His children to usher in a deeper faith and to anchor the church within salvation history. As central as martyrdom is to the story, however, it is not to be sought. Persecution, and ultimately martyrdom, is simply a reality for those following the Son of God in a fallen world. The West often repeats Tertullian's words from the third century that the "blood of the martyrs is the seed of the church." Perhaps those words are sometimes spoken flippantly by people who have not yet experienced severe persecution. While God uses even persecution for His ultimate purposes, martyrdom also leaves children without fathers, spouses without a loving mate, and believing bodies temporarily void of leadership. Martyrdom is tragic wherever and however it happens. *But it is especially tragic when it happens because of secondary reasons.*

Looking back on the recent history of Somalia, it appears that severe persecution visited the young and emerging Somali church at a delicate time in her history. And, sadly, it appears that the persecution largely arose for reasons other than witnessing to the life and resurrection of Jesus. Of course, God's story in Somalia is still being written, but at this point, and from a human point of view, it seems that the current generation has witnessed the almost complete annihilation of a reproducible faith within the land and among the peoples of Somalia. God always uses the blood of those who die for Christ to increase and deepen witness. Yet when the death of believers occurs more for their relationships with outsiders than their positive witness to the saving grace found in Jesus, then the positives that come from that "martyrdom" are severely reduced.

Few functions of the faith will lead to persecution more quickly than that of a believer's baptism—especially baptism encouraged and administered by an outsider. This article will reflect on the issues surrounding the baptism of MBBs within cultures of persecution and violence. It will outline some of the unique challenges related to baptism and then suggest some missiological perspectives that could reduce the frequency of persecution *for secondary reasons.*

Somewhat surprisingly, the goal of this article—and the goal of the mission enterprise itself—is not the elimination of persecution. In fact, the only way to eliminate persecution is to eliminate conversions to Jesus. The goal is not to bring persecution to an end. Rather, the goal is to be certain that, when persecution comes, it is grounded firmly in an individual's walk and witness as a follower of Jesus. Being put to death because of employment practices, worship circumstances, or because of possession of certain discipleship materials is not the same thing as being martyred for a positive, culturally sensitive witness to the death and resurrection of Jesus.

Reflections shared in this article are based on a sixty-country pilgrimage among believers in Jesus who experience persecution as a normal and ordinary part of the Christian walk. To date, approximately six hundred interviews have been completed. The persecution was framed by atheism, communism, Buddhism, Hinduism, as well as Islam. About three hundred interviews were conducted among MBBs. The persecuted, as well as their families and colleagues, were asked to contribute to the development of a missiology of suffering that would assist the western church in discipling itself as it seeks to fulfill the Great Commission in environments defined by violence and persecution. One of the explicit goals of this research was to find ways to reduce the persecution of local seekers and believers specifically related to the presence of outsiders.[1]

The Life and Death Lessons of Persecution

Much has been learned from the persecuted. What is perhaps most significant is the identification of the chief precursor of persecution. The primary cause of persecution globally is an individual's acknowledgement of Jesus as Lord and Savior. In praying about persecution on behalf of Christians in other parts of the world, the western church typically prays (with great compassion) that persecution would be eliminated, which can only happen if conversions cease. Obviously, the elimination of persecution, in itself, is not an appropriate goal or desire. But how, exactly, is it possible to guarantee that persecution is firmly grounded in a believer's walk and witness?

It is instructive to consider the concerns of the persecutors. What, precisely, do the persecutors forbid or seek to control? Often, persecutors withhold from the believing community the right to handle and control its own sacred scriptures and music. If corporate worship happens to be allowed in a fixed location, the persecutors prohibit the faith community from expressing its faith in other settings (for example, within homes). In settings where the faith community owns property, buildings, and possessions, the persecutors will find a way to hold believers hostage to their own material wealth. What seems to cause the persecutors the most trouble is a home-based faith community, led by emerging and locally-trained lay leadership, and characterized by competence in oral transmission of the truth.

Insights gained regarding Islam, the chief modern-day persecutor of the church, are especially important. For example, MBBs from the Horn of Africa were mentoring new western missionaries concerning insights into faith and practices within Islamic environments. One newly arrived missionary asked the nationality of these fifteen MBBs. Without hesitation the MBB elder stated, "We have no nationality as we have become Christians." Prior to Christian conversion, citizenship is inseparably linked to religious identity. To be a citizen of many particular countries is to be a Muslim. Saying, "I am a Saudi and I am a Muslim" is to make the same statement twice. Within this worldview, when MBBs become followers of Christ they not only lose their jobs, educational opportunities, and possibly their lives, but they also believe that they have sacrificed their national identities. A summary of the interviews suggests that MBBs new to the "Christian" faith may psychologically believe that they have taken on the nationality of the western missionary who assisted them into their new faith in Christ! Why?

For Muslims, the word "Christian" essentially means "western." And the word "western" essentially means "Christian." In the eyes of most Muslims, "Christians" are part of a culture defined by abortion, drug abuse, pornography, crime—and all the ills of western society. In addition, "Christians" are responsible for the invasions of Afghanistan and Iraq. "Christians" inevitably side with Israel. "Christians" are intent on "westernizing" the entire world. "Christians" are captive to materialism. The church would be wise to learn from criticism, even if it comes from unlikely sources, but the church would also be wise to manage its own glossary. Even if the labels are inaccurate or confused, Islam can teach the church a great deal.

The Unique Problem of Baptism

Especially helpful is the typical Muslim understanding of conversion to Jesus. Simply stated, Islam generally equates baptism with conversion. From the perspective of Islam, to be baptized is to be saved. A repeated emphasis through almost three hundred interviews with MBBs was the intensification of persecution immediately following the believer's baptism. Up to that point, it was not unusual for a "seeker" to be allowed to study the Bible, listen to Christian radio programming, attend a Christian Background Believer (CBB) church, and even to meet regularly and openly with western missionaries. Obviously, in some cases, there was significant resistance to such practices. But this often low-key persecution paled in comparison to the overt and intense persecution that began to surface immediately after the MBB experienced believer's baptism.[2]

Islam is convinced that it is at baptism that its sons and daughters have become separated from their former way of life. Islam identifies baptism as the time when the believer has died to the old way and embraced a new worldview. Though the image might be uncomfortable, it might even be suggested that baptism, given the worldview of Islam, is to a new believer in Christ what strapping on a belt of explosives is to a suicide bomber. For Islam, baptism is the point of no return. Though western Christians might be repelled by such an image, it seems that Islam, perhaps more than the western church itself, has truly grasped the weight and significance of baptism!

Baggage from Home

Most practitioners of the Christian faith, regardless of background, would agree at this point: baptism is critically important. Baptism is central to the expansion of the Kingdom of God and is, therefore, crucial to the mission enterprise. Baptism is extremely important in identifying the new believer with the faith community and all that it has to offer (including mutual support and nurture, accountability, creation of a new family, a setting for service, an environment for corporate worship, among many others).

When missionaries belittle or misunderstand the power and impact of a believer's baptism, defined and practiced locally, hey can unintentionally hinder emerging faith. How ironic that missionaries can baptize literally hundreds of MBBs—and yet those baptisms rarely result in a church that can survive the departure of the missionary. What the interviews suggest is that baptism is profoundly significant—but that an MBB and a western missionary will understand that significance in radically different ways. Missionaries are often captive to the doctrinal formulations of sending bodies, compelled to produce measurable results, often represented in the statistic of "baptisms", and desperate for some kind of observable "success." Given that worldview, they would quickly agree that baptism matters. What can be easily neglected, however, is the transforming impact of baptism within a culture of persecution and violence. The MBB will agree that baptism is staggering in its importance—but for entirely different reasons.

Matters of Timing and Setting

Within Islamic cultures, missionaries will generally encourage MBBs to embrace believer's baptism approximately three to six months after an MBB professes faith in Jesus. That statistic holds true regardless of how the process of conversion occurred. When an MBB baptizes another MBB, however, baptism might follow a declaration of faith by as much as three to five years. At this point, the difference in timing is not easy to explain. Missionaries will suggest that their desire to baptize quickly is an effort to be biblically obedient. MBBs will suggest that the delay allows a stronger grounding in the faith before the crucial step of baptism. This is clearly an area the calls for ongoing and candid dialogue.

Another highlight of the interviews focused on the connection between baptism and the planting of new churches. When a missionary baptizes an MBB, persecution of that person is often swift and devastating. Despite the fact that baptism of an MBB by an outsider can be administered in the dark of night and outside of the local community (perhaps even in another country), the family and friends of the MBB will learn of the baptism almost immediately. Regardless of whatever attempts are made, and leaving for now the question of whether or not secrecy is advisable, there is simply no way to keep a baptism secret. The rapid rate of communication in an oral culture rivals the speed of the internet. The only exception to this reality happens when an MBB is extracted for baptism—and then never returns home to family and friends. The motivation behind such a choice is, of course, easy to understand. Missionaries might be compelled by genuine love and concern for their newfound brother or sister in Christ—but the implications for the birth of church planting movements are profound. Unfortunately, the way that baptism is often administered does, in fact, lead to *reduced* rather than *increased* witness.

Open or Secret?

Given the relationship of baptism and persecution, missionaries often seek to baptize MBBs in secret. Despite the good intentions, the missionary inadvertently models fear and insecurity that will hinder the new believer's faith for months and years to come. When the persecuting family or community is asked about why they treated their child or neighbor so harshly for being baptized, the reply is often, "Our son/daughter/neighbor has participated in a secret, foreign religious ritual at the hands of a foreigner. He/she has been bought with foreign money. He/she has become a westerner and has taken sides against our own people." The missiological implications are clear. Persecution becomes a socially responsible, even necessary, reaction to a "foreign ritual' or even a perceived "foreign invasion." Couched in these terms, it is impossible for the local community to so much as consider the claims of Christ or the process of faith. Protection of the community from foreign influence is the only concern; faith questions are seldom considered. The entire experience has been reduced to the inappropriate influence of an outsider and the community's response to that.

As important as baptism is—and it is utterly crucial—it becomes apparent that even baptism is a secondary matter. To be persecuted because of baptism, regardless of how or by whom it is done, is not the same thing as being persecuted for who Jesus claims to be.

If Being Baptized Once is Good, is Being Baptized Several Times Even Better?

The interviews also reveal that most MBBs, within five years of their declaration of faith in Christ, regardless of whatever process they have been a part of, have been baptized and re-baptized three to five times. In countries where missionaries representing different agencies are beginning to partner and share statistics, it is clear that the number of annual baptisms of MBBs is significantly inflated as MBBs are baptized time and time again within different mission bodies. Seldom will these mission entities realize that a particular MBB has already been baptized by a sister organization. The baptism of one MBB might be counted by a number of different groups. It is not unusual to read that there are, for example, a thousand followers of Christ in a particular country—while in personal interviews it is possible to account for only two or three hundred. The difference can be explained by the fact that many MBBs have experienced repeated baptism through several different groups. What's more, *each time* the MBB is baptized, the potential for severe persecution escalates.

One of the motivations behind multiple baptisms is the connection of baptism to the opportunity for employment with a mission organization. Whether implied or explicit, the step of baptism is understood to be an entry requirement for a job, and MBBs willingly submit to that expectation. Additional pressure sometimes comes from missionaries themselves. It is difficult to delay baptism when home churches and sending agencies are evaluating the number of baptisms as a measure of missional effectiveness.

Mode and Meaning

The matter is complicated further by the theological, historical, and doctrinal differences represented by various mission organizations. It is not unusual for an MBB to receive believer's baptism by immersion at the hands of a Baptist missionary who explains to the believer the symbolic nature of baptism. Yet, some time later, either because of spiritual struggle or the opportunity for a new job, the MBB may gravitate to an Assembly of God missionary, receiving another baptism along with detailed teaching about being filled with the Holy Spirit. This same MBB might then be drawn to a Lutheran relief agency or, perhaps, one supported by Presbyterians. This pilgrimage might be the result of honest seeking—or it might be motivated by a desire for employment, education, a spouse, or a chance to live in America. Whatever the motivation, in a relatively short span of time this MBB could have been personally baptized by immersion, sprinkling, *and* pouring—every mode of baptism that the western church has practiced over its two thousand years of life.

For the MBB, generally speaking, the mode of baptism is not especially significant. The theological setting for baptism is also likely to be confused. MBBs do not come to Christ in a vacuum. In some cases, they have already been exposed to the church. In fact, in many cases, this historical church can pre-date Islam. As if by osmosis, these seekers and incipient believers have already been affected by different theologies and traditions regarding baptism. The impact on both the MBBs and their faith is deeply significant.

The Pilgrimage Illustrated

Imagine a man named Mohamed. He has experienced dreams and visions that have sent him on a spiritual pilgrimage. This season of searching lasts from three to five years. During this time, he has interacted with the Bible; he has read and studied. He has also had between twenty and thirty spiritual encounters with the gospel The Holy Spirit, time and again, has sent someone to Mohamed. The process repeats what happened often in Scripture: Joseph was sent to Pharaoh, Ananias was sent to Saul, Philip was sent to the Ethiopian eunuch. In the same way, many different people have been sent to Mohamed.

As a result of this good and godly witness, Mohamed makes a declaration of faith in Jesus. He then receives believer's baptism.

At this point in the story, it does not really matter who administers the baptism. Remarkably, when MBBs baptize each other, with a minimum of outside participation, the greatest influence on the *mode* of baptism does not come from Bible studies or even from discussions with other MBBs. What influences Mohamed and his friends the most is whether or not they have seen the *Jesus Film*! The most common mode of baptism comes from a movie.

So Mohamed receives a "Jesus Film" baptism. Often, he will describe his faith pilgrimage and speak of this baptism (which has come several years after his declaration of faith) as a symbol of his relationship with Jesus.

If Mohamed is married, he will go home to his family. Within three to six months, Mohamed will make a proclamation to his wife: "Woman, I am now a Christian. That makes this a Christian home. Therefore, you are now a Christian."

Of course, his wife is shocked. Because of his terrible indiscretion, she can divorce him or betray him to his family. But often, her dependence on her husband and her desire to obey him is so deeply ingrained that she will accept the fact that faith has been declared for her by her more informed husband. A few months later, he will baptize her.

In the interview, Mohamed will describe his own faith and the faith of his wife in different ways. In fact, he might say that his wife is not yet a "true believer." She is married to him, however, and her baptism (he will say) represents a sign that one day she will believe in her own right. One day, she will become a "true believer."

Mohamed is not quite finished. His faith has not been birthed within a vacuum. The religious environment surrounding him often includes Catholic and Orthodox churches. He has been influenced by these also. He gazes with love at his three-month-old son. He knows the difficulties that lie ahead for this child. He knows the struggle of being educated in an Islamic system. Mohamed may have many theological questions—but he is willing to take a chance that perhaps the Catholics and Orthodox are correct. So Mohamed will baptize his infant son, praying that this time baptism is actually salvific.

Notice that baptism has gone from symbol to sign to sacrament within one family and within a very short span of time. Perhaps Mohamed has been immersed. Perhaps his wife has had water poured over her head. Perhaps the infant son has been sprinkled. Mohamed has very little interest in the theology of baptism or in the proper mode of baptism. He has different and deeper concerns.

It is also likely that each of these baptisms has taken place with the participation of an outside community. Regardless of their level of theological or biblical understanding, Mohamed and his family experience increasing persecution with each step of the process. Quickly, they become outsiders even within their own community. If they happen to live in an environment where violence is common, missionaries will typically offer to extract them to a country of safety.[3] Often, the persecution that Mohamed and his family will experience will be precipitated by multiple baptisms with the involvement of outside missionaries or those within the CBB church.

Lessons to Be Learned

Perhaps Islam understands what the West has forgotten. Perhaps Islam understands an old way of living in community. Baptism represents a new alignment with the Kingdom of God and a new way of relating to family and friends. Quite simply, baptism represents a new life. It is startling to realize the Jesus never extracted one person from his or her country of origin. In every case, submission to the Lordship of Jesus, and sharing in the experience of baptism, was a local experience.

There is also a growing theological corruption that surrounds baptism when an MBB receives baptism by western hands. The interviews record numerous instances where godly missionaries have faithfully the meaning of baptism more profoundly than the church does. Baptism represents dying to sin, dying to self, and dying to witnessed, led Muslims through a process or experience of salvation, and baptized them. Rarely does this result in a church being planted, even when the missionary has performed in culturally appropriate ways and fulfilled the expectations of the sending body. Why? The interviews suggest that many MBBs have experienced serious persecution when their faith pilgrimage and baptism were traced to the ministry of the foreigner. In some settings, scores of MBBs went to jail and were severely beaten. When asked why they did not simply meet with other MBBs, evangelizing and administering the ordinances or sacraments of the church themselves, several trust issues and several theological corruptions were noted in almost every case.

MBBs will typically meet with one another—but only if the missionary is present. If the missionary is reassigned, goes on a furlough, or even takes an extended vacation, the MBBs refuse to meet together. When asked why this was so, since all of them went to jail for their association with the outsider, the reply is, "You cannot trust a person from this country." "Who do you trust," the interviews asked? "We trust the missionary." "But it was because of your relationship with the missionary that you went to jail." "Yes, that is true, but still, we trust the missionary."

Missiologically, understanding this apparent contradiction makes cultural sense. MBBs will trust the one who brings them to Jesus. "Timothy" will trust "Paul." And "Paul" will trust "Timothy" that he has come to know well. He has observed "Timothy" struggle through the faith process. He has watched "Timothy" begin to endure persecution. The trust is based on shared experience. MBBs will meet as a church with those they trust. Interestingly, the greater the role that outsiders play in bringing MBBs to faith, the less trust those MBBs will have for other MBBs.

Though they experience serious persecution as a result, most MBBs will bring themselves and scores of others to the missionary in order to pray the prayer of salvation and receive believer's baptism. Why? Why is it necessary for the missionary to be involved at this point in the process? Almost without exception, MBBs will say, "My baptism is *better* at the hands of a missionary who has known Jesus for years and who has such deep religious training." John 3:22 is perhaps the most definitive reference to the possibility that Jesus Himself baptized. But John 4:1 indicates that Jesus quickly delegated this task to His disciples. There, Scripture makes it clear that "it was not Jesus who baptized, but His disciples." The Apostle Paul addressed this issue of baptismal corruption in 1 Corinthians 1:13-17. He concludes with this telling word, "For Christ did not send me to baptize, but to preach the gospel."

More damaging is the almost universal statement from MBBs that, "My salvation is better at the hands of a missionary who knows Jesus so much better than any local person." This is a theological corruption. Unknowingly, the missionary can give credence to the development of a "first-class MBB" and a "second-class MBB" within a group of first generation believers. Such a desire to receive these blessings and functions at the hands of the missionary often leads to increased persecution. When these MBBs are arrested, the arresting authorities seldom question MBBs in regard to issues of personal faith. The persecutors demand information concerning the involvement of outsiders in the lives of local believers. They want to know from where the Bibles originated, who gave them the Jesus Film, who provided Christian witness, materials, and money. It is very common for MBBs to be arrested simply because of their relationships with outsiders. Issues of personal faith are seldom raised during the course of the persecution event.

The earthly ministry of Jesus took place within a hostile environment. Opposition from the Jewish leaders under the Roman occupation was serious. However, prior to Pentecost when thousands of believers emerged, Jesus, as a cultural insider, incarnated the Kingdom of God so effectively that not one follower was severely persecuted throughout the entire three years of his earthly ministry. No one went to jail. No one was beaten. Not one person was martyred.

Jesus, a cultural insider in an environment framed by religious and secular violence, ministered in a way so that thousands of souls eventually had the opportunity to hear, to understand, to believe, and to be gathered into believing communities before they were visited by severe persecution.

Theological and Missiological Suggestions

Several concluding observations are in order. First, the interviews suggest that baptism should be practiced in and among the host, believing community. Missionaries from the West seldom, if ever, make up that host, believing community. Clearly, baptism in the New Testament took place in local community. Baptism outside of a local community, if present at all, was a distinct exception to normal practice. The story of the Ethiopian eunuch in Acts 8:26-39 might be cited as the classic exception to the norm. But the comments of the persecuted on this story and the cultural setting are telling. In their view, it is significant that this Ethiopian was "...an important official in charge of all the treasury of Candace, queen of the Ethiopians." They point out that he was traveling in caravan and was, therefore, surrounded by community. He was riding in a chariot driven by a servant. Others were traveling with him. And that entire community, his community was able to observe what he experienced. To people in the west, the story suggests isolation and separation. But through MBB eyes, the baptism of the Ethiopian eunuch was clearly within community.

The biblical norm is baptism within community. The biblical norm is a setting where an individual's family members and friends are baptized together. In the New Testament, there is no evidence of secret baptism by outsiders in the middle of the night, certainly not in another country. John's baptism of Jesus, the baptism of the household of Cornelius, and the baptism of the Philippian jailor are all representative. The location and setting of the believer's baptism has great significance.

Ignored and rejected by western missionaries is the evidence that many MBBs experience psychological dysfunction after they come to Christ. This might include alcoholism, multiple marriages, sexual voyeurism, or depression. Why? Islam informs an adherent how to live life, how to exist in community, how to fill every moment of every day. It defines when to wake, when to pray, where to pray, the direction to face during prayer, and even the words to pray. It regulates life between genders. Islam touches on every aspect of daily life. Often when a young Muslim comes to Jesus, baptized by an outsider, he loses his family, and social identity. He has indeed died to, and been thrown out of, his old culture. But he has yet to be resurrected into real New Testament community. He and his evangelizer, baptizer, and discipler live in two distinctly different worlds. This new believer has lost his life structure—but it has not yet been replaced. Without community, this MBB is "lost"—even though he has been saved!

Second, reflecting on both the interviews and the New Testament, it is suggested that an in-culture or near-culture believer should baptize MBBs. The more the baptizer is viewed as an outsider, the more likely it is that intense persecution and theological corruption will result. In the West, the baptizer is generally set apart by seminary degrees, education, title, and ordination. Right or wrong, there is a clear delineation between clergy and congregation. Within environments of persecution, however, community is formed most quickly when baptism is lovingly administered by local hands: husband to wife, father to children, neighbor to neighbor. As in-culture and near-culture believers baptize, persecution for secondary reasons is sharply reduced and old communities of faith are transformed into new communities in Christ. When persecution does arrive, it is in direct response to who Jesus is and to the kind of transformed community that He is creating. And when persecution arises, an incipient community of support has already come into existence. This is not to suggest that Islam has the right to persecute those who turn to Jesus if a western missionary happened to be involved in that conversion. What is suggested is that missionaries need to work and minister with great sensitivity and wisdom.

It is not uncommon for MBBs to plead with believers from the outside to baptize them, even outsiders temporarily passing through their country. If MBBs are evangelized, baptized, financed, and gathered together by outsiders, what is their motivation to be in community? The interviews suggest that MBBs need to be locally accountable for witness and behavior among their family, friends and neighbors.

Clearly, a sound theology of baptism is important. The church for centuries has debated and divided over whether baptism represents a symbol, sign or sacrament. The church has persecuted itself over who has the authority to perform baptism and which mode of baptism is biblical: immersion, pouring or sprinkling. These are heavy and important issues. At the same time, the issues of theology and mode, as defined by the western church, were never raised by MBBs in the almost three hundred interviews globally! MBBs will experience multiple baptisms as they pass from one western mission family to another. They will usually receive something useful from each doctrinal experience, even if they acquiesce to multiple baptisms for the sake of employment. MBBs will pass from one agency to the next, expressing the feeling that "something is still missing." Generally, they will be baptized again and again until they receive believer's baptism at the hands of another MBB within their own community. Then, they will say, "I have come home. I have found true New Testament family. This is real church."

MBBs, in environments of persecution and violence, are concerned about only one doctrinal issue regarding their baptism. The question is this: "Have I been baptized into Christ and into a local community? Will this church care for me, hold me daily accountable, and share all things common? Will this new spiritual family care for me and my family if I lose my job, if we are excluded from my extended family, or thrown into prison or martyred for our faith?" Unfortunately, that concern is not always the central issue for missionaries and their sending bodies concerning baptism in cultures of violence. Sometimes, missionaries are more consumed with counting baptisms than with making baptism count.

At the point where baptism, MBBs, and missionaries converge, the overwhelming foundational issue is the nature of local community. What is church in its essence, stripped of property, buildings, and all the possessions collected throughout the centuries? What does i mean to belong—to belong!—to the Body of Christ?

Baptism is at the heart of church planting in environments framed by violence and persecution, especially in places where faith is emerging. At its heart, baptism is the midwife to the emerging church. Suggested here is a revealing and wonderful insight: when baptism is truly New Testament and culturally sensitive, it will always leave a church behind. Baptism births the church. It may be only one family, one clan, or an Ethiopian in caravan on his way home. But church will be the result. This is especially true in environments known for their hostility to faith in Jesus.

Certainly there is a longing for the day when Muslims by the thousands can be baptized into existing churches, filled and led by local MBBs. Until that day comes, belonging to a missionary community or even a local CBB church, is no substitute for practicing baptism in a theologically and missiologically sound manner. Practiced that way, baptism inevitably leaves in its wake a new, New Testament MBB church.

Some may read this article as yet another request for the western missionary to vacate remaining mission fields, especially those defined by violence. One might honestly wonder that f western workers precipitate persecution and theological corruption, why stay? Why bring such hardship upon more vulnerable, local believers? Primarily, western believers must remain obedient to carry out the Great Commission given to them by Jesus Himself as part of the global body of Christ. The command to go to all the people groups of the world stands strong. That command has neither repealed nor completed.

It is also important to hear again the hearts of the persecuted. MBBs do not want western missionaries to leave or cease from carrying the gospel into environments defined by persecution and violence. They admire and desire to mimic the call to the nations. They observe a cross-cultural witness that they seek to emulate. They see western missionaries model godly marriages and healthy parenting. MBBs thrill in discovering worship patterns that include the entire family around the throne of God. Local believers note the broad seed sowing that takes place among their people through the presence of believing westerners. This incarnation allows for thousands of spiritual conversations which occur alongside the arrival of a culturally and linguistically gifted foreign worker. These spiritual conversations are less frequent for Muslims without the presence of the western worker, as there are few safe persons with whom one can converse in regard to the claims of Jesus and the shortcomings of Islam. MBBs have heard the Word of God within the words of a film or a radio broadcast. It has taken on flesh and it has incarnated Christ in their midst.

This article is not a call for the western missionary to disobey the Great Commission. It is a plea for those sent into lostness to work smarter, not harder. Could it be that the western church has forgotten what it means to be baptized into real community, into the body of Christ, the church? Having forgotten the joy and accountability of "bringing all things common," the church in the West has reduced baptism to arguments about its mode, encased within increasingly hardened denominational positions.

Missionaries from the West, including those from diverse theological backgrounds, would be wise to model real community, church, among themselves. These missionaries should then guide and encourage new MBBs to embrace whatever form that real New Testament community, church, could be within the host culture. We can be certain that when healthy New Testament churches emerge among MBBs who are grounded in Scripture and led by the Holy Spirit, those communities will work out for themselves a theology of baptism that is both biblical and honoring of God. It may not completely match our hope or expectation, but it will be biblical nonetheless. On the other hand, missionaries can continue to superimpose a theology of baptism that emphasizes a particular perspective and a distinctly western flavor—and, yet, never leave an honest to goodness New Testament church behind. That, we would argue, would be a tragic choice.

MBBs do not ask for their persecution to end. They ask for the western church to pray that they will remain obedient in the midst of their persecution. When persecution comes, let it be for Jesus and not for secondary issues.

Notes

1. An electronic book summary of these interviews in their entirety is available by e-mail from nripken@attglobal.net.
2. One long-standing Somali mission agency had observed this trend for decades. They addressed the problematic connection of baptism and persecution by simply stopping the practice of baptism! Most evangelical mission agencies would find such a solution troubling.
3. Within cultures where violence if prevalent, up to seventy percent of all MBBs will be extracted to a country of safety.

Chapter Ten

Missions' Greatest Enemy, Greatest Violence

Ralph D. Winter

Probably few Evangelicals can easily imagine how the longstanding interpretation of Genesis 1:1 by a Dallas Seminary professor (Dr. Merrill Unger) could possibly lead to a momentous reinterpretation of our conventional concepts of Christian mission in terms of enemy and violence.

However, this paper actually has three different purposes:

This paper attempts to defend the trustworthiness of the Bible in the eyes of the average well-educated secular person by showing how the Bible does not necessarily conflict with the idea that the universe started with a bang and is immensely old, and that the Earth itself is very old and displays a steady progression of increasingly complex life forms. Even if all that all were true, what would it do to the Bible? While this paper accepts what most paleontologists believe for the sake of discussion, its conclusions do not depend on the validity of the views of contemporary paleontologists. And, for the record, it does not give an inch to the idea of Darwinian evolution or to a fallible Bible.

Secondly, it is a serious attempt to take the Bible literally and yet to be capable of belief in both "the young Earth" and "the old Earth" points of view. I feel sorry when I hear that a famous Bible College graduate faculty believes in "the old Earth" while the undergraduate faculty believes in "the young Earth," thinking they are contradictory.

175

Much more important, in a way, is the proposal that our current concepts of Christian mission work are good, but incomplete, and in fact are much too narrow if we are really setting out to glorify God who is constantly blamed for evil. The novel element here is the idea that the full implications of the New Testament's concept of Satan have been largely lost in Western Christianity to the extent that we have been influenced by Augustine's neo-platonic view of a God who, often with mysterious reasons, initiates both good and evil with Satan only a "bystander."

A larger interpretation of mission goes like this: we have been recruiting people all over the world into God's eternal family, which is an activity as basic and as significant as you can get. But while our new "recruits" are now all dressed up in their new uniforms they do not know they are *military uniforms*, and are more often hoping to flee evil rather than fight it. Personal righteousness, both "positional" and actual, would seem to be very thin if it does not turn around and fight evil.

Worse still—far worse—is the fact that if we let the world fight disease, corruption and violence, God is generally blamed for "allowing" such evils. We puzzle over evil if we think God is "behind" all evil—instead of "in front" making good out of evil. Such a theology requires books that help us to understand *When God Doesn't Make Sense*.[1] However, suffering and violence in a war against an intelligent enemy *don't need to be explained*, and for that reason neither does the verse, "All that will live godly. . . will suffer persecution." We *are* in a war!

Summary

Opening the AD 1611 King James Bible we read "In the beginning God created. . . ." Over the next 400 years this interpretation has been cemented in the minds of millions of people. It conveys the idea that the Bible begins by describing the beginning of the entire universe, not merely the new beginning of the human story.

However, not even in 1611 was the universe well understood. It was likely far less clear to the "holy men of God" writing in the days of Genesis.[2]

In fact, the "known world" of Moses would not have even included the idea of a planet, of a sphere hanging in space. Similarly, "The ends of the earth" in Isaiah 49:6 never referred to our planet but to the ends of the earthen plain ending abruptly where the "fertile crescent" of the Middle East is bounded by the mountains rising in Turkey and Iran.

In other words, the common interpretation of Genesis today—that the universe began 6,000 years ago—may simply be the result of reading later understanding into an earlier text. Such errors are called *anachronisms*. The error is understandable. However, the very serious result is to force the Bible (unfairly?) to say that the world is only 6,000 years old, and thereby to create the greatest stumbling block to modern man's trust in the Bible.

Curiously, as long ago as 1958 the chair of the Old Testament Department at Dallas Theological Seminary, Dr. Merrill Unger, taught that "the geologic ages" preceded Genesis 1:1 and that the events of Genesis 1 portray not THE beginning but "a relative beginning (*Unger's Bible Handbook*)."[3] His was not a new idea even then but today it is uncommon.

Our problem is that most of the world today assumes that both our planet and the universe are much older than 6,000 years. The grim result, then, is that the Bible appears wrong when in fact it may in fact be a very accurate description of things using terms that were understood in that day.

Thus, Unger's insight is what undergirds the tentative perspective of this paper, namely, that Satan fell long before Gen. 1:1, and began distorting all of nature from the Cambrian Period on, continuing that type of genetic distortion after Adam's fall, and although he was decisively routed at the turning point of the Cross, he stalks the land to this day, *his works casting blame on "the God of*

Creation." This then sets the stage for a radically expanded concept of Christian mission.

This presentation is both hypothetical and conjectural. It lays out the predominant secular interpretation of the history of the universe and more specifically the earth and life on earth, doing so whenever the phrase is employed "many scientists believe" simply describing not affirming. It does not give any credence to Darwinian evolution at all. But it does note that there is no necessary conflict with Genesis of the secular sequence and time spans, if, that is, Genesis 1:1 does not describe the origin of the universe but rather a new creation of the era of "image of God" humans.

The story is cast in narrative form for efficiency and digestible order. Credit is due to John Eldridge for the concept of "Acts" in a story. He has four Acts in his superb little book, *The Epic*.[4] I have split his third Act into Act III, the Edenic period and Act IV, the period after the Fall of Adam. Thus, I have five "Acts."

Act I: The Creation of the Universe

Thirteen and a half, or so, billion years ago, many scientists believe, a "Big Bang" occurred, *producing* the entire universe. (They don't like the word *creating*.)

• For various reasons mentioned below, such a creation event does not seem to be what Genesis 1:1 is describing.

Four and a half billion years ago, many scientists believe, planet Earth was formed.

About four billion years ago, many scientists believe, very small forms of life appeared on Earth. For the next 3.5 billion years life forms were still very small.

• This astounding slowness of the formation of progressively more complex forms of life may in this case imply that God has for millions of years been doing that work through intelligent, but finite, intermediate beings who have been at work in an incredibly complex, *and thus lengthy*, learning curve. Perhaps some of them have been small enough to work directly with DNA.

It took a century with thousands of intelligent engineers at work to "evolve" the Model T Ford into a Lincoln Continental. It did not happen without intelligent guidance at every point.

Prokaryotes were followed by Eukaryotes about two billion years ago, many scientists believe.[5] All angels were good at this time.

Then, about 530 million years ago the Ediacaron period displayed small animals with "radial symmetry" similar to starfish, as well as "bi-polar symmetry"—with a front and a back and four legs.

• Significantly this Ediacaron animal life revealed no predation or even defenses against predation! Still only good angels.[6]

Act II: The Fall of Satan

Next, relatively suddenly, the "Cambrian Explosion" took place. A wide variety of different types of animals now appeared, and, for the next 500 million years, all of them can be characterized as horrifyingly cruel predators or prey or both.

Note that this lengthy record of violent animal life does not seem to fit well into the first chapter of Genesis, even if the "days" spoken of there might be considered very long, since the animals described in Genesis are explicitly declared (v. 29) to be *noncarnivorous*.

• Here is a thought: this new and radically different 500-million-year period might have begun when an intermediate being, an archangel, in turning against his Creator in the "Fall of Satan" carried perhaps millions of equally rebellious angels with him, becoming what C. S. Lewis called "a hideous strength" or what Paul called the "god of this world."

• If the long story of the earlier, progressive, *creation* of non-predatory life had reflected God's infinite wisdom and goodness, now the pervasive *distortion* of that life, if not that of a Satanic foe, would seem clearly to *reflect negatively on God's character*. This negative reputation may be seen today in the very common attribution of tragedies not to Satan, but to "God's mysterious will." This absence of Satan in people's minds is what allows a book by the title of *When God Doesn't Make Sense*,[7] or a Harvard professor logically to remark that, "If the God of the Intelligent Design proponents exists, He must be a divine 'sadist' who creates parasites that blind millions of people."[8] How can we reply to such thinking if we do not recognize (point out and fight) "the works of the devil (I John 3:8)"?

Also, during the next 500 million years, many scientists believe, many asteroidal collisions blotted out life in various parts of the globe, as if in judgment—my thinking—of the prevailing violence and destructive nature of gruesomely distorted life forms.

• Forty-five of the resulting craters that have been found are fifteen miles across or larger. The largest, in the Antarctic, is 300 miles in diameter. It is believed to have occurred 275 million years ago, and is estimated to have extinguished ninety-seven percent of all life on Earth. Another large crater, at the north end of Mexico's Yucatan peninsula, is believed to have occurred 65 million years ago, and is 100 miles across. It is the one understood to have ended the one-hundred-million-year period of the characteristically violent dinosaurs. Many of these forty-five larger asteroids are understood to have been solid rock miles in diameter moving at the speed of a rifle bullet at the moment of impact.[9]

Following the extinction of the dinosaurs, many scientists believe, mammals came into their own, growing in size to tons of weight, existing virtually unchallenged until intelligent pre-humans began to drive them into extinction.

Finally, evidence of distinctive and unprecedented intelligence appeared, reasonably (in my opinion) the first true humans (but Satanically distorted, carnivorous, violent, cannibals, not the Genesis 1 type). The evidence in this case is not *fossil bones* but indications of highly intelligent *genetic breeding of both plants and animals*, that is, 1) the selective breeding of virtually inedible plants, deriving corn, wheat, rice, and potatoes, etc., and 2) the selective breeding of animal life, for example, dangerous wolves into friendly dogs. Both types of genetic engineering, many paleo-historians and paleontologists believe, took place about 11,000 years ago[10] (about five thousand years before the Genesis new beginning).

However, despite this early evidence of sudden, unprecedented intelligence, all fossils of human life that far back clearly reflect cannibalism and violence, in other words, durable evidence of intentional, *evil distortion*.[11]

Act III: A New Beginning and the Fall of Man

About 6,000 years ago, at the very beginning of the Jewish/Christian Bible, we find what may be a series of events which could possibly be the aftermath of a fairly small asteroidal collision in the Middle East

The idea of an asteroid wiping out all life in a local region of the earth is conjectural but not unrealistic. However, the idea of Genesis describing a new beginning *following* a major catastrophe has been fairly widely thought of by people such as C.I. Scofield, editor of the most widely used reference Bible of all time, the *Scofield Reference Bible;* by Merrill Unger, as mentioned earlier, a Dallas Seminary professor and editor of the 500,000-in-print *Unger's Bible Handbook*, published by Moody Press, and perhaps even John Eldredge (*Wild at Heart*, and *The Epic*).

The book last mentioned speaks of events "prior to Genesis" on page 19. On page 18 Eldredge says, speaking of Genesis 1:1,

> An important passage it is, to be sure. But to grasp this Epic, you cannot start there. <u>That is way into the story</u>. That is Act Three. It is a beginning, but it is the beginning of the *human* story, the story of life here on earth. As Hebrew scholar Robert Alter says, a better rendering of the Hebrew goes "When God began to create heaven and earth." When God began to create the life we know. And before this? There are events that have preceded this chapter, events we must know.

> If you want to look back into the once upon a time before all time,
> well, then you have to start with another passage, from the Gospel
> of John (1:1). (Underlining mine)

Genesis 1:2 is the rest of the sentence, describing what God had to
contend with in this particular new beginning. The English
translation "formless and void" is today widely understood not to be
a good translation of the Hebrew idiom, *tohu wabohu,* which more
often in the Bible means "destroyed and desolate."[12]

The result might then actually be "When God began to put things
back together, to reclaim the heavens and the earth, the (regional)
situation appears to have been destroyed and desolate."

The subsequent verses describe the initial total darkness surrounding
the entire planet, but, then, with light peeking through as the dust
settled.

• Note well that it is typical of even the smaller of these major
asteroidal impacts to kick enough dust into the atmosphere to block
out all light for a time around the entire planet. Gradually, however,
as the dust settles, dim light becomes noticeable once a day.
Eventually the direct rays of the Sun penetrate the remaining dust
and the Sun becomes visible. Later, the Moon. Later, the stars.[13]

These verses surely seem to be a "restoration sequence" rather than a
"creation sequence." If they are viewed as a *creation* series of events
many scholars have wondered how the dim light of day would have
been created before the sun appeared. The word *creation* is not even
used. The text simply says "Let there be light."

• Obviously those humans wiped out in this regional impact would
not have been able to report this sequence. On the other hand,
surviving humans scattered elsewhere around the globe would
certainly have been actual eye witnesses of the darkness and the
gradual reappearance of light, the sun, etc.. Egyptian scholars then
could have retained a record of such observations so as to be the
source of information Moses employed in Genesis.

• Many Bible expositors are either unaware of, or do not go along with, the fairly recent search for impact craters on the earth's surface. This search began in earnest only in 1970 after the first Moon landing unexpectedly revealed that the hundreds of pock marks on the Moon were not, as had been assumed, volcanic craters but were impact craters.[14]

• Beginning in 1812 hundreds of thousands of fossil bones of violent animals have been dug up which belong to thousands of now extinct forms of life. Since these animals cannot be the ones described in Genesis 1, where both animals and man are clearly described as non carnivorous,[15] they must have either come *before* Genesis or we must assume they were distorted into their violence and carnivorous nature *after* the Fall of man. The latter possibility would force enormous complexity into the last 6,000 years, including much extinction. Bones have been discovered for a thousand times as many animal species as survive today.

It would seem to be easier to believe, following Unger, that all of that violent life preceded Genesis, and that, then, Genesis is describing a new creation of non-distorted life in the "known world" of the writers. In fact, it may be unfair to the Bible to make it speak of a *planet* since at that time people did not know of such a thing. Indeed, most of the Old Testament is written by (KJV) "holy men of God who spake as they were moved by the Holy Spirit."[16] A key word here is "men." Unlike the *Qur'an* and the *Book of Mormon* (which are said to have been dictated by God) the Bible normally contains what these holy writers, guided by God, understood and their hearers understood. Reading later knowledge into earlier documents is a common mistake called *anachronism.*

• Similarly, the later judgment of the flood would reasonably be in "the known world." The table of nations in Genesis 11, the children of Shem, Ham, and Japheth, are nations which Bible maps locate in the Middle East. There are no Incas or Eskimos. This would certainly be fair to the Bible. Some of the faculty at Wheaton College have believed and taught a regional flood for fifty years.

• Thus, Genesis may be regional, and, if so, the Edenic events would thus not be the first or only "new beginning." The flood is another "new beginning." The selection of Abraham is another "new beginning." Isaac instead of Ishmael is another "new beginning." The selection of Jacob/Israel instead of Esau is another "new beginning." The Exodus is another "new beginning." The return from Babylon is another "new beginning." The coming of Christ and the breakthrough to the Gentiles in the NT is another "new beginning." The Reformation is another new beginning, and so on and so forth.

In any case, the vast majority of all scientists today, if we continue to tell them that the Bible teaches that all forms of life are no more than 6,000 years old, will continue to feel forced to believe that the Bible cannot be trusted.

Luther and Calvin interpreted Psalm 19 to mean that the Sun revolved around the earth, as against Copernicus' view that the earth revolved around the Sun. Unfortunately, people later on did not say Luther and Calvin misinterpreted the Bible. They said the Bible must be wrong. However, science in that case did not contradict the Bible. Science contradicted a misinterpretation of the Bible!

• Thus, it is not to criticize the Bible, but to defend it, if we recognize that the phrase "to the ends of the earth" in Isaiah 49:6 only refers to the flat plain of earth leading up to the mountains of Eastern Iran and Turkey. Only fairly recently in European languages has the word *earth* (soil) meant *the Earth* (a planet), and it still is not usually used that way.

Genesis 1 may then present the non-carnivorous type of life, animal and human, which we see again at the end of time in Isaiah 6 and 11 (the lion lying down with a lamb). Once Adam and Eve are seduced by Satan and turned out of Eden, the "sons of God" (the new type of humans created in Eden in the image of God?) marry the "daughters of men" (previously distorted and depraved humans beginning 11,000 years ago?). In that case we can understand why the life spans of the Edenic humans gradually shorten.

Further, it would seem reasonable that the Edenic type of non-carnivorous human and animal life, by interbreeding with the distorted, carnivorous life outside of Eden, would gradually revert to the life-destroying carnivorous behavior of the pre-Edenic, pre-Genesis 1:1, distorted life. Eventually the non-carnivorous Edenic version of human and animal life would have had virtually disappeared into the genetically distorted earlier gene pools. This may be one way of understanding original sin as something we cannot wish away easily, it being inherited genetically—something illuminating Romans 3:23, "All have sinned and come short of the glory of God." This also would enable us to understand why being "born again" does not change all our inborn wayward traits even though it allies us with our Father in Heaven against hardwired genetic evil within which we still must fight—the sort of conflict we read about in Romans 7.

Act IV: Wartime

Far more important is the fact that this scenario describes a great length of time Satan has been at work distorting God's creation, producing the incredible vastness of his corrupting work *of which we are mostly unaware*. As one theologian put it, "The greatest achievement of Satan is to cover his tracks."[17] The crucial facts would thus be that 1) we underestimate what Satan has done and is doing, and 2) we do not consider it our mission to fight it, and for that reason 3) *we very often attribute the works of Satan to God*. Remember the Harvard professor mentioned earlier who quite logically remarked that "If the God of the Intelligent Design proponents exists He must be a divine 'sadist' who creates parasites that blind millions of people." I cannot forget that damaging statement, even though it is alarmingly misinformed. (Why can't the Intelligent Design people admit that some of what they see in nature is evil design, not to be blamed on a supreme being?)

If Satan exists and opposes God in every way possible, we might then expect two things to happen: physical distortions and intellectual delusions.

Diabolical Distortions

Obviously, if the time of the Cambrian Explosion were to mark the point when Satan turned against God, it would mean that Satan began distorting the larger forms of life genetically a very long period of time before the events in Genesis even begin. It also seems logical that he would have been twisting bacteria into dangerous germs, creating destructive viruses, and inventing extremely clever and deadly parasites like malaria. Are we supposed to fight germs? Is that part of the verse "The Son of God appeared for this purpose, that He might destroy the works of the devil (1 John 3:8)"?

Is this what Jesus meant when He taught us to pray "Thy Kingdom come, Thy will be done in earth as it is in heaven"?

Augustine and Calvin were unaware of germs, yet even our theologians or TV preachers today do not speak of deadly germs being the work of Satan, to be destroyed as an intentional mission of Christ and of those who follow Him—not wanting to blame disease on God. But if you identify and recognize the enormous global impact of disease-induced suffering as a sphere of diabolical distortion, then both the great violence introduced by the fall of Satan and the fall of Adam become a major reality. In that case, Satan becomes the enemy and the Christian life and mission must be seen as part of an all-out war, a war to be fought not "in addition to winning souls to Christ" but as a means of glorifying God and thus empowering our evangelism. Disassociating God from the works of the Devil becomes then both the means and the end of winning souls to Christ.

Diabolical Delusions

A second dimension of Satanic evil to become aware of *and to be fought as a Christian mission* is what could be called *diabolic delusions*. Millions of people suffer horribly and die prematurely not only because of disease, but because of misunderstandings about the origins of disease. The whole history of medicine has been, in one sense, the mysteriously delayed understanding of the real causes of disease. Just three of actually hundreds of examples of this mysterious delay are the fact that the common cold, tuberculosis, and duodenal ulcers were thought for many centuries not to be the direct result of destructive germs but rather to be the result of, respectively, 1) getting cold, 2) sleeping in damp, cold places and 3) being subject to stress.

There are many other types of diabolical delusions. Here are merely four of them:

• Down through history in India thousands and thousands of widows have been burned on their husbands funeral pyres because of the *delusion* that they would thereby be reincarnated at a higher level.

• Thousands of young women have contracted AIDS in South Africa due to the widespread *delusion* that a man with AIDS can be cured by having intercourse with a virgin.

• We are *deluded* if we think that the world's largest business—the American medical/pharmaceutical industry—is tracking down the primary *sources* of disease. Why are we deluded? Because all of its money comes from people who are already sick and are paying to be *healed*. However, treating the sick and eradicating pathogenic sources of illnesses are usually very different activities. For the latter the available money is microscopic.

• In Africa, due to mistaken *delusions*, 140 million women have undergone "female genital mutilation," which often leads to ruptured bladders (at the time of childbirth) and a resulting life of being social outcasts.

These are some of the destructive *delusions* which need to be fought in the Name of Christ.

Evangelical Fatalism?

However, Evangelicals, instead of fighting to destroy the "works of the devil" have gotten accustomed to a plainly fatalistic understanding of them as "the mysterious will of God." This is the relentless message of the book already mentioned, *When God Doesn't Make Sense* (by no less than James Dobson). In other words, if there is no Satan, much of life really "does not make sense," and our concept of the Christian life and mission becomes diabolically reduced.

What to Do?

Many may think, "What can I as an individual do? What should I do differently? Isn't it still important to win people to the Lordship of Christ even if I can't explain to them how their lives can make a difference in the identification and destruction of the works of Satan?"

Yes, winning people to Christ is still bedrock. But two other things are also true.

1. More and more people can't even be won to Christ because they are deeply confused by the "good news" of a loving God who would seem to have created a world of suffering, or to have at least been unwilling or unable, in general, to rescue us from earthly horrors of evil and pain until the next world.

2. People who are won to Christ rarely understand that they have been recruited to become soldiers in an all-out war.

Of course we know that individuals on their own can't "win a war." To win a war you need a whole lot of things. The United States during the Second World War would be an example. Swarms of "servicemen" (including women) swirled about on planes, trains, and buses, heading off to ports of departure for the various "theaters of war" around the world. Eleven million were sprayed out across the globe in the Army, Air Corps, and the Navy. But 200 million "civilians" staying behind *were equally occupied by the war.*

As millions of men disappeared from their jobs women took their places. A largely women's workforce ("Rosie the Riveter") built entire ships one every fourteen days, medium bombers one every hour. Nylon was needed for parachute cords—no more stockings. No more coffee, incoming ships had no room for such trivialities because more crucial goods took their place. Any idle moments or unused material were instantly challenged by "Don't you know there is a war on?" You could get a huge fine for unnecessary driving—driving *unrelated to the war*, like, yes, a family outing on Sunday! Gasoline had other more crucial uses.

Today, when Evangelical believers get together they don't compare notes on how to win the war against the "works of the devil." They compare prices on home furnishings, vacations, adult toys. Truly, *they don't know there is a war on!* We act like we don't live in a wartime economy but in a time of peace.

Organize, Organize, Organize

Obviously, individuals need to organize. Do we need dozens of new specialized mission agencies? Note that there is not one Christian institution in the world dedicated to eradication of disease pathogens. Our entire, mammoth medical/pharmaceutical industry is ninety-nine percent focused on the needs of people who are already sick, rather than on ways of eradicating the disease origins.

Our pastors tend to define "Christian service" as activity in and for and through the local church, not the labors of the forty-hour week. If, as Rick Warren says, he wants to transform his "audience into an army," and other pastors by the thousands would follow him, a veritable revolution might occur. But his *Purpose Driven Life* book contains not a single line about the forty-hour week, much less does it recognize that the forty-hour week is exactly where, in a major way, we can best actually fight evil, corruption and disease, efforts crucial to restoring glory to God and credibility to our evangelism. (In a conversation about this he told me he is going to write another book.) This sphere is nowadays being called "Public Theology."

However, although we hear of pastors around the world *losing their lives* because of their faith, it is not often we hear of laymen in the USA even *losing their jobs* because of, say, being honest or opposing deception.

Basically, the incredible violence we must fight against *in the Name of Christ* constitutes an all-out war. Neither laity nor clergy are well aware of that war. Thus, all true believers, not just "full time workers," must be willing to organize against evil, to be creative, and to measure every vocation not by its pay scale, but by its contribution to that war.

It seems very clear that we must recruit people for this war as well as for heaven. If we can't do both *we will ultimately fail at both*. This is why the Christian mission is far more complex and demanding than we thought.

I would hope existing mission agencies could lead the way in the discovery and the defeat of both 1) Satanic *indirectly-inspired human* evil such as war, and such as the corruption that guts almost every secular type of humanitarian aid, and 2) *direct Satanic* evil such as genetic distortions of man and animal, the creation of disease germs and diabolical delusions. This means seeing mission in very much larger terms. It also gives a much larger role to laymen than check-book missions or "after hours Christianity" centering on work in and for the church.

Figure 1: An Overall View

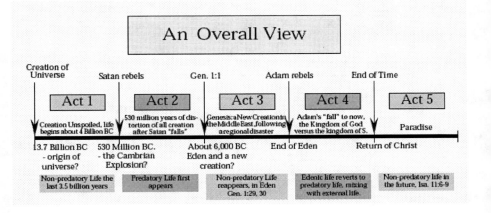

Figure 2: The Enigma of Life

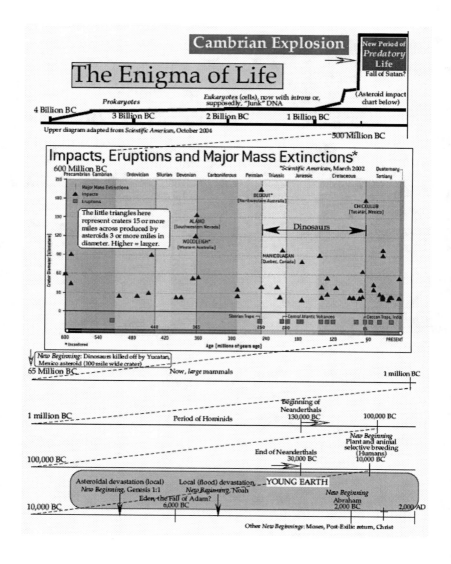

Notes

1. James Dobson, *When God Doesn't Make Sense* (Illinois: Tyndale House, Inc., 1997).
2. 2 Peter 1:21, KJV.
3. Merrill F. Unger, *Unger's Bible Handbook* Chicago: Moody Press, 1967.
4. John Eldredge, *Epic* (Nashville: Thomas Nelson, Inc., 2004).
5. Luann Becker, "Repeated Blows," (*Scientific American*, March 2002: 76-83).
6. Richard Fortey, Life: A Natural History of the 1st 4 billion Years of Life on Earth. (New York: Alfred A. Knopf, 1998).
7. James Dobson, *When God Doesn't Make Sense* (Illinois: Tyndale House, Inc., 1997).
8. Steven Pinker, quoted in David Van Biema. "Can You Believe in God and Evolution?" *(Time,* August 7, 2005).
9. Luann Becker, "Repeated Blows," (*Scientific American*, March 2002: 76-83).
10. Melinda A. Zeder and Brian Hesse. "The Initial Domestication of Goats (Capra hircus) in the Zagros Mountains 10,000 Years Ago" *Science (*24 March 2000).
11. "Once Were Cannibals," by White, Tim D.. *Scientific American*, August 2001, Vol. 285 Issue 2, p58, 8p; "Clear evidence of cannibalism in the human fossil record has been [considered] rare, but it is now becoming apparent that the practice is deeply rooted in our history." [*Abstract from author*].
12. Tsumura, David Toshio.
13. 1988a Tohu in Isa 45:19. Vetus Testamentum. 38: 361-364.
14. 1988b AXYB Pattem in Amos 1:5 and Ps 9:7. Vetus Testamentum. 38: 234-236.
15. 1994 Earth in Genesis 1. In "I Studied Inscriptions from before the Flood": Ancient Near Eastern, Literary, and linguistic Approaches to Genesis 1-11. Richard S. Hess and David Toshio Tsumura, eds. 310-328. Winona Lake, IN: Eisenbrauns.
16. Luann Becker, "Repeated Blows," (*Scientific American*, March 2002: 76-83).
17. Walter Alvarez, *T. Rex & the Crater of Doom*, . (Princeton, NJ: Princeton Univ. Press, 1997).
18. Gen 1:29-30.
19. 2 Pet. 1:21, KJV.
20. Pastor Gordon Kirk, Lake Avenue Church, Pasadena, CA. Graphic: *Scientific American*, October 2004, *Scientific American*, March 2004.

Chapter Eleven

"Violent Words" in a Shrinking World: A Biblical Response

Chris Lindley and Molly Wall

The world is quickly shrinking. Globalization has brought far away peoples closer to one another than ever before. As a result, what is said publicly in one sphere has an increased likelihood of reaching listeners in other spheres at an ever-expanding rate, and with greater opportunity for misunderstanding and conflict. The Christian world is not immune to this growing phenomenon. When Christian leaders, authors, and public figures speak negatively of Islam or the prophet Muhammad on home soil, as has happened with increasing frequency in recent days, their message quickly makes its way around the world, falling on countless Muslim ears.

What effects are these statements having on Muslim-Christian relations, and in particular, on Christian efforts to share Jesus with Muslims? When it comes to sharing the gospel message in the context of an established religious, cultural, and political system, like Islam, what lessons can we learn from Jesus' life and teaching? This paper explores these important questions, while also highlighting implications for all who are seeking to introduce the Prince of Peace into a climate of growing Muslim-Christian hostility.

"Violent Words" and Their Effects

When Christian leaders speak out against Islam as a religion, against Muslims, or against their messenger Muhammad, their actions do not go unnoticed. What are they saying, and what has been the effect of these powerful words on both Muslims and Christians at this time in history where a "clash of civilizations" continues to escalate? Within the past four years, noted Christian leaders have publicly described the messenger of Islam, Muhammad, with words such as: "Islam was founded by Muhammad, a demon-possessed pedophile[1] or, "Muhammad was a terrorist . . . he was a violent man, a man of war."[2] One leader, in response to Muslim outrage over the recently published cartoon drawings of Muhammad said, "These people are crazed fanatics, and I want to say it now: I believe it's motivated by demonic power. It is satanic and it's time we recognize what we're dealing with."[3] Another prominent leader called Islam "a very evil and wicked religion."[4] These quotes are a sampling of statements toward Islam made public through various media, including internationally viewed television and news broadcasts.

However, Christian authors have also represented this growing tide of anti-Islamic sentiment in their writings. One author known for finding redemptive themes within various tribal cultures, said of Islam,

> The more digging I did into the Koran the more I realized when it comes to Islam the redemptive-analogy approach cannot work. Therefore, I had to look at the religion—its founder and its teaching—through a different lens, something antithetical to redemptive analogies.[5]

Another author gives warning to the dangers of Muslims immigrating to the West,

> We have seen that elements of Islam fiercely resist secularism, as well as relativism and indifferentism. Some Muslims are suspicious of non-Muslim cultures and will not assimilate into them, just as they begin to overwhelm them numerically. If anything is certain in the future, it is that these elements will cause more conflicts, and that the West should be prepared for them.[6]

What effect do these statements have on Christians?

This question came home for me on a recent flight. I was seated next to a Yemeni international student on his first trip to the U.S. It was pre-September 11; I had Yossef Bodansky's book on Osama bin

Laden with me, and was about halfway through. With my active imagination, reading an account of the world's number one terrorist was not contributing to good relations with the Muslim gentleman next to me! As he reached into his backpack, I speculated about what he was doing, nervous something might explode or some weapon might emerge. The worst part, though, was his occasional trips to the restroom. I had read of operations where a bomb was assembled in the bathroom. Each time he left my fears escalated that he was readying for attack. They grew so great I could not read and could only pray and hope I was ready for life beyond the grave.

Why was I reacting this way? Why did I assume this Muslim young man was a terrorist plotting my demise? Islam has received an increasingly bad image in the Christian West due to the actions of a small minority of Muslims who literally interpret the Qur'an and its more violent passages, using them to justify their *jihad* (holy war) against the U.S. for its policies towards Muslims. Christian persecution in Muslim lands, suicide bombings, kidnappings, televised executions, and media reports with the latest *fatwas* (religious edicts) and diatribes against modern-day Crusaders all contribute to a rising fear and misunderstanding of Muslims from the Christian West. When Christian leaders and authors speak words that "confirm" these suspicions, many Christians' attitudes toward Muslims begin, like mine, to degenerate into fear and mistrust.

What effect do these statements have on Muslims?

Before answering this question directly, it is important to first ascertain how men and women in the Muslim world can sometimes understand these comments. The most common misunderstanding among Muslims is that there is cohesive sentiment among Christendom and Western governments regarding Islam, such that statements made by Christian leaders represent positions of both Christendom and the government. The author of *Imperial Hubris* explains,

> Clerical comments most U.S. citizens disregard are taken as threatening by Muslims because their societal frame of reference is one in which there is no separation of church and state. Thus,

198 MISSIONS IN CONTEXTS OF VIOLENCE

words of little consequence in U.S. politics and society are heard
and remembered in the Islamic world as threats and blasphemy,
earning America increased Muslim hatred.[7]

Christians in the U.S. feel free to distance themselves from an
inflammatory statement made by a Christian leader, and quickly
disregard the comments as statements from an individual not
representative of the entire Christian community, or of their
government. However, this dichotomy cannot be assumed in the
Muslim world. What is seen as irresponsible and probably innocuous
to Christians in the West is received as violent and inflammatory to
Muslims who hear the words of Christian clerics as representative of
both Christendom and the governments of the West. Note how these
statements will naturally reflect upon all Western representatives
who enter Muslim lands, including those who seek to liberate a
country from totalitarianism, provide relief and development, or
possibly gospel witness. As a result of Christendom's public face,
soldiers, development workers, and missionaries alike may all
receive the same scornful and possibly even violent treatment.

Inflammatory words have in some cases, especially when
misunderstood, led to violent actions. As an example, the statement
accusing Muhammad of being a terrorist led to protests in New York
and Kashmir, as well as to violent scuffles between Hindus and
Muslims in Solapur, India, where eight people died.[8] Although the
violent actions taken by those responding to the statement were not
the sole responsibility of the offender, it is true the anger, riots, and
loss of life are a heavy consequence. If the intent of such a
declaration was for Muslims to see the messenger of their religion in
new light, the use of the word "terrorist" as a description during
President Bush's "War on Terror" likely furthered misunderstanding.
If Muhammad truly were a terrorist, would not his followers then be
the likely recipients of just such a war? Words such as these may
contribute to the Muslim suspicion, and further misunderstanding,
that the U.S. and the Christian West are engaged in a holy war
against Islam.

Recognizing this volatile climate and rampant misunderstanding, one
might conclude these negative Christian public statements or

opinions are, in fact, *violent words,* or words of war, whose impact will be dangerous if not fatal for Christian workers in the Muslim world. As globalization continues to thrust nations, peoples, and religions closer together, the Christian West will face new challenges and obstacles. Violent words vilifying Islam may end up further distancing Christians from those who Jesus, the founder of their faith, admonished them to love. The stakes are too high for the Christian community to ignore this current situation.

Learning from the Life and Teachings of Jesus

Cognizant of this real and mounting conflict, Christians remain convinced of their task, to "Go . . . and make disciples of all the nations" (Mt. 28:18, NIV). About 37% of the yet unreached nations are Muslim peoples. 1.2 million of the world's population are adherents to some form of Islam.[9] The mission community today faces unprecedented challenges, and must begin to think and act differently if the Good News of the gospel is to be introduced into this religious and cultural system in such a way it grows "like yeast through the dough" (Mt. 13:33). How can Christians communicate Jesus and His Kingdom within a Muslim context so that it truly is Good News? If negative statements about the religion are inflammatory, violent, and harmful to God's work among Muslims, how should Christians respond when encountering actual sin, evil, and false understanding in the hearts and minds of Muslims they meet?

A starting place is Scripture, studying the life and teaching of Jesus. He, too, entered a volatile cultural and religious system (Judaism). He lived, worked, and died within it, brought the Kingdom to it, and planted the gospel message within it. He also confronted its leaders, deceptions, and evil beliefs and practices. At the same time, Jesus engaged with those from other religious systems (e.g. Samaritan woman - Jn. 4, Syrophoenician woman - Mk. 7, Geresene demoniac - Mt. 8). What was His message within each of these contexts? How did He handle the sin and evil present within the people He met and the religious systems they adored?

What was Jesus' message to men and women of the religious systems He encountered?

Understanding Jesus' message requires Christians in the (far removed) West to rediscover the life and teachings of Jesus framed in the religious, cultural, historical, and political time in which He walked the earth. Jesus was a brown-skinned Palestinian Jew whose land was under foreign (Roman) occupation. He spoke to Middle Eastern peoples, in a Middle Eastern context. His ancient culture parallels that of peoples in the modern East far more closely than it does that of Americans and Europeans of the modern West. What message did Jesus bring to these peoples?

From the outset of Jesus' public ministry, his message was one of calling for repentance and belief because ". . . the Kingdom of heaven [had] come near" (Mt. 4:17, NIV). This is the same message He gave his disciples to speak upon sending them out on two occasions (Mt. 10:7, Lk. 10:9). Matthew's gospel alone records over thirty times Jesus speaks of the Kingdom of heaven. He spoke of entering the Kingdom (e.g. Mt. 5:20, 18:3), its characteristics (e.g. parables of Mt. 13), and its nature (e.g. Mt. 5:3, 5:19). He spoke of the gospel of the Kingdom (e.g. Mt. 24:14). He walked into a hostile religious, political, and cultural context and spoke primarily of another system that superseded any of the world's systems, including the Jewish religious system to which he belonged. What is this Kingdom? Jesus preached this gospel of the kingdom before His death and resurrection (Mt. 24:14); what is this Gospel?

A clearer understanding of Jesus and His message may help refine the message that gets communicated cross-culturally from Western Christians to Eastern Muslims. The need for this becomes apparent when we understand "Muslims' reasons for rejecting Christianity usually swing around to perceiving Christianity as part of the colonialist endeavor, and perceiving Christ as a Westerner with no relationship to Eastern culture." [10] It is possible the Muslim rejection of Jesus is based on a rejection of all things Western, and not necessarily on the actual person and teaching found in the Gospels. Jesus' message focused on the Kingdom of God, and on a call to repentance, righteousness, Kingdom service, and belief.

How did Jesus confront sin and evil in the people and systems He encountered?

While Jesus spoke of a spiritual Kingdom, He also spoke directly into the religious, political, and cultural systems of the day. He did not come to abolish them (e.g. Mt. 5:17), nor did He come to uphold or build them (Jn. 18:36). Rather, He came to build His Kingdom that would then grow in and through these systems, eventually jumping across these contexts into others until it penetrated and drew followers from among all the nations of earth. Along the way, Jesus rejected some religious and cultural traditions, made use of others, and even transformed a few, bringing new meaning to dead practice.[11] What Jesus rejected, He spoke openly and publicly against. He also taught His followers how to respond to attack and hatred from enemies. What insight does Jesus give for those seeking to speak Truth about the Kingdom in a world where words can be deadly?

Throughout Jesus life and public ministry, He encountered and practiced aspects of the Jewish religious system. Being a Jew, He faithfully carried out the Law, and even many of the Jewish traditions (i.e. Lk. 4:16, Lk. 5:14). These Jewish practices were not necessary practices for His Kingdom (as the apostles later recognized in Acts 15), yet they were not harmful, and, in many ways, were helpful to understanding God and His plan within that cultural context. On occasion, however, Jesus encountered traditions that were sinful and counter to His Kingdom. In these cases He was quick to speak and act against them and those who practiced them, as when the Pharisees complained about His eating with tax collectors and sinners (Lk. 5:13), or when He found the court of the Gentiles used for trade, not prayer (Lk. 19:45-46). In some cases, He took a practice and transformed it, or gave it new meaning, as with ritual washing (Lk. 11:37-40). Jesus did confront, and forcefully, yet He did so selectively, focusing on specific areas of sin within the person or system rather than the religious system itself. Even when confronting non-Jews, Jesus pointed away from the religious system practiced, and toward a spiritual Kingdom. Just as His Kingdom message transcended religious, cultural, or political systems, so did His focus on addressing sin and calling for repentance.

Jesus' use of violent words

There are instances where Jesus used provocative words to reject deceptive or wicked aspects of a religious system. It is evident the recipients of Jesus' harshest criticisms were the Jewish traditions and the religious authorities of the day, including the Pharisees and Sadducees. Jesus' criticisms included, ". . . you hypocrites! You shut the kingdom of heaven in men's faces. You yourselves do not enter, nor will you let those enter who are trying to." (Mt. 23:13, NIV) He called them "blind guides" (Mt. 23:16, NIV), "blind fools" (Mt. 23:17, NIV), "whitewashed tombs" (Mt. 23:27, NIV), "snakes" and "brood of vipers" (Mt. 23:33, NIV). More than likely, these words did not bring about repentance, humility, and belief among the religious rulers. These violent words actually incited them to further oppose Jesus, defending their power and influence. In fact, the effect of these words was violent, even fatal against Jesus and some of His followers.

Has Jesus modeled an example of how His followers ought to confront religious rulers and authorities, and their empty traditions, if they also are keeping people from entering God's Kingdom? Perhaps Jesus had divine authority to challenge the current religious rulers because of his own status as God's Son, because He knew the hearts of men. One must examine these words together with His other teachings on confronting sin. However, the following observations are revealing.

• Jesus confronted those who were leading others away from the Kingdom of God and toward a religious system.

• He spoke to the leaders of the religious system to which He Himself belonged. He rebuked the leaders with whom He lived and worked.

• Jesus focused on those sinful attitudes and beliefs that kept people from entering the Kingdom, not practices keeping people from entering another religious system (i.e. Judaism, Christianity).

• Jesus directly confronted and addressed the leaders who He had witnessed teaching and proclaiming deceptions or exhibiting sinful attitudes.

Do Jesus' followers today have the same authority to vehemently confront religious rulers within their own faith for actions that keep people from Jesus? It seems so, in keeping with the guidelines given for confronting a brother in sin (e.g. Mt. 18, I Tim. 5:19). Can they also apply this practice to leaders in other faith communities? It seems one cannot derive this conclusion from this example. We have no example of Jesus speaking this way against leaders of a religious system outside Judaism.

Jesus' teachings on responding to those who mistreat you. In Matthew 5, Jesus begins teaching his disciples and the crowds that the teachings they have heard about the law, sometimes misrepresentations, are not operating principles of the Kingdom (v. 21-48). In their place should be love for one's enemies (v. 44), turning the other cheek (v. 39), and going the second mile (v. 41). The ultimate example of this comes at the culmination of Jesus' earthly ministry, His arrest. Jesus rebukes Peter for his violent actions saying, "Do you think I cannot call on my Father, and he will at once put at my disposal more than twelve legions of angels?" (Mt. 26:53, NIV) Jesus willingly gave up his life although he had the power to prevent his murder. He Himself modeled in His dying moments His command to ". . . bless those who curse you, pray for those who mistreat you." (Lk. 6:28, Lk. 23:24, NIV) Jesus taught and lived a message of love and blessing for one's enemies, even those who might attack and mistreat others.

In Matthew 7, Jesus teaches His disciples about judging others saying, "First take the plank out of your own eye, and then you will see clearly to remove the speck from your brother's eye" (v. 5, NIV). Following this principle, it seems before making any judgments against Islam as a religious system, or against individual Muslims, including Muhammad, Christians must follow Jesus' powerful injunction. In a recent television interview, the president of a Christian seminary responded to another Christian leader's statement about Islam saying, ". . . any belief system that keeps persons from coming to Christ we would see as a manifestation of demonic power." [12] In some ways, this statement reflects Jesus' rebuke of the religious rulers for keeping people out of the Kingdom of God. It may be that some teachings and practices of Islam have, can, and do keep Muslims out of the Kingdom of God. Could one also say some teachings and practices of Christendom have, can, and do keep people out of the Kingdom as well? It behooves the Christian community to first admit and address the failures within its own system before judging the failures of those of another.

For example, Globalization has now opened the door to a massive exportation from West to East of materialism, pornography, individualism, secularism, and other temptations that have bombarded and begun to erode Muslim religious and family structures. Unfortunately, Muslims do not always differentiate these "secular" sins from Christianity in the West, due to the misunderstanding surrounding separation of church and state. On the other hand, how active has the Christian West been in opposing this exportation of its own sin? Has apathy prevented Christendom from publicly setting itself apart, and thus been found guilty by association in the eyes of Muslims? David Bloesch argues, ". . . the revelation of Jesus Christ stands in judgment over all religions, including institutional Christianity. The beliefs and experiences in all religions need to be purified and tested by God's self-revelation in Jesus Christ" (1992). Again, Jesus addresses sin and judgment in a way that transcends systems, including religious systems, and points to a spiritual Kingdom where love and righteousness prevail, and where kindness leads to repentance.

When it comes to sharing the gospel message in the context of an established religious, cultural, and political system, like Islam, Scripture reveals the focus of that message is the Kingdom of God, not a religious system (e.g. Christianity, Judaism), and a call to repentance from sin, and then belief. The Kingdom of God is not an offensive Western concept to Muslims, and can open the door for further discussion of the King. When it comes to recognizing and confronting sin within other people or systems, Jesus models and teaches rebuke for sinful attitudes and practices within one's own religious system, while he also shows ways to use and bring new meaning to many aspects of a corrupt religious and cultural system. This gives little ground for attacking Islam or rebuking individual Muslims from the outside, while giving plenty of ground for lifting up the Kingdom of God within an existing cultural context, including Islam. It is significant that Jesus did not call for the fall of any religious systems (Jewish or Gentile), but rather for the rise of the Kingdom within every context and the fall of unrighteousness and unbelief.

Biblical Principles for Bringing Peace

Even if the Christian leaders and authors quoted above spoke against Islam and Muhammad from sincere hearts, desiring to expose the lies and evil within Islam in order to see Muslims enter relationship with Jesus, we can see from the consequences that good intentions alone are insufficient for bringing about this desired outcome. If the message is perceived as an attack, it might lead a Muslim understandably toward a defensive posture, leaving him or her unwilling to engage in dialogue. Jesus instructed His followers to be ". . . as shrewd as snakes and as innocent as doves" (Mt. 10:16, NIV); how might we apply this principle to the volatile situation at hand? Is there a way to peaceably introduce Jesus, who bears the title Prince of Peace (Is. 9:6)? Jesus' life and teachings reveal much about His message and methods for confrontation. Would a continued search of Holy Scripture reveal a method of living out this gospel of the kingdom among Muslims by interacting gently and with respect?

Biblical Principles for Interaction. To gain a context and platform for communicating a message, Christians must interact with Muslim friends, neighbors, co-workers, and even strangers on airplanes. Whether informally or formally through arranged meetings, conferences, or other inter-faith dialogue venues, interaction should be built on models provided by Jesus, Paul, and other men of faith.

Communication: Building Bridges. A careful study of the book of Acts reveals the variety ways the apostle Paul preaches the Good News to his many audiences. When speaking to Jewish audiences, he makes assumptions about the culture, traditions, and religious system Jews and the Greek God-fearers of the 1st century would commonly understand (see chap. 13, 22-23). However, when Paul traveled to Greek areas and presented the Gospel to those with no Jewish background, his approach differed notably. When speaking to the Athenians in Acts 17, Paul begins by affirming the good he already sees within the culture. "Men of Athens! I see that in every way you are very religious" (v. 22, NIV). Note he does not begin by chastising them for their worship of false idols, nor defaming their gods and prophets, or by calling them evil, wicked people. Rather, he spends time observing and learning about the people and their religious practices (v. 23). He then acknowledges what he has found, that they are people searching for god (v. 23). He even uses one of their altars inscribed "TO AN UNKNOWN GOD" as a connection to God, and a starting point for sharing the message (v. 23)! He even says to the group, "Now what you worship as something unknown I am going to proclaim to you" (v. 23, NIV). He connects Almighty God to a pagan altar, recognizing Creator God by a name by which they could recognize Him. He acknowledges a measure of good in their seeking after a god, ignorant though they may be of Jesus at this point. Paul went deep within the pagan religious system to find traces of God at work.

Paul goes on to describe Creator God and how He has been at work among all nations since the beginning of time. He shows them how God's Story is really their story. He even quotes their poets in the process (v. 28). Lastly, he speaks of accountability now in effect, that with Jesus' act on the cross, all men from every nation should repent and worship only the one God. Not once does Paul accuse the Athenians of being under a satanic religion or demonic influence, nor do his words communicate disdain or intent to provoke. He respectfully speaks within their context, using real and present aspects of their religion and culture as a springboard to declare a greater revelation beyond what they currently possess. Note he does not introduce a new god, encourage them to leave their religious and cultural system and join another, or call them to renounce all their old beliefs, yet He calls them to repent (v. 30). Paul was open to looking for God's handiwork already evident in the people with whom he interacted.

Are there evidences of God's hand already at work within the peoples and religious system of Islam? Might Christians make such exciting discoveries as they build relationships with and learn from Muslims? Fouad Accad addresses this issue in *Building Bridges.*

> Most people living in a Western environment know very little about Muslims and have little interest in learning about Muhammad's life or his intent in Islam. These people may occupy great positions in the world and in the church, but their ignorance of real facts leads them to conclude that Islam and Muhammad should be totally rejected. In some cases these people will point to the Qur'an as a book that is counter to the gospel, not even realizing that the Qur'an itself is largely pro-Christian. This kind of myopia has led to many unnecessarily fruitless debates, strife, and even bloodshed. (1997)

Many Christians are unaware there are numerous passages in the Qur'an that speak highly of Jesus. This does not negate the fact there are passages that deny basic Christian teachings about Jesus; it simply informs that the majority of Qur'anic passages do give a positive outlook, and a ready place to begin interaction. Muslims already revere Jesus as a prophet in a succession of prophets, with Muhammad being the last and final one. However, Qur'anic accounts are consistent with Biblical accounts of Jesus on the following topics: Jesus' virgin birth (Surah 4:171, 21:91, 66:12), the affirmation of Jesus' messiah-ship (Surah 3:45), Jesus describing Himself as the Word of God (Surah 3:39). Also on His miraculous acts, including raising the dead (Surah 3:49), creating life from nothing (Surah 3:49, 5:110), although taken from an apocryphal account, and lastly, His return at the day of judgment (Surah 43:61).

Christians that desire Muslims to know the Jesus of Scripture should also encourage Muslims to re-visit their Holy Qur'an to discover a Jesus they may have overlooked in their rejection of Western Christianity, as it is better to allow Jesus and the gospel to be an offense, nothing else. Perhaps this, a search to understand more about Jesus, could be the starting point of greater inter-faith dialogue, as both faith communities grapple with the teachings and theology of Jesus in their respective scriptures.

Inter-faith dialogue. How might Christians interact with Muslims in such a way they clearly, but gently, represent Truths of Scripture, yet at the same time, respectfully point Muslims towards Jesus? There are often venues available for inter-faith dialogue, ranging from academic to online settings, and hosts often invite Christians to participate. What is the intent of the inter-faith dialogue? Is it an effective way to interact with Muslims? First, one must recognize the model itself, a formal gathering for discussing religious beliefs and practices among various religious systems, as extra-biblical. That understood, biblical principles must guide a Christian's decision to participate and manner of interaction.

Some may see the role of the inter-faith dialogue as an opportunity to publicly buttress the positions of those in the Christian religious system against those of other religious camps. Others may see the dialogue as opportunity to look for universal commonalities, avoiding any religious absolutes on any side, so they may preserve harmony, even over truth. Neither option seems compatible with the ways Jesus or the apostles invested their time and efforts. However, could an inter-faith dialogue be used for interaction with Muslims, or those of other religions, in a way that fulfills the original Abrahamic covenant, blessing the families of the earth (Gen. 12:3), and Jesus' Great Commission to make disciples of all ethnic groups (Mt. 28:19)?

These dialogues often focus heavily on doctrines and practices, so participating effectively would require the Christian to go carefully about the task of boring out the Gospel from his/her own all-encompassing culture and civilization. Christian witness in any context and in an inter-faith discussion in particular, cannot be effective if it presents a biblical faith inseparable from the communicator's own cultural expression and civilization. This leaves adherents to Islam or other faiths faced with adopting or rejecting Western traditions, values, and practices, rather than simply accepting or rejecting Jesus' message. Vincent J. Donovan describes this important function.

> The gospel is, after all, not a philosophy or set of doctrines or laws. That is what a culture is. The gospel is essentially a history,

at whose center is the God-man born in Bethlehem, risen near Golgotha . . . . I spoke before about the necessity of peeling away from the gospel the accretions of the centuries, and of Western, white, European, American culture, to get to the kernel of the gospel underneath. This involves separating it from the philosophies and theologies with which we have long identified it—even from good philosophy and good theology. (2003)

Again, Jesus' message was of a spiritual Kingdom, one that can enter and grow within any cultural context (Lk. 13:21). It is this transcendent power of the Kingdom of God, to remain apart from the world, yet express itself within every culture, that largely distinguishes it from any other religious message.

Biblical Principles for Action

A maxim commonly attributed to St. Francis of Assisi reads, "Preach the gospel. And if necessary, use words." Jesus was reputed as being powerful "in word and deed before God and all the people" (Lk. 24:20, NIV). Certainly it is true the works of Christians speak at least equally as loudly as do words. In a day when violent words have incited anger and hatred, how might works and deeds instead speak loudly of peace?

Service. Further reflection on Jesus' life leads quickly to the realization He was devoted to service. He served the Father (Jn. 17:4). He explained to His disciples He ". . . did not come to be served, but to serve . . ." (Mt. 20:28, NIV), so service was His purpose in coming. Who did He serve? To His disciples He said, ". . . I am among you as one who serves . . ." (Lk. 22:27, NIV). Jesus served His disciples and followers, but also those who were in need and ultimately all mankind as He ". . . [took] the very nature of a servant . . . and became obedient to death . . ." (Phil. 2:7-8, NIV). The discipline of service runs counter to the world's values. Yet Jesus demonstrated service as an indisputable Kingdom value, "The greatest among you shall be your servant" (Mt. 23:11, NIV). Jesus taught His followers to serve God, and to serve one another.

Muslims often perceive the Christian West as an agent of colonialism and Western imperialism. If the latter does not change its approach, Muslims will continue to perceive it in this way. And perhaps the West will continue to act in this way in many cases. Aspects of both systems have clearly reflected the world's value system, not that of the Kingdom. Could widespread practice of the Christian discipline of service begin to undermine the colonialist and imperialist tendencies of the West? Might a life of true service enable Jesus' followers to reach out in very practical yet selfless ways to the Muslim community? It seems Christians will only communicate the Jesus of Scripture effectively through following His example of humility and service.

What does a life of service look like for a Christian approaching a Muslim community?

1. What if Christians were to approach Muslim communities and ask the leaders how they might best serve them, rather than announce a plan or just begin working? The answers may not be what Christians expect, but how different this approach is from arriving in a Muslim community and jumping to conclusions the West knows and has the necessary solutions for problems of the Muslim world. Service involves helping a community identify and solve the problems that matter to them, in ways that bring health and life to families and communities.

2. Service involves meeting needs. Jesus instructed His disciples to, "Heal the sick, raise the dead, cleanse those who have leprosy, drive out demons" (Mt. 10:8, NIV). Service involves providing assistance and relief to those in need.

3. The true power of service comes through humility and the laying down of one's life for the sake of others (Jn. 15:13). Service involves a willingness to die for the sake of the gospel, and giving a life in exchange for the advance of the Kingdom on earth.

Bernard of Clairvaux said, "Learn that you need a hoe, not a sceptre, to do the work of the Prophet." All Christians offer is the very life of Jesus living within them; that life is demonstrated through the towel rather than the sword or scepter.

A Role for Peacemakers. Isaiah gives Jesus the title "Prince of Peace" (Is. 9:6, NIV), and it is prophesied He will, ". . . guide our feet into the path of peace" (Lk. 1:79, NIV). Paul explains how,

> Now in Christ Jesus [the Gentiles] who once were far away have been brought near through the blood of Christ. For he himself is our peace, who has made the two one and has destroyed the barrier, the dividing wall of hostility . . . (Eph. 2:13-14, NIV)

Jesus is peace. He not only blesses those who work for peace and guides men into peace, He also is able to bring hostile groups together in peace! If God did this for Jews and Gentiles, can He not do it now for His followers from among Christianity and Islam? Paul continues,

> His purpose was to create in himself one new man out of the two, thus making peace, and in this one body to reconcile both of them to God through the cross, by which he put to death their hostility. He came and preached peace to you who were far away and peace to those who were near. For through him we both have access to the Father by one Spirit. (Eph. 2:15-18, NIV)

A comfort in this time of violent words and growing hostility is that Jesus preaches peace to Christians and Muslims alike, putting to death hostility of both through the cross. May Jesus again create one new man out of the two!

Jesus taught, "Blessed are the peacemakers, for they will be called sons of God" (Mt. 5:9, NIV). What does it look like to be a peacemaker among Muslims? What does a peacemaker do?

1. Peacemakers work to promote the reconciliation that Paul describes, recognizing it is only possible through God's work through Jesus, not man's, which returns us to effectively communication Jesus' Kingdom message.

2. Peacemakers work to bring wholeness to families and communities. Malachi prophesies, "He will turn the hearts of the fathers to their children, and the hearts of the children to their

fathers . . ." (Mal. 4:6, NIV). What Muslim who values his family and community above all would not resonate with this desire?

How are families and communities restored? Through the same preaching of peace that restores peoples (Gentiles and Jews), so the message is central. However, there are many ways to serve communities that build up families, ranging from teaching to counseling to family-focused development, eventually introducing the gospel into the family, which can become the fellowship of faith. A peacemaker seeks both to reconcile men to God, and men to men, recognizing that the Prince of Peace alone has power to bring lasting peace.

The interaction Christians have with Muslims in coming days will largely determine the course of future events. Avoiding violent words, while simultaneously adhering to biblical models of communication and service, will more quickly usher in the peace of Christ to a broken situation.

Conclusion

Recently, a Muslim friend inspired me with his courage and humility to look introspectively and critically upon actions and beliefs within his own faith community. His paper confronted sin within his own cultural and religious context, exhorting his faith community to a higher standard of righteous living. As a result of his example, I have sought to do the same. This paper traced the effects of violent words spoken in recent days by Christian leaders, recognizing the consequences are negative and significant for Western workers in the Muslim world. In response, we find through study of Scripture instruction about both the Kingdom message Jesus preached, and the manner in which He confronted sin and evil. Furthermore, we find biblical principles that direct us in living and serving among Muslims.

Ruminating on my flight experience, I wonder how things might have gone differently if these practices were evident in my life at that time. Would this have changed my limited interaction with the Yemeni student sitting next to me? Might I have found a way to lift up Jesus and His Kingdom, transcending the differences in our religious systems? Might I have demonstrated that followers of Jesus are different than what he imagined or expected, by beginning to counter through my words and deeds the damage caused by others' violent words and misperceptions? May we understand well the times, and wisely lift up Jesus, sowing the gospel of peace among Muslim peoples worldwide. And let the following scripture be the operating principle as Christians speak the truth in love to Muslims, "But in your hearts set apart Christ as Lord. Always be prepared to give an answer to everyone who asks you to give the reason for the hope that you have. But do this with gentleness and respect" (1 Peter 4:15, NIV).

Notes

1. CNN, 2002, 2.
2. Moore, 2002, 2.
3. BBCNews, 2006, 7.
4. Foust, 2002, 4.
5. Richardson, 2003.
6. Spencer, 2002.
7. Anonymous, 2004.
8. BBCNews, 2002.
9. Barrett & Johnson, 2001.
10. Mallouhi, 2000.
11. Common Ground Consultants, personal communication, June 1-4, 2005
12. Roach, 2006.

Bibliography

Accad, Fouad Elias. (1997). <u>Building Bridges: Christianity and Islam</u> Colorado Springs, CO: NavPress.

214   MISSIONS IN CONTEXTS OF VIOLENCE

Ali, Abdullah Yusuf. (2001). The Qur'an: A Translation. Elmhurst, NY: Tahrike Tarsile Qur'an, Inc.

Barrett, David B. & Johnson, Todd M. (2001). World Christian Trends, AD 30-AD 2200. Pasadena, CA: William Carey Library.

Bernard of Clairvaux. (1982). Five Books On Consideration: Advice To A Pope. Kalamazoo, MI: Cistercian Publications, Inc.

Bloesch, David. (1992). A Theology of Word and Spirit: Authority & Method in Theology. In William L. Osborne & Ralph D. Winter (Eds.), Global Civilization: Ancient World Reader: Vol. 2 (3rd ed., pp. 58B-1). Pasadena, CA: William Carey Library.

Donovan, Vincent J. (1978). Christianity Rediscovered. Maryknoll, NY: Orbis Books.

Falwell 'sorry' for Mohammed remark. (2002, October 13). BBCNews. Retrieved on April 6, 2006 from http://news.bbc.co.uk/2/hi/americas/2323897.stm.

Foust, Michael. (2002, July 16). Mohler defends Franklin Graham, Vines in New York Times letter. BPNews. Retrieved on March 30, 2006 from http://www.bpnews.net/bpnews.asp?ID=13834.

Imperial Hubris. (2004). Dulles, VA: Brassey's, Inc.

International Bible Society. The Holy Bible, New International Version. (1999). Nashville, TN: Cornerstone Bible Publishers.

Mallouhi, Christine A. (2000). Waging Peace On Islam. Downers Grove, IL: InterVarsity Press.

Moore, Art. (2002, October 4). Falwell: Intent not to attack Muhammad. WorldNetDaily. Retrieved on March 30, 2006 from http://www.worldnetdaily.com/news/article.asp?ARTICLE_ID=2.

175 Muslims angered by Baptist criticism. (2002, June 23). CNN. Retrieved on March 30, 2006 from http://archives.cnn.com/2002/ALLPOLITICS/06/13/cf.crossfire.

Richardson, Don. (2003). Secrets of the Koran. Ventura, CA: Regal Books.

Roach, David. (2006, March 20). Mohler, on 'O'Reilly Factor,' discusses Islam, demonic power. *BPNews*. Retrieved on March 28, 2006 from http://www.bpnews.net/bpnews.asp?ID=22876.

Spencer, Robert. (2002). <u>Islam Unveiled: Disturbing Questions About the World's Fastest-Growing Faith.</u> San Francisco, CA: Encounter Books.

Top US evangelist targets Islam. (2006, March 14). *BBCNews*. Retrieved on March 30, 2006 from http://news.bbc.co.uk/2/hi/americas/4805952.stm.

Area or Thematic Specific Studies

of Contexts of Violence

Chapter Twelve

The Ethiopian Church and Mission in Contexts of Violence: Four Historical Episodes

E. Paul Balisky and Lila W. Balisky

The country of Ethiopia provides a unique historical setting in which to investigate the church and mission in the context of violence. For over sixteen centuries, the Orthodox Church[1] of Ethiopia, with its often turbulent history, has been embedded as Christendom and a territorial church. This ancient church has penetrated the pagan strongholds of southern Ethiopia with her evangelists and withstood the onslaught of Arab Muslim power with her own armies. Italian Colonialism was warded off in 1896 by the military strength of Menilek's army, but from 1935–1941 the Orthodox Church, as well as the nascent 'new churches', experienced the renewed military vengeance of Italian colonialism.[2] Atheistic communism dealt a severe blow against the Ethiopian church and worked havoc on the minds of the student population from 1974–1991, as well as violence upon the Christians. Of recent years, the Orthodox Church has struggled with her own identity, as she is no longer the "state" church. She has occasionally lashed out against the 'new churches' that are making inroads into what was formerly her "territory".

Islamic Assault Against the Ethiopian Orthodox Church in the Sixteenth Century

In 1529 Ahmad Gragn led his Muslim military forces from eastern Ethiopia against Christian Ethiopia, located in the central highlands. The technically advantaged military might of the Muslims wreaked immense havoc and destruction on Christian Ethiopia.[3] The many ornately decorated Churches were a special target of Ahmad Gragn and his soldiers. Ahmad Gragn's sixteenth century chronicler describes the glory of these churches and relates in detail the loot that was taken from them on the Lake Tana islands.

> They carried off the gold ... there were crucifixes of gold and silver which were carried away by a hundred men, chandeliers of gold in great quantity, books with cases and bindings of gold, and countless idols of gold.... They also took a vast quantity of cloth and silk.[4]

There were three significant factors that brought about the downfall of Christian Ethiopia in the 16th century under the military leadership of Ahmad Gragn. First, there was disunity within Christian Ethiopia. During the fourteenth and fifteenth centuries there was an unusual expansion of Christianity deep into the pagan South. Except for King Zar'a Ya'iqob (1434–1468), no other Ethiopian monarch attempted to Christianize his subjects and to bring unity and a sense of nationhood among newly baptized yet ethnically disparate communities.[5] Ahmad Gragn's tactic was to further divide these nominal Christians and conquer. And second, the new technical advances in warfare and firearms from the Ottoman Turks gave the Ahmad Gragn army superiority. Together with this military superiority and the revival of Islam in the Red Sea region, Ahmad Gragn led his tribal forces from the semi-desert parts of eastern Ethiopia to completely overwhelm the Christian empire of Ethiopia.

During those tumultuous times, Emperor Lebna Dengal became a fugitive in hiding. In desperation, in 1530, he sent a messenger to the King of Portugal for military assistance. Finally, in 1541 the 400 handpicked Portuguese troops armed with muskets and led by Dom Christavao de Gama arrived in Ethiopia. Lebna Dengal was now dead and his son Galawdéwos was made emperor. In 1542 the two united Christian armies pitched battle against the Muslims on the plains of Dambeya, north of Lake Tana. The combined Portuguese and Ethiopian troops did not fare well. Thousands of Ethiopian Christian warriors and over one/half of the Portuguese soldiers, including their leader, Dom Christavao, were killed in battle. Nearly one year later the two forces, Christians against the Muslims, once again took up their battle positions in Wayna Daga, Western Begemder. At this critical time in Ethiopia's history, the Christians had the ascendancy, because many of Ahmad Gragn's Turkish mercenaries returned to their homelands, thinking victory had been achieved. In 1543 Ahmad Gragn was killed in battle, probably by a bullet from a Portuguese musket. His son Mohammad was taken prisoner. The fourteen years of Muslim ascendancy over Christian Ethiopia finally came to an abrupt end—but not without considerable loss of life, material devastation and the aftermath of confused intermingling of Christians and Muslims.[6]

What are some of the lessons Christian mission may learn from this historical episode? First, weak Christianity is subject to disintegration from within and attack from without.

Second, cooperation among Christians is essential if we are to be successful. Catholic Portugal came to the assistance of Orthodox Ethiopia. There are instances when cooperation of disparate Christian groups may be essential in protecting the larger church or mission from violence.

Italian Colonialism against the Ethiopian Orthodox Church and the 'New Churches' from 1935–1941

The Italian invasion of Ethiopia in 1935 was prompted in a large measure to redress the 1896 Italian defeat at Adwa. But in 1935 the Ethiopian military were no match for the Italians who came well-prepared fielding 170 war planes, 280 cannons and thousands of troops armed with modern rifles, hundreds of tanks and vast quantities of mustard gas at their disposal.[7] Dr. John Melly, head of the British Red Cross Unit wrote on April 13, 1936,

> This isn't a war—it isn't even a slaughter—it's the torture of thousands of defenseless men, women, and children, with bombs and poison gas. They're using gas incessantly, and we've treated hundreds of cases, including infants in arms.[8]

After the Ethiopian military was crushed, the Italian fascists attempted to make a truce with the Orthodox Church. Some of the

Orthodox Church leaders were initially conned into appeasement. The insignificant membership of the New Churches did not initially draw the attention of the fascists, but after the attempted assassination of the Italian military commander, Graziani, on the porch of the Haile Selassie palace in 1937 by two Eritrean assassins, the Italian military carried out a cruel and terrifying three-day massacre upon the innocent population of Addis Ababa. The fascist vengeance was then vented upon the priests and monks at Debre Libanos, located some 120 kilometers north of Addis Ababa. It was surmised by the fascists that the perpetrators of the assassination were housed within the confines of the Debre Libanos monastery. Some 150 of the Orthodox clerics were loaded onto trucks, which transported them several kilometers from the Debra Libanos monastery. The innocent clergy were then off-loaded and shot in cold blood. It was now clear to the Orthodox leadership that the fascists could no longer be trusted as Christian friends.

The nascent New Church movements in Dembi Dollo, Wellega in western Ethiopia (planted by the American Presbyterian Mission) and in Wolaitta, southern Ethiopia (planted by SIM missionaries) were now without expatriate missionaries, as they were deported. These two groups were viewed by the Italians as collaborators with foreign powers and the Ethiopian patriots. Informers to the Italians reported that these believers prayed regularly for the safety of exiled Emperor Haile Selassie and his soon return. The night meetings of the believers were viewed as a patriot clandestine operation by the Italians. For this reason about sixty Wolaitta house churches were destroyed by the Italians and their leaders imprisoned. Several of them, such as Wondaro Däbäro, Toro Dubusho, and Gäfäto Jagiso were severely beaten by the fascists. After the Italians were defeated by the combined British and Ethiopian forces in 1941, the New Churches in Wolaitta multiplied very rapidly. By December 1946 Walter Ohman reported that there were 207 local churches in Wolaitta.[9] Similar church growth was reported from Dembi Dolo in Wollega by the Presbyterians.[10]

Some significant lessons gleaned from the fascist violence against the Ethiopian churches include the following:

First, the Ethiopian Orthodox Church leadership began to understand that the kingdoms of this world, the Ethiopian government and the Italian colonial powers, were not the Kingdom of God. Second, the New Churches movement in western and southern Ethiopia realized they could now rely upon their own spiritual resources rather than relying on the spiritual resources of the evicted expatriate missionaries who brought them the faith. Third, the New Churches movement developed a wholesome self-identity. With this growing self-identity came the creation of their own spiritual hymnody— phrases adapted from scripture and Bible stories communicated line by line by antiphonal singing, sung to work song tunes. Fourth, the joy and peace so evident among the believers was contagious, with the result that many became adherents of the New Churches movement. And lastly, members of mission societies who once served in Ethiopia, as well as concerned friends in foreign countries, prayed earnestly for the suffering believers within Ethiopia.[11]

Marxism against the Ethiopian Orthodox Church and against the New Churches (1974–1991)

In 1974 Ethiopia's Emperor Haile Selassie was deposed by a military junta, who declared themselves to be Marxist and established themselves as the Provisional Military Government of Ethiopia. When the Orthodox Patriarch Tewoflos publicly criticized the newly established military regime, he was silenced by death in July 1979. And in the same year *Kes* Gudina Tumsa, General Secretary of the Ethiopian Evangelical Church Mekane Yesus, was strangled to death by henchmen of the revolutionary regime.[12] His anti-revolutionary stance was interpreted by the leaders of the Marxist junta as political.

When gospel songwriter and soloist Tesfaye Gabbiso became popular with his songs that blessed the persecuted Ethiopian church[13], he was imprisoned in southern Ethiopia, severely beaten and placed in solitary confinement for seven years. Miraculously, he was spared martyrdom.

Hundreds of New Churches were confiscated and converted into Marxist teaching centers. The nationalization of Orthodox Church agricultural properties greatly reduced the income for the local clergy. Thousands of Christians, both those from the Orthodox Church, as well as those of the New Churches, were imprisoned.[14] Many were beaten; others were placed in solitary confinement in prisons far from relatives and friends.[15]

The expatriate missionary force from over twenty missionary societies was drastically reduced during the period from 1974–1991, because visa entry permits were nearly impossible to obtain. Our own missionary agency, SIM, gave us as a family freedom to remain or leave Ethiopia during the Red Terror when hundreds of students were shot dead and their bodies left bleeding on the streets of Addis Ababa and other urban centres. In 1976 while we were stationed in Bonga Kaffa, an evangelists working with us, Ato Tessema Dube was killed in a violent reaction stirred up by revolutionary students. His speared and bleeding wife escaped into the forest and struggled for three days with her young family before she found her way to other Christians. This was a shocking martyrdom very near to our hearts and home. During 1977, we lived in ambivalence; "Should we remain in this land of violence or should we go home?" We finally decided to stay at a new posting, teaching in a diploma theological institution at Jimma some 325 kilometers southwest of Addis Ababa in Kafa Province. In March of 1978, a political "shake-up" began, which resulted in our being put under house arrest together with the entire student body and staff of Grace Bible Institute. After seven days of surveillance and harassment, the communist government issued orders that we be evicted from our home and our place of ministry. We were given twenty-four hours to leave, completely empty-handed. As we boarded the Ethiopian Airlines plane at the Jimma airport we faced the realization that we were now suddenly bereft of our ministry, our friends, our vehicle, as well as our home and all our personal possessions. We suffered the trauma of loss. Although we experienced that local expulsion from Kafa Province and never returned there for fifteen years, we were part of the small core of SIMers who were allowed to remain in greater Ethiopia throughout the Marxist years 1974–1991.

There were two major responses of the Orthodox Church to the anti-Christian onslaught of Marxist atheism. A positive response was that

Orthodox adherents, as a public statement, generously donated funds to construct large lavish church buildings in many urban centers. Another response was that the Orthodox began to face the realization that the separation of church and state had occurred. Ethiopia could no longer call herself a "Christian nation" with a state church.

There were a number of responses of the New Churches to the attacks of Marxist atheism. First, because of the closure of regular places of worship, many secret house churches led by lay people were established in urban centers. Second, indigenous hymnology flourished among these house churches. Third, former denominational hostilities were broken down. Christians were bonded together in a time of suffering. Fourth, a new understanding and practice of indigeneity was achieved as believers relied on their own financial and leadership resources. And fifth, the New Churches movement grew in spiritual depth as they prayed for one another, visited the imprisoned, assisted the wives and children of the imprisoned and nurtured themselves in the scriptures.

The responses of the mission societies involved with mission in Ethiopia varied. First, a small core of those who remained in Ethiopia bore the burdens of the persecuted and suffering church. Second, mission societies which withdrew the majority of their personnel from Ethiopia organized special prayer outside the country for the suffering Ethiopian church. Third, arrangements were made for seminars and particular biblical teaching. Christian young people were instructed in communistic tactics and what to guard against. The book of Nehemiah became a popular book for study. Fourth, Christians from outside Ethiopia came to share. One such couple was Pastor YuKwong Hsueh and his wife Lily, with long experience in China, visited Ethiopia some seven times in order to bring spiritual counsel and nurturing to church leaders as well as Christians in government. Lastly, for the second time in Ethiopian church history, mission agencies were made aware that the Ethiopian church, guided by the Holy Spirit, is quite capable of functioning without external assistance.

During this Marxist period in Ethiopian history, both churches, the Orthodox and the New Churches were dealt a cruel blow by atheistic communism. It was as if a dark evil cloud had settled over what was once called the Christian "island" of Ethiopia.

The following are some missional lessons we learned during this Marxist period of violence. First, inexperienced mission personnel should not be assigned to potential situations of violence. For example, during the turbulent years of the Ethiopian communist revolution, there was a ten-year hiatus when no new SIM missionaries were brought in. Second, we felt the pain of personal misunderstanding and suffering as we were isolated from the local churches. Third, we learned to work together with communist leaders implementing community development for the betterment of Ethiopia.

And, fourth, as we lived under the authority of an atheistic government, we had to deal with our own responses such as bitterness, anger, self-pity, frustration, and temptation to exaggerate our own situation.

Internal Church violence: The Ethiopian Orthodox Church Attempts to Suppress the New Churches

After the Italian occupation of Ethiopia, the returned Emperor Haile Selassie invited western missions to assist in rebuilding the educational and medical infrastructure of Ethiopia. But with the condition of the Government drafted Missions Decree of 1944, mission agencies were given freedom to open schools, hospitals and clinics in the so-called "Pagan" south and Muslim east. These were identified as "Open Areas". The northern provinces of Ethiopia, which are predominantly Orthodox, were "closed" to missions.

The Orthodox Church functioned within a "Christendom" model. Their leadership, against the sentiments of Haile Selassie, viewed all of Ethiopia, whether pagan or Muslim, as their domain. Western mission agencies, with their propensity to launch New Churches were seen as a threat to the Orthodox Church. The Orthodox Church leadership, in cooperation with local southern administrative authorities, made a protracted effort to curtail the planting of New Churches during the 1950s in southern and western Ethiopia.

Expatriate personnel were prevented from itinerant ministry among the local population.

Evangelists and local church leaders were imprisoned and beaten. Mrs. Edna Ratzliff described the following atrocity against New Church believers in a letter to her family on 20 May 1951.

> It seems that part of hell has at least broken loose. Our compound has become a refuge for over a hundred people from Ocholo [in Gamo Gofa province] who have been forced to flee their homes. They were given a choice, either deny their faith or get out. Some did deny their faith and signed with their fingerprints to a paper to prove it.... I've cried so much these days. I feel like the Psalmist who said, "Tears have been my meat day and night."[16]

As recently as 2002, the New Churches have experienced a martyrdom instigated by the Orthodox Church leadership. The account of the death of Damtew Demelash, a New Churches pastoral leader in the Full Gospel Church near Bahir Dar, is a sad chronicle of violence, which has left its sting.[17] Violence is irrational and may erupt unexpectedly when people are stirred up. As Christians, missions or church, we should never instigate a provocative response.

The role of mission societies was threefold during this period when the Orthodox Church regularly persecuted the fledgling minority groups of New Church believers. First, certain individual missionaries, together with church leaders, appealed to higher Ethiopian government offices to achieve justice for the persecuted. Second, missionaries visited the imprisoned and provided them with food and blankets. And third, mission societies continued to carry on their medical and educational ministries in a professional manner.

Conclusion

In this brief glimpse into four episodes of violence in Ethiopian history, we have seen examples of religious violence from without against a state church, colonial violence against all churches, Marxist violence against all churches, and state-church violence against the new churches. Philosophy, government and church may all be perpetrators of violence.

It is inevitable that when the church moves out in mission, it will suffer persecution and violence. Our Master predicted it (Matt. 5:10–11; John 15:20), the early church experienced it (2 Cor. 12:10; 2 Thess. 1:4), and persecution and violence has been the lot of the church and her mission throughout history to the present. It is imperative that we move forward in mission with tact and wisdom (Matt. 10:16), equipping ourselves with spiritual armor (Eph. 6:10–17), practicing vigilant prayer for one another (Eph. 6:18–20; Phil. 1:19), and practicing forgiveness (Matt. 6:14–15; Luke 11:4).

Notes

1. The term "Orthodox Church" will be used throughout the article, indicating the Ethiopian Tawahedo Orthodox Church, and with the understanding that before 1958, this church, through its long affiliation with Egypt, was known as the Ethiopian Coptic Church.
2. Throughout this paper, the term 'New Churches' designates the non-Orthodox and non-Catholic churches, the majority of which were initiated by external missions.
3. See J. S. Trimingham, *Islam in Ethiopia,* London: Oxford University Press, 1950, 84–93 for a detailed and authoritative account of the 16th century Muslim impact upon Christian Ethiopia.
4. Richard Pankhurst (ed.), *The Ethiopian Royal Chronicles,* Addis Ababa: Oxford University Press, 1967, 65.
5. Taddesse Tamrat, *Church and State in Ethiopia,* London: Oxford University Press, 1972, 300–302.
6. Richard Pankhurst, *The Ethiopians,* Oxford: Blackwell Publishers, 1998, 92, 93.
7. Pankhurst, The Ethiopians, 233.
8. As quoted in Pankhurst, *The Ethiopians,* 234.
9. E. Paul Balisky, "Wolaitta Evangelists: A Study in Religious Innovation in Southern Ethiopia, 1937–1975", Ph.D. Thesis, University of Aberdeen, 1997, 190.

10. As reported by J. Edwin Orr, *Evangelical Awakenings in Africa,* Minneapolis, MN: Bethany Press, 1975, 168.

11. Rees Howells, a personal friend of Haile Selassie, called for special prayer meetings at his Bible College in Wales to pray for the persecuted Ethiopian evangelicals. See Orr, 1975, 167.

12. Ovind M. Eide, Revolution and Religion in Ethiopia: The Growth and Persecution of the Mekane Yesus Church 1974–1985, Addis Ababa: Addis Ababa University Press, 2000, 175–182.

13. Lila W. Balisky, "Theology in Song: Ethiopia's Tesfaye Gabbiso," *Missiology,* Vol. XXV, No. 4, 1997, 447–456.

14. See Nathan B. Hege, *Beyond Our Prayers: Anabaptist Church Growth in Ethiopia, 1948–1998,* Scottdale, PA: Herald Press, 1998, 182–192 for an account of prison life for the believers.

15. John Cumbers, *Count it all Joy: Testimonies from a Persecuted Church,* Kearney, 1995, 60. After 1974, the SIM missionary force was drastically reduced from over 300 to 38 by the Marxist government.

16. Ed and Edna Ratzliff, *Letters from the Uttermost Parts of the Earth,* Abbotsford, British Columbia: Self–published, 1987, 116,117.

17. See www.DACB.org under the Ethiopia section for the story of Damtew Demelash.

Chapter Thirteen

The Benefits of Chaos: Missionary Reflections on Zimbabwe's Decline

Robert Reese

Since 2000, the nation of Zimbabwe in southern Africa has been sliding into chaos. Following the rejection by voters of a proposed new constitution that year, the government reacted by permitting its supporters to invade white-owned farms.[1] Not only were several thousand white farmers violently displaced, but also hundreds of thousands of African farm workers were forcibly ejected from the land and from employment. This government-instigated violence had repercussions that continue to reverberate throughout the small country.[2] The agricultural sector, which was the backbone of the economy, collapsed causing widespread hunger;[3] the economy moved rapidly toward hyperinflation and the accompanying shortages of basic commodities, including fuel;[4] unemployment and poverty escalated dramatically; a climate of general lawlessness began to prevail.

What impact did the lawlessness and violence have on ministry by both western missionaries and African Christians? This paper is experiential, based on the author's personal reactions and observations.[5] Following the initial crisis, after some time, the author was able to see some unique benefits of the slide into chaos. His initial reactions, however, were confusion, fear, and anger.

Confusion

Since gangs of thugs were moving across the land, many apparently sponsored by the government, the author's basic western assumptions were challenged as confusion reigned. First, the government became the instigator of violence against its own citizens. From a western viewpoint, governments are supposed to be allies of the people in the desire for peace, justice, and progress. Government propaganda continued to claim that this was indeed the goal of the farm invasions. Rather than being able to back up that claim with any positive results, the government continued to lurch from crisis to crisis; the situation in Zimbabwe has continued to deteriorate rapidly for the past six years.

Second, a western viewpoint sees progress as the norm, and much missionary work aims to ensure that positive result, expecting government cooperation to some extent. Of all its tasks, the government's most basic one is to ensure that its people do not starve. Now here was a government whose ideology seemed not to care about the consequences of its actions on the most weak and vulnerable of its citizens. The deterioration in the country did not actually begin with the farm invasions, as the author witnessed a steady decline in the economy throughout the previous two decades there. The deterioration was simply much more rapid, and much more stressful. Infrastructure and businesses that had taken generations to build were being systematically destroyed and the owners chased away, sometimes right out of the country. People began to realize that something had been broken that might never be fixed in their lifetime. The country has passed the point of no return in its leaders' quest for some ill-defined goal.

Third, from a missionary standpoint, projects that aimed at improving the lives of Zimbabweans were rapidly undermined by government decisions and actions. If agricultural projects depended on trucking a product to market, government decisions created shortages and hyperinflation that prevented the transportation of products and rendered valueless the currency used to pay the farmers. When missionaries worked to have local churches become self-supporting, members were soon barely able to pay their most basic bills such as food, rent, utilities, and school fees. Nothing was left over for health care, so diseases spread rapidly and life expectancy dropped. Missionaries aimed to increase body life in local churches, yet government policies sent church members scattering into neighboring countries in search of a livelihood. Eventually, it became a crime to transport sizeable quantities of food to those desperate for it, as the government insisted that it alone had the right to distribute food to the people. Zimbabwe, once prosperous, has become a man-made humanitarian crisis because of its elected leaders.

Fear

Beyond confusion, a climate of fear reigned as the government pursued its perceived enemies beyond the farms into businesses. White people perhaps felt more fear because the initial target of violence was white farmers, but no sector of the population was spared the consequences of mindless violence. The police turned out to be the enemy of the people, as they no longer protected those who were targeted as government enemies. Fear now manifested itself in many forms: fear of sounds in the night, fear of being watched or followed, fear of supposed friends who might betray you as an alleged enemy of the government for a secret grudge, or fear of physical violence. Ordinary thugs took advantage of the situation to pass for politically motivated *povo*,[6] so regular crime increased in addition to political violence. The American missionary population held meetings with representatives from the American embassy to try to understand the situation, but found that embassy personnel wanted information from them about what was happening on the ground. This merely added to the uncertainty, but possible evacuation plans were discussed and local American wardens[7] were appointed just in case.

Anger

After the initial reactions of confusion and fear, anger set in. Anger can be a luxury that arises when one realizes that the greatest fears were of things that never happened. Anger was not only directed at the government but also at the disturbing tendency to be so afraid. Fear paralyzes and anger follows to counteract paralysis. In preparing a series of lessons on the Ten Commandments, the author realized that these lessons were suddenly potentially subversive. The government was systematically violating several of the commandments, as basic as they are. Could a preacher in Zimbabwe preach the Ten Commandments without referring to their daily violations? Could it just be overlooked that politicians seemed to maintain that false testimony, covetousness, theft, and murder were politically justified and therefore justified for anyone?

Anger drove people to Scripture in order to explain God's perspective on the situation and this began to overcome fear and paralysis. After all, does not Scripture say, "Do not call conspiracy everything that these people call conspiracy; do not fear what they fear, and do not dread it. The LORD Almighty is the one you are to regard as holy, he is the one you are to fear, he is the one you are to dread" (Isaiah 8:12-13)? And did not Jesus say, "Do not be afraid of those who kill the body but cannot kill the soul. Rather, be afraid of the One who can destroy both soul and body in hell" (Matthew 10:28)?

Drawing Strength from Scripture

From reading Scripture, the realization dawned that fear and violence were common for Bible writers. They drew strength from communion with God and wrote it down for our benefit. Even anger was evident, as the imprecatory Psalms indicate. It seems that turmoil was often the place where biblical writers found themselves.

Imprecatory Psalms – Studying these Psalms, it became clear that the writers were projecting back to God what they hoped would happen to their persecutors. They channeled anger they felt about those who harassed them to an all-powerful God who could take vengeance on their behalf. Furthermore, since the writers were in covenant fellowship with God, this meant that those who treated them unjustly were subject to all the curses God has ever placed on His enemies. Imprecatory Psalms are a way of restating these curses without trying to carry them out personally. Righteous indignation is allowed to vent frustration, fear, and confusion by telling God all about it and letting Him act as He sees fit. Retaliation is wisely left up to God. Before the chaos in Zimbabwe, the author had never understood imprecatory Psalms, but then he used them in daily devotions as his personal cry to God in the situation.[8]

Persecution in the New Testament – The New Testament also indicated that persecution was the expected life of the disciples and church of Jesus Christ. In fact, the chaos in Zimbabwe was not a direct persecution of Christians unless the church seemed to be opposing the government. It was more a persecution of the whole population by the government and its supporters. Nevertheless, the New Testament teaching about persecution was relevant, starting with Jesus' blessing, "Blessed are you when people insult you, persecute you and falsely say all kinds of evil against you because of me" (Matthew 5:11). Peter spoke of the blessedness of suffering unjustly because it identifies the disciple with Jesus' suffering (1 Peter 2:21-24; 3:14-17; 4:12-19). Suffering then took on deep significance as the disciple put himself or herself in Jesus' position to try to understand and identify with His terrible experiences.

Suffering became a refining experience (1 Peter 1:6-7) and it purged not only the individual ("He who has suffered in his body is done with sin" 1 Peter 4:1), but also the church. Christians had two reactions to the violence: either to be driven to deeper dependence on God and to greater fellowship with the body of Christ or to be driven away. The parable of the sower predicts that when trouble or persecution comes because of the message of Christ, some will quickly fall away (Matthew 13:21). Paul not only experienced continual persecution but also accepted this as normal (2 Timothy 3:12). In other words, living a life without persecution indicated a lack of true discipleship.

Drawing Strength from the Church Fathers

Persecution is a well-known characteristic of the early church. Christians were unjustly accused of all sorts of crimes such as atheism, cannibalism, orgies in worship, incest, and political subversion. Atheism, because they refused to worship idols and worshipped an invisible God; cannibalism because they were said to eat the flesh of their God and drink his blood at their secret

Eucharist; orgies in worship because they greeted one another with a holy kiss; incest because they called each other brother and sister; and subversion because they refused to sacrifice to Caesar as Lord. Famous martyrs filled the ranks of early church leaders, beginning with Jesus, Stephen, and the apostle James, but going on to include most of the apostles, and later people like Ignatius, Polycarp, Justin Martyr, and Cyprian. Apologists rose up to defend Christianity against the multitude of false charges. Naturally then, the writings of the early church fathers shed light on how Christians understood and coped with persecution.

Eusebius – For this author, Eusebius of Caesarea is the early church writer who explained persecution most graphically and placed it in a historical framework. Called "the father of church history,"[9] Eusebius was born around AD 260 and his life coincided with the last great persecutions of Christianity in the Roman Empire, followed by the benevolent reign of Constantine. Having survived the onslaughts of Maximin Daia and then Licinius, Eusebius welcomed the rule of Constantine as the culmination of history and vindication of Christianity. He structured his church history around ten great persecutions, noting that ten was "a perfect number."[10] With the advent of Constantine, however, he could rejoice that "from now on, a cloudless day, radiant with rays of heavenly light, shined down on the churches of Christ throughout the world."[11] So severe and purifying had the ten persecutions been, in Eusebius's view, that the church was entering into a type of millennial bliss with the cessation of persecution and official recognition of Christianity.

In graphic detail, Eusebius described how the persecutions both decimated the young churches and also added new members who marveled at the brave testimony of martyrs. Weaker Christians were either strengthened or lapsed through the awful purging. Origen's influence persisted at Caesarea where Eusebius studied in the theological school,[12] and the church historian noted how persecution had shaped the young Origen. During a persecution of Christians under Roman Emperor Septimius Severus at Alexandria when Origen was only a boy, Eusebius noted, "Such a passion for martyrdom possessed Origen, boy though he was, that he wanted to court danger and plunge into the conflict."[13] When he learned that his father had been arrested, he urged him to become a martyr and tried to join him, but his mother hid his clothes so he could not venture outside.[14] Left destitute when his father was martyred, Origen adopted the life of an ascetic philosopher whose students and converts often went willingly to martyrdom.[15]

One of those influenced by Origen was a soldier named Basilides who was ordered to lead a Christian virgin girl named Potamiaena to execution. Seeing that Potamiaena had already endured a terrible beating and had been threatened with rape by gladiators, but refused to deny Christ, Basilides determined to treat her kindly and prevented the crowds from harassing her. She in return promised to pray for him and to repay him for his kindness. Then she was slowly killed by boiling tar being dripped all over her body. Some time afterwards, his fellow soldiers were surprised to find that Basilides had become a confessing Christian, so he too was imprisoned and sentenced to execution. When some of Origen's flock visited Basilides in prison, he declared that Potamiaena had appeared to him three days after her death, placed a crown on his head, and said the Lord had answered her prayers that Basilides would soon join her in martyrdom. The Christians baptized Basilides in prison and the next day he was beheaded for his new faith.[16]

Such stories helped to cement a picture of the early church whose entire life was often defined by persecution. Certainly it would be difficult to understand the early church and the kinds of decisions made and directions taken without knowledge of the part played by persecution. Eusebius painted an unforgettable picture of the effects of the attempts by the Roman Empire to stamp out Christianity and this helps modern Christians to regain perspective on how much the church has been lulled by peaceful prosperity into an unreal view of worldly powers.

Augustine – About a century after Eusebius, when Augustine was writing *City of God*, he was not impressed by Eusebius' scheme of persecution ending when Constantine became emperor. Nor did he accept the idea of counting ten persecutions to coincide with the ten plagues of Egypt, in order to indicate freedom for God's people once they were complete. He asserted, "No limit can be set to the number of persecutions which the Church is bound to suffer for her training."[17] Not desiring to speculate about future persecutions, he was nevertheless certain that there would be at least one more severe persecution: that of the Antichrist.[18]

Augustine himself did not live in a time of great persecution, and in fact is accused by many of becoming a persecutor of sects he deemed heretical like the Donatists. Aside from that, however, this author benefited from reading *City of God* for the perspective it gives on how Christians are to operate in earthly kingdoms. Some today accuse Augustine of being the architect of the excesses of Christendom, but this is not the picture of *City of God*. Rather, Augustine was pessimistic about what lasting good earthly kingdoms can accomplish. Christians, on the other hand, belong to the eternal city of God, and therefore, often have conflicts with earthly rulers.

Despite living in a supposed Christian empire, Augustine warned that the earthly city worshipped its gods "so that with their assistance it may reign in the enjoyment of victories and an earthly peace, not with a loving concern for others, but with lust for domination over them. For the good make use of this world to enjoy God, whereas the evil want to make use of God in order to enjoy the world."[19] For Augustine, the two cities constituted opposing systems. The earthly city was man-made, finite, but also arrogant about what it could achieve; the heavenly city was eternal, God-made, and was the city to which Christians of all races and cultures in the world belonged. There was little in common between the two.

Augustine asserted that the earthly city cannot achieve justice because it is ruled by demons: "When a man does not serve God, what amount of justice at we to suppose to exist in his being? . . . And if there is no justice in such a man, there can be no sort of doubt that there is no justice in a gathering which consists of such men."[20] Since the earthly city is such a gathering of non-Christians, Augustine did not expect to find justice in it. "Because God does not rule there the general characteristic of that [earthly] city is that it is devoid of true justice."[21]

In the earthly city, Christians can only expect to find violence. Looking at the original creation, Augustine observed that God "did not wish the rational being, made in his own image, to have dominion over any but irrational creatures, not man over man, but man over beasts."[22] Domination of one human over another resulted from the fall into sin, and the apparatus of the state slowly built up to combat sin, starting with parental discipline in the family. The lust for domination characterizes life from the family level on up in the earthly city, and that is what makes life on earth dangerous and unpredictable. "If then, safety is not to be found in the home, the common refuge from the evils that befall mankind, what shall we say of the city? The larger the city, the more is its forum filled with civil lawsuits and criminal trials."[23] At the national level, this amounts to civil wars, and at the international level to wars of imperialism.

For Augustine, then, persecution of Christians was an expected part of the earthly city. Regarding the sack of Rome by barbarians in AD 410, he faced the violence squarely rather than trying to explain it away. He saw it as a physical ill involving rape and pillage upon Christians and pagans alike, but physical ills are not the worst kind. He commented that physical ills "are the only evils dreaded by fools. . . . As for moral ills, those fools accept them not merely with patience, but with delight; and those are the evils which make them evil."[24] Physical ills like persecution might have a salutary effect by bettering the person, but moral ills can kill the soul. Thus, Augustine did not see anything to fear in persecution by itself.

Augustine helped this author to understand how he has tended to glorify the role of governments, making them more than what they are in God's sight. He commented, "Remove justice, and what are kingdoms but gangs of criminals on a large scale? What are criminal gangs but petty kingdoms?"[25] By emphasizing that Christians belong to the eternal city of God more than to earthly kingdoms, Augustine helps us gain perspective about violence instigated by governments as well as by gangs of thugs. All violence is simply part of this life.

Drawing Strength from African Christians

Finally, this author realized that his suffering was far less than that of African Christians, but they reacted with greater patience and more faith. Sometimes they too would become upset by the circumstances, but they seldom reacted with the same chain of confusion, fear, and anger. Rather, they had more equanimity. With their long history of experiencing oppression, as well as their trust in God, they clearly have much to teach western Christians about reacting to unjust treatment. While western missionaries were discussing evacuation with the representatives of the most powerful nations in the world, African Christians had no such options and most never contemplated leaving the bad situation. They reacted calmly and prayerfully and went about their daily lives the best they could in the difficult circumstances. They continued to spread the gospel because they are survivors through all sorts of turmoil, yet they have hope in their Savior.

African Christians teach western Christians that we have become soft through living in a time of unparalleled peace and prosperity. We have come to expect that governments should cater to our needs, protect our rights, and keep us prosperous. Africans expect little from governments except pain and exploitation. Justo Gonzalez remarked, "The cultures that have emerged at the end of the colonial age bear the mark of the colonial period, and therefore are better equipped to cope with the challenges of the still dominant cultures of the North Atlantic."[26] That is, some like the Africans have learned to cope with extreme challenges that make them resilient survivors in an unjust world. Others, like North Americans have not experienced hardship and so are not prepared to face the same challenges, including persecution. Similarly, Wilbert Shenk noted that "the Christian movement worldwide is comprised essentially of two classes,"[27] those who know persecution and those who know only peace and prosperity. He concluded, "The greatest integrity and vitality of faith today appears to be found in those churches that have suffered and known martyrdom firsthand."[28]

The author had the privilege of visiting a unique indigenous African church, L'Eglise Protestante Baptiste Oeuvres et Mission,[29] in the West African country of Ivory Coast. This church grew from a handful of members in Abidjan in 1975 to a hundred thousand members spread out over the Ivory Coast and neighboring countries. Part of the strength of the church lies in its eschatology. Anticipating that persecution will be one of the main factors of the impending end times, the church is divided up into thousands of cell groups with trained leaders. Church leaders explained that they could not rely on their central headquarters and main sanctuary being permanent in the end times. Therefore, they spread out all church functions into decentralized cell groups, so that the church could effectively go underground at short notice. Although persecution has yet to come in the form expected, the nation has entered a period of civil war, in which the church is already prepared for violence. This is another indication that Africans have much to teach western Christians about coping with violence while continuing to minister. How many western churches have made any preparation for persecution at all? How many western churches would long survive persecution if it hit?

In Zimbabwe, the author noted that while the chaotic situation tended to impair the missionaries' effectiveness, it tended to strengthen the African Christians' leadership. A rapidly declining economy adversely affects the operation of technology, on which western missionaries tend to base their work, but it does not diminish the local people's ability to operate as such. While missionaries became increasingly frustrated by the situation, Zimbabwean Christians managed to become better evangelists living as those who have genuine hope during a crisis. Missionaries also felt more vulnerable during the chaos, but local people had lived through it all before. Thus, the chaos in Zimbabwe also hastened the transition in the author's mission from external leadership to local leadership, as missionaries gave way to Zimbabweans. Perhaps this was the greatest benefit of all.

Conclusion

The author's limited experiences of ministering cross-culturally in a situation of violence allowed him to see some benefits of chaos. He first drew inspiration from Scripture, which indicated that ministering in violent situations is normal and part of God's plan.

The church fathers, Eusebius and Augustine, also helped him see how early Christians were not overcome or overawed by violence or threats. Rather, these experiences caused them to grow, showing that physical danger is not the worst kind of danger. Finally, African Christians, operating out of a history of oppression by various powers local and foreign, showed more equanimity and less fear than western missionaries in violent situations. All this helped the author overcome his initial responses of confusion, fear, and anger to be able to minister God's word more effectively in the situation.

Above all, he came to understand that governments are not always friendly and people look in vain for justice from them. Our future lies less in being patriotic than in being strong in our churches, especially when these churches are geared for persecution. Our hope lies less in democratic institutions than in the crucified Savior who overcame violent death to become the Risen Lord. Such lessons may be obvious, but sometimes it takes chaos to make them real.

Notes

1. http://news.bbc.co.uk/2/hi/africa/670755.stm (Feb. 23, 2007).
2. http://en.wikipedia.org/wiki/Zimbabwe (Feb. 23, 2007).
3. http://www.wfp.org/country_brief/indexcountry.asp?country=716 (Feb. 23, 2007).
4. http://www.zwnews.com/ issuefull.cfm?ArticleID=13696 (Feb. 23, 2007).
5. The author was born and raised in Zimbabwe, later became a missionary there from 1981-2002, and continues to spend about a month each year there.
6. *Povo* is the Portuguese word for the politicized masses who in Marxist theory rise up to rebel against oppressors. It is widely used in Zimbabwe since many of the guerrillas who fought for independence from white rule were based in Mozambique.
7. A warden is a volunteer American citizen who agrees to be a link of communication between Americans and their embassy.

8. Psalm 55 is an excellent example of an imprecatory Psalm.
9. Paul L. Meier, Eusebius—*The Church History: A New Translation with Commentary* (Grand Rapids: Kregel, 1999), 9.
10. Ibid., 345.
11. Ibid., 346.
12. Ibid., 11.
13. Ibid., 207.
14. Ibid., 208.
15. Ibid., 208-210.
16. Ibid., 211-212.
17. Augustine, Concerning the City of God against the Pagans, trans. John O'Meara (London: Penguin, 1984), 837.
18. Ibid., 838.
19. Ibid., 604.
20. Ibid., 883.
21. Ibid., 891.
22. Ibid., 874.
23. Ibid., 859.
24. Ibid., 136.
25. Ibid., 139.
26. Justo L. Gonzalez, For the Healing of the Nations: The Book of Revelation in an Age of Cultural Conflict (Maryknoll, NY: Orbis, 1999), 6.
27. Wilbert R. Shenk, *Changing Frontiers of Mission* (Maryknoll, NY: Orbis, 1999), 190.
28. Ibid.
29. http://www.epbomi.net/cicomis (Feb. 23, 2007)

Chapter Fourteen

From Barbarians to Barbarians:
Celtic Missionary Spirituality in the Dark Ages

David K. Strong

The world changed forever on September 11, 2001. Or did it? We see ourselves conducting mission in an age of violence, yet mission has always occurred in violent contexts. As we seek the wherewithal to minister in such settings, who better to teach us how to flourish than those who have traveled the same path and traveled it well? One worthy example is the Celtic missionary movement, which began in the fifth century.[1] As the Roman Empire collapsed before the migrations of the barbarian tribes, a remarkable missionary movement began among those whom the Romans had considered the most barbaric of the barbarians.[2] Converted barbarians from Ireland evangelized the barbarian tribes of Europe during the period popularly called the Dark Ages, indeed during the darkest part of the Dark Ages.[3] The Celts possessed a spirituality that sustained them in their mission, and we might well ask whether we should or even could foster a similar spirituality?

In this paper I explore the spiritual sustenance that nourished the Celtic mission in a context of violence. In order to do this I will limit my examination to three prototypical Celtic missionaries—Patrick, Columba[4], and Columbanus.[5] I will first introduce the missionaries and their sources, before establishing the violence of their contexts. I will then examine each of their spiritual lives, often quoting the sources in order to offer a flavor of their thought world, and I will conclude with suggestions for developing a modern missionary spirituality for violent contexts.

The Missionaries and Their Sources

Patrick, of course, is credited with evangelizing Ireland. He was not, however, the first recorded Celtic missionary beyond the Roman frontier.[6] That honor goes to Ninian, who evangelized the southern Picts and built a church at Whithorn in Bernicia.[7] Nor was he the first missionary to Ireland, for Prosper of Acquitaine records in 431 that "Palladius was ordained by Pope Celestine and sent to the Irish believers in Christ as their first bishop."[8] Patrick was, however, the first Celtic missionary about whom we have more extensive information. He apparently came from northwestern Roman Britain; his father was a deacon and decurion (member of the ruling class), and his grandfather was a priest.[9] Some might well object that Patrick does not represent the Celtic missionary movement, because he was not Irish. Indeed he was a Briton, but as Hanson observes, "The Britons were for the Romans a congeries of tribes displaying all the usual characteristics of Celtic culture and tradition."[10] While the dates of ministry are debated (432–461, or more likely 461(?)–493), he went, not as a missionary, but as a bishop to minister to Christians in northeastern Ireland.[11] Kathleen Hughes further concludes that, since the south was already Christian, his ministry likely extended to the north, the west, and the center of the island.[12] Of particular interest for our purposes is the fact that we possess his Confession and his Letter to the Soldiers of Coroticus through which we intend to enter his spiritual world.

Columba has often been considered the first of the great Irish missionaries. Born into a powerful ruling family, the Uí Néills, around 520–522, he studied in one of the best schools in Leinster and established monasteries at Durrow and Derry[13] before embarking upon perpetual pilgrimage to Iona off the west coast of Scotland. His hagiographer Adomnán would have us believe that he "sailed away from Ireland to Britain choosing to be a pilgrim for Christ."[14] A second explanation, dating to the eleventh century, links his exile to penitence for supporting his northern Uí Néill kinsman against the high king, Diarma it mac Cerbaill, in a battle. A third suggests that he was excommunicated by his synod for trivial offenses that were later proved unfounded. Richard Sharpe, however, believes that Columba left in order to pursue a religious life, which he could not do because of the political entanglements of his family.[15] Whatever the case,

Columba crossed the narrow channel to Dalriada, an Irish settlement on the west coast of modern Scotland that was surrounded by Picts, and received permission to settle on Iona off the Isle of Mull. Bede records:

> In the year of our Lord 565, when Justin the second took over the control of the Roman Empire after Justinian, there came from Ireland to Britain a priest and abbot named Columba, a true monk, in life no less than habit; he came to Britain to preach the word of God to the kingdoms of the northern Picts which are separated from the southern part of their land by steep and rugged mountains.[16]

From Iona his disciples evangelized the Picts, and ultimately over the next one hundred years Northumbria and the English Midlands.[17] It should be noted, however, that Columba's mission was different than that of Patrick and Columbanus. He was essentially a pilgrim, but never completely broke his ties with Ireland and while in Scotland ministered primarily to the Irish *Scotti*.[18] In order to enter Columba's spiritual world, we will rely upon the *Life of St. Columba* by Adomnán, Columba's descendent and the ninth abbot of Iona, who wrote almost a century after Columba's death, but drew upon excellent informants and an unbroken oral tradition.[19] The written tradition, in fact, extends back to within twenty-seven years of Columba's death.[20] We shall also investigate the theology of the poem *Altus Prosator* ("The High First-Sower"), which tadition attributes to Columba.[21] Even if Columba did not write the poem himself, as is more likely, it nevertheless reveals the Columban spirituality of Iona, compressing "into its twenty-three stanzas all the most essential information about the world, as an early medieval Christian saw it."[22]

Although certainly not the first Irish missionary on the Continent,[23] Columbanus inspired much of the later missionary impulse. He was born around 543 in southeastern Ireland. As a young man he met a woman hermit who challenged him, saying:

> If the weakness of my sex had not prevented me, I would have crossed the sea and chosen a better place among strangers as my

home. But you, glowing with the fire of youth, stay quietly on your native soil; out of weakness you lend your ear even against your own will, to the voice of the flesh, and think you can associate with the female sex without sin.[24]

She reminded him of Eve, and Delilah, and Bathsheba, and counseled him to flee. Reportedly he departed, stepping over his prostrate mother who begged him not to leave, saying "Has thou not heard, 'He that loveth father or mother more than me is not worthy of me?'"[25] He sought spiritual direction from Comgall, first at a monastery near Lough Erne and later at Bangor, which belonged to the most austere federation of Irish monasticism. In 591 he departed for Brittany, and from there proceeded to establish monasteries in Annegray and Luxeuil (in eastern France), Bregenz (on the eastern shore of Lake Constance in Austria), and Bobbio (northeast of Genoa, Italy).[26] To understand the spirituality that sustained such a steadfast missionary, we will examine Jonas's *Life*, which was written shortly after Columbanus' death and drew on eyewitnesses, as well as Columbanus' monastic rule and sermons.

A Violent Age

The context of the Celtic mission was every bit as violent as our own. We find evidence of violence in the writings of pre-Christian Romans, artwork, archaeological remains, pre-Christian Irish sagas, Christian prayers, and in the lives of the missionaries themselves.

The Romans perceived pre-Christian Celtic culture as particularly violent. The first century geographer Strabo commented on Celtic culture generally when he wrote:

The whole race which is now called both "Gallic" and "Galatic" is war-mad, both high-spirited and ready for battle, but otherwise simple and not uncultured. . . . As for their might, it arises partly from their large physique and partly from their numbers. And on account of their trait of simplicity and straightforwardness they easily come together in great numbers, because they always share in the vexation of those of their neighbours whom they think wronged.[27]

He appears, however, particularly horrified by the barbaric nature of the Irish.

> [Ierne's] inhabitants are more savage than the Britons, since they are man-eaters as well as heavy eaters [or perhaps better 'herb-eaters'], and since, further, they count it an honourable thing, when their fathers die, to devour them, and openly to have intercourse, not only with the other women, but also with their mothers and sisters; but I am saying this only with the understanding that I have no trustworthy witnesses for it; and yet, as for the matter of man-eating, that is said to be a custom of the Scythians also, and, in cases of necessity forced by sieges, the Celti, the Iberians, and several other peoples are said to have practised it.[28]

Besides Strabo's testimony, the statue of the Dying Gaul, dating from the late third century, reveals that Celtic warriors fought naked except for a *torc* neck ornament, believing that this practice provided supernatural protection.[29]

Historian Nora Chadwick cautions, however, against over-exaggerating the pre-Christian violence, for the Irish did not go into battle like Roman legions did. Ireland's mostly pastoral population lay scattered across the island, and towns did not even exist until the coming of the monasteries. In order to survive feuds and nuisance raids, common folk surrounded their small houses with a timber palisade, stone wall, bank, or ditch. They also constructed artificial islands (*crannog*) in lakes and rivers from layers of timber, stone, clay, and peat. For the aristocracy, however, warfare was something else. They constructed larger hill-forts, and thousands of ring-forts survive. Bands of young warriors (*fianna*) left their own tribal areas to hunt and to fight. This was perhaps more sport than true warfare, but one could easily die in the process. In fact, the Irish saga of Cú Chulainn suggests that decapitation and headhunting were acceptable goals of such encounters. Although the evidence for a culture of violence predates the Celtic missionary efforts, Chadwick contends that there was little cultural change in the 400 years prior to the coming of Christianity.[30]

As we enter the Celtic missionary era, we find that violence continues. Patrick decries the brutal slaying of newly baptized Christians, who were still in their baptismal garb, and requests the return of others who had been taken captive. He notes that young baptized women were being distributed as prizes and is particularly incensed that the soldiers of Coroticus treated the whole affair as a "big joke."[31] Patrick himself had been taken captive by the Irish at the age of sixteen "along with thousands upon thousands of others."[32] He describes the experience as full of tribulations and many setbacks.[33] After his escape he claims to have come near starvation,[34] and many years later he was again taken captive for two months.[35] Twelve times he faced mortal danger.[36] On one occasion kings to whom he had given gifts "took me and my companions captive. On that day they avidly sought to kill, but the time had not yet come. Still they looted us, took everything of value, and bound me in iron."[37]

As mentioned above, Columba may well have been personally involved in violence. Brendan Lehane describes Columba's times as "rough, if apostolic, days," noting that monks participated in military service until the ninth century and "remained so devoted to their martial experience that inter-monastic skirmishes were as common as competitive sports among their modern successors!"[38] According to one story Columba secretly copied the only copy of the Vulgate in Ireland, which belonged to Finnian of Moville. When Finnian laid claim to the copy, Columba refused to return it, so Finnian laid his case before High King Diarmait. Diarmait favored Finnian, and Columba stirred up his kin, the Uí Néills.[39] In the ensuing battle of Culdreihmne (561), Columba prayed and fasted, and an angel in the shape of a giant soldier so terrified the enemy that three thousand lost their lives. According to one story, the angel demanded that he embark on permanent exile; according to another, Columba sought suitable penance from a saint, and the saint told him to leave Ireland and win as many souls as had been lost in battle.[40]

On the Continent Columbanus faced the brutal, nominally Christian culture of the Merovingian Franks, who had converted under Clovis only one hundred years before. The Frankish bishops apparently sent murderers to loot the populace, and churches accepted bribes to permit the slaughter of those who sought sanctuary within.[41] In Burgundy, Columbanus aroused the ire of Brunhilda, mother of King Theuderich, when he refused to bless her illegitimate grandsons. With characteristic Irish bluntness he said, "Know that these boys will never bear the royal sceptre, for they were begotten in sin."[42] As a consequence Brunhilda began to persecute his monasteries, and eventually Columbanus was seized and banished.[43]

Despite the brevity of our survey of three great Celtic missionaries' experiences, and Celtic society in general, we clearly see that Celtic missions proceeded from first to last in an age at least as violent as our own. We are consequently left to ask, upon what spiritual resources did they draw in order to minister in such a setting?

Patrick's Spirituality

Patrick's spirituality embraces a number of concepts vital for missionary spirituality. He has been overwhelmed by the grace of God, and he has a clear and compelling missionary call. He lives, moreover, in the biblical world, in which the end is near, the Spirit remains active, and we need not fear death.

Above all else Patrick's spirituality is grounded in an understanding of God's grace. Patrick clearly sees himself as a sinner. The first words of both the Confession and Letter are "I am Patrick. I am a sinner" and "Patrick, a sinner." Based on this fundamental self-identity, he recognizes that God exercised both judgment and mercy in his captivity. God both protected him and led him to an awareness of Himself.[44] He recognizes that "I was like a stone lying in the deepest mire; and then 'he who is mighty' came and, in his mercy, raised me up."[45] Therefore God has given him a great gift in placing him in a situation in which he "fiercely sought" and found God.[46] He has received the gift of both knowing and loving God,[47] so that now he knows both the love and fear of God.[48] But beyond his salvation, Patrick views his missionary ministry as a gift of God. He does not feel himself worthy of ministering to his former captors, yet acknowledges that God has given him "great grace" toward them, which he would not have thought possible as a youth.[49] "Truly," he says, "I am greatly in God's debt. He has given me a great grace, that through me many peoples might be reborn and later brought to completion; and also that from among them everywhere clerics should be ordained [to serve] this people."[50] He believes that God frequently forgave his "stupidity and negligence" when he hung back from accepting God's clear call because others were forbidding his mission.[51] Consequently as he draws toward the end of his Confession, he writes from the depths of gratitude, "Therefore, 'I shall give to him for all the things that he has given to me.' But what shall I say to him? What can I promise to give my Lord? I have nothing of value that is not his gift!"[52]

Welling up from his understanding of God's gracious work in his life Patrick feels a deep sense of obligation to testify. He records his experience in captivity "because this is how we return thanks to God . . . . [We] glorify and bear witness to his wonderful works in the presence of every nation under heaven."[53] As a consequence of his salvation, he believes, "I ought to cry out with all my strength and render thanks to the Lord for his blessings are indeed great, here and in eternity, and beyond all that the human mind can imagine."[54] As he contemplates the grace of missionary ministry, he asks in wonder, "'Who am I, O Lord' and what is my vocation, that you have cooperated with me with such divine [power]? Thus today I constantly praise and glorify your name wherever I may be among the nations both in my successes and in my difficulties."[55]

Patrick's testimony, however, moves beyond the need to testify to God's grace, to a clear and compelling call to worldwide missionary service. He identifies himself as God's ambassador and believes that he is among those who have been "called and predestined" to missionary service.[56] As he tells it, he received his call in a dream.

> 'I saw a vision of the night': a man named Victoricus—'like one' from Ireland—coming with innumerable letters. He gave me one of them and I began to read what was in it: 'The voice of the Irish.' And at that very moment as I was reading out the letter's opening, I thought I heard the voice of those around the wood of Foclut, which is close to the western sea. It was 'as if they were shouting with one voice': 'O holy boy, we beg you to come again and walk among us.' And I was 'broken hearted' and could not read anything more. And at that moment I woke up.[57]

Besides the dream, however, Patrick provides biblical justification for careful, urgent, and worldwide evangelization. He begins with Jesus' commands in Matthew 28:19–20, Matthew 24:14, and Mark 16:15–16. (Notably, he makes a slight emendation of the Great Commission: "Go therefore *now* and teach all nations.") To this he adds Peter's promise of the universal Spirit (Acts 2:17–18; Joel 2:28–29) and Paul's instruction that God is calling to himself not only Jews, but also Gentiles (Rom. 9:25–26; Hos. 1:10, 2:23).[58] Moreover, Patrick bears the nations on his heart. He sees himself as living among the nations[59] as a light to the nations;[60] he preaches the gospel as a testimony to all nations;[61] and as a result many peoples and nations are coming to Christ from the ends of the earth.[62] Even Coroticus himself might turn to Christ![63] Based upon this understanding, he is consumed by missionary zeal. He expends himself that others might know of Christ;[64] he is "bound by the Spirit" and under orders to minister to the Irish;[65] and he has sworn to God that he will teach the nations.[66] Thus Richard Fletcher observes that, as far as we know, Patrick was the first Christian who truly grasped the scope of the Great Commission and the responsibility to preach the gospel to barbarians even outside the Empire.[67]

Patrick appears deeply aware of the Holy Spirit's work in his life. The Spirit worked fervently within him to bring him to faith and to increase his love and fear of God,[68] and the Spirit bound him for missionary ministry.[69] Moreover it is the Spirit who prays within him, prompts him, and chastises him.[70] Finally, the Spirit even gave him voice to cry for help when Satan attacked him and he had lost power over his limbs.[71]

Patrick's spirituality included belief in the revelatory power of dreams. In the Confession he records eight visions, which he saw in dreams.[72] As we have seen, a dream proved instrumental in his missionary call, but Patrick also believed his dreams provided direction, comfort,[73] warning,[74] and foreknowledge of what would come to pass.[75] His contemporaries held dreams in equal esteem. He tells of one noblewoman who became a nun after "divine communication from a messenger of God which advised her to become a virgin of Christ."[76] It should be noted, however, that

Patrick's dreams are "not worked up and rationalised as most dreams recounted for edification by medieval writers are. Patrick's dreams are convincing because they have the inconsequence, the surrealist atmosphere, of dreams."[77] Equally intriguing in light of contemporary interest in dreams and visions is his apparent lack of interest in signs and wonders. Later hagiographers embroider his life with numerous miracles (cf. Murichú and Tírechán), but Patrick himself records none. His only mention of signs and wonders refers to the revelatory nature of his dreams.[78]

Patrick viewed his ministry within an eschatological framework, which provided a powerful motive for evangelization. With the empire collapsing and preaching at the ends of the earth, Patrick believed he was living in the last days.[79] In his Letter he observes that the Lord "has wonderfully and mercifully planted [his law] in Ireland in these final times."[80] He gives evidence of the belief that he is living in the last days, not only by quoting Joel 2:28–29 (Ac 2:17–18),[81] but most clearly when he writes, quoting Matthew 24:14:

> It is he who 'in the last days' heard me, so that I—an ignorant man—should dare to take up so holy and wonderful a work as this: that I should in some way imitate those men to whom the Lord foretold what was about to occur when 'his gospel [of the kingdom will be preached throughout the whole world] as a testimony to all nations' before the end of the world. And this is what we see: It has been fulfilled. Behold! We are [now] witnesses to the fact that the gospel has been preached out to beyond where any man lives.[82]

Clearly his eschatological beliefs provided impetus for faithful preaching in difficult circumstances.

Despite dangerous surroundings, however, Patrick did not fear death. He trusted God and even looked forward to death, because it was the doorway to glory. He had offered his life as a living sacrifice[83] and states that "not a day passes but I expect to be killed or waylaid or taken into slavery or assaulted in some other way. But for the sake of the promise of heaven I 'fear none of these things.'"[84] He can adopt such an attitude because, as he goes on to say, "I have cast myself into the hands of God, the almighty one who rules everywhere."[85]

Not only is he fearless, but he even sought death. At one point he says, "if I be worthy I am ready to give my life right now 'for his name's sake,'"[86] and at another he actually prays for martyrdom:

> And, if at any time I have 'imitated something that is good' for the sake of my God whom I love, then I ask him to grant me that I may shed my blood 'for his name's sake' with those proselytes and captives, even if this means that I should lack even a tomb, or that my corpse be horribly chopped up by dogs and wild beasts, or that 'the birds of heaven devour it'.[87]

Patrick prayed this because he firmly believed in the promise of resurrection glory. He sought to comfort those martyred by Coroticus with the promise "it is as faithful baptized people that you have left this world to go to Paradise"[88] and he concluded his prayer for martyrdom with the bold assurance that "there is no doubt that on the day we shall arise . . . we shall be 'sons of the living God' and 'fellow heirs with Christ' and 'conformed to his image'; 'for from him and through him and in him' we shall reign."[89]

Finally, it is important to note that Patrick thoroughly immersed himself in the biblical world. As Hanson observes, he "has no acquaintance with any book, so far as we can ascertain, except the Latin (pre-Vulgate) Bible. But that book he knows very well and uses constantly, even when biblical quotations are not called for."[90] Thus, O'Loughlin's translation of the Confession, which runs to less than seventeen printed pages, cross-references no less than three hundred references or allusions to the Bible! Patrick's mind is so filled with scripture that the language of scripture fills and shapes his very thought world.

Having examined Patrick's missionary spirituality, we conclude with Hanson that he indeed deserves the title "Apostle of the Irish People." Greater than this, however, is his legacy to the Irish church, for he bequeathed it his missionary zeal. Certainly "anybody who read his Confession might be infected by it."[91]

Columba's Spirituality

In turning to Columba, we have less access to his spirituality than with Patrick, for besides the *Altus Prosator* we must rely upon hagiography. Still, several observations can be made.

The second preface to the *Life* reveals three noteworthy facts about the saint. First, "when he was forty-one, Columba sailed away from Ireland to Britain, choosing to be a pilgrim for Christ." Chadwick argues that such pilgrimage is simply part of early Irish asceticism and bears no relationship to mission work.[92] Sharpe too notes that pilgrims who left Ireland exercised greater self-denial and did greater penance than those who simply retreated to a monastery in Ireland.[93] James Bruce, however, challenges the idea that Columba was not a missionary, noting that, while he may not fulfill the modern concept, he nonetheless fulfilled Adomnán's idea, and we should consequently investigate what mission entailed in the sixth century.[94] Second, Adomnán records a prophecy placing Columba's birth "in the last days of world." Thus, as with Patrick, Columba's ministry occurred within an eschatological framework. Finally, Adomnán refers to the saint as an "island soldier," as he does throughout the *Life*, referring both to the saint and his monks.[95] Their identification as soldiers indicates that the monks are highly disciplined, under command, and responsible to fulfill the duty of a superior.

Lives of the saints were written for three basic purposes: to edify, to exalt the saint, and above all to encourage imitation of the saint. Thus, as Jean Michel Picard explains, sixth century hagiographers emphasized the saint's character and virtue as an example for holy living. Saints were consequently presented as imitating Christ's lifestyle and character, not just his miracles. In the seventh century, however, saints' characters had become stylized and miracles came to the fore. The aim was, therefore, no longer edification, but rather satisfaction of a public craving the miraculous, and propaganda for a particular monastic community.[96] It is no surprise, then, that Adomnán's *Life of St. Columba* reflects these propagandistic aims, because he seeks to present Columba as equal to continental saints. With respect to the miraculous, however, he demonstrates concern for the credibility of his evidence and carefully cites the reliability of his witnesses.[97] This is different than other Irish *Lives*, which, according to Picard, lack the rationalizing influence of Rome and reflect Irish enjoyment of fantasy and an oral tradition rooted in mythology.[98]

In Book II Adomnán records the saint's miracles, miracles for the most part of an evangelical sort that "comfort human misery or restore man's dignity."[99] In most Irish *Lives* evangelical miracles play a minor role, so that the *Lives* belong more to the realm of the folktale, as in Tírechán's and Murichú's tales of Patrick. In Columba's case the aim is evangelical and confirms the mission of the saint.[100] In fact, some have argued convincingly that the miracles demonstrate the coming of Christ's eschatological kingdom in and through Columba's ministry. Reading the miracles, we enter into the biblical world of Jesus, the prophets, and the apostles. Like Jesus, in the first recorded miracle Columba turns water into wine.[101] He stills storms[102] and directs others to a catch of fish.[103] He even raises the dead, the supreme evangelical miracle.[104] Like the prophets, he turns bitter fruit into sweet,[105] obtains water from a rock so that he can baptize a boy,[106] and destroys evil men who had scorned him when he asked that they return their plunder.[107] He tames wild beasts, including the first recorded encounter with the Loch Ness monster, in which even the heathen "magnified the God of the Christians,"[108] and like Patrick in Ireland the snakes on Iona can do no poisonous harm.[109] In one delightful account Columba even fasts and prays all night so that a wife who loathed her husband and refused to sleep with him lives out her days in wedded bliss.[110]

The final book of Adomnán's *Life* contains accounts of angelic apparitions, which were either revealed to others about Columba or to him about others, and special phenomena of bright, heavenly light. Picard observes that such accounts sometimes simply follow the prescribed literary form or are symbolic, but Adomnán insists that these were real and takes care to cite excellent witnesses.[111] Some of the apparitions are clearly meant to highlight Columba's special nature. Thus, his mother saw an angel who announced that her child was "destined by God to lead innumerable souls to the heavenly kingdom"[112] and his foster-father saw a fiery ball near his sleeping head, which indicated the outpouring of the Holy Spirit.[113] The presence of heavenly light served a similar purpose. On one occasion "the grace of the Holy Spirit was poured upon him in incomparable abundance," and though he remained in his house "rays of brilliant light could be seen at night, escaping through the chinks of the doors and through the keyholes."[114]

Of special importance for our purposes, however, are the appearances of angels in spiritual battle, especially at the time of death. Angels came to his aid as he prayed against "a line of foul, black devils armed with iron spikes and drawn up ready for battle" that intended to attack and kill the monks at his monastery.[115] On another occasion Columba said, "we must bring the help of our prayers to some of St Comgall's monks who are drowned in Belfast Lough at this time. See, even now, they are battling in the air against the powers of the Adversary who are seeking to snatch away the soul of a visitor who was drowned along with them."[116] The account reveals the deep-seated beliefs that heavenly warfare lies behind earthly circumstances and that angels and demons battle for the souls of the dead. Picard observes that the devil appears prominently in the continental *Lives*. Misfortune and accident were viewed as his work; evildoers were also his agents—whether bad monks, flirtatious women, brutal bullies, or murderers; and the devil appears in the form of animals—whether serpents, rams and goats, or dragons. In the Irish *Lives*, however, the devil is not so omnipresent; evildoers are simply human (except for the wizards); animals are simply animals; the devil is simply the devil.[117] In Adomnán's *Life*, besides fighting for the souls of the dead[118] and seeking to inflict physical harm directly on the monks,[119] demons were believed to be active in other ways as well. The devil is said to have prompted a man to kill Columba.[120] Another story recounts a devil hiding in the bottom of a milk pail, because the milkman had failed to make the sign of the cross before pouring in the milk,[121] and the devil had clouded the minds of the Picts so that they worshiped a certain well.

The devil's agents are shamans or wizards. Sharpe hesitates to call them 'druids', because Adomnán uses the Latin term *magus*, which portrays pagan priests as magicians and shamans. Besides, the term 'druid' has precise but different meanings in Gaul, Britain, Wales, England, and Ireland, none of which applies to the Picts.[122] The *Life* contains accounts of several power encounters with the wizards. On one occasion Columba was saying vespers, and some wizards tried their best to make him stop, for fear that their people would hear God's praise. Knowing this, Columba chanted Psalm 45. His voice sounded like thunder, so that his listeners were filled with fear.[123] In another account, wizards watched as Columba and his companions washed and drank from a well, which the people regarded as a god because of its ill effects. They expected harm to come to the party, but it did not. In fact the demons departed and the well became a place of healing.[124] In still another encounter, when a new-believer's son lay dying, wizards "began to make a mock of the parents and to reproach them harshly, making much of their own gods as the stronger and belittling the God of the Christians as the feebler."[125] Columba arrived after the child had died, but prayed to Christ and commanded the boy to rise. In one final instance, a wizard who held power over wind and mist told Columba that he would not be able to sail. Columba replied, "The almighty power of God rules all things, . . . and all our comings and goings are directed by his governance."[126] When the time came to sail, a great mist did indeed cover the loch and a stormy, contrary wind was blowing. Adomnán observes, "One must not be surprised that such things happen occasionally by the art of devils—when God permits it." Columba simply called on Christ, ordered the men to hoist the sail, and the boat moved off rapidly into the wind. In all of these instances, there is clear demonstration of the power of God over the power of the heathen gods and devils.

Finally, we should note the attitude toward death that is revealed in the *Life*. Four years before his death, Columba reveals:

> A long time ago I earnestly asked the Lord that at the end of this thirtieth year he would release me from this dwelling and call me straightaway to the heavenly kingdom. This is why I was so glad, . . . for I saw the angels sent from the throne on high to lead my soul from this body.[127]

His time had not yet come, however. Four years later, when the angel of the Lord returns to take him home, Columba is filled joy. He views his life as the loan of a "sacred soul entrusted to him by God," and the angel had simply come to "recover a loan dear to God." He describes his coming death as his sabbath: "Scripture calls this day the Sabbath, which means 'rest'. Today is truly my sabbath, for it is my last day in this wearisome life, when I shall keep the Sabbath after my troublesome labours."[128] Life, then, is laborious, and we should anticipate our departure with joy.

The *Altus Prosator* simply confirms the Celtic view that life is but a brief stop in a transient world, and consequently we should concentrate upon the unseen world.[129] Consisting of twenty-three stanzas of six lines each, with each stanza beginning with the next letter of the Latin alphabet, it introduces the modern mind to a strange new world. As the very title suggests, it portrays God as the High First-Sower, sowing, tending, and reaping his creation. After beginning with a strong Trinitarian affirmation, roughly one-third of the poem focuses upon the angelic world, one-third upon God's providential care for the physical world, and one-third upon eschatological realities. Humans are surprisingly absent. The poet mentions their creation along with that of the heavens and earth and every living thing:

> The High One, looking forward to the system of the universe and its harmony, made the heaven and the earth; Brought forth the sea, the waters, the shoots of grass, the trees of the woods, the sun, moon, stars, fire, and all things needed, birds, fish, cattle, beasts, and everything that lives. Then, at the end of his works, [he made] the first-formed human so that he could rule with knowledge.

The fall receives mention only in the context of the demons' second fall (the first was from heaven to earth; the second from earth to hell):[130]

> Having loitered around and seduced our two first parents, the Devil and his horde fell a second time. The ugliness of their [demonic] faces and the sound of their flying strikes fragile humans with such terror that they cannot see with their eyes of flesh those who are now bundled in the bonds of prison labor camps.

Kings rule only briefly, and only Moses appears by name. In fact, as Jane Stevenson observes, there is "no direct mention of any part of human history between Exodus and the Apocalypse."[131] Instead we are introduced to "the world of unseen things—God on his throne, his mysterious and all-governing providence, angels and demons, and things to come."[132] Not surprisingly, then, the poem ends with the refrain:

> Who can please God 'in the final time,'
> With the various orders of truth made plain?
> *Only those who have contempt for the world.* (emphasis added)

One finishes the *Altus Prosator* with the distinct impression that we pass through life in a world for which God providentially cares, but we are surrounded by a spiritual battle, and we are heading swiftly toward judgment. The *Altus* calls us to live in light of such truth.

Columban spirituality confronts us with a fleeting life and a welcome home-going. Like Patrick, Columba resides in a biblical world of unseen spiritual powers, dependent on God's providence and the Spirit. He also calls us to become pilgrims and soldiers for Christ.

Columbanus' Spirituality

Columbanus provides an example of missionary spirituality on multiple levels. Like Patrick he too has a clear call to missionary service, and his effectiveness increases due to his character and knowledge of scripture. Like Columba he performs evangelical miracles and engages in power encounters. Like Patrick and Columba he receives prophetic revelations and displays their characteristic attitude toward life and death. He is, however, perhaps best remembered for his extreme asceticism.

Columbanus departed Ireland with a clear missionary call, and in this sense resembles Patrick more than Columba. As we have seen,[133] some have argued that the Irish *perigrini* were not missionaries, but extreme ascetics bent on the salvation of their own souls. To some extent Tomás Ó Fiaich concurs. "The exodus of the Irish monks and scholars had little of the modern foreign missionary movement about it," he writes. "For one thing, the primary motive was ascetical rather than evangelical"[134] He does allow that a secondary motive did subsequently arise, namely, to spread Christ's kingdom.[135] Wolfgang H. Fritze, however, has demonstrated that Pope Gregory the Great actively promoted a universal mission, reflected in sending missionaries to England.[136] It would therefore not be surprising if Gregory's contemporary, Columbanus, was among the first to implement such a vision.

More pointedly, Columbanus' hagiographer, Jonas, clearly develops the saint's call, as well as his missionary activity. He departed the monastery at Bangor in specific obedience to God's command to the prototypical missionary Abraham: "Leave your country, your people and your father's household and go to the land I will show you" (Gen. 12:3, NIV). In departing he confessed to Comgall that he had been meditating on the Lord's word in Luke 12:49: "I have come to bring fire on the earth, and how I wish it were already kindled!" (NIV). The verse anticipates a division between believers and unbelievers dependent upon their response to Jesus Christ, and Columbanus states that the Lord had kindled this same desire in his own heart.[137] Elsewhere he attributes his departure from Ireland to his "love for Christ."[138] From the beginning of their ministry on the Continent, the saint and his companions desired to "sow the seeds of salvation; or in case they found the hearts of the people in darkness, go on to the nearest nations," where presumably they would also preach,[139] for everywhere he went he "preached the Gospel"[140] He "preached the word of God" to condemned prisoners;[141] when he encountered a group of Swabians offering sacrifice to the god Wodan, "he reproved them in the words of the Gospel, and commanded them to cease from such offerings."[142] Finally, he considered a mission to the Wends,[143] the earliest evidence of Western missionary interest in this Slavic people.[144]

Columbanus' character enhanced the power of his preaching. Jonas notes that "his teaching was adorned by eloquence and enforced by examples of virtue" and goes on to catalog specific virtues of the saint and his monks. Selected for mention were humility, modesty and moderation, meekness and mildness, patience and love. On the other hand, pride and haughtiness, scorn and envy, sloth and dissension "were banished." "No one dared to return evil for evil, or to let fall a harsh word; so that people must have believed that an angelic life was being lived by mortal men."[145] Jonas further emphasizes the power of Columbanus' character through his reports of the saint's special relationship with animals. Animals were drawn to him in a special way,[146] and dangerous animals would not harm him.[147]

Columbanus' effectiveness rested not only upon virtuous character, but also upon his knowledge of scripture. Jonas explains that as a youth Columbanus placed himself under the tutelage of Sinell, "who at this time was distinguished among his countrymen for his unusual piety and knowledge of the Holy Scriptures."[148] Sinell, impressed by his pupil's ability, instructed him thoroughly and carefully, so that Columbanus memorized great quantities of scripture and even as a youth "expounded the Psalter in fitting language and [made] many other extracts worthy to be sung, and instructive to read."[149] In contrast to the continental church, Irish monasteries emphasized the scriptures. They focused upon biblical memorization and instruction. In fact, when continental bishops wanted to study scripture they went to Ireland.[150] When Columbanus left Sinell for Comgall's instruction at Bangor, he entered an abbey renowned for biblical instruction, one that held to a high standard of Latin and even some Greek.[151] As a result Columbanus would have known his Bible well. Small wonder then that his monastic federation restored a thorough knowledge of the Old and New Testaments on the Continent and that even lay disciples began to read the Bible.[152]

Even more than his character, Columbanus remains famous, or infamous, for his rigid asceticism. At Bangor, while under Comgall's direction, he "gave himself entirely to fasting and prayer, to bearing the easy yoke of Christ, to mortifying the flesh, to taking the cross upon himself and following Christ, in order that he who was to be a teacher of others might show the learning which he taught ...."[153] When at Annegray, "he settled there with his followers in spite of the entire loneliness, the wilderness and the rocks, mindful of the proverb that, 'Man shall not live by bread alone,' but shall have sufficient food from the bread of life and shall never hunger."[154] Jonas testifies to his rigorous discipline, when he writes:

> He was so attenuated by fasting that he scarcely seemed alive—
> nor did he eat anything except a small measure of the herbs of the
> field, or of the little apples which that wilderness produces and
> which are commonly called *bolluca*. His drink was water. And
> as he was always occupied with other cares, he could not get
> this regularly; at least during the time when he was performing
> his vows.[155]

The ascetic life was regularized in Columbanus' Rule, which outlines "a hard and fierce régime."[156] It was most likely modeled after the rule at Bangor, with further influence from Eastern monasticism, particularly through the rules of Basil the Great and Cassian and through an emphasis upon singing Psalms during nightly vigils.[157] The Rule consisted of two texts, the Communal Rule and the Rule for Monks. The Communal Rule is noteworthy for the detailed way in which it prescribes penances for violations of monastic discipline. The Rule for Monks, except for the long chapter on the Choir Office, deals primarily with the monk's spiritual life, that is, with obedience, silence, fasting, poverty, vanity, chastity, discernment (which is set in the context of spiritual warfare), mortification, and ultimately perfection. The final chapter on perfection will suffice to offer a flavor of the whole:

> Let the monk live in a monastery under the direction of a single
> father, in the company of many, so that he may learn humility
> from one, and patience from another. One may teach him silence
> and another gentleness. Let him not do as he wishes, let him eat
> what he is told to eat, let him keep what he has received, let him
> carry out his duties and be obedient to someone he would not have
> chosen. Let him come tired to his bed and sleep while he is still
> walking, and let him be made to rise before he has slept enough.
> Let him be silent when he suffers wrong, let him fear the superior
> of the monastery as a lord, and love him as a father, believing that
> whatever he commands is for his own good. Let him not pass
> judgment on the opinion of an elder; his duty is to obey and carry
> out what he is commanded to do, as Moses says: 'Hear, O Israel,'
> and the rest (Dt 6:4).[158]

Thus, as Ó Fiaich observes, "For an Irish monk obedience was everything and the details of community life could be safely left to the decisions of a wise and inspiring abbot."[159] In focusing on obedience rather than providing detailed rules for monastic life, the Rule of Columbanus provides a striking contrast to the Rule of St. Benedict.

Mention must also be made of the Penitential, for it had enormous impact upon continental Christianity. When Columbanus arrived on the Continent, Jonas observes, "At that time, either because of the numerous enemies from without, or on account of the carelessness of the bishops, the Christian faith had almost departed from that country. The creed alone remained. But *the saving grace of penance and the longing to root out the lusts of the flesh* were to be found only in a few."[160] The Penitential addressed this deficiency. Columbanus' monks confessed their sins privately twice a day and received an appropriate penance. When this practice was extended to the laity, Columbanus wrote the Penitential. He believed that we overcome a sin by practicing its opposite virtue. So, for example, talkativeness required silence, gluttony/fasting, sleepiness/vigils, and desertion/banishment. To modern Christians the penances appear severe. Drunkenness or gluttony required a week on bread and water; someone who stole a domestic animal not only had to provide restitution, but also faced 120 days on bread and water; perjury required three years on bread and water and two additional years without meat or wine. Still, in light of the fact that the continental system met the same sins with excommunication, the Penitential offered hope of restoration.[161] Riché goes so far as to say that the new system of private confession with penance proportional to the seriousness of the sin actually deepened the understanding of sin and led to more frequent participation in the Eucharist. In short, historians consider the impact "as a real spiritual revolution."[162]

Columbanus' severity naturally raises questions in modern minds. Indeed, it should be noted that other Irish monks were more moderate and humane.[163] Moreover, as Hughes observes, "the violence of Columbanus' régime, willingly undertaken, must be compared, not with the civilization of a later age, but with the violence of Merovingian Gaul, involuntarily endured."[164] Still, in spite of his severity, Columbanus genuinely loved his monks and moments of gentleness offset the harshness of his rules.[165] When Brunhilda and Theuderich seized him to banish him to Ireland, for example, he wrote to his monks at Luxueil:

> Peace be to you . . . and salvation and eternal charity. With Him may the Trinity grant you these three gifts, and preserve them amongst you with my prayer. The greatness of my zeal for your salvation is known to Him alone who gave it, and my longing for the advance of your instruction . . . .[166]

Clearly he views his severity as essential to their spiritual progress.

Like Adomnán and Patrick before him, Jonas believed in the power of dreams and visions. He records that Columbanus' mother had a dream prophesying the importance of her child.[167] Columbanus also dreamed of a battle between his nemesis King Theuderich and his brother Theudebert.[168] Through revelation he prophesied that Theuderich and his family would all die within three years[169] and advised Chlotar that he would receive both the kingdoms of Theuderich and Theudebert.[170] In addition, a vision led Abbot Caramtoc to provide food for his party at Annegray,[171] and through a revelation he learned of the illness of his monks near Luxeuil in time to intervene.[172] Lastly, the angel of the Lord directed him regarding his place of ministry.[173]

Like Adomnán, Jonas also emphasized his saint's miracles, particularly with respect to provision of food, healings, and nature miracles. On at least six occasions God miraculously provides food for Columbanus, his monks, or the needy, like he did for Israel in the wilderness or for Elijah with the jug of oil.[174] The need for such miracles reflects both the austerity of the monks, as well as the difficult circumstances in which they ministered. In language reminiscent of the ministry of Jesus, Jonas also reports a number of instances of healing.

> Then crowds of people and throngs of the infirm began to crowd about St. Columban in order that they might recover their health and in order to seek aid in all their infirmities. When he was

unable to rid himself of their importunities, obeying the petitions
and prayers of all, through his prayers and relying upon the divine
aid, he healed the infirmities of all who came to him.[175]

On different occasions Columbanus healed a severed finger and a
cut in the forehead with his saliva[176] and a blind man and a barren
couple by his prayers.[177] In one instance sick monks who arise at
his command to thresh grain are healed, while those who do not
are subjected to lengthy illness.[178] The conclusion that Jonas draws
is this:

> Wonderful compassion of the Creator! He permits us to be in need,
> that He may show His mercy by giving to the needy. He permits us
> to be tempted, that by aiding us in our temptations He may turn the
> hearts of His servants more fully to Himself. He permits His
> followers to be cruelly tortured that they may delight more fully in
> restored health.[179]

Jonas also records incidents of Columbanus' saintly power over
nature, miracles that sometimes reflect biblical events and sometimes
demonstrate God's protection. Through his prayers a stream of water
sprang from a rock,[180] and he instructs his disciples to a catch of
fish.[181] When the saint, onboard a boat and under guard, desired to
visit the grave of St. Martin of Tours, the wind prevailed against the
oarsmen and blew the boat into the harbor.[182] When the bishop of
Nantes and count Theudebald attempted to repatriate Columbanus to
Ireland, the boat ran aground, and they came to recognize that God
did not want Columbanus to return home.[183] The saint also enjoyed
divine protection. When the king's master of horse intended to kill
him with a lance, God made his hand lame, so that he dropped his
lance and was forced to depend upon Columbanus for healing.[184]
Reflecting on such events, Jonas concludes:

> Nor did he lack defence, because in all things he had the aid of the
> Creator, and He who keeps Israel under the shadow of His wings
> never slumbers. Thus truly He shows by granting all things to all
> men, that He wishes to be glorified by all in proportion to the
> greatness of his gifts.[185]

Like Adomnán, Jonas records instances of demonic activity, but unlike Adomnán such activity does not relate to wizards. Jonas does not mention wizards, instead Columbanus' earthly foes are secular and religious powers, namely kings and bishops. He does, however, battle the demonic, as illustrated in the following exorcism:

> When he arrived [in Paris], he met at the gate a man having an unclean spirit, who was raving and rending his garments, while babbling. The latter addressed the man of God complainingly: 'What are you doing in this place, O man of God?' From afar he had been crying out for a long time with his growling voice as he saw Columban, the man of God, approaching. When the latter saw him, he said: 'Depart, evil one, depart! Do not dare to possess any longer the body washed by Christ. Yield to the power of God, and invoked by [sic] the name of Christ.' But when the devil resisted for a long time with savage and cruel strength, the man of God placed his hand on the man's ear and struck the man's tongue and by the power of God commanded the devil to depart. Then rending the man with cruel violence so that bonds could scarcely restrain him, the devil, issuing forth amid great purging and vomiting made such a stench that those who stood by believed that they could endure the fumes of sulphur more easily.[186]

On other occasions, Columbanus reportedly healed twelve demoniacs and five mad men on the same day.[187] Since a band of mad men is elsewhere described as "tortured with savage fury" by demons,[188] it may be that madness was viewed as possession. Through his prayers, the saint likewise healed a demon-possessed youth, who was "wounded by the devil's art."[189] In each of these instances Jonas identifies the exorcisms as healings.[190] One final incident can be compared to Columba's encounter with the devil in the milk-pail. Columbanus exorcises a devil from a cask of beer that the Swabians were about to offer to Wodan, and they are so impressed that they heed his preaching and are baptized.[191] For Columbanus, however, spiritual warfare does not consist solely of power encounters, healings, and exorcisms. It also entails ascetic practices aimed at controlling the sinful nature, for as Jonas notes, "By their extreme severities every lust of the flesh was expelled, so that the plunderer and robber of all virtues fled."[192] Thus in his Rule, Columbanus explains,

The word *discernment* comes from distinguishing, therefore, since in us it distinguishes between good and evil, the mediocre and the perfect. For from the beginning good and evil have been divided like light and dark after evil began to exist through the Devil by the corruption of the good . . . . [193]

The remainder of the chapter distinguishes between good and evil, pressing the monks to pursue the good and to avoid the evils cunningly designed by the devil.

There are not many angelic apparitions in Jonas's *Life*, but as with Columba, one instance associates angelic appearances with death. The account poignantly reveals once again the Celtic monks' attitude toward life and death.

When at one time the man of God was staying at Luxeuil, one of the brethren, who was also named Columban, was stricken with a fever and, lying at the point of death, was awaiting instantly a happy release. When he wanted to draw his last breath, confident of the eternal reward which he had sought in his long service, he saw a man clothed in light coming to him, and saying, 'I am not able now to free you from your body, because I am hindered by the prayers of your father Columban.' When the sick man heard this, sorrowfully as if he had been awakened from sleep, he began to call his attendant Theudegisel . . ., and said, 'Go quickly and summon our father Columban to me.' The attendant went swiftly to Columban weeping in the church, and asked him to hasten to the sick man. Columban came quickly and asked him what he wanted. The latter told him, saying, 'Why do you detain me by your prayers in this sorrowful world? For those are present, who would lead me away if they were not hindered by your tears and prayers. I beseech you; remove the obstacles which retain me that the celestial kingdom may open for me.' Columban, struck with fear, made a signal that all should come. His joy lessened his grief at the loss of his holy companion. He gave the dying man the body of Christ as a viaticum, and after the last kiss began the death-song. For they were of the same race and name and had left Ireland in the same company. [194]

As touching as Jonas' account is, I have found Columbanus' view of life nowhere more powerfully and more poetically expressed than in his homily. He writes:

> Human life, fragile and marked for death, how many have you deceived, beguiled, and blinded? While in flight, you are nothing; while in sight, you are a shadow; while you rise up, you are but smoke. Every day you depart and every day you return; you depart in returning and you return in departing, different ending, same beginning, different pleasure, the same passing, sweet to the foolish and bitter to the wise. Those who love you do not know you, and those who condemn you really understand you. Thus you are not true but false; you present yourself as true but prove yourself false. What are you then, human life? You are the wayfaring of mortals and not their living; your beginning is in sin and in death your end. You would be true if the sin of the first human transgression had not cut you short so that you became unsteady and mortal and marked all who tread your way for death. And so you are the way that leads to life, but not life itself, for you are a true way, but not an open one: brief for some and long for others, broad for some and narrow for others, joyful for some and full of grief for others, but for each and every one, you hurry on and cannot be called back. A way is what you are, a way, but you are not evident to all. Though many see you, few understand that you are indeed a way. You are so cunning and alluring that it is given to few to know you as a way. Thus you are to be questioned and not believed or credited, you are to be traversed and not inhabited: wretched human life. For a road is to be walked on and not lived in, so that they who walk upon it may dwell finally in the land that is their home.[195]

As with Patrick and Columba before him, Columbanus viewed life not only as a material but also as a spiritual pilgrimage. Their home was not on earth, but in heaven, so they did not cling to this life and freely gave their lives away to God.

Celtic Spirituality for Modern Mission

Having acquainted ourselves with three great Celtic missionaries and their spiritual worlds, what lessons can we learn to sustain ourselves in contexts of violence? Celtic spirituality cannot be repeated,

Chadwick concludes, because it emerged from a world without the temptations of city life, materialism, and money.[196] I would suggest, however, that these three missionary giants bequeath the modern church in mission at least four spiritual counsels.

First, they call us to embrace the biblical thought world. As we have seen, all three monks had thoroughly memorized scripture, so much so that the biblical thought world became their world. They lived in a world in which God supervised the tiniest details. In such a world, *peregrini* did not fear setting forth in small *coracles*, abandoning themselves to the wind and the waves, because God controlled the wind and waves. They did not fear retreating to rocky islets where they depended upon small pockets of soil and bird eggs for food, because this simply required total dependence upon God. Moreover, even if we do not regard the hagiographa as factually true, they most certainly reflect the Celtic belief that the kingdom of God had become a present reality. The works of Jesus, the apostles, and prophets continued in their midst. Unencumbered by Enlightenment skepticism, they inhabited a cosmos in which angels, demons, and their agents were active, but a cosmos that was quickly passing away. As we have seen, Patrick viewed the surrounding violence simply as a sign of the end, and Columba also believed himself living in the last days. We too might view our present violence as a sign of the end, but as it did in the case of the Celts, such violence might simply accompany a major turning point in history. In such days we should live as they did, aware of spiritual realities behind current events and utterly dependent upon God's sovereign care.

Second, these three legendary missionaries bequeath us a clear and compelling call to missionary vocation in the midst of violence. It could be argued that the contemporary threat is different than the one faced by the monks. Violence today is anonymous, faceless, even banal, while ancient violence had a personal face. Nevertheless, fear of possible violence remains the same, and fear did not paralyze the monks. Instead they maintained steadfast confidence in God's protection and providential care. More than this, however, Patrick and Columbanus in particular knew their vocation in the midst of violent days was to reach the nations, to extend Christ's kingdom. By the time of Columbanus, the Roman church had done little to evangelize beyond the borders of the Empire. Pope Gregory the Great, however, reversed this failure by dispatching Augustine to England in 596, and Friedrich Prinz argues that Columbanus was one of the first actually to embrace Gregory's goal of systematic evangelization.[197] His monasteries subsequently became the "nurseries of missionaries" that transformed the Continent.[198] The Celtic missionaries would call us to follow them into missionary service in spite of the dark days in which we find ourselves.

Third, they call us to reexamine the relationship between asceticism and mission. With Columbanus in view, we might easily dismiss Celtic asceticism as un-Christlike, as world-renouncing rather than world-affirming. Yet Christ's simple, unmarried lifestyle was not our own, and Davies observes that on the whole the Celts held a deeply incarnational theology that led to "a wonderfully life-affirming and exuberant kind of Christianity."[199] God inhabited every aspect of their world down to the smallest detail, and they did not divorce spirituality from physicality. This enabled the Celts to embrace singleness and allowed them to function more easily in the midst of potential violence. This is no new insight, for the Apostle Paul had argued the same thing five centuries earlier.[200] Should we not proactively encourage young people to embrace a single lifestyle for the sake of world evangelization? Not only this, but instead of simply dismissing asceticism as a Pelagian attempt to attain salvation and perfection, we should note the impact of their testimony. Riché remarks,

> Merovingian bishops were horrified and indeed scandalized by the ascetic exploits of the insular monks: prayer with arms extended, immersion in icy water, perpetual fasting and so forth. Yet these acts of ascetic prowess were what made Columbanan monks so popular with the laity. If it was a choice between a clergy living a comfortable secular existence and men 'mad for God', the choice went to the madmen.[201]

Could it be that we in the North American church have sided with the bishops? Faced with a world that lives in daily poverty, should we adopt more of the ascetic simplicity of the monks?

Finally, Patrick, Columba, and Columbanus call us toward our heavenly home. They viewed life as a pilgrimage, a departure from family, clan, and homeland to follow Christ toward their heavenly home. Patrick had offered his life as a living sacrifice and even looked forward to the privilege of martyrdom. In the *Altus Prosator* Columba sets this life in the larger context of eternity, thus calling into question our preoccupation with this life. He thus calls us to focus on things above, to beware the temptations of the devil, and to prepare for the Second Coming.[202] Columbanus, likewise, warns of the dangers of setting up house on the roadway of life, rather than walking on the road toward our heavenly home. In facing the challenge of violence in our day, we can do no better than to reflect upon the call that he issued to his flock faced with the violence of their day.

> And so, turning our back on all evil and laying aside all apathy, let us strive to please him who is everywhere, so that we may joyfully and with a good conscience pass over from the road of this world to the blessed and eternal home of our eternal Father, moving from present things to absent ones, from sad things to joyful ones, from passing things to eternal ones, from earthly things to heavenly ones, from the region of death to the sphere of the living, where we shall see heavenly things face-to-face, and the King of Kings, ruling his realms with an upright rule, our Lord Jesus Christ, to whom be glory from age to age. Amen.[203]

Notes

1. On the anachronistic nature and shortcomings of the concept of 'Celtic' see Oliver Davies (1999, 3–6; Fletcher 1999, 92; Bruce 2004, 5).
2. Although often called barbarian invasions, the decline of the Roman Empire resulted from the vast tribal migrations in the 5th century precipitated by the pressure of the Huns from Central Asia upon the Germanic Goths, and followed by movements of Visgoths, Burgundians Vandals, and Saxons (Brown 2003, 43–48, 101–102).

3. I use the term "Dark Ages" reservedly. The term originally denoted the loss of civilized Roman culture, but later decried a superstitious form of Christian faith. I use the term to express our relative lack of written records (especially in the British isles, as a result of the Anglo-Saxon invasions) and what to us appears to be the violent nature of the times (cf. Hanson 1989, 42–43; de Paor 1993, 95; Brown 2003, 17–23).

4. Columba. 1999. "The High First-Sower." In *Celtic spirituality*, trans. Thomas O'Loughlin, 405–410. New York: Paulist Press. (Columcille)

5. Columbanus. 1970. *Sancti Columbani opera*. Translated and edited by G. S. M. Walker. Dublin: Dublin Institute for Advanced Studies. (Columban)

6. Hughes, Kathleen. 1966. *The Church in early Irish society*. Ithaca, NY: Cornell University Press. (Hughes 1966, 26)

7. Bede. 1994. *The ecclesiastical history of the English people*. Oxford World's Classics. Edited by Judith McClure and Roger Collins. Oxford: Oxford University Press. (Bede iii.4).

8. Can't Match (Chronicle).

9. Confession 1; de Paor 1993, 88–89.

10. 1989, 24.

11. de Paor 1993, 89–91.

12. 1966, 31.

13. so Bieler 1963, 26; but see Sharpe 1995, 255 n. 54.

14. Ibid.

15. 1995, 9–14. For still other theories see Lehane (1968, 117–119).

16. iii.4.

17. Bede iii.3–5; Lehane 1968, 143–146.

18. Ó Fiaich 1989, 103) The ancient sources identify the Irish as Hibernians and Scots. The indigenes of modern Scotland were the Picts (Ó Fiaich 1989, 102).

19. Hughes 1966, 61.

20. Bruce 2004, 2 n. 4.

21. Davies 1999, 475 n. 184.

22. Stevenson 1999, 327, 368.

23. Riché 1981, 61; Ó Fiaich 1989, 106.

24. Jonas 8.

25. Jonas 8.

26. Walker, G. S. M., ed. 1970. *Sancti Columbani opera*. Dublin: Dublin Institute for Advanced Studies. (Walker 1970, ix–xxxiv, Ó Fiaich 1989, 107–111; Lehane 1968, 148–150; Bullough 1997.

27. 4.4.2.

28. 4.5.4.

29. Chadwick 1970, 134.
30. 1970, 107, 125–138.
31. Letter to the Soldiers of Coroticus 2, 19.
32. Confession 1.
33. Conf. 15.
34. Conf. 19.
35. Conf. 21.
36. Conf. 35.
37. Conf. 52.
38. 1968, 117.
39. Lehane 1968, 118–119.
40. Bieler 1963, 11.
41. Lehane, Brendan. 1968. *The quest of three abbot: The golden age of Celtic Christianity.* Hudson, NY: Lindisfarne Press. (Lehane 1968, 152)
42. Jonas. 1897. The life of St. Columban. Medieval Source Book, Vol. 2, No. 7, ed. Dana C. Munro. Philadelphia: University of Pennsylvania. Available online http://www.fordham.edu/halsall/basis/
43. columban.html; accessed December 31, 2005. (Jonas 32).
44. Jonas 32–34.
45. Conf. 2–3.
46. Conf. 12.
47. Conf. 33.
48. Conf. 36.
49. Conf. 16, 44.
50. Conf.. 15.
51. Conf. 38.
52. Conf. 46.
53. Conf. 57.
54. Conf. 3; cf. 5, 33.
55. Conf. 12.
56. Conf. 34.
57. Conf. 56; Letter 5, 6.
58. Conf. 23.
59. Conf. 40.
60. Conf. 48.
61. Conf. 38.
62. Conf. 35.
63. Conf. 38, 39.
64. Letter 21.
65. Conf. 51.

66. Conf. 43.
67. Letter 1.
68. 1999, 86.
69. Conf. 16, 33.
70. Conf. 43, Letter 10.
71. Conf. 25, 46.
72. Conf. 20.
73. 17 [2x], 20, 21, 23, 24, 25, 29.
74. Conf. 17.
75. Conf. 35.
76. Conf. 45.
77. Conf. 42.
78. Hanson 1989, 33.
79. Conf. 45.
80. Hanson 1989, 33.
81. Hanson 1989, 5.
82. Conf. 40.
83. Conf. 34.
84. Conf. 34.
85. Conf. 55.
86. Conf. 55.
87. Conf. 37.
88. Conf. 59.
89. Letter 17.
90. Conf. 59.
91. 1989, 40.
92. 1989, 43; cf. Fletcher 1999, 86.
93. 1970, 206.
94. 1995, 283 n. 122; cf. Adomnán i.22.
95. 2004, 206 ff.
96. cf. i.2, 14, 29, 32, 35; ii. 4, 14, 43; iii.5, 8, 24.
97. 1981, 99–100.
98. Sharpe 1995, 57.
99. 1981, 100.
100. Picard 1981, 92.
101. 1981, 92–93.
102. ii.1.
103. ii.12.
104. ii.19.
105. ii.32.
106. ii.2.

107. ii.10.
108. ii.22.
109. ii.27.
110. ii.28.
111. ii.41.
112. 1981, 94.
113. iii.1.
114. iii.2.
115. iii.18.
116. iii.8.
117. iii.13.
118. 1981, 93.
119. iii.6, 13.
120. iii.8.
121. ii.24.
122. ii.16.
123. 1995, 334 n. 287.
124. i.37.
125. ii.11.
126. ii.32.
127. ii.34.
128. iii.22.
129. iii.23.
130. Columba 1999.
131. O'Loughlin 1999, 525 n. 32.
132. 1999, 332.
133. Moore 2005, 2.
134. see p. 8.
135. 1989, 103.
136. 1989, 104.
137. 1969, 84 ff., 95 f., 106 ff.
138. Jonas 9.
139. 36.
140. 9.
141. 11.
142. 34.
143. 53.
144. 56.
145. Bullough 1997, 21.
146. 11.
147. 25, 30.

148. 15, 55.
149. 9.
150. 9.
151. Riché 1981, 63.
152. Ó Fiaich 1989, 107.
153. Riché 1981, 68–69.
154. Jonas 9.
155. 12, cf. 14.
156. 16.
157. Hughes 1966, 59.
158. Bieler 1963, 32; cf. Davies 1999, 40.
159. Rule for Monks 10.
160. 1989, 109.
161. 11; emphasis added.
162. Ó Fiaich 1989, 109–110.
163. 1981, 68.
164. Hughes 1966, 59–62.
165. 1966, 59–62.
166. Bullough 1997, 12.
167. Letter IV.
168. 6.
169. 57.
170. 43.
171. 48.
172. 14.
173. 20.
174. 56.
175. 14, 18, 28, 45, 46, 54.
176. 14.
177. 23, 24.
178. 22, 41.
179. 20.
180. 46.
181. 16.
182. 19.
183. 42.
184. 47.
185. 38.
186. 47.
187. 49.
188. 39.

189. 41.
190. 40.
191. 39, 40, 41, 46.
192. 53.
193. 14.
194. 8.
195. 29.
196. Sermon 5.
197. 1970, 219.
198. It has been popular in Evangelical circles to dichotomize the Celtic and Roman branches of the church and to bemoan the loss of the Celtic church after the Synod of Whitby in 664 (e.g., Hunter 2000, 38ff.). Sharpe, however, notes that "It has become a common misconception in Great Britain that the Synod of Whitby in 664 meant the end of 'the Celtic church', an idea which is meaningless to anyone better versed in the Irish sources" (1995, 96); he then traces the history of such popular views (1995, 96–99; cf. Fletcher 1999, 92). Columbanus, most certainly, considered himself a staunch defender of the Roman Catholic faith (cf. Riché 1981, 66; de Paor 1993, 141; Bieler 1965, 85–86). For a helpful defense of a softer sense of Celtic spirituality see Davies (1999, 7–12). (1981, 76, 80).
199. Riché 1981, 65.
200. 1999, 12.
201. 1 Cor. 7:25 ff.
202. 1981, 66–67.
203. Moore, T. M. 2005. Poetry as spiritual discipline: Theme, structure, and focus in *Altus Prosator. Ars Poetica.* Available online http://www.pfm.org; accessed March 15, 2006. (Moore 2005)
204. Sermon 8

Bibliography

Adomnán of Iona. 1995. *Life of St. Columba.* Translated by Richard Sharpe. New York: Penguin Books.

Bede. 1994. *The ecclesiastical history of the English people.* Oxford World's Classics. Edited by Judith McClure and Roger Collins. Oxford: Oxford University Press.

Bieler, Ludwig. 1963. *Ireland: Harbinger of the Middle Ages*. London: Oxford University Press.

Brown, Peter. 2003. *The rise of Western Christendom*. 2nd ed. Malden, MA: Blackwell Publishing.

Bruce, James. 2004. *Prophecy, miracles, angels, and heavenly light: The eschatology, pneumatology, and missiology of Adomnán's Life of St. Columba*. Waynesboro, GA: Paternoster.

Bullough, Donald. 1997. The career of Columbanus. In *Columbanus: Studies on the Latin writings*, ed. Michael Lapidge, 1–28. Woodbridge, Suffolk, UK: Boydell Press.

Chadwick, Nora. 1970. *The Celts*. New York: Penguin Books.

Columba. 1999. The High First-Sower. In *Celtic spirituality*, trans. Thomas O'Loughlin, 405–410. New York: Paulist Press.

Columbanus. 1970. *Sancti Columbani opera*. Translated and edited by G. S. M. Walker. Dublin: Dublin Institute for Advanced Studies.

———. 1999. Rule for monks. In *Celtic spirituality*, ed. and trans. Oliver Davies, 246–256. New York: Paulist Press.

———. 1999. Sermons. In *Celtic spirituality*, ed. and trans. Oliver Davies, 353–362. New York: Paulist Press.

Davies, Oliver, ed. and trans. 1999. *Celtic spirituality*. The Classics of Western Spirituality. New York: Paulist Press.

de Paor, Liam. 1993. *St. Patrick's world: The Christian culture of Ireland's apostolic age*. Notre Dame: University of Notre Dame Press.

Fletcher, Richard. 1999. *The barbarian conversion: From paganism to Christianity*. Paperback ed. Berkeley: University of California Press.

Fritze, Wolfgang H. 1969. *Universalis gentium confessio*: Formeln, Träger und Wege universalmissionarischen Denkens im 7. Jahrhudert, *Frühmittelalterliche Studien* 3: 78–130.

Hanson, R. P. C. 1989. The mission of St. Patrick. In *An introduction to Celtic Christianity*, ed. James P. Mackey, 22–44. Edinburgh: T&T Clark.

Hughes, Kathleen. 1966. *The Church in early Irish society.* Ithaca, NY: Cornell University Press.

Hunter, George G., III. 2000. *The Celtic way of evangelism: How Christianity can reach the West again.* Nashville: Abingdon.

Jonas. 1897. *The life of St. Columban.* Medieval Source Book, Vol. 2, No. 7, ed. Dana C. Munro. Philadelphia: University of Pennsylvania. Available online http://www.fordham.edu/halsall/basis/columban.html; accessed December 31, 2005.

Lehane, Brendan. 1968. *The quest of three abbot: The golden age of Celtic Christianity.* Hudson, NY: Lindisfarne Press.

Murichú. 1993. Murichú's Life of St. Patrick. In *St. Patrick's world: The Christian culture of Ireland's apostolic age*, ed. and trans., Liam de Paor, 175–197. Notre Dame: University of Notre Dame Press.

Ó Fiaich, Tomás. 1989. Irish monks on the Continent. In *An introduction to Celtic Christianity*, ed. James P. Mackey, 101–139. Edinburgh: T&T Clark.

O'Loughlin, Thomas. 1999. Hagiography: The Patrick tradition. In *Celtic spirituality*, ed. Oliver Davies, 27–31. New York: Paulist Press.

———, trans. 1999. The High First-Sower. In *Celtic spirituality*, trans. Thomas O'Loughlin, 405–410, 524–528. New York: Paulist Press.

Patrick. 1999. [Confession.] Patrick's declaration of the great works of God. In *Celtic spirituality*, trans. Thomas O'Loughlin, 67–83. New York: Paulist Press.

———.1999. Letter to the soldiers of Coroticus. In *Celtic Spirituality*, trans. Oliver Davies, 84–89. New York: Paulist Press.

Picard, Jean Michel. 1981. The marvellous in Irish and continental saints' Lives of the Merovingian period. In *Columbanus and Merovingian monasticism*, eds. H. B. Clarke and Mary Brennan, 91–104. British Archaeological Reports International Series, 113. Oxford: B.A.R.

Prinz, Friedrich. 1981. Columbanus, the Frankish nobility and the territories east of the Rhine. In *Columbanus and Merovingian monasticism*, eds. H. B. Clarke and Mary Brennan, 73–90. British Archaeological Reports International Series, 113. Oxford: B.A.R.

Prosper of Acquitaine. 1993. Chronicle. In *St. Patrick's world: The Christian culture of Ireland's apostolic age*, ed. and trans. Liam de Paor, 72–87. Notre Dame: University of Notre Dame Press.

Riché, Pierre. 1981. Columbanus, his followers and the Merovingian Church. In *Columbanus and Merovingian monasticism*, eds. H. B. Clarke and Mary Brennan, 59–72. British Archaeological Reports International Series, 113. Oxford: B.A.R.

Sharpe, Richard. 1995. Introduction. In *Life of St. Columba*. Adomnán of Iona, 1–99. New York: Penguin Books.

Stevenson, Jane. 1999. *Altus Prosator*. *Celtica* 23:326–368. [Available online http://www.celt.dias.ie/publications/celtica/c23/c23–326.pdf; accessed March 14, 2006]

Strabo. 1988. *The Geography of Strabo*. Loeb Classical Library. Translated by Horace Leonard Jones. Cambridge, MA: Harvard University Press.

Tírechán. 1993. Bishop Tírechán's account of St. Patrick's journey. In *St. Patrick's world: The Christian culture of Ireland's apostolic age*, ed. and trans., Liam de Paor, 154–174. Notre Dame: University of Notre Dame Press.

Chapter Fifteen

Ministry in the Context of Suffering and Trauma in Southern Sudan

Enoch Wan and Karen Fancher

The country of Sudan is at the crossroads of North and South Africa. It is also the center of the conflict between those who seek to promote and impose Islam, and the Christians and animists who have resisted this pressure. Thus, it is a strategic field of ministry with global implications.

Southern Sudan has experienced incredible devastation during the past twenty-one years of civil war, instability and oppression. Millions of men, women and children have been traumatized. Children under the age of twenty have grown up only knowing the context of war. With the recent signing of the Peace Agreement in Nairobi in January of 2005, tentative peace has been achieved between the Islamic government of the North and the Sudan People's Liberation Army of the South. This opens the door of opportunity for missionaries to have access to people and places in Southern Sudan that were otherwise virtually isolated during the war.

In light of this opportunity, it is vital for missiologists to carefully discern which approaches will be the most effective for ministry in a region that has experienced suffering and trauma of immense proportions.

The purpose of this study is to report about and describe the situation in Southern Sudan, where people have experienced long-term instability and trauma, and to derive missiological implications for Christian ministry. This paper is based upon three presuppositions:

Contextually, it is imperative that Christian workers recognize that those who have experienced long-term trauma have unique needs that should be acknowledged and addressed accordingly.

Strategically, a primary role of missionaries is to prepare local churches and ministry leaders to serve in ways that are sensitive to the unique needs of those who have experienced suffering and trauma.

Longitudinally, Christian leaders should strive to address the core issues of those who have experienced suffering and trauma, in order to establish a foundation for the health and vitality of the church of the next generation in Southern Sudan.

The data for this study were collected by means of archival research and ethnographic interviews. The fieldwork was conducted in trips to Southern Sudan on three occasions to interview individuals who had experienced war-related trauma.

Definition of Key Terms

For the sake of clarity, several key terms are defined below:

Suffering. In this paper, "suffering" refers to enduring physical or emotional pain, discomfort or tribulation as a result of violence, injustice, physical ailments, death of and/or separation from loved ones, and/or lack of basic resources necessary to sustain life. Extreme suffering can result in trauma.

War-related trauma. "War-related trauma" is the emotional shock that is experienced as a result of war; including the experiences and fear of bombings, attacks, rapes, capture and other acts of violence. War-related trauma can also result from a sustained sense of uncertainty, and of being violated. This likely includes helplessness due to economic disruption, displacement, hunger, death of loved ones or lack of knowledge as to their location or well-being, or disruption of social structures such as jobs and schools. In a war, the trauma can be multifaceted and sustained over a long period of time.

Thus, war related trauma is a unique phenomenon.

Holistic Ministry. "Ministry" is the work of the followers of Jesus Christ, his church, to demonstrate the love and truth of God, by the enabling power of the Holy Spirit. Ministry takes place as people allow God to use them to fulfill his purposes, through his Spirit and for his glory. "Holistic ministry" is a comprehensive approach in which those ministering embrace the foundational premise that human beings are multi-faceted and integrated beings; with physical, psychological, spiritual, and social dimensions. Holistic ministry addresses each of these dimensions at both personal and societal levels.

Spiritual and Emotional Healing. "Spiritual and emotional healing" is healing that includes both spiritual and psychological dimensions. Spiritually, healing refers to the restoration of relationship with God. This is evidenced when one is able to trust in God's goodness, faithfulness, compassion and sovereignty, in and beyond the distressing situation that one is experiencing. Psychologically, healing is indicated by a return to the level of functional performance in daily tasks and relational roles that is on par with, or stronger than, levels before experiencing the traumatic event.

In both of these definitions, healing does not imply the absence of pain, memories and trials in daily life. It is the ability to cope with the pain and trials in a way that allows one to continue to follow one's convictions, and to be engaged with and invest in family and community in meaningful ways. A renewed sense of hope and purpose are evidence that one has experienced healing.

Contemporary History and Socio-Cultural Profile

Civil War. Geographically, Sudan is the largest country in Africa. It has experienced civil war since it gained independence in 1956. The last phase of the conflict began in 1983. A comprehensive peace agreement was signed in Nairobi Kenya in January of 2005, bringing the civil war officially to an end. However, the peace is fragile, and there are still outbreaks of violence and instability. The International Rescue Committee described the conflict that fueled the war in this way:

> The conflict [. . .] is primarily between the government in Khartoum, dominated by an Arab, Islamic identity, and the peoples of the South and periphery, largely of African origin. However, the war has also involved internecine conflict among myriad rebel factions, government-aligned militias and tribal groups. The complex cultural factors fueling the conflict— religion, ethnicity, political ambitions, and colonial history—are further complicated by the struggle for control over the country's vast natural resources—oil, fertile land and water—located primarily in the south.[1]

Impact of the War. Sudan's civil war was the longest ongoing civil war in the world. Southern Sudan experienced incredible devastation and many atrocities were committed against civilians. One result of the conflict is that a generation of young people has grown up knowing only the context of instability and violence. During the war, the Sudanese government in the north acquired helicopter gun ships and advanced weaponry, which were used against both the Sudan People's Liberation Army[2] (henceforth referred to as SPLA) and civilians in the south. Villages were ravaged and looted, cattle stolen or killed, crops burned, women raped and mutilated, men massacred, and women and children forced into slavery. Many bombing raids targeted civilian populations, including schools, churches and hospitals. It is estimated that more than 1.5 million people were killed in Southern Sudan between 1955 and 1973; an additional 2 million were killed and more than 4 million people were displaced from 1983 to 2005. The U.S. Committee for Refugees provides some of the following statistics:

At least one out of every five Southern Sudanese died during the civil war.

Nearly 5.5 million Sudanese were uprooted at the end of 2003, including nearly 5 million internally displaced. (This is approximately 80% of the population.)

Nearly 600,000 Southern Sudanese have fled Sudan and are now refugees in other countries.[3]

Ideology of the Southern Resistance. In the foreword to *War and Faith in Sudan*, Francis Deng differentiates between the two phases of the civil war. The first phase erupted in 1955 and continued until 1972. According to Deng, this was a battle for separatism, and in the end the South was granted limited autonomy. In 1983, the Northern government formally broke that agreement and sought to impose *Sharia* law in Southern Sudan. In this second phase of the war, the goal of the South in fighting against the North seemed not necessarily secession, but rather equal rights. Francis Deng states:

> While the first was separatist, the declared objective of the second, championed by the Sudan People's Liberation Movement and Army (SPLA/M), was and continues to be the restructuring of the country to be free from discrimination on the basis of race, ethnicity, religion or culture.[4]

Thus, a primary goal of the people of Southern Sudan is to be a catalyst for change in the very structure of the government and society. This war of ideologies will continue long after the last weapon is laid down.

Instability Caused by Internal Factors

Tension in the Darfur Region. According to Deng, the focus on restructuring, equal rights and protection gained support from some in the North, especially in the non-Arab regions. The Nuba of Southern Kordofan and the Ingassana of Southern Blue Nile were some of the first to join the SPLA/M in the struggle. In 1991 a group of Darfurians staged a rebellion. They were ruthlessly defeated by the Sudanese government armed forces. Twelve years later, two non-Arab groups in Darfur—the Justice and Equality Movement (JEM)[5] and the Sudan Liberation Movement and Army (SLM/A)[6]—began another rebellion. The current conflict and suffering in the Darfur region are the consequence of this rebellion. The Sudanese government reacted against the rebellion with a strong show of force, and provided support for the *Janjaweed*, or militias. The *Janjaweed* have terrorized the region: burning and pillaging villages, and raping and killing civilians. Since 2003, the ongoing genocide in Western Sudan (Darfur) has resulted in the slaughter of up to 300,000 in just the past 3 years. No one knows the exact numbers, but the devastation is immense. Thousands of people each week continue to die as a result of this crisis.[7] This further foments mistrust of the Northern Government.

Tribal Divisions. Tribal divisions provide additional challenges for missionary work in Southern Sudan. Many tribes still have enmity and distrust of one another, and violent attacks erupt on occasion. In general, the lack of infrastructure and myriad tensions in the south opened doors for violence of southerners against southerners. The "2005 UN and Partners Work Plan for Sudan" states,

> Localized conflict within Southern Sudan remains a concern. Competition for resources, sometimes violent, has been exacerbated by local political opportunism and the absence of a common enemy. Significant security threats remain and violence against civilians continues too frequently with impunity. Efforts to promote South-South dialogue have begun with the aim of offering wider participation in developing governance structures in Southern Sudan.[8]

Denominational Divisions. In addition, there is division among Christian denominations. After the British left Sudan, certain regions were designated to specific religious orders (e.g., Catholic, Episcopalian, Presbyterian, etc.) If a ministry from one denomination enters an area without the blessing of those already there, tensions may rise.

Economic Concerns. Another internal factor is the economic situation in Southern Sudan. Unfortunately, the Comprehensive Peace Agreement has not brought an end to the suffering and violence. Insecurity in the south and east continues. Many communities in the south still lack food and water. BBC news reports that up to six million people have been displaced from Southern Sudan and will be moving back in the near future. Many were displaced in neighboring countries, or in camps within Sudan itself. As masses of people start to move back to the South, there is little infrastructure in place to support them. Many are attacked and robbed by bandits on the routes of return. Some return to Khartoum after finding the situation in the South still too difficult.[9]

The division of Sudan's oil reserves is a critical concern. Under the agreement, these reserves are supposed to be equally shared between the North and the South. According to Sudan analyst Peter Moszynski, the government of the South is getting far less oil revenue than it had expected, due to disputes over whether some oil wells are in the territory of the North or the South.

In a report on October 4, 2005, the U.N. Integrated Regional Information Networks stated that malnutrition levels in Southern Sudan were alarmingly high. Roger Persichino, an Action Against Hunger officer, said that the prevalence of malnutrition was comparable to what we have in Niger or in Darfur. Although the overall rate of malnutrition in Southern Sudan is similar to Niger at approximately 20.7%, it is more acute in Upper Nile and Bahr-el-Ghazal, where rates have reached 29% and 64% respectively. Action Against Hunger reported that people have gotten used to the malnutrition in this area, and are focusing on development rather than alleviating the nutritional crisis. Many of the international relief funds allocated for Sudan are getting earmarked for Darfur, at times to the neglect of the south. In addition, many governments have not yet fulfilled pledges of financial assistance promised through the U.N. Often the difficulty of access to outlying areas exacerbates the problem.[10]

Instability Caused by External Factors. The instability in Southern Sudan has been augmented by the terrorism of the Lord's Resistance Army, a cultish group, which originated in Uganda and has ravaged through Southern Sudan and the Congo. The LRA has terrorized and mutilated civilians, kidnapping children and forcing them into being child soldiers or concubines. Joseph Koney is a spirit medium who has led the cultish group for the past 19 years, with no clear political goal.[11] The LRA has disrupted resettlement and relief operations in Southern Sudan. During the civil war, the LRA was backed by the Sudanese government to bring terror to the south. Many southerners believe that the northern government has continued to support the LRA.[12] Negotiations are currently underway to disarm the LRA, and there is hope that this entity, which has contributed to the suffering and trauma of civilians in southern Sudan, will soon be abated.

Ministry Considerations in the Context of Suffering and Trauma

When ministering in Southern Sudan, the impact of trauma must be addressed. It is important to examine how people process and respond to traumatic experiences, and the impact of the trauma upon their communities and social relationships. Such an understanding is essential in order to accurately assess and effectively respond to the needs.

Theological Understandings. Each person's theological constructs are impacted by life experiences. It is essential to seek insight into the influence of the experience of trauma on how believers in Southern Sudan perceive God, his purposes and their relationship with him. For example, how might the experiences of an orphan of war influence his understanding of the attributes of God? Is God perceived by such a child as a distant, powerless, unmerciful and angry deity? Individuals impacted by trauma may have difficulty appreciating their personal worth in God's sight. After all, if God really cared for them, would he allow such a thing to happen?

Another important theological concept to address is justice. How do God's justice and mercy work in harmony? Implicit in this theological tension is also the concept of hope. What is the foundation and focus of hope for Christians? How is that concept lived out practically in the midst of conflict and violence? The challenge and mandate for Christian workers in Southern Sudan is to support believers in the process of developing a theology that allows them to understand and apply Scriptural truth in the context of their life circumstances. This is especially important for those who have experienced trauma.

Social Dimensions. Trauma takes place within a social context affecting families and communities. Social issues repeatedly surfaced during the interviews of traumatized individuals from Southern Sudan.

1. Separation and Displacement. Approximately 20 women were interviewed during a visit to Yei, Sudan in December of 2004. One of the authors of this study listened to their concerns and prayed with them. The devastating reality of having husbands absent for years without knowing whether they were dead or alive resulted in the victims' poverty, uncertainty, grief and fear. Some felt abandoned and wondered if their husbands would ever return. One woman, whose husband was a soldier, shared that their infant child died while her husband was off fighting. Before the death of the child, they had maintained consistent contact while he was away. Since the death of the child, he had not come home or contacted her at all. The trauma of the death of her child and her uncertainty in the midst of war was compounded by relational difficulties with her husband. Other women shared that many of the young people had little sense of hope and purpose, and were often getting drunk or "messing" around. This was slang way of saying that they were being sexually promiscuous, even though they knew about the danger of HIV/AIDS.

2. Forgiveness. Others demonstrated a skewed understanding of forgiveness. One woman told the story of her drunken brother attacking her with sticks. She was seriously wounded and hospitalized for some time. As a Christian, she had been taught that she needed to forgive him. To her, this meant that she should not take action against her brother or report him to the police, even though he continued to stalk and threaten her. Learned helplessness, addictions and anti-social behavior were frequent themes in the interviews, and seemed to often be evidenced in those who had not been able to cope with the impact of war-related trauma.

3. Violence. The experience of Grace (not her real name), illustrates the severity of the concerns within the societal structure. Grace came to our leadership training conference, and told us the story of losing her parents and being given to a man as his wife when she was 14 years old. Her husband mistreated and abused her. Soon she became pregnant. After her baby boy was born, she focused all of her attention on him, and that brought her joy for a time. However, while still an infant, her little son died. Grace suffered an emotional breakdown, and ran into the bush wanting to commit suicide. She was rescued by relatives, who shielded her from her cruel husband for several months. As she was walking to the conference, her husband saw her, beat her and stripped her naked, leaving her in the street. A western woman found her, clothed her, and brought her to the church compound. The multiple traumas of losing parents, being abused, facing the death of a child, and living in fear of her husband, together form an overwhelming cycle of misery that a sixteen-year-old woman could not escape from or bear on her own.

Psychological Dimensions. Trauma has a psychological impact, which is often manifested in the form of depression, social isolation, anger outbursts, hyper-vigilance, irrational behavior, nightmares, agitation, difficulty in concentrating, racing thoughts, emotional numbness, flashbacks, etc. Psychological damage may result in increased fatigue, sleep difficulty, dramatic changes in appetite, severe headaches, muscle ache, etc. As indicated above, social relationships may become unstable as a result.

Child victims of trauma often have more difficulty forming healthy attachments to others, and have a lowered sense of personal worth or self-esteem. There can be a learned helplessness that results and a compulsion to take risks. Others may dissociate from the trauma and avoid anything that may remind them of the traumatic event.

Obviously, these psychological impairments hinder normal social relationships and proper functioning in a community.

Cultural Dimensions. Culture impacts the way people perceive, experience and process trauma, and consequently their conceptualization of God. As missionaries, we must not assume that we understand either what is traumatic to an individual, or the most effective way for that person to process the trauma. Our goal should be to facilitate biblically and culturally appropriate forms of expression and to be aware of cultural norms by asking questions such as these:

- Is there a sense of shame involved in expressing grief or pain, and is it acceptable to cry in public?
- Is it culturally appropriate to talk about traumatic personal experiences? If so, in what social contexts and to whom?
- Are there rites and rituals for celebration and mourning within the cultural context?

It is also important to allow for and recognize differences between individuals of the same culture and background. Missionaries must use caution, as shame and social ostracism can compound the traumatic experience. Secondary consequences of the trauma—for example, being displaced and forced to live among members of another tribe whose language one does not speak well—can also add to the intensity of the traumatic experience. We cannot assume that what may invoke a crisis of faith, or cause a sense of being violated, will be the same in the cultural contexts of Southern Sudan and the USA.

Implications for Ministry. Having a grasp of how the social, psychological and cultural dimensions are impacted by traumatic experience is essential to the formulation of a ministry strategy which can bring hope and healing to victims. It is imperative to humbly learn of the host culture before we teach cross-culturally, especially when addressing the concerns of those who have experienced trauma. We must listen intently, so that we will be sensitive and respond to their questions and concerns.

If we present theological concepts outside of the social, psychological and cultural frames of reference of the individual, false concepts of God may result. For example, if we are working with young Sudanese believers who have no foundational knowledge of God's holiness and justice, yet we insist that victims of atrocities of war should pray for and forgive those who persecute them, we could easily create confusion and the truth of God could be distorted. They may come to the conclusion that God treats evil lightly or that he does not care about their pain. The grace of God, which is the foundation for forgiveness, must be taught in the context of the justice of God.

Christian Understanding of Suffering and Trauma

Scriptural Examples of Suffering and Trauma. In order to consider how to respond to those who have experienced trauma, it is important to look at some of the biblical passages that provide a proper understanding of trauma and an appropriate Christian response to suffering. This paper does not allow for an exhaustive study; but does present a few passages and selected principles.

At the outset, we must acknowledge that the Scriptures reveal many different reasons why people suffer traumatic events. Four examples from the Bible are chosen as illustrations.

1. God's Sovereign Purposes Beyond our Comprehension. Our first example is Job. The Book of Job reminds us that our faith is not dependant upon our circumstances, but upon the knowledge and character of God. It also clearly demonstrates that both the righteous and the unjust will suffer in this world. We are taught in this book that there is a purpose to what we experience, and the ability to identify or understand that purpose may be beyond human comprehension. We are called to trust God's character and to be faithful to Him.

2. A Consequence of Rebellion. The second example is King Nebuchadnezzar, who suffered what seemed to be delusions and insanity due to his pride (Dan. 4:25–26). At times, suffering may be a result of rebellion against God, as evidenced in the life of this king.

3. That We May Become More Like Christ. Third, we see the example of Christ, who suffered because of his obedience to the Father's will and to fulfill His priestly role for our sake (Heb. 8–10). The character of Christ is evidenced in his suffering. As we remain faithful to God and seek to be humble in the difficult circumstances that we face, we can become more conformed to the image of Christ. Thus, we can be used more effectively by God for his purposes (Luke 24:46).

4. For the Sake of the Gospel. The final example is the apostle Paul, who suffered for the sake of the Gospel and his apostolic ministry (2 Cor. 11; Phil. 3:10).
The emphasis in Scripture has never been to avoid pain or to remove all discomfort. Rather, the goal is that God be made known and be glorified in our suffering, as we live in the light and hope of the eternal promises of our God.

Theological Foundations. Following are a few key theological concepts and Bible verses which are helpful for ministering to those in the midst of suffering and trauma.
God is attentive to our circumstances and to our cries to for his help. He has not forgotten us, and will execute his perfect judgment against the unjust (Ps. 92:12).

- Affliction can be a tool of God to remind us of our need for him, and to encourage us to turn from sin and to follow him (Ps. 119:67).
- God is true to his word and his righteous character (Ps. 119:75).
- God allows affliction, but he is also the one who blesses and restores (Ps. 107:41).
- God does not delight that we suffer, however, he does allow it for a greater purpose. Lamentations 3:31–33 says, "For men are not cast off by the Lord forever. Though he brings grief, he will show compassion, so great is his unfailing love, for he does not willingly bring affliction or grief to the children of men." The Book of Lamentations speaks of suffering and trauma, and exhorts us to hope in the Lord and to wait upon him.

Christian Response. In general, Christians in the West have been shielded from experiencing suffering and trauma on a regular basis, and consequently may have difficulty ministering to others in such situations. We must be humble learners, sensitive listeners, faithful servants and persistent intercessors. When we speak we must do so thoughtfully and prayerfully, and we must have a strong biblical understanding of suffering and be ready to provide a Christian response. Our goal is to gently support and assist believers to face suffering in godly way. As Christians, we are called to patient endurance, waiting for God's deliverance in due time. "Be joyful in hope, patient in affliction, and faithful in prayer" (Rom. 12:12). The following are some guidelines for a Christian response to suffering:

- We are called to rejoice if we suffer for the sake of Christ (1 Pet. 4:12–14, 16).
- We are called to be conformed to the image of Christ and to be used for his glory (Rom. 5:3).
- We are called to keep an eternal perspective (Rom. 8:18).
- We are called to speak out against injustice and on behalf of the helpless (Jer. 22:16).
- We are called to pray for those who persecute us (Matt. 5:44; Rom. 12:14).

Missiological Implications

Missiological implications are the thoughtful responses within the context of missionary service that may impact or alter the way the missionary endeavor is undertaken. Several missiologically derived implications are presented below.

Identifying Commonly Held Missionary Presuppositions. The first task of the missionary working in a context of suffering and trauma is to identify the presuppositions s/he brings to the ministry. Our presuppositions will affect our theology and the way that we respond to the suffering of others. The challenge is to step out of our cultural framework and emotional response, and continually seek a biblical model.

For example, some believers in Southern Sudan have been persecuted for their faith. At times soldiers from the Northern Army have tried to force people to deny their faith in Christ and convert to Islam. Those who refused faced the possibility of being tortured or killed. How do we as Christians respond to the reality of such persecution? A few common erroneous presuppositions are listed below.

1. "Something is very wrong if the church is facing persecution." Actually, the opposite is true. Persecution usually takes place when there is a vital Christian witness in a primarily non-Christian context. Persecution is biblically and historically normal in the emerging church. Horrific persecution may come to Christians, with justice apparently nowhere to be found. Yet, we should not be surprised when such circumstances arise. Christ has forewarned us (Matt. 24). Dr. Gupta (not his real name), is a Christian researcher on persecution of Christians. He has collected over 600 interviews of believers who had faced some kind of persecution for their faith in over sixty countries. The results of his study are noted in his article "Servants in the Crucible" as quoted below:

> Organizations have arisen globally that report, measure and intercede on behalf of the persecuted, often with the intent of eliminating persecution and punishing the persecutors. A biblically sound missiology and theology of suffering might lead to a different focus. Persecution is biblically and historically normative for the emerging Church; it cannot be avoided or eliminated. The task is to reduce persecution for secondary reasons. Believers in the midst of persecution, victorious in their walk with Christ, share many commonalities. Two of the most important issues are that they have claimed their freedom and they have lost their fear, as was noted earlier. Such components of faith are foundational to incarnating Christ within environments of persecution. [13]

Gupta challenges believers to be wise, not fearful. He also shares the concern that many believers are not persecuted for their faith in Christ and Christian testimony, but rather for secondary reasons such as associating with foreigners or receiving financial benefits from an outside source. He challenges missionaries that these secondary reasons for persecution must be eliminated.

2. "We shouldn't send people in until it is safe." Southern Sudan is still politically unstable and insecure. Many missionary organizations do not yet want to send missionaries into Southern

Sudan as they cannot assure their safety. Although caution and wisdom are traits to be lauded, especially when we are responsible for the well-being of others, we must always be convinced that our first goal is eternal, and that it is worth taking risks for sharing the good news of Jesus Christ. Missionaries must be willing to face the risks that they are asking others to take for the sake of the Gospel Gupta remarks,

> The nature of witness among the persecuted has the missionary asking seekers and new believers to place themselves and their families at risk for the sake of the gospel. Shared suffering validates both the message and the messenger. Asking others to place their lives at risk while the witness resides in relative safety undermines the validity of the testimony and calls into question the missionary's moral right to witness.

> Sending bodies need to be clear. They are sending their representatives out as "sheep among wolves." Missionary safety is important. Yet the interviews show that missionary safety should become secondary to the goal that all peoples hear and have the opportunity to respond to the gospel of Jesus Christ. Churches must recapture the biblical truth that positive responses to the gospel and persecution have always been biblical and historical partners. For millions of believers in the world, persecution is the norm. Persecution is neither sought nor avoided. Persecution just is.[14]

Many people in Southern Sudan have suffered at the hands of the Northern army, which represents a fundamentalist Muslim regime. Churches and schools have been burned, women raped and children captured as slaves.

3. *"They must be heroes of the faith if they have suffered at the hands of the Northern army."* Three strands of this presupposition, followed by clarification, are listed below. One implicit belief underlying this statement is that all Southerners are Christians. Another belief is that all who claim to be Christians truly are followers of Christ. The third belief is that all those who suffered were persecuted because of their Christian testimony.

A great number of people in the South are either animists or nominal Christians, although some Muslims also reside there. Many who say they are Christians do not understand the implications of the Gospel, but have made the decision that they do not want to be Muslims. As Southern Sudanese, they often associate themselves culturally with Christianity. All who suffer for their faith are not necessarily "heroes" who would want attention called to themselves, but rather are individuals who have been mistreated. There are some who refuse to deny Christ, even under extreme pressure, and maintain a faithful witness. These truly are heroes of the faith. Gupta challenges Christians to be very careful when reporting persecution for the Christian faith. For example, in Southern Sudan many people are persecuted for racial, economic or political reasons. Gupta asserts that when we over-report persecution for Christian testimony, we lose credibility and minimize the impact of the lives and testimonies of those who truly suffer for their Christian faith.

Socio-Cultural Context of Ministry

Growth of the Church. In the midst of incredible suffering, there is also reason for hope. Southern Sudan is comprised mostly of people of black African descent. A large number of the tribal people in Southern Sudan are animists and practice the tribal religions of their ancestors. However, there is a strong Christian influence. In the midst of the turmoil, numerous people are professing faith in Christ daily. Some do so as a cultural alliance and a reaction against the fundamentalist Muslim government of the North, without truly understanding the lordship of Christ. Others sincerely submit their lives to Christ in faith and trust Him as their Savior.

The challenge for these believers is the lack of resources, such as Bible and Christian literature, available for their Christian growth and maturity. When traveling in Sudan, one of the authors of this study had the privilege of meeting many outstanding Christian men and women who preached the gospel wherever they went. Yet, some did not possess their own copy of the Word of God. These men and women must be equipped to apply biblical truths to the present realities. It is the authors' firm conviction that the church is uniquely positioned to become an agent of healing and hope to those who have been traumatized in Southern Sudan. As God works to restore lives, many doors for the Gospel may open. However, there must be intentional equipping of leaders who can then walk with others, in order for this function of the church to be fulfilled.

The socio-cultural factors mentioned previously also have implications for ministry. Missionaries must be prepared to speak to issues that are indicative of the daily experiences of those whom they serve. They must show that the Word of God is relevant to people's lives in all circumstances. Issues such as grief, comfort, prayer, repentance, and forgiveness must be addressed in the context of families in crisis: e.g. a father has been gone for three years, a daughter was taken as a slave, a son is drinking and "messing around," or a husband is having an affair with a woman who has AIDS. Violence in the context of the homes should be an issue that the church addresses. It would be more effective if the missionaries could help present or facilitate biblical teaching concerning these issues, and then let the local Christian community determine how those will be applied in their context. Tribal and denominational divisions must also be addressed so that the church can truly be the vehicle for inter-personal healing and unity. Since so many people in Southern Sudan have lost their primary support system or sense of community, there is a tremendous opportunity for the church body to step up and fulfill this role.

Animism and Folk Religion. In Southern Sudan, there is a strong influence of animism and folk religion. Paul Heibert has identified the difference between formal religion and folk religion in the following manner:

> Formal religion deals with the questions of ultimate origin, purpose and destiny of the universe, society and self. Folk religion deals with meaning in this life and the problem of death, well-being in this life and the problem of misfortunes, knowledge to decide and the problem of the unknown, and righteousness and justice and the problem of evil and injustice.[15]

Heibert contends that Christian missionaries often present the answers to questions of origin and ultimate destiny, while leaving adherents to folk religion with little or no answers to the problems of daily life and misfortune. Thus, they often maintain the practices of their folk religion under the umbrella of nominal Christianity.

The challenge for missionaries working with individuals who practice animism or come from animistic backgrounds will be to discern what aspects of African culture can be expressed in genuine Christian worship and what elements cannot. At the same time, missionaries must develop strategies to answer the questions posed by practitioners of African traditional religion, and to show that YHWH is involved in our day-to-day struggles and activities. Discernment in contextualization will require careful study of the subtleties of symbols and rituals and the meanings they convey.

The Christian missionary must demonstrate that Christian faith is not just relevant for eternal truth, but gives us principles by which we can cope with the practicality and difficulties of life, especially in the midst of trauma. Failing to address these issues could leave the door wide open for syncretism.

Contextualization. It is imperative that local believers be a part of the process in determining how biblical truths are to be applied in the homes and communities. They should be given the task to process application of biblical truths, such as how they should respond to Northern soldiers who come into their villages now that the war is over. As the Scriptures are presented and explained, they should be invited to take up the task of theologizing for themselves in their own context.

Teaching on grief should also take place within the cultural context. Only biblical principles should be shared, allowing the community to apply them as deemed appropriate. Children should not only be provided with food, clothing and opportunities to learn, but the church should also seek to provide opportunities for children of war to form healthy attachments with other members of the church body and community. Core issues such as fear, anger, hopelessness and worthlessness must be addressed over time in the context of a caring community.

A balanced understanding of a temporal and fallen world and eternal hope in Christ should be presented. Many believers in Southern Sudan have much more of an eternal perspective than Christians in the West. In one church service in Southern Sudan the congregation was singing "obi-obi-la": "we are going to our heavenly home." Even in the midst of extreme difficulty, they could celebrate the reality of their salvation and eternal hope.

The context of war and its spiritual applications must also be addressed. A unique ministry task is to help believers separate the political concerns from the spiritual Although they may greatly impact one another, it is important to keep them distinct. Many in the SPLA stated that they were fighting for the freedom to practice the Christian faith, and numerous Southern soldiers became Christians. The South has fought for religious freedom and to opt out from being under the *Sharia* law. Although the Lord is actively working in and through governments and authorities, his kingdom is not of this world and our hope is not based upon these structures. Christians must be taught to focus primarily on building the eternal Kingdom of God, and to truly pray for those who persecute them.

The Relationship of Missionaries to the Community

Above all, missionaries must model total commitment to the cause of Christ as a response of their love for him. The love of Christ must be demonstrated naturally in words and deeds. Missionaries are called to serve with humility and in unity; they are to learn from, listen to, and serve with local people at individual and tribal levels.

Mading Ngor Akec Kual, in an article entitled, "NGOs in Southern Sudan: Polluting or Solving our Woes," challenges NGOs that have workers living in comfort and enjoying many amenities, as they serve among local people in abject poverty[16]. It is often difficult for nationals to have access to some NGO workers, who live and work behind barricades and employ unfriendly watchmen. Many Sudanese observe that NGOs operate as businesses, with many of the funds going to serve the foreign workers, and little being accomplished on the ground. Other nationals feel used or dishonored in the way missionaries speak about them to their agencies or supporters in their countries of origin. Teaching is often not done in a culturally sensitive manner. The charges of Kuai's article are serious and severe, and expose areas of concern that need to be addressed by the missionary community. Jok Gai states, "It has been common knowledge that NGOs evacuate their staff members once they sensed danger and leave the innocent civilians to the mercy of the enemy only to reappear later claiming to help. How will they help those who died when they had evacuated?"[17]

The underlying message of these comments is that those we serve must know that we identify with them and that we deeply care about them. Our goal should be to invest in people, not just in projects. Empowerment and leadership development are essential. Most of all, we must be willing to face hardship alongside our Sudanese brothers and sisters in Christ, loving them as Christ loved us.

Holistic Approach to Ministry

As we have examined some of the social, psychological, physiological, and spiritual aspects of suffering and trauma, it seems clear that ministry in this context must be holistic. As biblical truths are being presented in word and story, tangible expressions of care must be shown to those who have experienced suffering and trauma. Physical needs must be attended to as much as possible and consistent support structures, such as Sunday school meetings, schools, prayer groups etc, should be put in place. Practical skills such as conflict resolution and trade skills should be taught to help people and community both to function and survive.

Social Concerns. The church is called to be the agent of reconciliation; first to God, and then to others. Strategies to bring tribal reconciliation and healing to families should be developed. Homes for children of war may be established, providing supportive and healing relationships. Some social concerns are not consequences of the war, but rather due to tribal traditions. It is important that these are addressed by the church as well. For example, beating and mistreating one's wife is a common and acceptable practice in many tribes. It will be most effective if these issues are addressed by male church leaders, who exhibit sensitivity and wisdom, allowing the church to once again study the Scriptures and establish guidelines for Christian family life. Church leaders will also need to seek ways to provide and support widows and orphans (Jas 1:27).

Emotional Concerns. In Southern Sudan, there are very few trained counselors or resources for people who have experienced trauma. Therefore, the church has an opportunity, and an obligation, to provide supportive and consistent relationships for those who are experiencing trauma. It would be helpful for churches to teach about the physiological and emotional responses to trauma, so that people are not ostracized or being judged as "crazy" when they exhibit trauma symptoms. Individuals who are having physiological symptoms from trauma (e.g. such as racing mind or heart, sleep difficulty, etc.) can be taught ways to relax and relieve stress without prolonged periods of anxiety. Safe relationships in which to share, cry as appropriate, or just learn to reconnect are vital. Cultural expressions such as dance, song and drawing may also be beneficial in expressing emotion for healing. Small prayer groups and committed lay people can make a significant difference in providing hope, stability and comfort. Teaching on the character of God, his justice, grief, comfort, forgiveness and hope are important as well.

Physical Concerns. There are many physical needs for medication, food, clean water and health care in Southern Sudan. The lack of infrastructure has prevented development of community resources. Tangible resources, such as seeds to plant crops or micro-finance loans to help people reestablish their lives after all of the cattle have died or been stolen, will not only save lives, but will help the church to be seen as relevant to the needs of the community. With the coming peace, these forms of assistance should begin to occur on a large scale. Concern must be taken that people are empowered and given a sense of control, rather than fostering dependence on others.

Spiritual Concerns. The most effective way to teach theological truths is in the ongoing process of discipleship and nurturing relationships. Spiritual concepts should be developed within the framework of the questions and the concerns of daily life. Teaching should be presented in a sequential manner, thus gaps in understanding can be more effectively avoided. Discipleship, in this context, must be focused on helping people to know God in the midst of difficult circumstances. Systematic teaching of spiritual truths allows for a consistent framework within which people can experience freedom, learn to respond to God, and deal to with emotions such as anger, bitterness, pain and despair.

A true and dynamic relationship with God is the ultimate goal of ministry. As people understand that they are loved and created for a purpose, hope can begin to be restored. Realizing that God will walk with them in every circumstance of life—drawing them to himself, and molding and using them for his eternal purposes and glory—is the most healing reality a person can experience. We are called to be the hands and feet of Jesus to others. Most importantly, we must show them his scarred hands and let them find comfort in his presence; knowing that he loves them, he identifies with their suffering, and he gives hope beyond the pain of this world—eternal life in his wonderful presence. Propositional truth can bring understanding, but hope and healing are realized in a personal transforming relationship with our living Lord.

Conclusion

God is opening new doors for Christian ministry in Southern Sudan. The church is at a key stage in its development, and poised to be an instrument of healing and restoration. Western missionaries must be wise to ascertain when to step in and when to pull out. We must be sensitive to the unique needs of those who have undergone long-term suffering and trauma. Cultural sensitivity and allowing those we serve to be a part of the process of contextualization are imperative. Ministry in such a context is most effective if done holistically. The core concerns of those who have experienced suffering and trauma must be addressed. To do so successfully, missionaries need to first set aside their own cultural presuppositions. The incarnation of Christ must be our model and the Great Command of "loving God and neighbor" should be our motto when carrying out the Great Commission in the context of suffering and trauma.

Notes

1. *International Rescue Committee*, Dec. 2003. http://www.theirc.org/ 2nd_files/2nd-html.html> (Feb. 20, 2007).
2. The SPLA was formed in 1983 under the leadership of John Garang to oppose the imposition of *Sharia* law upon the citizens of Southern Sudan. It was the principle military force of the insurgency in the last phase of the civil war. The SPLM, or Sudan People's Liberation Movement, is the political arm of the SPLA. They are often referred to as one entity the SPLA/M. For more information on the SPLA/M see "Sudan People's Liberation Army," *Intelligence Resource Program*, updated Jan. 5, 2000. <http://www.fas.org/irp/world/para/spla.htm> (September 9, 2006).
3. "World Refugee Survey 2004 Country Report", *U.S. Committee for Refugees*, 2004.<http://www.refugees.org/countryreports.aspx/> (Sept. 22, 2006).
4. Gabriel Meyer, Foreword by Francis M. Deng. *War and Faith in Sudan*, (Grand Rapids, MI, 2005). ix.
5. JEM is a faction of the Sudanese Liberation Army (SLA) that is fighting the Government of Sudan military (GOS) and the *Janjaweed*, militia groups, whom the GOS has supported. Their goal is to demand socio-economic and political justice for the region of Darfur. For more information on the JEM and SLA/M, see *GlobalSecurity.org*, modified August 16, 2006, <http://www.globalsecurity.org/military/world/para/ darfur.htm/> (September 19, 2006).
6. The SLA/M was formerly known as the Darfur Liberation Front. They have no formal connection with the SPLA/M of the South. The SLA is led by Mini Arkoi Minawi, and states that its goal is to "create a united, democratic Sudan." The SLA is backed by Eritrea. For more information on the SLA, *Global Security.org*.
7. Russel Smith, "How Many Have Died in Darfur?" *BBC News*. February 16, 2005. <http://news.bbc.co.uk/1/hi/world/africa/4268733 .stm> (April 3, 2006).
8. "2005 United Nations and Partners: Work Plan for Sudan", revision of the original document June 29, 2005. *Relief Web*, November 30, 2004. <http://www.reliefweb.int/rw/RWB.NSF/> (September 22, 2006).
9. David, Loyn "Sudan Struggles As Millions Head South", *BBC News*, September 30, 2005. <http://news.bbc.co.uk/1/hi/world/africa/4297508 .stm> (April 6, 2006).

10. "IRIN: SUDAN: Malnutrition Levels in South Alarmingly High", *Webbolt Newsroom*. October 4, 2005. <http://webbolt.ecnext.com/coms2/description_54926_SUDAN041005_SUS> (April 2, 2006).
11. "Profile: Ugandan Rebel Joseph Koney ", *BBC News*. October 7, 2005. <http://news.bbc.co.uk/1/hi/world/africa/4320858.stm> (April 3, 2006).
12. "Ugandan Rebel Attack Shocks Sudan", *BBC News*. September 14, 2005. <http://news.bbc.co.uk/2/hi/africa/4246276.stm> (April 3, 2006).
13. Gupta (pseudonym), *Servants in the Crucible* (unpublished article), 2004. 58.
14. Ibid., p. 56.
15. Paul G. Heibert, Daniel Shaw, and Tite Tienou, Understanding Folk Religion, A Christian Response to Popular Beliefs and Practices. (Grand Rapids, MI, 1999). 74.
16. Akec Kuai, Mading Ngor, "NGOs in Southern Sudan: Polluting or Solving our Woes?" *The Bor Globe Network. November 6, 2006.* <http://www.borglobe.com> (September 23, 2006).
17. Ibid.

Bibliography

Anderson, Joy. "Behold! The Ox of God?" *Evangelical Missions Quarterly* 34.3 (1998).

Byang, Kato. "History Comes Full Circle." *Evangelical Review of Theology* 2.2 (April 2004): 130–139.

Crim, Keith, Ed. *The Perennial Dictionary of World Religions.* San Francisco: Harper and Row Publishers, 1989.

"Darfur Liberation Front." *GlobalSecurity.org.* modified August 16, 2006. <http://www.globalsecurity.org/military/wold/para/darfur.html> September 19, 2006.

Dattilio, Frank M. and Arthur Freeman, Ed. *Cognitive-Behavioral Strategies in Crisis Intervention, 2nd ed.* New York: Guilford Press, 2000.

Deng, Francis Mading. *The Dinka of the Sudan.* Prospect Heights, Illinois: Waveland Press, Inc., 1984.

Flannery, Raymond, B., Jr. *Post-Traumatic Stress Disorder*. New York, NY: Crossroads Publishing, 1998.

Gehman, Richard J. *African Traditional Religion in Biblical Perspective*. Kijabe, Kenya: Kijabe Printing Press, 1989.

Gupta, Leila. "Follow-Up Survey of Rwandan Children's Reactions to War Related Violence From the 1994 Genocide." *UNICEF*. Nov. 13, 2004. <http//www.unicef.org/evaldatabase/index-14242.html> Dec. 4, 2004.

Gupta (pseudonym). Servants in the Crucible. (unpublished manuscript) January 2004.

Hiebert, Paul G., Daniel Shaw and Tite Tienou. *Understanding Folk Religion, A Christian Response to Popular Beliefs and Practices*. Grand Rapids, MI: Baker Books, 1999.

International Rescue Committee, Dec. 2003 <http://www.irc.org>April 1, 2006.

"IRIN: SUDAN: Malnutrition Levels in South Alarmingly High." *Webbolt Newsroom*. October 4, 2005. <http://webbolt.ecnext.com/coms2/description_54926_SUDAN04 1005_SUS> April 2, 2006.

Jones, Gregory L. *Embodying Forgiveness, A Theological Analysis*. Grand Rapids: William B. Eerdman's Publishing Company, 1995.

Kilbourn, Phyllis, Ed. *Healing the Children of War*. Monrovia, CA: Marc Publishers. 1995.

Laurenz, Mel, and Daniel Green. *Life After Grief.* Grand Rapids: Baker Books, 1995.

Levi, William O. *The Bible or the Axe*. Chicago, IL: Moody Publishers. 2005.

Loyn, David "Sudan Struggles As Millions Head South." *BBC News*. September 30, 2005.

<http://news.bbc.co.uk/1/hi/world/africa/4297508.stm> April 6, 2006.

Lubit, Roy and Wilfred G. Van Gorp, Nancy Hartwell, and Spencer Eth, "Forensic Evaluation of Trauma Syndromes in Children." January 17, 2002. <www.puc.cl/psicologia/buentrato/pdf/est_inv/maltra/mi.lubit.pdf> December 4, 2004.

Lyne, C.M., W.R. Saltzman, G.M. Burlingame, R.F. Houston, R.S. Pynoos,. "Evaluation of Program Efficacy: UNICEF School-based Psychosocial program for War Exposed Adolescents as Implemented During the 1999-2000 School Year." BHG 2000/009:(2000) <http://www.unicef.org/evaldatabase/index-14165.html> December 4, 2004.

Meyer, Gabriel. *War and Faith in Sudan*. Grand Rapids, MI: Eerdman's Publishing, 2005.

Mollica, R.F. and Lopes B. Cardozo, H.J. Osofsky, Raphael B. Ager and P. Salama. "Mental Health In Complex Emergencies." *Lancet*, December 4, 2004: Vol. 364 Issue 9450, 2058. EBSCO Host, Academic Search Premier, December 17, 2004.

The NIV Study Bible, New International Version. Kenneth Barker Gen. Ed. Grand Rapids, MI: Zondervan Bible Publisher, 1985.

Oborji, Francis Anekwe. "In Dialogue with African Traditional Religion: New Horizons." *Mission Studies*, Vol. 19, Issue 1, 2002, 13–35.

Profile: Ugandan Rebel Joseph Koney" *BBC News*. October 7, 2005. <http://news.bbc.co.uk/1/hi/world/africa/4320858.htm.> April 3, 2006.

Robertson, Chris and Una McCauley. "The return and Reintegration of Child Soldiers In Sudan: The Challenges Ahead." *Forced Migration Review.* (Oxford University, UK) September 30, 2000. <http://www.fmreview.org/FMRpdfs/FMR211.pdf> December 16, 2004.

Save the Children. "Bringing Hope in Darfur." November 24, 2004. <http://www.savethechildren.org/home.shtml> December 4, 2004.

Schafer, Jessica. "Supporting Livelihoods in Situations of Chronic Conflict and Political Instability: Overview of Conceptual Issues." *Overseas Development Institute*, 2002. <www.livelihoods.org/static/jschafer-NN167.gtml-15k> December 4, 2004.

Smith, Russel. "How Many Have Died in Darfur?" February 16, 2005. *BBC News*. <http://news.bbc.co.uk/1/hi/world/africa/ 4268733.stm> April 3, 2006.

Stoop, David. *Forgiving the Unforgivable*. Ann Arbor, MI: Servant Publications, 2001.

"Sudan People's Liberation Army." *Intelligence Resource Program*. Updated January 5, 2000. <http://www.fas.org/irp/world/para/spla.htm> September 19, 2006.

"Ugandan Rebel Attack Shocks Sudan." *BBC News*. September 14, 2005. < http://news.bbc.co.uk/2/hi/africa/4246276.stm> April 3, 2006.

UN Resident Coordinator. "2005 United Nations and Partners:Work Plan for the Sudan." Revision of the original document June 29, 2005. *Relief Web*. <www.reliefweb.intl/rw/RWB.NSF.> September 22, 2006.

U.S. Committee for Refugees. "World Refugee Survey 2004 Country Report." 2004. <http://www.refugees.org/countryreports.aspx> September 22, 2006.

Wainri, Barbara Rubin and Ellen L. Bloch, *Crisis Intervention and Trauma Response*. New York, NY: Springer Publishing, 1998.

Werner, Roland, William Anderson and Andrew Wheeler. *Day of Devastation Day of Contentment*. Nairobi, Kenya: Paulines Publications Africa, 2001.

Wiger, Donald E., and Kathy J. Harowski. *Essentials of Crisis Counseling and Intervention*. New Jersey: John Wiley and Sons, Inc., 2003.

Chapter Sixteen

Lessons from Ministry in the Context of Violence in Eastern Europe

John Moldovan

Eastern European Christians and churches are gradually emerging from the dark night of Communist persecution. Even now, it is impossible to assess the full impact of that persecution on believers and their institutions. So many people suffered under Marxist-Leninist regimes that no exact figures can be extracted to indicate how many agonized primarily because of their faith. Some religious groups, particularly Baptists, experienced harsher treatment than others.

Baptists in Europe have been the most consistent and persistent advocates of religious liberty. They believe that no civil or ecclesiastical government has the right to curb or hinder the freedom of men to assemble together, to organize themselves, and to propagate the truth as they perceive it. This radical concept was forged, advanced, and defended in times of fierce persecution. Within the evangelical community, Romanian Baptists offer probably the best example in recent times of the struggle to retain growth, integrity, and spiritual vitality in the midst of tremendous government pressure and violence.

The tenacity and progress of Romanian Baptists during forty-five years of systematic persecution under the Marxist-Leninist regime came as a surprise to many in the West who sought to understand the constant interplay between the political and religious sectors. Despite some excellent reporting by journalists and the availability of publications on topics related to religious persecution, Western observers had little real understanding of the daily struggles believers were facing. Many Christians in the West failed to understand the sophisticated system of Communist repression of religion and its impact on individual believers, churches, and society. Even after the 1989 Revolution, many remain puzzled and unable to comprehend the life of an evangelical Christian under Communism.

It is not the purpose of this paper to explore the full impact of Communist persecution on all aspects of Christian life and ministry. Rather, the purpose is to examine the significant growth in a context of hostility and violence and identify specific lessons for effective interaction with a culture infused with intolerance and violence.

Both primary and secondary sources are examined meticulously in order to assess the effects of restrictive and punitive measures on various facets of ministry. In pursuing empirical research, this writer is faced with the difficult task of preventing the intrusion of subjective material. He will compensate for the ideological bias that inevitably accompanies such studies by employing methods to check the reliability of the results, including the consultation of a wide range of sources in order to verify their correctness.

Brief Historical Overview

Romania is a land of contrasts and paradoxes and a vast museum of ancient heritage.[1] Historically, Romania emerged from the Roman province of Dacia established by Emperor Trajan in A.D. 106. The Dacians,[2] who lived in the Carpathian-Danubian area as early as the Iron Age, battled the Greeks, Persians, Romans, and barbarian tribes.

Burebista (70–44 B.C.), a strong Dacian ruler, brought the Dacian state to the pinnacle of its centralization and independence. Later, following two successful campaigns (A.D. 101–2 and 105–6), the Roman emperor Trajan defeated the Dacians and captured their capital, Sarmizegetuza, after a prolonged siege.[3] The Dacian leader Decebalus escaped, but to avoid being captured he committed suicide. Dacia became a Roman province, received Roman colonists, and remained Roman until A.D. 271.[4]

Available evidence shows that the Daco-Roman population accepted Christianity as early as the third century, long before the arrival of the Slavs.[5] About A.D. 380, Latin-speaking missionaries such as St. Nicetas of Remesiana, called "the Apostle of the Romanians," evangelized the area south of the Danube River.[6]

From the third to the twelfth century, waves of barbarian invaders from the east surged through the country. The Germanic Goths came first. As the Goths moved steadily onward, the Slavs filled their place, permeating the whole Balkan peninsula. They were followed in the sixth century by the Avars and, toward the end of the seventh century, by the Bulgars who became assimilated with the Slavs and, after the conversion of their king, Boris, about 865, spread the Byzantine form of Christianity to the ancestors of the Romanians.[7]

At the beginning of the thirteenth century, the Vlachs[8] or Wallachs of Transylvania established themselves south of the Carpathian Mountains[9] in two distinct regions that became known as Wallachia and Moldavia. In 1290, Prince Basarab founded the principality of Wallachia that was semi-independent of Hungary. Subsequently, an independent Moldavian state emerged about 1359 under Prince Bogdan. Soon afterwards, the newly created Eastern Orthodox metropolitan sees from these principalities came directly under the authority of the Patriarch of Constantinople. Under the auspices of this Orthodox hierarchy, Slav culture was fostered, with Orthodox monasteries playing a leading role. Slavonic came to be used not only in the liturgy, but also in the chancelleries of the princes.[10]

Toward the end of the fourteenth century, the Ottoman Turks extended their empire into this part of Europe. Several Romanian leaders became prominent in their struggles with the Turks.[11] Between 1716 and 1821, the Turks reasserted their control over the principalities. Meanwhile, the peoples in this area found themselves driven back and forth between the armies of Russia, Austria, Hungary, and Romania. Russia briefly occupied Moldavia. Austria took the area of Bucovina[12] in 1775. Then, in 1812, Russia seized the district of Bessarabia. Hungary incorporated Transylvania in 1865 and governed it until 1918. During this period, the Hungarian leaders initiated a relentless campaign of Magyarization.[13]

In 1857, the assemblies of Wallachia and Moldavia voted to create a union of principalities. In 1881, Prince Carol was proclaimed King Carol I of Romania. After a forty-eight year reign, he died in 1914, leaving his nephew, Prince Ferdinand, to succeed him. The stage for the creation of a "Greater Romania" was set during the First World War. After two years of neutrality, Romania joined the Allies in 1916 and declared war on Austria-Hungary. The 1920 Treaty of Trianon recognized Transylvania, Crisana, Maramures, and northern Banat as integral parts of the Romanian nation.[14]

In the years following the creation of the Romanian national state, a process of consolidation took place through economic recovery, agrarian reform, and the introduction of universal suffrage. The assertion of more democratic and progressive currents led to the creation of new political parties and groups. Among them, the Workers' Party, which assumed the name of Socialist Party in 1918, organized political demonstrations and strikes and carried on intensive political and ideological activities. On May 11, 1921, the General Congress of the Socialist Party decided, by a large majority, to transform the party into a Socialist Communist Party affiliated with the Third Communist International. The following year, the Second Congress of the party adopted a new name, the Communist Party of Romania, and elected its first Central Committee. This party continued its activity underground until August 23, 1944.[15]

The failure of the Western democracies to offer military assistance and the constant threat of Soviet communism drove Romania into Hitler's camp.[16] By 1939, the Romanian economy was almost entirely controlled by Germany.[17]

The secret protocol to the 1939 pact between Stalin and Hitler cleared the way for the annexation by the Soviet Union in 1940 of Bessarabia and Bucovina. This action was a signal for other nations to take advantage of Romania's plight. Two months later, Hitler and Mussolini imposed the so-called Vienna Award,[18] transferring northern Transylvania to Hungary. Eight days later, Germany induced Romania to return southern Dobrogea to Bulgaria. In two months, Romania "lost over a third of its territory and some five million citizens, three million of them Romanians."[19] The popular reaction was so strong that King Carol II was forced to abdicate. His son Michael became King Mihai I.

The Soviet deputy foreign minister, Andrei Vyshinski, arrived in Bucharest to speed up political development there. He demanded the appointment of Petru Groza as premier.[20]

The Communists secured the most important ministries in this government. In August 1945, the king demanded Groza's resignation, but, confident of Soviet backing, Groza proceeded to rule without royal assent. The 1947 Peace Treaty with Romania, signed in Paris, cancelled the Vienna Diktat and recognized Romania's legitimate right to Transylvania. Shortly afterward, a wave of arrests, deportations, and executions of the democratic parties' leaders took place, followed by the dissolution of those parties. Under these circumstances, the monarchy was regarded as an anachronism. On December 30, 1947, Groza and Gheorghiu-Dej had a stormy meeting with King Mihai and forced the king to abdicate. On the same day, Romania was declared a People's Republic. With their accession to power, these Communists virtually subordinated the national Romanian interests to those of the Soviet Union.[21]

After 1947, the Communist government followed the Soviet model of agricultural collectivization and forced industrialization. A Soviet-type constitution was adopted in 1948, followed in 1952 by a revised constitution, analogous to that of the Soviet Union. A struggle developed between the pro-Russian and pro-Romanian elements in the Communist Party. Gradually, the Moscovites were ousted from power, but a general "de-Russification" of the country did not begin until 1961, as the Romanian leadership displayed increasing independence of the Soviet Union. The principal political figure of this post-war period was Gheorghe Gheorghiu-Dej, General Secretary of the Romanian Communist Party [RCP] and First Secretary from 1955 to his death in 1965. Dej was succeeded by Nicolae Ceausescu as First Secretary of the party. Under a new constitution, adopted in 1965, the country's name was changed to the Socialist Republic of Romania.

Romania's adamant commitment to a rapid development of heavy industry entailed large imports of advanced technology and equipment and led to a huge increase in foreign debt. The drastic austerity program, initiated by President Ceausescu in the 1980s, led to severe food and energy shortages and triggered massive protests.[22] In addition, the Romanian government was increasingly accused of human rights violations and religious persecution. Ceausescu's "systematization plan," announced in March 1988, intended to urbanize almost half of Romania's 13,000 villages[23] by bulldozing private homes, churches, and even historical sites and moving the inhabitants into "agro-industrial complexes."

A combination of these factors, accentuated by the suppression of religious freedom, ignited a spontaneous revolution that began on December 15, 1989 in Timisoara city, quickly engulfed the entire nation, and led to the downfall of the totalitarian communist government. In spite of heavy fighting by the highly trained, well-armed, and loyal secret police force, Nicolae Ceausescu and his wife Elena were caught. On Christmas Day, they were tried and executed. The hastily constituted National Salvation Front appointed Ion Iliescu as president. On May 20, 1990, the country experienced its first free election since 1937. With a majority of the vote, Romanians elected Iliescu as president. Anti-Communist demonstrations took place in several cities, the largest ones occurring in Timisoara and Bucharest. In an attempt to end the demonstrations, Iliescu brought thousands of miners loyal to him into the capital. Armed with truncheons, they ransacked opposition party offices and newspapers and brutally beat the peaceful demonstrators, mostly students and intellectuals.

Baptist Beginnings in Romania

The history of Romanian Baptists is both fascinating and complex. While part of the complexity is due to internal developments, the historical perspective cannot be adequately understood and appreciated apart from that of the Continental Baptists.

The First Baptist Church in Romania. The beginnings of the Baptist churches in Romania are closely related to the ministry and influence of Johann Gerhardt Oncken.[24] Karl Johann Scharschmidt, a carpenter by trade who was baptized by Oncken in Hamburg in 1845, came with his wife, Augusta, to Bucharest, Romania, in 1856, following several years of witness in Hungary. The two shared their faith with fellow Germans attending meetings in their home. A German Baptist church was organized in 1856. This was the first Baptist church on Romanian soil. Its members adopted Oncken's motto: "Every Baptist a missionary." Scharschmidt organized a tract society and distributed thousands of tracts among the twenty thousand Germans in Bucharest. At their request, Oncken sent August Liebig as pastor. The following year, the church would print and distribute tracts in the Romanian language. The tract distribution constituted the first attempt to evangelize the Romanian people.[25]

Meanwhile, persecuted German Baptists from the Ukraine sought refuge in the area of Dobrogea near the Black Sea and in 1862 established a Baptist church in Cataloi. Twenty-two converts were baptized in the month of November 1865. In 1869, Oncken visited both the church in Cataloi and the church in Bucharest.

Left without a pastor for eleven years, the church in Bucharest preserved its spiritual vitality through the reading of Spurgeon's weekly sermons during the worship services. In 1878, the church called Daniel Schwegler, manager of the Bible distribution center in Bucharest, to be their pastor, a position he held until 1886. Johann Hammerschmidt, whose influence extended beyond the German population, succeeded him.[26]

The First Romanian Baptist Church. During Hammerschmidt's pastorate, in 1896, the first two Romanian converts were baptized and accepted as church members. However, the most celebrated Romanian convert was Constantin Adorian, a pharmacist who spoke German fluently. Following his conversion in 1902 and baptism in 1903, the German Baptist Church agreed to initiate an independent mission among the Romanian people. In preparation, the church encouraged Adorian to study at the Baptist Theological Seminary in Hamburg. Upon his return, on Sunday, December 29, 1912, in Bucharest, he organized the first Romanian Baptist Church. The first meeting place was a room in the house of Lady Bekesh, a member of the German Baptist church. On that occasion, Adorian preached a moving message from 2 Cor. 12:15. On May 26, 1913, the church held its first baptism service at a nearby lake. During the same year, the church held eight additional baptism services with a total of ten converts.[27]

On February 14–16, 1920, at the first Baptist Congress held in Buteni, a village in Transylvania, the Romanian Baptist Union was formed, and Constantin Adorian was elected president.[28] At the time of its inception, the Union consisted of six hundred churches with a total membership of 18,751. There were approximately fifty-three ordained and 638 non-ordained preachers.[29] A fervent missionary spirit animated them. Plans were made to reorganize and expand the evangelistic efforts as well as to start a theological seminary. Thus, in September 1921, a seminary was instituted in Buteni. Its director, Ioan R. Socaciu, attended the Southern Baptist Theological Seminary in Louisville, Kentucky and returned to Romania to train pastors. A number of Romanian Baptists from the United States also returned. Evidently, a new phase of Baptist development began.[30]

As part of the 1920 agreement of the Baptist World Alliance (BWA) London Conference, Southern Baptists received the mandate of assisting the Romanian Baptists in their work..[31] Their greatest contribution was in the field of education. Through the efforts of the Foreign Mission Board and especially those of Dr. Everett Gill, its representative in Europe, theological training of ministers and laymen was made possible. The sudden suspension by the police of the seminary in Buteni precipitated its relocation to Bucharest in 1922. Then, in 1924, the seminary was moved to a newly erected building funded by the Southern Baptists. The first Southern Baptist missionary to Romania, Dan Hurley of North Carolina, arrived in Bucharest in 1923. He and Dr. Gill taught courses at the seminary.[32]

From the beginning, Baptists in Romania regarded evangelism as their primary responsibility. They devoted ample time and efforts to public proclamation and personal evangelism. Preachers tenaciously spread the gospel, gathering thousands of converts into churches. During these services, several preachers frequently shared the platform. In the process of affirming the truth, they developed extensive knowledge of the Bible and good apologetic skills. With love and tact, they concentrated on winnable audiences and reached out to persons in transition. Most of these preachers were farmers

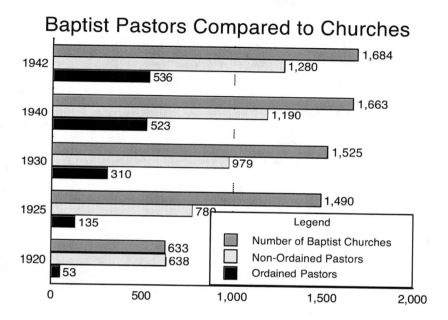

Baptist Pastors Compared to Churches

1942	1,684 / 1,280 / 536	
1940	1,663 / 1,190 / 523	
1930	1,525 / 979 / 310	
1925	1,490 / 78? / 135	
1920	633 / 638 / 53	

Legend
- Number of Baptist Churches
- Non-Ordained Pastors
- Ordained Pastors

0   500   1,000   1,500   2,000

who worked alongside their constituencies and identified with the problems faced by their listeners. On some occasions, however, government officia ls capitalized on their lack of formal education in order to discredit the Baptist movement. In reality, these preachers compensated for their lack of proper training with extraordinary fervor and inspiration.[33]

By 1927 there were a total of 915 pastors, mostly non-ordained. In fact, for over twenty years lay pastors carried the ministry work in most churches.[34] Sharing the good news, however, was not confined to preachers. Many believers had taken seriously their responsibility to witness. Primarily they were seeking to reach unbelievers in their intimate social networks. On Sunday afternoons, groups of eight to fifteen members of larger churches traveled to localities where only three or four believers lived. There, in members' backyards, they held meetings attended by neighbors and curious townspeople. After some singing, they answered questions regarding the Baptist faith. An open-air evangelistic service followed, resulting in many decisions. Post-baptismal training of converts played an important part in ensuring spiritually mature congregations.

Within a comparatively brief period, leaders realized that, in order to carry out their functions and accomplish their mission, churches must develop several organizations. As early as 1924, the Romanian Baptist Youth's Union was constituted followed in 1926 by the Sunday School Union and the Baptist Women's Union. Throughout the country Baptists experienced a surge of compassion manifested in the creation of special shelters for the elderly, widows, and handicapped as well as numerous orphanages.[35] Moreover, a mission among the leper colony in Tichilesti was started in 1935. In addition, Baptists sponsored a home mission work among the gypsies where a church was formed.

Foreign missions activity also received attention. One project was started in September 1935 with the appointment of Avram Balgradeanu as missionary among Romanians in Yugoslavia.[36] The following year Bessarabian Baptists sponsored a Foreign Mission Board missionary to Africa.

Adversity

As Baptists churches strengthened and expanded their work, they experienced remarkable growth so that by 1930, over a ten-year period, the number of churches and members had more than doubled.[37] This growth was achieved in the face of increased persecution which stemmed from a number of factors.

The Eastern Orthodox Church helped the nation in its survival and kept the national spirit alive during periods of foreign domination. Accordingly, the church considered conversion to any other form of the Christian faith an act of treason. The rationale was based on the assertion that the terms "Romanian" and "Orthodox" are synonymous; being Romanian meant being an Orthodox Christian. Consequently, it became politically expedient for the leaders in government, who wanted to keep their constituency united, to side with the Orthodox clergy in the promotion of the national religion.

Moreover, the Baptist faith was categorized as foreign; an "American sect" detrimental to the nation. Since Baptists included a considerable number of minorities, they were viewed with suspicion and portrayed as alienated, sold to the foreigners, or victims of magyarization efforts.[38]

To a certain degree, Baptist traditions, based upon the principles of democratic church organization, local autonomy, and true equity among baptized believers, were alien to the prevailing authoritarian mindset of the time. Evidently, the majority of governmental officials, political leaders, and local authorities were unaware or misinformed about Baptists.

Finally, a major cause of the hostility toward Baptists was their unequaled success in winning over thousands of Romanians, mostly of whom came from an Orthodox background. Baptists were frequently accused of ardent proselytism. The Orthodox church complained about the 'illegal methods' of recruitment employed by the sectarians. As a consequence of all of these factors, Baptists came to be considered among the most dangerous religious groups in the country.

Severe Waves of Persecution

The First Wave of Persecution. Despite the fact that Law XLIII from 1895 was still valid in Transylvania and that the Baptist denomination was officially recognized by the Hungarian government in 1905, Baptists in Romania, especially those living in the newly acquired territories of Transylvania, Bucovina, and Bessarabia, faced varying degrees of pressure and persecution. In Buteni, Transylvania, the authorities issued Order No. 244 dated June 13, 1919, prohibiting Baptist services on Sunday afternoon and evening and limiting Sunday morning services to only two hours. In August, several churches were closed as a result.

At the instigation of local Orthodox priests, agitated mobs opposed the burial of Baptists in the local cemeteries. In other cases, preachers and elders were assaulted by officers. For instance, in 1919, in Coronini Village, at the instigation of priest Pavel Bufanu, Baptist believer Gheorghe Moldovan was publicly beaten by a Serb officer until he lost consciousness. The officer ordered the soldiers to tie a large rock around his neck and throw him into the Danube River. On the way to the execution spot, those God fearing soldiers spared his life by allowing him to run while they discharged their rifles into the air. Moldovan, who converted to the Baptist faith in a Russian prison camp, was accused of spreading Bolshevism in the area, following his return.[39]

Such persecutions afflicted not only individual believers but also congregations, such as the one in Lupeni. On March 10, 1920, the Lupeni police chief and his men assaulted Teodore Munteanu's pregnant wife in her home and then, followed by a group of armed soldiers, entered the church, cancelled the service, and arrested all present. While in police custody, these Baptists were cruelly beaten and sentenced to prison terms ranging from three months to a year.[40] Various interventions and appeals of Baptist Union leaders and pastors on behalf of churches and believers received little attention and rarely ameliorated the situation.

On June 26, 1920, BWA commissioners Charles A. Brooks of New York and James H. Rushbrooke of London arrived in Bucharest in order to reestablish contact with the Romanian Baptists and to assess their situation. As they learned about the treatment of Baptists, they appealed to the President of the Ministers' Council, Alexandru Vaida Voevod, asking for his intervention to restore the "full religious liberty to which all good citizens are entitled, included unrestricted liberty of worship, the right to preach without let or hindrance, and complete protection of person and property."[41]

On their return to London, Brooks and Rushbrooke submitted a report to the Baptist World Alliance Conference held in London in July 1920. The main points of the report are highlighted in the following section:

We submit with this report extra documents duly signed and witnessed. We have seen others . . . and we have listened to direct testimony including exact details . . . . From our notebooks we add a number of instances described to us.

(a) Local magistrates (Stuhlrichter) supporting the interference of the gendarmerie with Baptist services.

(b) Elders severely beaten, and in consequence incapacitated for several days.

(c) Imprisonment of elders on the initiative of a local chief of police (only three months ago).

(d) Baptist propaganda forbidden, so that meetings have had to be held in the woods. (Several instances of this.)

(e) Beating of a Baptist by officers, who kicked him after he had collapsed under their blows, beat him again, and subjected him to such other ill-usage that he had to keep his bed for three months.

(f) Entry of officer with eight soldiers (with fixed bayonets) into a service. Savage striking of those present, Bibles seized and carried off . . . . All imprisoned in separate cells . . . . (Names of officers concerned, and numbers of their regiments given, as well as other confirmatory details.)

(g) Meetings forbidden three months ago by military, and still forbidden. Bibles and hymn books seized.

(h) Trial by court-martial followed by two weeks' imprisonment. (At least five such cases occurred in May of this year.)

(i) Savage bullying of Baptist soldiers. (On this matter we submit documents.)

We pressed our brethren closely upon several issues, but their answers were unhesitating and clear. Had they taken part in political activities directed against the new Government? Had there been among them, even on the part of a negligible minority, any teaching such as that of the unlawfulness of bearing arms? Was there any kind of justification for the epithet of "Bolshevist" sometimes hurled at them? In all cases the negative reply was clear, definite and emphatic.[42]

Circular Order No. 42078, issued on November 9, 1920, by the Minister of Cults,[43] Octavian Goga, officially sanctioned the persecution. Goga's erroneous interpretation failed to acknowledge the legality of Baptist confession, granted in 1905 by the Hungarian government, prompted a strong reaction on the part of Baptist leaders who met in Bucharest on November 16, 1920. They agreed that this medieval type of treatment of religious groups in the twentieth century civilized society is outrageous. C. Adorian, V. Berbecar, T. Sida, R. Tasca, A. Pascu, and I. R. Socaciu signed an appeal requesting the cessation of persecution.[44]

Meanwhile, in December 1920, civil and military authorities issued new ordinances prohibiting all Baptist activity and practically closing all the churches. Baptist leaders presented a new petition to the President of the Ministers' Council, General Averescu, emphasizing the unjust suffering of Baptist believers. Also, on March 28, 1921, they met the Minister of War, General Rascanu, who immediately responded by writing his resolution on their petition pledging to remove the restrictions placed on Baptist activities. On the same day, he issued Circular Order No. 25973, mandating the cessation of persecution and the reopening of all Baptist churches.[45]

However, the Minister of Cults felt that Rascanu's order granted too much freedom. Therefore, on April 1, 1921, Goga issued Circular Order No. 15831/1921, which specified that only local church organizations with special permits are recognized and all preachers must obtain permits and limit their preaching to only one location. As a result, the Baptist Union lost its legal right of representation, house churches were closed, and preachers who usually ministered to several churches were prevented from reaching them. Two weeks later, J. H. Rushbrooke and T. R. Glover returned to Bucharest and, during a special meeting with the Minister of Cults, were assured that Order No. 15831/1921 would be rescinded and the Baptist problem be addressed in a special law. Despite these promises, Goga failed to rescind Order No. 15831.[46]

These issues also caused heated debates in the Romanian Parliament. On December 9, 1921, Socialist Senator Gheorghe Grigorovici recounted many abuses of Baptist rights. In his long Senate speech, he admits that Baptists

> . . . are the most moral people who have an impeccable life and that they are Christians, but of another color. If our priests want to win on behalf of our church, they should do it through propaganda. . . . Arrests take place daily in all villages, and these arrests are not only of individuals but they are done in bloc. . . . There is nothing

holy for gendarmes and priests, for they are now the rulers of the country. . . . The adherents of these oppressed sects are simple people who are terrorized, carrying with them the ordinances of Mr. Goga and Rascanu and showing them without any result to priests and prefects.[47]

On December 18, 1921, after his return to the capital, Rushbrooke submitted a letter documenting the persecution of Baptists to Tache Ionescu, the new prime minister. The letter described the empty promises made by the former Minister of Cults, Octavian Goga, and the lamentable predicament of Baptists. On the same day, Rushbrooke was personally assured by Dumitrescu-Braila, the new Minister of Cults, that Baptists would be granted freedom. Thus, on December 24, 1921, Circular Order No. 68135 accorded "absolute freedom" to the Baptist cult but failed to void Order No. 15831/1921. Finally, on January 17, 1922, another Circular Order, No. 2143, voided Order No. 15831/1921 and brought a momentary lull to the suffering of Baptists.[48]

The Second Wave of Persecution. Although the last two orders were clear and precise, they did not bring "absolute freedom" to Baptists. Actually, these orders were circulated only to high-level officials; most local authorities were not aware of their existence. In addition, both orders contained a "secret formula" which in fact negated the presupposed religious liberty. This hidden clause granted freedom except when state security and public morals were affected. The contradiction is obvious: either Baptists are not dangerous and should therefore enjoy absolute freedom, or they are a threat to state and society and thus their freedom should be curtailed.

This ambivalence was exploited by those in the Ministry of Cults who resented Baptists. Persecution continued and even took new forms. In January 1922, through an official directive, Lazar Zaharia was accused of Baptist propaganda and expelled from his village. In Gepis, on a Sunday afternoon in March 1922, the Orthodox priest, Andrei Martian, in plain view of villagers, bludgeoned Baptists on their way to church.[49] Gendarmes interfered with baptismal and funeral services. In Caprioara, Timis District, on June 13, 1922, the body of Baptist Lazar Petrescu was exhumed, after he had been interred for fourteen months, and reburied in a cow pasture. His son, Simion Petrescu, was forced to pay all related expenses.[50]

In many places, Baptist school children were ridiculed, forced to make the sign of the cross, compelled to attend Orthodox services, beaten, and even expelled from school. Parents were fined for refusing to have their children christened.[51]

Many churches were closed without any justification. Baptist believers and pastors were excluded from the agrarian reform, interrogated, arrested, and traumatized. On the identification card of preacher Tafratov, the authorities had written that he must be arrested wherever he is found. Conversely, the press added to the insult through a campaign of slander and disinformation. Articles about Baptists bore suggestive titles such as "Talks with Our Most Miserable Brethren" and "Baptist Fanaticism."[52]

In July 1922, several articles published in the *Times* of London drew attention to the sufferings of Romanian Baptists. These articles were followed in August by a meeting in London between a BWA delegation and Nicolae Titulescu, the Romanian delegate to the League of Nations.[53]

Well-documented articles on the persecutions in Romania continued to be published in London by Rushbrooke throughout 1923. Moreover, Adorian's speech at the BWA Congress held in Stockholm in July 1923 described the sufferings of Baptists in Romania. Consequently, under world wide public pressure, the Minister of Cults issued Order No. 21641/1924 calling for the removal of all restrictions imposed on Baptists.[54]

In general, the order was respected. Yet cases of repression still existed, although fewer than before. On January 29, 1925, the Minister of Cults and Arts issued a brief directive, No. 5734, referring to the Baptist confession as an "association." This subtle maneuver placed Baptist organizations in a totally different category, together with associations for hunting, fishing, and other sports. It meant that Baptist activities would be regulated by other laws, not by religious laws. The preamble of this directive stated that the freedom accorded to Baptists until now "does not mean their recognition as an organized cult."[55] This signaled the beginning of new restrictions.

Baptists were prohibited from traveling outside their places of residence, their names were removed from the agrarian reform lists, and their newborn children were registered as belonging to the Orthodox church. Baptist soldiers were forbidden to attend church services. Engaged couples were refused marriage licenses. Similarly, Baptist craftsmen lost their trade licenses. Peasants were denied access to forests and pastures. Burial rights in local cemeteries were refused. Baptists were frequently beaten, fined, put on trial, and even imprisoned. Preachers were especially targeted. Their ministry was limited to their local church; those who traveled to other churches paid heavy fines, were beaten, and escorted out by the gendarmes.

Many churches were closed. In churches still open, authorities interfered with services. Transfers to the Baptist faith were prohibited. Nevertheless, as the Minister of Cults painfully admitted, despite all restrictions, "the adherents of these sects are multiplying."[56] For this reason, he instructed the local authorities to take "the most severe measures against the Baptist preachers who are engaging in propaganda outside their place of residence."[57]

Baptist Union leaders responded to these new challenges with a number of petitions presented in 1925 to all possible levels of authority, including King Ferdinand. Concurrently, the Baptist World Alliance initiated a massive campaign to obtain freedom for Romanian Baptists. Numerous articles on this topic were published in the international press.[58]

Meanwhile, the Romanian press attacked Rushbrooke and published defamatory articles, claiming, among other charges, that foreigners pay a reward of five thousand dollars for every converted Baptist. The idea of a free church was presented as a national threat.

In July 1927 the new Minister of Cults, Alexandru Lapedatu, promised a Baptist delegation that he would halt the persecution. He pleaded with them to help end the international campaign initiated on behalf of Romanian Baptists. Without any written order, all persecutions ceased by August 1927.[59]

Within a brief period, the Ministers' Council recognized the organizational statute of the Baptist confession, and in January 1928 the Minister of Cults approved it. The General Association of Orthodox Clerics fomented intense protests against the "mistake" of Baptists' recognition.

Heated debates concerning the proposed Law of Cults took place in the Romanian Senate. Finally, on March 31, 1928, the overwhelming majority of senators voted in favor of the new Law, followed by a similar result in the Deputies' Chamber on April 6. Article fifty-three of the new Law of Cults stated that "the rights recognized to the Baptist community through the Ministers' Council's Provision No. 2680 from November 21, 1927, are maintained."[60]

Defending the Faith

Encouraged by their new legal status, Baptists mobilized their communities for effective evangelism and expanded their work throughout the country. For two consecutive years, 1928 and 1929 they reported phenomenal growth. However, beginning with 1931, their activities were limited by a number of restrictions reminiscent of earlier periods.

On February 10, 1931, the Minister of Internal Affairs issued Order No. 802/A which again treated the Baptist confession as a "religious association." This measure induced authorities to require detailed statistics from churches and certificates for preachers. A second order, No. 10197, issued on November 25 specifically banned the use in Baptist churches of poetry, drama, and dialogues, under the pretext that they were not part of religious services. Occasionally, preachers were arrested, school children were harassed, and churches were closed. Baptist leaders expressed their disapproval through letters of protest and personal meetings with government officials, including King Carol II. These interventions produced some temporary relief.[61]

The persecution of Baptists was resumed in 1933 with the coming to power of the National-Peasant government.[62] At the end of 1934, the persecution reached striking proportions. Accused of trying to win converts many churches were closed, sealed, and guarded. Transfers of membership to the Baptist confession were virtually stopped. Many preachers were arrested and tried. Children of Baptists were not promoted in school and were beaten because they refused to attend Orthodox services. The Baptist Union was declared invalid.[63]

As the persecution intensified, Rushbrooke was officially invited to Romania. His meetings with several ministers, in September and October 1935, resulted in Baptists regaining their legal rights.[64]

Solidarity and Protest

For almost a year, Baptist churches enjoyed peace and freedom. Yet, "isolated" cases of harassment began to surface at the end of 1936. There were rumors at the Ministry of Cults and Arts that a new order restricting Baptists was being contemplated. In January 1937, Rushbrooke received assurances from the Minister of Cults, Victor Iamandi, that no adverse directives affecting Baptists would be issued. Nevertheless, Iamandi failed to fulfill his pledge.

On April 17, 1937, Iamandi signed Directive No. 4781, which was stricter than previous orders. All local Baptist organizations must obtain a new approval of the organizational statutes within six months. To be approved, a religious association was required to have at least one hundred men, heads of families, who could officially document that they did not belong to another religious group. The activities of preachers were limited to the local church. Moreover, the Baptist Union was nullified and religious "proselytism" strictly prohibited.

The Baptist Union's reaction was to call all churches and believers to a day of prayer and fasting. At the London meeting of the BWA Executive Committee, a letter of protest addressed to the Romanian government was signed and published. A commission which included George W. Truett, the president of the BWA, J. H. Rushbrooke, and other distinguished world Baptist leaders delivered the letter to the Romanian minister in London. In addition, the BWA leadership sent Romanian Baptists a letter of encouragement. A rushed meeting between the general secretary of the RBU, Ioan Cocut, and the Minister of Cults, Iamandi, secured the suspension of Directive No. 4781. This latest Baptist victory remains to this day an enigma.[65]

Fight for Freedom

Events of 1938 precipitated major changes and created political instability, with the dissolving of all political parties by King Carol II and the establishment of his own government presided over by the Orthodox Patriarch Miron Cristea. A new constitution was published and "accepted" in a plebiscite. During this period, the persecution took a more systematic course, threatening the very existence of the 1,602 Baptist churches. Despite Rushbrooke's continuing efforts in March and April 1938 to stop the closing of churches in some parts of the country, events went from bad to worse. Two months after Rushbrooke's meetings in Bucharest with the king and the new governmental leaders, the new Minister of Education and Cults, Orthodox Bishop Nicholae Colan, signed Directive No. 26208/1938, which was almost identical with the suspended Directive No. 4781/1937.

Thousands of protests regarding the new directive were received from Baptists across the country. The RBU assigned September 18, 1938, as a day of fasting and prayer. The six-month deadline for the application of the directive expired on December 14, 1938. On that date, all 1,602 Baptist churches in Romania, comprised of 77,420 members, were closed and sealed. Thus began one of the greatest periods of suppression. Scores of preachers were arrested, tried, and imprisoned. Believers were brutally persecuted. Burial, wedding, and baptismal services were forbidden. Despite these sufferings, Baptists "have adopted a calm and dignified attitude, refusing to invite collision with the police by breaking the official seals that have been placed on their churches, but quite firmly insisting that wrong has been done which calls for redress, and claiming the freedom to which Christian men and Christian churches are entitled."[66]

Voices of protest were heard from all over the world; the persecution was cruel and unworthy of the twentieth œntury. The executive secretary of the Foreign Mission Board of the Southern Baptist Convention (SBC), Charles E. Maddry, encouraged Baptists everywhere "to express their protest to the Rumanian government and to urge King Carol to see that his nation fulfills her Versailles pledge to give 'full religious freedom' to her minorities."[67] Scores of letters, petitions, and appeals protesting the persecution in Romania passed through the offices of the Foreign Mission Board en route to the officials of the Romanian government. Twenty-five hundred Baptist students from four hundred colleges and universities sent an appeal requesting that "this repressive edict may be annulled, and that full liberty of worship may be accorded to all Rumanian citizens."[68] The Federal Council of Churches made a similar plea in its letter to the Patriarch Miron Cristea. Furthermore, speaking for millions of Baptists, the president and the general secretary of the BWA, George W. Truett and J. H. Rushbrooke respectively, recorded their most solemn protest against the implementation of Directive No. 26208/1938 and demanded the granting of full religious freedom to their Romanian brethren. Likewise, the president of the Southern Baptist Convention, L. R. Scarborough, urged Southern Baptists to continue their efforts to bring religious freedom to Romania.[69]

These expressions of Christian solidarity seemed to have played a positive role, for, in March 1939, the Minister of Internal Affairs telegraphically transmitted Circular Order No. 26003 to permit the reopening of Baptist churches. The new situation was fragile, since Baptists' rights were not recognized and the restrictive Decision No. 26208/1938 was not rescinded. Not satisfied with the simple "tolerated" status, Baptist leaders submitted a statute for approval, but instead of recognition, the Baptist confession was targeted by a new directive, No. 31999/1939, with a content almost identical to previous directives. Within three months, local churches were again asked to submit documents in order to be authorized. Churches failing to meet the deadline were to be closed. Thus, on October 12, 1939, most Baptist churches were closed. Yet, on February 6, 1940, the newly constituted government released Directive No. 5657, which restored the legal status of the Baptist confession and revoked Directive No. 31999/1939.[70]

Growing Pains: Persecution Under the Nazis

Shortly after the abdication of King Carol II and the constitution of the dictatorial government of General Ion Antonescu, the new Minister of Cults approved a directive banning all religious associations. Nine days later, in September 1940, he was replaced and his directive suspended.

On February 30, 1942, the general secretary of the Minister of National Culture and Cults, Aurel Popa, signed Directive No. 10091, which canceled Directive No. 5657/1940 and reinstated Directive No. 31999/1939. Most churches were closed and believers were carefully watched. In October 1942, the Minister of National Culture and Cults, Ioan Petrovici, signed a new directive legalizing previous abuses. The most cruel persecution occurred in Bucovina, where Baptists were tortured.

Based on the arguments that Baptists, Adventists, and Christians According to the Gospel [Brethren Church] promote a current of spiritual anarchy, have a foreign origin, and destroy the national unity, in December 1942, General Antonescu signed the Decree-Law No. 927 abolishing all religious associations and Article 53 of the Law of Cults. Although all Baptist churches were closed, the confession abolished, and all archives confiscated, General Antonescu signed a second decree-law abolishing religious associations. Under its provisions, the Southern Baptist mission in Bucharest and all its properties, including the Baptist Theological Seminary, were declared state property.[71]

Europe has not known a persecution similar to the one endured by Baptists in 1942–44 since the seventh century. Baptist churches were transformed into dance halls, sleeping quarters for arrested Jews, warehouses for grain, and even livestock stables. Baptists in Bucovina, Bessarabia, and Moldova suffered the most. The martial courts were busy sentencing Baptists to long prison terms of from five to twenty-five years. Many of the arrested believers were taken without a trial to the Dniester River and shot. At the insistence of Orthodox Patriarch Nicodim Munteanu, General Antonescu approved an order to effect a mass deportation of Baptists, Adventists, and Christians According to the Gospel in the area of Bug, Transdniester. Lists containing the names of believers to be deported were produced. However, the serious defeat at Stalingrad stopped these deportations.[72]

Between February 20, 1942, and October 1, 1944, Baptists continued their activities illegally. They held secret meetings in homes, fields, and forests. Ordained elders and preachers officiated at baptisms and administered the Lord's Supper. In towns, several families gathered for meetings; to avoid suspicion, they arrived and left individually or in groups of two. Blankets were placed on the windows to muffle the singing and preaching, which usually were done in a hushed tone. Burials were more difficult, since the Orthodox priests had orders to administer them. Also, Baptists organized special ministries to collect and distribute food and money for the imprisoned believers.[73]

Attempts to further demoralize and compromise the believers proved, in most part, useless. For instance, the former general secretary of the Baptist Union, Ioan Ungureanu, and Alexandru Ruja, former pastor of the Romanian Baptist church from Ketegyhaza, Hungary, were recruited by the Orthodox Bishop, Andrei Magieru, to attempt to convert Baptists back to the Orthodox faith. They were authorized to travel, engage in discussions, and even hold meetings in the Baptist churches which were closed. Similar efforts to reconvert Baptists transpired in prisons. In one case, the Orthodox priest and the prison director managed to obtain the signature of forty-four condemned believers who "returned" to the true Orthodox faith. As a result, they were pardoned in a special prison ceremony and set free. Nevertheless, the majority of condemned believers, several hundred of them, remained steadfast. In most cases, Baptists demonstrated a kind spirit and tenacity in the face of impossible conditions.[74]

On August 23, 1944, the fascist dictatorship was overthrown. At the end of September 1944, all Baptist churches were reopened, and on October 31, 1944, King Mihai I signed Decree-Law No. 553

recognizing the Baptist confession in the entire country. As an expression of their gratitude to God, Baptist believers held special thanksgiving services. With the reopening of churches, a striking discrepancy between the number of believers before the closing and after the reopening was noticed. During the period of persecution, many converts were baptized. Also, soldiers converted during the Second World War returned home and joined the churches. For a period of ten years, the baptisms reported from Romania represented more than thirty-five percent of the total baptisms reported on all mission fields of the SBC.[75] Although Baptist believers and churches suffered great material losses during the various periods of persecution, they did not contemplate any acts of retaliation. Instead, they demonstrated magnanimity toward their persecutors.

Significant Lessons

The history of Baptists in Romania is one of repression and growth. From the beginning, believers enthusiastically bore witness to their newfound faith and started churches. Additionally, they opened schools, orphanages, and leprosaria.

Their phenomenal growth drew the attention of the whole country. An analysis of the period between 1919–42 shows that there was no consistent pattern of growth during the various years of persecution. In light of these findings, it is difficult to sustain the theory that persecution automatically leads to church growth. However, one should avoid falling into the other extreme of ruling out any impact. There are some interesting trends. For instance, for the years 1921, 1925, 1927, 1935 and 1942, when persecution subsided, Baptists reported low growth. At the same time, during some (author's emphasis) periods of intense persecution, such as 1922, 1926, 1934, 1937, and 1938 there was phenomenal growth. In fact, the highest growth rate occurred in 1938 when churches were sealed. These cases seem to indicate not only the great power of human perseverance, but a level of spiritual maturity characteristic of those who have completely identified with Christ and His gospel

Moreover, the world-wide protests of Baptist leaders to publicize the plight of their Romanian brethren illustrates the effectiveness of spiritual solidarity among the Baptists. Evidently, the years of relative freedom, 1928–29, 1939, and 1940 brought substantial growth for Romanian Baptists.

Baptists labored even for people who rejected them and their message. In their work they encountered indifference, suspicion, hostility, persecution, and imprisonment. Insinuations of disloyalty were falsely made against them. At times, their churches were desecrated and their lives threatened. They were astonished at the barbaric methods employed by their enemies, methods totally unfit for a civilized society.

In the midst of these turbulent events, Baptists displayed a courageous spirit and an absence of malice. Persecutions, which drastically affected them and temporarily halted their advance, left scars on individuals, families, and churches. Instead of breaking their spirit, these afflictions united them, confirmed the faithfulness of God, and strengthened their resolve to carry on their mission. The resilience shown by Baptists during this period caused them to face the postwar period with optimism. However, the Communist era was an even greater test.

Marxism-Leninism and Christianity in Romania

The end of World War II brought new freedoms to Romanian Baptists. At first there was coexistence between church and state. Baptist churches were left relatively undisturbed in their activities. The Baptist advance between 1944 and 1947 was remarkable. The war provided Baptists with the opportunity of demonstrating their loyalty and value to their country through their participation in the liberation of Romania from the Nazis. Church leaders also made great efforts to prove their sincerity.

However, the rise in 1947 of the Romanian Communist Party [RCP] drastically altered the relationship between church and state. Guided by a Marxist-Leninist ideology[76] and following the Soviet Union's model, the RCP brought all religious groups under its direct control. Churches became useful instruments in promoting the Party's policy. Since the Marxist-Leninist ideological approach to religion consists of deductions from the postulates, assumptions, and sporadic judgments of Karl Marx and Vladimir I. Lenin, it is necessary to understand their views on religion in general and Christianity in particular.

The Marxist-Leninist Understanding of Religion

Marxism-Leninism regards religion not only as the ideology behind a corrupt social order, but as a fantasy of alienated man. This concentration on the social sources of religion severely limits the Marxist-Leninist understanding of religion. The interpretation of religion on the basis of man's fear of natural and social forces denotes a failure to distinguish between religion and superstition. Religion is a much more complex phenomenon. The Marxist-Leninist assertion that religion derives from social alienation has been proven false. Even atheists concede that in countries where the major sources of social alienation have disappeared, religion not only persists, but appears to gain momentum.

In its own estimate, Marxism-Leninism constitutes the only truly scientific reflection of reality. James Thrower suggests two reasons why one must reject the claim of Marxist-Leninist 'scientific atheism' to be the only true science of religion. The first reason is its inability to formulate any empirically verifiable explanation about religion. Despite its adoption of the term "science" to suggest objectivity, precision, and authority, Marxism-Leninism provides only a partial explanation of religious phenomena. The claim that Marxism-Leninism is confirmed by science is quixotic. The second reason   for rejecting the Marxist-Leninist claim is the inability of 'scientific atheism' to account for the motives underlying the personal religious quest, the inability to come to terms with the reading of the   human condition.

In reality, the Marxist-Leninist study of religion is ideological, dogmatic, and closed to critical philosophical analysis. Its actual purpose is to further the understanding of religion in order to suppress it. Any rapprochement with religion seems impossible. 'Scientific atheism' must criticize religion and set forth the atheist ideals of the Communist society. This ideological antagonism toward religion has translated into a long history of persecution of Christians by Communist governments.

The Ethics of Communism

Communism denies the reality of moral law. Marx and Engels state that "Communism abolishes eternal truths"[77] which are used by classes to defend their interests.

Truth-telling is deemed a capitalist sentimentality. "We must be ready," Lenin wrote, "to employ trickery, deceit, lawbreaking, withholding and concealing truth."[78] For Communists, an idea has value only if it advances the interests of the proletariat. They have a class morality. The concept of honor, as Christians know it, does not exist in Communist thinking. They will urge a person to dishonor his parents if it advances the Party.

Hate occupies an important place in Communist "morality." Communist leaders encourage Christians to "discard kindness, mercy, meekness, self-sacrifice, charity, honesty, and brotherly love as capitalist nonsense and not needed in the atheist paradise on earth."[79] The class conflict must be intensified, not eliminated.

For the Communist, good is what man chooses. But this does not mean that man has complete freedom. Men will believe what they are told to believe and "choose" what is authorized by the state.

The commandment "Thou shall not kill" (Deut. 5:17) is irrelevant to Communists. Revolution, torture, and murder are welcomed if they serve the interests of the Communist state. During Stalinist rule, millions of innocent people in Russia were killed.[80]

In light of this concept, Lenin's hostile attitude toward religion was more than a consequence of his Marxist materialism. Religion was the basic ideological tool used by the ruling class to maintain dominance over the exploited classes. Lenin refused to allow room for any compromise. Lenin added little to the classic Marxist critique of religion. He was content to repeat Marx's conclusions.[81]

Romanian Christians Under Communism

The Soviet Union's approach to religion has served as the model for most Eastern European countries, including Romania. Soviet military occupation of Romania was the prelude to the establishment of a Communist regime. The Communist takeover was accomplished in several stages. Nevertheless, the 'peaceful transition to Socialism' and the consolidation of Communist power involved a certain degree of violence.

In general, the policies of the Communist government followed two basic approaches. The first approach, prevalent during the Stalinist period, called for the prohibition of religious activities, confiscation of church property, and imprisonment of church leaders and clergy.[82] The Romanian Communists modified this approach to fit their own situation and applied it selectively to the Roman Catholic Church,[83] the Uniate Church,[84] and the "Lord's Army Movement." [85] The government also dissolved the Young Men's Christian Association (YMCA) and confiscated buildings, libraries, and equipment.[86]

The second approach considered the Christian church as a deeply rooted historical, cultural, social, and even political force that must be tolerated within strictly defined limits. Religious liberty was limited to freedom of worship. Coercive policies set the stage for RCP control of all aspects of religious life. All church activities required state approval Governmental decisions were often arbitrary, based on strict regulations, and not even published. Those who actively opposed the regulations were subjected to harassment, intimidation, fines, searches, arrests, beatings, and even imprisonment. The government did not tolerate any use of religious meetings, the church building, the pulpit, the sermon, or the prayer for the purpose of directly or indirectly subverting the state. The regime kept constant pressure on the churches through its local administrative organs.

What was the main reason for such an attitude? The Communist party successfully eliminated all other political and social organizations. The Christian church remained, in fact, the only major institution that promoted a diametrically opposed ideology to Marxism and provided a focus for potential dissent.

Most churches accepted the conditions of "normalization," including extensive government control over their activity. Religious denominations such as Orthodox, Lutheran, and Reformed offered a policy of acquiescence or patriotic endorsement of the government. They continued to "function as ritualistic organizations expounding doctrines of allegiance to communism to frightened and politically inactive members of rapidly waning congregations." Other churches maintained their spiritual commitment and gained respect for their dedication and integrity.

The Communists purged the ideologically suspect clergy. Tactics pursued by the regime combined severe repressions against the "recalcitrants" with token concessions for those ministers who cooperated. Some church leaders opted for selling out altogether.[87]

The new Romanian constitution enacted on April 13, 1948, subsequently amended in 1952, formally guaranteed freedom of conscience and freedom of religious worship to all citizens. In practice, subsequent laws and their interpretation and administration limited these liberties. The 1948 Law of Cults granted fourteen denominations legal authority to function. At the same time, this law drastically curtailed the activities of religious denominations, subjecting them to rigorous administrative control.[88] Leaders of religious denominations were required to take an oath of allegiance promising "to defend the Rumanian People's Republic against internal and external enemies." The Ministry of Cults was empowered to control all assets and revenues of churches and supervise their use. All denominational and private schools of all types were expropriated. The only schools allowed in the entire country were a limited number of theological seminaries for training of the clergy: two for the Orthodox Church, one for the Catholic Church, and one for all Protestant churches.[89]

Broadly speaking, evangelicals in Romania have been called *neo-Protestants*. They are considered the left-wing descendants of the Protestant Reformation with a primary emphasis on a biblically-oriented community consisting of individuals regenerated by divine power. In the Romanian context, neo-Protestants include Baptists, the Brethren (Christians According to the Gospel), Pentecostals, and

Seventh-day Adventists. A number of unofficial groups such as the Nazarenes, the Reformed Adventists, and the Lord's Army are related to neo-Protestants. The neo-Protestants were frequently accused of threatening the national unity.

Baptists Under Communism

Baptist statutes were approved in 1950 by Decree No. 1203. Relations with the state were carried through the Ministry of Cults office, replaced in 1957 by the Department of Cults attached to the Council of Ministers. At first many Baptists hoped that the democratic government, established in 1947, would help to reduce the harassment of believers. Baptist leaders expected to maintain the freedom to evangelize by submitting to the Communist regime. Later, they realized the naivete of such an approach.

Communists used the denomination to promote their political propaganda in several ways. First, they demanded extensive coverage of the issue of peace. The denominational magazine *Îndrumatorul Crestin* published many articles on the topic, comparing the peace-loving attitude of the Communist countries to the imperialist promotion of the arms race. Messages preached by pastors followed the same topic. Secondly, the denominational publications carried extensive articles emphasizing the religious freedom enjoyed by Christians in the Soviet Union, including special references to Baptists. Thirdly, attempts were made to secularize the Christian religion. The Baptist denomination was asked to get involved in the special education of the public, particularly the Christian public, on topics such as health, agriculture, and scientific discovery. As a result, the publication came to resemble more an official political journal than a Christian magazine.

Beginning in 1954, the state commenced to interfere seriously with Baptist activity. The RBU president, Ioan Dan, refused to sign the new restrictive regulations imposed by the state. The government immediately pressed for the 'election' of a new president and new church officials.

The new leaders accepted the restrictive regulations, but additional rules followed, further quelling the activities of churches. By 1964, four hundred Baptist pastors, from an approximate total of 540, lost their licenses.[90] Furthermore, in the early 1960s, the Baptist Union was 'persuaded' to close three hundred 'redundant' churches. The government also requested the names of candidates for baptism. As a result, a list of candidates had to be approved first by the inspectors of the Department of Cults.

Baptists carried with them into the new political order old legacies of suspect loyalty, charges of proselytism, and dubious international contacts. In the late 1950s, Baptists, especially in Transylvania, were imprisoned. They were regarded as agents of foreign powers and American imperialism.

With the emergence of a new generation of Baptists who were better educated, versed in the Marxist-Leninist philosophy, and less inclined to compromise, the denomination took a new turn and began to see signs of revival. By the early 1970s revival had begun in Baptist and other evangelical churches. Leading Baptist evangelists called for repentance and a renewed commitment to Christ. Thousands of converts, mostly from the Orthodox Church, were added to the already overcrowded churches.[91]

Church and State Tensions

In the fall of 1973, Iosif Ton,[92] then a teacher at the Baptist Seminary in Bucharest, wrote and circulated a paper entitled "The Present Situation of the Baptist Church in Romania" in which he analyzed the relations between the Baptist church and the state since 1954. Ton exposed the intolerable interference of the state in the affairs of the church and the unfortunate submissiveness of Baptist leaders to the oral instructions of the Department of Cults. He considered these attitudes illegal and a threat to Christ's lordship over His Church. By 1973, the church considered its right to choose pastors and leaders, to baptize openly without first submitting a list of candidates for the Department of Cults' approval, to open new churches, to repair and extend existing ones. The paper concluded with a warning that "if faced with a conflict of loyalties, we will be obliged to put our loyalty to God first." [93]

Ton's paper triggered a variety of responses. His ideas caught the imagination of young preachers. They renounced self-censorship in their preaching and discovered the positive impact of their messages upon the listeners. At the same time, older Baptists, while agreeing with the correct assessment of the situation, entertained doubts about the value of Ton's solutions.[94] Ton's pastoral colleagues were more cautious. However, a group of four pastors from the Bucharest Association wrote in November 1973 a petition with a content similar to Ton's paper. The petition was signed by fifty pastors, out of the 157 pastors throughout the country, and presented to the Council of State. No reply was received from the Council, so these pastors began to administer their churches according to the statutory position. They held baptisms without the customary submission of names to the Department of Cults, prepared to hold independent elections of local church officers, and invited 'unauthorized' preachers to their pulpits.[95]

A revival spirit predominated in the churches. Baptist believers gained confidence, and many pastors started to claim their legal rights. The chains of fear had been broken, and the authorities lost their main lever of control. Gradually, the practice of referring baptisms and the appointment of local officers to the Inspector of Cults was abandoned. RBU leaders, supported by the European Baptist Federation, began negotiations with the Department of Cults for official sanction of the activities already adopted by a good number of churches.[96]

On May 24, 1974, at the Inaugural Congress of the United Socialist Front, Nicolae Ceausescu reassured the Romanian citizens of their right to religious freedom.[97] In the fall of 1974, Ton sent his second paper directly to President Ceausescu. He questioned whether atheism was necessary to socialism and underscored atheism's destructive impact on morality. Additionally, he called attention to the persecution of evangelicals and stressed the constructive role that neo-Protestants could play within Romanian society.[98] Some pastors felt that Ton's paper touched upon the forbidden area of political ideology, while others considered his approach of trusting the government for an understanding of the Christian role in a socialist society too naive.

During this period the secret police carried out house searches in Bucharest and throughout the country, confiscating Christian books, tapes, letters, and personal notes. Intense investigations of prominent Baptists followed. Several pastors, displaying an uncompromising attitude, had their licenses suspended. Among these was Liviu Olah, a pastor from Timisoara. The broadcasting of these events on Radio Free Europe caught the interest of the general public. Curious to learn more about the Baptists, Romanians began to attend services and were exposed to sound evangelistic preaching, and many were converted and baptized. For instance, Liviu Olah, who became the pastor of the Second Baptist Church in Oradea, baptized during his first baptismal service at the church 136 converts. In 1974 Olah baptized a total of 356 candidates.[99]

In 1976, after banning his preaching and monitoring all his moves, the authorities finally 'persuaded' Olah to emigrate. The Baptist Congress, held in February 1977, sparked spirited and frank discussions, putting the Union leadership on the defensive. The question of closed churches was one of the most significant matters addressed. Pastors complained about the long delays suffered by congregations. Some churches waited fifteen years for opening permits. In addition, the issue concerning the fining and imprisoning of Baptists under Article 153 of the Penal Code, referring to hooligans, vandals, and anarchists, was hotly debated. Yet, the new Baptist leadership was still too divided and insecure to stand up to the government. Vasile Talos, pastor of Mihai Bravu Church in Bucharest and a lawyer by training, analyzed the legal position of the denomination and emphasized the autonomy of the individual churches. This was the first instance when Baptists publicly questioned the fairness of state laws.[100]

Shortly after the Baptist Congress, six evangelical Christians circulated two important documents exposing discrimination against evangelicals and calling on believers to cast off fear and seek to please God. The result was that, in April 1977, the members of this group were arrested, interrogated, and later released. Yet, in a clever move, their case was handed over to the Baptist Union and their respective denominational leadership for punishment. Baptist Union officials strongly denounced the views expressed in the document.[101] The movement for greater freedom continued to grow among Baptists. At the same time, there were no signs that the violations of religious freedom would cease. On the contrary, increasingly new cases and methods of religious persecution surfaced. Consequently, in 1978, a group of nine Baptists founded an organization called "Comitetul Crestin Român Pentru Apararea Libertatii Religioase si de Constiinta" (ALRC) [The Romanian Christian Committee for the Defense of Religious Freedom and Conscience] affiliated with the international organization Christian Solidarity International (CSI) based in Zürich, Switzerland. Its main spokesman was Pavel Nicolescu, an outstanding preacher and friend of Ton. Members of the committee were first and foremost committed to the task of evangelization of their country. The group was comprised of preachers, evangelists, deacons, Sunday School teachers, church planters, leaders of prayer and Bible study groups, and representatives of the Baptist student movement. All of them were effective soul-winners. In July the committee sent an appeal to the Council of State, the Minister of Justice, the Department of Cults, and the Baptist Union calling for an end to the persecution of Christians and for "a free church in a free state." The document was signed by twenty-five Baptists, one Pentecostal, and one Orthodox. It contained a letter from Aurel Popescu, a lay-preacher, and Iosif Ton expressing their approval of the committee and its objectives, although they declined to become members. The signatories stated their desire "to make a modest contribution to the defense of the fundamental human rights, to the respect for constitutional guarantees, and to the raising of Romania's international prestige."[102]

The concerns of ALRC were interdenominational, defending the causes of persecuted Orthodox, Uniates, Pentecostal, Brethren, Catholics, and others in addition to those of Baptists. Believing that their actions were serving both the Christian churches and the state, they covered a large spectrum of religious concerns such as evangelism, preaching, baptism, open-air services, new churches, religious personnel, literature, censorship, use of media, religious instruction, theological training, social ministries, ideological discrimination, and approval of Billy Graham's visit to Romania. Earl Pope called the document "the most far-reaching statement made up to that time."[103]

Encouraged by this bold example, Christians of various denominations began to provide ample documentation of abuses, harassments, and persecutions. The similarity of the complaints only increased their credibility. However, during an extraordinary session of its executive committee on August 30, 1978, the Baptist Union expelled from the denomination the nine founding members of ALRC, the leaders of the First Baptist Church in Caransebes, and Aurel Popescu. Popescu was expelled for his refusal to stop preaching. Absent from this expulsion list was Ton, who had been criticized by his supporters for his eagerness to make peace with the Union council and for his silence on the expulsions.

Ton's relationship with Popescu, Nicolescu, and other supporters collapsed in October 1978 as Ton remained silent on the imprisonment of his Baptist friends from the church in Caransebes. To the dismay of his colleagues and supporters, Ton refused to comment on the right of Baptist Union officials to intervene in a local church situation or on the brutal beatings of those arrested in the presence of church members. In his open letter, Popescu charged that Ton's "silence and change of position in favor of the Union" had encouraged the secret police to persecute those who supported him.[104]

The government was determined to act strongly and quickly against the freedom movement. Popescu and Nicolescu were forced to emigrate to the United States. Other members of ALRC "were imprisoned, some, 'treated' on an 'outpatient' basis—beaten regularly, given truth drugs, threatened with death."[105] Most of its original members were driven into exile, but the remaining members continued to function, requesting special prayers on behalf of the persecuted believers and churches and occasionally producing documents. Nevertheless, the freedom movement set a vital precedent for evangelicals in Romania by demonstrating an excellent understanding of the real concept of religious freedom, as espoused in the resolutions of the BWA, and calling for respectful relations between the church and state.

In the 1980s the situation continued to deteriorate. Evangelical Christians were attacked in the press, smear tactics were used against pastors and evangelists, heavy fines were imposed on believers for participation in 'illegal' meetings, scores of church buildings were demolished, and active believers and church leaders were intimidated through arrest and interrogation.

Bibles imported legally into the country were always in short supply. Most Bibles made available to believers were smuggled. Edmond Perrett, former secretary of the World Alliance of Reformed Churches' European Assembly, announced in September of 1980 that "the Romanian authorities had approved a presentation of 10,000 Hungarian Bibles to the Reformed Church on this historical meeting."[106] Romanian authorities "referred to their Bible import agreements as proof of their 'good faith' toward religious groups and minorities." Their statements were contradicted when reports of Bibles converted into toilet paper surfaced in hearings before Congress, during the negotiations on Most Favored Nation status.[107]

Some Romanian Baptists assumed that President Ceausescu was completely unaware of the real situation and would intervene on behalf of their constitutional rights. In August 1982, sixty-six Baptist pastors sent a letter to the President listing seven points of concern. Following the appeal, the signatories were interrogated by the secret police and were pressured to withdraw their names. Ten pastors eventually withdrew their signatures, but fifty-six remained firm. There was no reply from President Ceausescu and no improvement in the situation.[108]

The triennial Baptist Congress was postponed twice, and, in 1984, when the Department of Cults finally permitted the meeting, it lasted one day. The number of delegates was limited, and no foreign observers were allowed. The following Baptist Congress, due in 1987, was delayed because the delegates failed to present candidates acceptable to the Department of Cults. Baptist churches continued to encounter opposition, harassment, and persecution up to the dramatic events of the 1989 Revolution. However, they maintained their courageous witness and experienced steady growth.

Significant Lessons

The Communist system cannot accept any competition from other ideologies. As a result, it develops a method to marginalize the alternative ideologies. The Romanian Marxist-Leninist government developed a complete organization of research and psychological laboratories for the purpose of planning and implementing its anti-religious strategy.

The Communist attack on religion affected every aspect of the church's ministry. The authorities infiltrated the hierarchical structure from the Baptist denominational leadership to the local church pastor. Prohibitions on "proselytizing," the interference in appointments of church leaders, and the destruction of church facilities hampered the church in its mission. Yet, there were pastors and church members who continued to minister and accept the consequences of their actions.

A church which preaches the cross must itself be marked by the cross. It becomes a stumbling block to evangelism when it betrays the gospel or lacks a living faith in God, a genuine love for people, or scrupulous honesty in all things including promotion and finance. The church is the community of God's people rather than an institution, and must not be identified with any particular culture, social and political system, or human ideology.

The fact that Baptists have often been restricted and persecuted is reflected in their confessions. In the explanation of the relationship between the church and state, the Lausanne Covenant states:

> It is the God-appointed duty of every government to secure conditions of peace, justice, and liberty in which the church may obey God, serve the Lord Christ, and preach the gospel without interference. . . . We also express our deep concern for all who have been unjustly imprisoned, and especially for those who are suffering for their testimony to the Lord Jesus. We promise to pray and work for their freedom. At the same time we refuse to be

intimidated by their fate. God helping us, we, too, will seek to stand against injustice and to remain faithful to the gospel, whatever the cost. We do not forget the warning of Jesus that persecution is inevitable.[109]

The passage in Rom. 13:1–7 extolling Christians to be obedient to the ruling authorities is not a blanket statement on the conduct of Christians regarding the state, but rather a set of theological principles intended to guide them in deciding how best to relate to the government. The same is true for the passage in Matt. 22:15–22, where Jesus responded to the question concerning the obligation of paying taxes to the government. These verses must be seen in the overall context of Scripture. While Jesus acknowledged the believer's responsibility toward government, He emphasized the believer's responsibility to God.

Jesus' critical attitude toward government is seen in several instances. He called King Herod "that fox" in Luke 13:32. Also, in Mark 13:9 Jesus warns his disciples that they would be punished by the state for their beliefs: "You must be on your guard. You will be handed over to the local councils and flogged in the synagogues. On account of me you will stand before governors and kings as a witness to them."

Biblical passages extolling the believer to obey the state should not be taken to mean total submission in all instances. When the state conflicts with God's commands, the believer must follow Christ. Christians "under normal circumstances" should obey and pray for the government, but when the government "usurps the place and prerogatives of God" it must be resisted. Romans 13 is not a systematic endorsement of the state.

The Communist religious policies succeeded in driving a wedge between leadership and ordinary church members. Broun concludes that "few leaders are not compromised to some extent, and fewer dare to speak out when they should."[110]

Believers must experience reconciliation themselves before trying to proclaim it to others. Now is the best time for church leaders who opted to save the denomination by compromising their integrity to repent from this decision.

The model of Communist leadership found in Romania was strictly hierarchical. All initiatives, ideas, and solutions originated at the top and were communicated to the lower levels of the hierarchical structures. The main intent of the Communists was not to rid the church of leaders but to press its leaders into conformity with the Communist mold. In this way the church can be weakened from within until it is no longer a true church.

Some Baptist leaders were willing to cooperate with the regime because, in their view, the policies of the party reflected the teachings of Christ. Some leaders were motivated by patriotism to collaborate with the government.

It is wrong to assume that all Baptist leaders were puppets of the government. Many pastors were sincere and unwavering. These men were accused of subverting young people, organizing Bible study groups, and holding illegal meetings. Most pastored several churches at one time and often were questioned, threatened or targeted, or had their licenses revoked.

Most civilized governments recognize their constitution as the law of the land. However, in the Marxist-Leninist setting, one can see constitutional crises triggered by subsequent laws which are intended to dilute or nullify the constitutional guarantees of freedom of religion and conscience. Frequently, Communist officials "explained" to the zealous pastor invoking his constitutional rights that the constitutional provisions are primarily intended for foreign consumption and not open to the individual's interpretation. Their pragmatic argument was reflected in the statement, "We are the law! We make the law! Your duty is to obey the law!" Rarely, if ever, did the Romanian Supreme Court declare a law unconstitutional.

The situation was aggravated by 'oral laws' and unwritten regulations invoked by representatives of the Department of Cults. Their insistence on full compliance with these laws and regulations was met with resistance from well-trained and informed Baptist ministers and believers.[111]

In summary, the balanced Baptist position, affirmed by these uncompromised ministers, was that the government's refusal to follow constitutional provisions in the formulation of subsequent laws and the introduction of unwritten laws amounts to an intentional breaking of the law. Thus, in their thinking, the government's moral authority was lost. Secondly, the believer's ultimate allegiance was to a higher law. When this law and human law come into conflict, the believer's only alternative is to obey God. This is clearly illustrated in the classic passage of Acts 4:17–20, where Peter and John were prohibited to speak or teach in the name of Jesus. The ban had legal power, being issued by the authoritative Sanhedrin. Yet the two apostles decided to ignore this authority and suffer the consequences. Their reply to the members of the Sanhedrin poses a similar challenge to those in authority today who demand total obedience even in spiritual matters: "Judge for yourselves, whether it is right in God's sight to obey you rather than God" (Acts 4:19).

In practical terms, the believer is required to submit to those in authority and to pray for them. God's desire is order, not chaos. Jacques Ellul's suggestion, which Michael Bauman concluded, that the Christian should consider adopting an anarchist position in the society is unbiblical and seriously defective.[112] However, when the tension between the state's demands and the dictates of the individual's conscience reaches a dangerous level, the Christian must entrust his case to God, do what God directs him, and suffer the consequences of disobeying the human laws and authorities. This suffering for conscience's sake was praised by both Jesus and Peter. Under those circumstances, the Christian joined in the tradition of the real prophets of God.

Silviu Brucan, a member of the Communist elite, confirmed what many have said all along, that the secret police "was an abominable and monstrous institution. Its huge apparatus not only was an effective instrument of terror—it frightened, tortured, and even killed hundreds of people whose names are not even known—but a specialized division spread rumors and disinformation using the most modern techniques of psychological warfare, as directed by a tyrant against his own people. Securitate's hold on the nation was so tentacular and omnipresent that it appeared as a sort of Frankenstein exerting considerable power in keeping everyone cowed and frightened. For a long time, Securitate made the Romanians a nation of sheep."[113]

Baptists strived for pure and righteous living. Along with other evangelical Christians they were called by unbelievers "Pocaiti" [Repenters]. They earned a reputation for integrity and concern for other people. The Baptist work ethic and performance attracted attention and provided points of contact with unbelievers. When Baptists openly refused to be intimidated, large numbers of new believers were attracted to the faith.

Baptists have developed remarkable abilities to adjust their lives in order to meet new challenges. Among evangelical bodies, Baptists face a peculiar situation due to their growing spiritual influence over the masses. Forty-five years of continuous persecution has forced them to re-evaluate their priorities and allegiances.

Religious persecution does not automatically result in church growth. However, the remarkable growth of Baptists in this century is unprecedented. Among the evangelical communities, Baptists have attracted the greatest measure of attention. In 1982, the BWA reported 164,000 registered members. According to Lotz, at the end of the 1980s, membership exceeded 300,000 with more than 2,000 registered churches. Earl Pope reports that by 1991 Romanian Baptists had 325,000 members, 1,700 churches, and 170 pastors.[114]

Persecution had also a negative impact upon believers. It introduced a spirit of mistrust on both individual and group levels. It forced outstanding preachers and evangelists into exile, hampered evangelistic efforts through restrictions placed on their activities, and caused controversies which threatened denominational unity, yet not to the point of splitting the denomination as in the case of Russian Baptists.

On the positive side, persecution prevented the spread of nominalism among believers, secured a purer theology, enhanced personal righteousness, brought a spirit of revival confirmed by observers worldwide, revealed the courageous attitude of believers in the face of persecution, demonstrated the power of God, affirmed the sovereignty of God. Additionally, it enabled the church to show kindness, love, and compassion to other suffering believers. Furthermore, special prayers were offered for informers, the Inspector of Cults, and other official 'guests' who in reality represented the most spiritually resistant people.

God's people continued to do His work under adverse circumstances. One could hope that such commitment would inspire modern-day believers.

Notes

1. Situated in southeastern Europe, on the Black Sea, Romania is nearly as large as the state of Oregon, covers an area of 91,699 square miles [*The New Encyclopædia Britannica*, 1992 ed., s.v. "Romania"] and borders Ukraine on the north, Moldova on the east, Bulgaria on the south, Yugoslavia on the southwest, and Hungary on the west. The official name of the country is România. In English-language sources, however, several spellings have been used: Romania, Rumania, and Roumania. These designations carry different connotations and must be used carefully, since they relate closely to the whole question of the country's origin and history. The official designation in French has been "Roumanie" and in German "Rumänien." For works in English, Romanians prefer the term "Romania."

2. Herodotus called them "the bravest and most honorable of all the Thracian tribes," while Ovid, the Latin poet who lived among them and wrote poetry in their language, said that their appearance reminded him of Mars, the god of war. See Everett Gill, *Europe and the Gospel* (Richmond: Foreign Mission Board of the SBC, 1931), 57; and Cornelia Bodea and Virgil Cândea, *Transylvania in the History of the Romanians* (Boulder, Colo.: East European Monographs, 1982), 1.

3.   To commemorate his victory, Trajan commissioned his engineer-architect-sculptor Apollodorus to erect a column carved with reliefs picturing the campaigns in Dacia and topped by a statue of Trajan. The two thousand figures of these 124 panels depict the figure of king Decebalus, Dacian men, women, and children caught in the turmoil of war. Their physical appearance, clothes, and footwear seem identical to that of Romanian peasants. Will Durant, *The Story of Civilization*, Part 3, *Caesar and Christ* (New York: Simon & Schuster, 1944), 412.

4.   *Mic Dictionar Enciclopedic* [Small encyclopedic dictionary] (Bucharest: Editura Enciclopedica Româna, 1972 ed.), s.v. "România" and Durant, 410.

5.   During the Diocletian persecution (A.D. 303–4), many Christian soldiers and colonists were martyred at Tomis (present day Constanta); Octavian Bârlea, *Romania and the Romanians*, trans. G. Muresan and E. Motiu (Los Angeles: American Romanian Academy of Arts and Sciences, 1977), 185–86; and David Barrett, ed., *World Christian Encyclopedia: A Comparative Study of Churches and Religions in the Modern World AD 1900–2000* (New York: Oxford University Press, 1982), s.v. "Romania." Furthermore, a Gothic bishop named Theophilus from the Black Sea area attended the Council of Nicæa in A.D. 325; Socrates, *Ecclesiastical History*, Book II, Chap. 41. Latourette states that, as a bishop of "the Christians in Gothia," Ulfilas labored among his people north of the Danube River. Kenneth Scott Latourette, *A History of the Expansion of Christianity*, vol. 1, *The First Five Centuries* (Grand Rapids: Zondervan Publishing House, 1970), 213. See also Philip Schaff, *History of the Christian Church*, vol. 3, *Nicene and Post-Nicene Christianity* (Grand Rapids: Wm. B. Eerdmans Publishing Co., 1910), 624; and Vladimir Gsovski, ed., *Church and State Behind the Iron Curtain* (New York: Frederick A. Praeger, 1955), 257.

6.   Bârlea, Romania and the Romanians, 187.

7.   Ferdinand Schevill, *History of the Balkan Peninsula: From the Earliest Times to the Present Day* (New York: Frederick Ungar Publishing Co., 1950), 72–73; *New Encyclopædia Britannica*. There is no evidence as to the exact period in which the Byzantine (Slavonic) rite was adopted by the Romanians, but it seems reasonable to suppose that it took place in the ninth or tenth century.

8.   This is the generic name given by the Slavs and others to the Romanic peoples. However, they called themselves <u>Rumîni</u>, Rumanians. Various sources refer to them as <u>Volohi</u> (Russian source: *Nestor's Chronicle*, late ninth century), <u>Vlachs</u> (Byzantine source), <u>Blasi</u> (the chronicle of

King Béla's Anonymous Notary, early tenth century), <u>Blaci</u>, <u>Blachi,</u> <u>Balak</u>, <u>Olah</u> (Hungarian), and <u>Wallachen</u> (German). Andrei Otetea, ed., *A Concise History of Romania,* trans. and ed. Andrew Mackenzie (London: Robert Hale, 1985), 153; Bodea and Cândea, 4–5.

9. This southward movement was due to the consolidation of Hungarian feudal power in Transylvania, to the arrival of German colonists, and to the growing proselytizing zeal of the Hungarian Catholic kings. *New Encyclopædia Britannica.*

10. For a pertinent discussion of the Slavic culture's impact on the religious life, see Bârlea, 209–13.

11. The first of these was Mircea the Old (1386–1418) of Walachia. He and Vlad the Impaler (1456–62) had some success fighting the Turks. The Moldavian ruler Stephen the Great (1457–1504) defeated the Turks and built nearly fifty monasteries and churches. Still, Michael the Brave (1593–1601) is the leading Romanian national hero, chiefly because for the first time he brought the Romanians from Moldavia, Wallachia, and Transylvania under one rule to fight the Turks. Schevill, 205–6; *Mic Dictionar Enciclopedic.*

12. A northern province containing Romanian population.

13. The Hungarian parliament "voted for the Magyarization of the names of Transylvanian towns and villages. Romanian family names were Magyarized extensively. Railway stations were given Hungarian names. The Romanian Press was banned and so was the use of the mother tongue in Romanian schools." Otetea, 23. See also R.W. Seton-Watson, *A History of the Romanians* (Cambridge: University Press, 1934), 377; Trond Gilberg, *Nationalism and Communism in Romania* (Boulder Colo.: Westview Press, 1990), 174. After World War I, the tables were turned.

14. New Encyclopædia Britannica; and Castellan, 153–66.

15. Constantin C. Giurescu et al., *Chronological History of Romania* (Bucharest: Editura Enciclopedica Romana, 1972), 276–82; Otetea, 429–43; Georges Castellan, *A History of the Romanians,* trans. Nicholas Bradley (Boulder, Colo.: East European Monographs, 1989) 186–87.

16. Andrea Deletant and Dennis Deletant, comps., *Romania,* World Bibliographical Series, vol. 59 (Denver, Colo.: Clio Press, 1985), xiv; and Otetea, 472.

17. Otetea, 452; and Castellan, 171–74.

18. This was also called The Vienna Diktat. Public reaction in Romania was outrage. Huge anti-Hungarian and anti-German demonstrations took place in the major cities. Castellan, 205; <u>New Encyclopædia</u>

Britannica; and Otetea, 475. For a detailed discussion on the national and international reaction to the Diktat, see Bodea and Cândea, 77–81.

19. Castellan, 205.

20. Vyshinski was said to have presented his demands to King Mihai in a violent manner with much table-pounding. David Floyd, *Rumania: Russia's Dissident Ally* (New York: Frederick A. Praeger Publishers, 1965) 24.

21. Castellan, 219–35; Giurescu, 333–45; *New Encyclopædia Britannica*; and Floyd, 4–27.

22. In November 1987, thousands of angry citizens assailed the town hall and Communist Party headquarters in Brasov, shouting anti-Ceausescu slogans. *New Encyclopædia Britannica*.

23. Many of these targeted villages were situated in Transylvania and inhabited by ethnic minorities, primarily Hungarians.

24. J. G. Oncken was one of the greatest pioneers of the Baptist faith in Europe. Called both the "Father of Continental Baptists," and the "Father of German Baptists," he displayed a deep love for the Bible and a passion for souls. In 1823, he returned to Germany as a colporter representing the Continental Society and, after 1828, worked for the Edinburgh Bible Society, reporting in 1879 that he distributed no less than two million Bibles. By 1826, he had doubts about infant baptism and, through personal study of the Bible, he sought believer's baptism but had no one to perform the ordinance for him. During his sabbatical in Germany, Barnas Sears, an American professor at Hamilton College, who had learned about Oncken's desire, baptized him, his wife, and five others in the Elbe River on April 22, 1834. On the next day, they formed a Baptist church in Hamburg with Oncken as its pastor. Their boldness and growth provoked opposition. The believers faced considerable persecution and Oncken was himself imprisoned a number of times. He adopted the motto "Jeder Baptist ein Missionar" which guided his entire ministry. As a representative of American Baptists, Oncken conducted preaching tours all over Europe and the United States, and made special visits to Baptist churches in Russia and Romania. Rushbrooke, *The Baptist Movement*, 17–27; Henry C. Vedder, *A Short History of Baptist Missions* (Philadelphia: The Judson Press, 1927), 377–80; and McBeth, 470–73.

25. Alexa Popovici, *Istoria Baptistilor din România Volume I: 1856–1919*, [The history of Baptists in Romania, Volume I, 1856–1919] (Chicago: Editura Bisericii Baptiste Române, 1980), 13–18; James Henry Rushbrooke, *The Baptist Movement in the Continent of Europe* (London: Kingsgate Press, 1923), 157–58; and Parker, 216.

26. Rushbrooke, The Baptist Movement, 158.
27. Popovici, Istoria Baptistilor Vol. I, 21; 122–23.
28. Popovici, Alexa, "Constantin Adorian," *Luminatorul* [The Illuminator], Feb. 1994, 19–20.
29. Popovici, Istoria Baptistilor Vol. II, 18, 328.
30. Ibid., 80; and Alexa Popovici and Petre N. Popa, "Profesorul Ioan R. Socaciu," *Îndrumatorul Crestin Baptist* [The Baptist Christian guide], March-April 1959, 8–10.
31. J. D. Hughey, *Europe—A Mission Field?* (Nashville:Convention Press, 1972), 76.
32. J. R. Socaciu, "Training in Rumania," *Third Baptist World Congress*, 112–13; Gill, *Europe and the Gospel*, 81; and Popovici, *Istoria Baptistilor Vol. II*, 80–81.
33. See Everett Gill, "Roumania: Annual Report," in *Annual of the SBC; Memphis, Tennessee: May 9–12, 1929*, n.p., 256.
34. This figure was given by Grigorie Comsa in his 1928 address to the Romanian Senate. Popovici, *Istoria Baptistilor Vol. II*, 40.
35. Orphanages were started in Lupeni (1925), Prilipeti, Caras district (1927), and Simeria (1938). Viorel Garoiu, "Istoricul Orfelinatului Crestin Baptist din Prilipeti," *Calendarul Îndrumatorului Crestin* [The Christian guide calendar], 1947, 145–53; *Farul Mîntuirii*, Jan.-Feb. 1926, 14; *Farul Crestin* [The Christian beacon], July 1938, 5; and Popovici, *Istoria Baptistilor Vol. II*, 334–37.
36. Balgradeanu died of tuberculosis contracted on the mission field and died in December 1938. Ibid., 39, 48; Everett Gill, "The Word of God Grew and Multiplied in Rumania," in *Annual of the SBC; Fort Worth, Texas: May 16–20, 1934*, n.p., 223; and Popovici, *Istoria Baptistilor Vol. II*, 397.
37. In 1920 there were 633 churches with a total membership of 19,901. In 1930, there were 1,684 churches with 44,828 members.
38. Grigorie Comsa, *Baptismul în România* [The Baptist belief in Romania] (Arad, Romania: n.p., 1927), 18–22.
39. Popovici, Istoria Baptistilor Vol. I, 199–200.
40. Idem, Istoria Baptistilor Vol. II, 99.
41. Charles A. Brooks and James H. Rushbrooke, Baptist Work in Europe: Report of Commissioners of the BWA, Presented at the Conference in London July 19, 1920 (London: Baptist Union Publication Department, 1920), 56.
42. Ibid., 53–54.
43. In the Romanian context, the term "cult" designates a denomination, church, confession, creed, or form of worship. In the past, however, it

was frequently used to designate evangelical groups rather than major denominations such as Orthodox, Reformed, or Catholic. For instance, while the official name for the Orthodox denomination was the Romanian Orthodox Church, the official name for the Baptist denomination was the Christian Baptist Cult. Although in the Romanian context the term "cult" was not used in a pejorative sense and did not carry the negative connotation it carries in the West, the term did suggest an inferior status, a form of alienation, or a threat to the official ideology.

44. The appeal was personally given to Octavian Goga by Adorian during the November 15, 1920, and then recorded under No. 44913/1920.
45. The original petition with the General's hand written resolution is found at the museum of The Baptist Theological Seminary in Bucharest. Popovici, *Istoria Baptistilor Vol. II*, 102–4.
46. Ibid., 105–7.
47. *Monitorul Oficial* [Official Monitor], no. 6/Dec. 13, 1921, 54–56. Excerpts translated by the author.
48. Popovici, Istoria Baptistilor Vol. II, 109–11.
49. Ibid., 120.
50. RBU's protests registered in Bucharest under No. 39970/July 31, 1922 and No. 40075/Aug. 1, 1922.
51. RBU's protests registered in Bucharest under No. 47253, No. 47255, and No. 47256, dated May 24, 1922; Protest No. 7/Jan. 6, 1923, No. 104 and No. 105/Nov. 27, 1923, No. 36/Feb. 28, 1924, to the Minister of Public Instruction. See also Adorian, "Rumania: Persecution and Consolidation," 51–54.
52. See "De Vorba cu Cei Mai Nenorociti Frati ai Nostri," *Libertatea* [Liberty] (Orastie), no. 30, July 20, 1923, 2 and A. Filimon, "Fanatismul Baptist," *Solia Dreptatii si Gazeta Hunedoarei* [The message of justice and Hunedoara's gazette] (Deva), no. 32, Aug. 8, 1923, 1.
53. "Baptisti Americani si Englezi la Legatia Româna din Londra" [American and English Baptists to the Romanian legation in London], *Farul Mîntuirii*, no. 2, 1923, 5–6.
54. Adorian, "Rumania: Persecution and Consolidation," 51–54.
55. Directive No. 5734 published in *Monitorul Oficial*, Jan. 29, 1925.
56. Order No. 37301/1926 published in *Monitorul Oficial* of District Hunedoara, no. 13/Sept. 16, 1926.
57. Order No. 25557/Oct. 19, 1926 of Arad Prefecture.
58. Rushbrooke wrote several articles in the *Times* (London) as well as an article in a denominational publication entitled "Romania—Will There

Be a Change?" Other articles were published in the *Daily News* (London), *British Weekly* (London), *New York Times*, and *Christian Science Monitor.* See *Baptist Times*, (London), Feb. 25, 1926, *Boston Independent*, vol. 117, no. 3991, Nov. 9, 1926, 605–6 and J. H. Rushbrooke, "Romanian Papers and the Baptists' Claim for Freedom," *Baptist Times*, Apr. 1927, 266. A petition requesting the end of persecution, signed by sixty distinguished American personalities and another thirty thousand people from all social strata, was delivered to the Romanian minister in Washington, D.C. Also, BWA meetings in Budapest and London in 1926 focused on the persecutions in Romania.

59. Popovici, Istoria Baptistilor Vol. II, 151.

60. *Monitorul Oficial*, no. 89/Apr. 22, 1928, 3607–13.

61. Ion Ungureanu, "Persecutii Împotriva Baptistilor," [Persecutions against Baptists] *Dimineata* [Morning] (Bucharest) Feb. 5, 1932; and N. Ionescu, "Delegatia Baptista la M.S. Regele Carol II" [Baptist delegation to His Majesty King Carol II], *Farul Mîntuirii*, nos. 10–14, 1931, 8–9.

62. The Minister of Cults and Arts issued Directive No. 114119/1933 in which the Baptist confession was again called a "religious association." The directive stated that churches can operate only with authorizations, preachers must have special permits, and changes in statistical data should be reported every six months. Its real intent, as journalist I. Teodorescu reveals, was to drastically limit the number of converts and stifle church growth. In his article he rhetorically asks, "Since when has it become a crime . . . to propagate one's belief and attempt to win followers? Where would we all be if this method were to be applied to all of us?"

63. I. Teodorescu, "Iar Persecutii Religioase," [Religious persecutions], *Dimineata*, Aug. 11, 1929, 1. When Baptist Union president Ioan Socaciu published a protest in the newspaper *Dimineata*, opponent Nichifor Crainic published an article entitled "Baptists' Impertinence," maintaining that "as we well know, Baptists were never recognized as a religious cult." Nichifor Crainic, "Obraznicia Baptistilor," *Calendarul* (Bucharest), Sept. 10, 1933.

64. Popovici, Istoria Baptistilor Vol. II, 386–87.

65. Minister of Cults and Arts, Circular Order No. 175154/20611 and No. 175155/20612 dated Oct. 8, 1935.

66. "Communicat" [Communiqué] *Farul Crestin*, no. 19, 1937, 6; and *Farul Crestin*, no. 24, 1937.

67. J. H. Rushbrooke, "Rumania: The Latest Phase," *The Commission*, Mar. 1939, 72.

68. "Rumanian Baptists Persecuted," *The Commission*, Jan. 1939, 12.
69. "An Appeal of Baptist Students to Rumania," *The Commission*, Feb. 1939, 44.
70. "We are not through with our battle in Rumania. We must go on. With Baptist preachers in jail for conscience's sake, the world cannot be happy. The word 'closed' on a Baptist church door is a world tragedy. . . . We must open these doors." L. R. Scarborough, "Facing the World Task," *The Commission*, May 1939, 135.
71. For details see Directive No. 5657/Feb. 6, 1940 published in *Monitorul Oficial*, no. 34/Feb. 10, 1940, 566–67.
72. Popovici, Istoria Baptistilor Vol. II, 448.
73. Ibid., 445–46, 448–49.
74. Ibid., 458–61.
75. Ibid., 454–55, 458–59.
76. Gill, *Europe and the Gospel*, 83; and Rufus W. Weaver, "The Background of Rumanian Baptists," *The Commission,* Jan. 1939, 13.
77. In modern times, unfortunately, the terms "Marxism" and "Communism" have come to be used interchangeably, not only in the West but within the Marxist camp itself. However, the word "Communism" includes a great deal more than some people realize. It is the name of a philosophy of life which consists of atheism, dialectical materialism, class warfare, moral relativism, and a doctrine of progress. It also refers to an international political movement. The official doctrine of the Communist parties under Soviet leadership is called Marxism-Leninism Many non-Soviet Marxists dismissed Marxism-Leninism as "Vulgar Marxism." Marxism-Leninism is also identified as Scientific Marxism and Dominant Marxism.
78. Critical Marxism, known as Western Marxism or Marxist Humanism, denotes a philosophical movement which shows a greater concern for the individual and which claims to be truer to Marx's thought. The term "Eurocommunism" identifies the doctrine of Western European Marxist parties.
79. Throughout this study, the terms "Communism" and "Marxism-Leninism" will be considered synonymous. They will be used interchangeably with reference to the doctrine of the RCP and other Eastern European Communist parties.
80. Karl Marx and Frederick Engels, *The Communist Manifesto* (New York: International Publishers, 1948), 29.
81. Canon A. E. Baker, "Why Communism?," citing *The Infantile Disease of Leftism*, Christian News Letter, Mar. 30, 1949, 19.correct to tur

82. O. K. Armstrong and Marjorie Moore Armstrong, *Religion Can Conquer Communism* (New York: Thomas Nelson & Sons, 1964), 220.

83. Conservative estimates suggest over fifteen million people were killed. In his special report to the 20th Congress of the Communist Party of the Soviet Union, Khrushchev denounced Joseph Stalin and his crimes, accusing Stalin of discarding the Leninist method and using "mass arrests and deportations of many thousands of people, execution without trial and without normal investigation." Nikita S. Khrushchev, "The Crimes of the Stalin Era," *The New Leader*, annotated by B. I. Nicolaevsky, 1962, 15.

84. The essence of Lenin's position on religion is best expressed in his article "The Attitude of the Workers' Party to Religion," written in May 1909: "Marxism is materialism. As such it is as relentlessly hostile to religion as was the materialism of the eighteenth-century Encyclopaedists or the materialism of Feuerbach. . . . We must combat religion—that is the ABC of all materialism, and consequently of Marxism. . . . The combatting of religion cannot be confined to abstract ideological preaching. . . . It must be linked up with the concrete practice of the class movement, which aims at eliminating the social roots of religion." V. I. Lenin, *Collected Works*, vol. 15 (Moscow: Foreign Languages Publishing House, n.d.), 405–6.

85. In his book, *The Anti-Humans*, D. Bacu chronicles the 're-education' which took place, in 1948–51, in selected Romanian prisons. He was an eyewitness of the "Pitesti Experiment" officially known as "The Center for Student Re-education." At these internment camps a process known as "unmasking" or coerced political indoctrination took place. It included both extreme physical and mental torture. All methods were allowed and "all means for attaining the calculated goal were . . . sanctioned." These unmaskings were carried out by fellow students who had already been through the process of re-education. The goal of these unmaskings was not "to destroy individual man but the human species itself." For example, at one prison, students were forced to defecate into their soup bowls and, after continuous beatings, coerced to eat their own feces. Christian believers were singled out for the cruelest punishment; the Communists theorized that if they could break these "fanatics," they could certainly control others. Christianity was reviled with blasphemous acts. The most notorious was known as "Christ's Robe." One student was adorned with a white bedsheet and a phallic symbol made of soap was hung around his neck. He would be forced to walk around the room, "the Golgotha way," while being beaten with broomsticks. His fellow students would have to make the

sign of the cross, kiss the symbol, and say, "I pray to your omnipotence, only true master of those who believe." The 'experiments' were stopped in 1951 and local officials were tried and convicted of these crimes, while the Communist Party officials denied culpability. D. Bacu, *The Anti-Humans: Student "Re-education" in Romanian Prisons* (Englewood, Colo.: Soldiers of the Cross, 1971), 61, 186, 89.

86. The Catholic press, monastic orders, convents, schools, seminaries, welfare organizations, foundations, and hospitals were eliminated. By March 1948, ninety-two priests had been arrested, and fifty-one of these were still in prison in October 1948. Gary MacEoin, *The Communist War on Religion* (New York: The Devin-Adair Co., 1951), 79–80.

87. This is known as the Eastern-rite Catholic Church. In 1948, the church, with an estimated one million members, was liquidated because it resisted attempts to compromise. As a result it was forcibly assimilated into the Orthodox Church, and all twelve bishops and hundreds of clergy and laity were imprisoned. "Persecution of Religion in Rumania," Rumania National Committee, Washington, D.C., Nov. 1949, 25–28.

88. The Lord's Army [Oastea Domnului] is a lay renewal movement within the Orthodox Church founded in the 1920s by Iosif Trifa, an Orthodox priest from Transylvania. Since its inception, the movement challenged the Orthodox Christians to become soldiers of Christ and to struggle against all evil. The Lord's Army represents a reformation movement or an awakening in the Orthodox Church. Trifa's vision for the Lord's Army contains four main themes: the centrality of Christ and the cross, moral renewal, both at the individual and national levels, strong commitment to the laity, and total commitment to the Scriptures. In addition to church meetings, members gather in homes for Bible study and prayer. The hymnology and poetry are Romanian. By the time of the Communist takeover, the Lord's Army was a strong grass roots movement with its own publishing house and newspaper. The movement was officially banned in 1948 and its leaders were imprisoned. In 1958, five hundred prominent members were reimprisoned; many of them were not released until 1964. After 1965, active members were fined rather than incarcerated. One of its committed leaders, poet and hymn writer Traian Dorz, spent almost twenty years in prison prior to his release in 1982. Despite fierce persecution, the movement continued its activities underground. In fact, this group has all the characteristics of a true underground church.

Due to its clandestine existence, the membership in the Lord's Army has been difficult to determine. The 1986 edition of Patrick Johnstone's *Operation World* estimates 300,000 members and another 200,000 sympathizers. The Lord's Army has no "sister" denominations or parallels outside Romania. The traditional Orthodox Church still regards the members of the movement to be neo-Protestants in disguise. Since the 1989 Revolution, the Lord's Army has been officially recognized by the government. Its greatest challenge is to remain true to its mission of spiritual revival, evangelism, and preaching of the crucified and risen Christ. Iosif Trifa, *Ce Este Oastea Domnului?* [What is the Lord's Army?] (Sibiu, Romania: Editura Tipografiei Oastea Domnului, 1934), 122–231; Tom Keppeler, "Romania's Army of the Lord," *Evangelical Missions Quarterly* 29, no. 2 (April 1993): 132–38; "Evangelical Wing of the Orthodox Church in Romania," *Religion in Communist Lands* (RCL) 3, no. 6 (1974): 15–18; and Earl A. Pope, "Protestantism in Romania," in *Protestantism and Politics in Eastern Europe and Russia: The Communist and Postcommunist Eras*, ed. Sabrina P. Ramet, Christianity Under Stress Series (Durham, N.C.: Duke University Press, 1992), 193–4.

89. *New York Times*, Oct. 22, 1949, sec. 7, p. 1.
90. Robert Tobias, *Communist-Christian Encounter in East Europe* (Indianapolis: School of Religious Press, 1956), 321.
91. Law No. 62 published in *Monitorul Oficial* no. 51/Mar. 2, 1948.
92. Decree No. 177, Article 49, published in *Monitorul Oficial*, no. 178/ Aug. 4, 1948.
93. Janice Broun, *Conscience and Captivity: Religion in Eastern Europe* (Washington, D.C.: Ethics and Public Policy Center, 1988), 210. Davies' figures are slightly higher than Broun's since they include the affiliated churches and lay ministers. Thus, he claims that, of the 1,196 Baptist churches and preaching stations, 532 were closed as 'unnecessary.' Also, of the 952 pastors, 787 lost their licenses because of 'irregularities.' R. E. Davies, "Persecution and Growth," *The Baptist Quarterly*, Apr. 1970, 269.
94. Broun, 210.
95. Between 1969 and 1972, Ton studied theology at Regent's Park College in Oxford. The circumstances surrounding his visit to England as a tourist and the 'permission' to study at Oxford eluded even his closest friends. At a time when no Romanian Baptist was allowed to study abroad, many wondered how it was possible for him to receive the rare concession for such a study. Moreover, some asked, "Why did

the Romanian Communists grant him permission to return?" Although some answers were circulated, none of them proved satisfactory.

96. Josif Ton, "The Present Situation in the Baptist Church of Romania," *Religion in Communist Lands [RCL]*, supplementary paper no. 1 (November 1973): 7, 18.

97. Scarfe attributed this attitude of believers to Ton's earlier years when he became disillusioned, underwent a ten-year period of spiritual decline by staying away from the Church, embraced atheism, and was separated from his wife. Evidently, as Scarfe stated, "those who remembered his past failure hoped that his present public activity would not lead him down the same road." Alan Scarfe, "Romanian Baptists and the State," *RCL* 4, no. 2 (Summer 1976): 17; see also Edward Plowman, "Josif Ton's Fight for Rights," *Christianity Today*, May 20, 1977, 41.

98. Alan Scarfe, "A Call for Truth: An Appraisal of Rumanian Baptist Church-State Relationships," *Journal of Church and State* 21, no. 3 (Autumn 1979): 436–37.

99. Ibid., 437.

100. *Scînteia*, May 25, 1974.

101. Joseph Ton, "A Christian Manifesto to a Socialist Society," *RCL* supplementary paper no. 2, 1976; republished in 1985 by Joseph Ton, under the title *Marxism: The Faded Dream* (Great Britain: Marshall Pickering).

102. Scarfe, "A Call for Truth," 442; and Davies, 270, 273.

103. Broun, 211.

104. Ibid.

105. Romanian Christian Committee for the Defense of Religious Freedom, "Statement of Constitution," Documents nos. 1, 2, 3, July 5, 1978; Private Collection of John Moldovan, Dallas.

106. Pope, "Protestantism in Romania," 181.

107. Aurel Popescu, "Open Letter to Brother Joseph Ton—Who Are You, Josif Ton?," Scappose, Oreg., Feb. 1979.

108. Broun, 213.

109. Pope, "Protestantism in Romania," 166.

110. Congress, House, Committee on Ways and Means, Subcommittee on Trade, "The Hungarian Reformed Church in Romania," *Most-Favored-Nation Trading Status for the Socialist Republic of Romania, the Hungarian People's Republic, and the People's Republic of China*, June 10, 1986 (Washington, D.C. GPO., 1986), 281–84; Peter Keresztes, "The Bible as Romanian Toilet Paper," 26; Wall Street

Journal, June 14, 1985; Breakthrough, Slavic Gospel Association Newsletter, 1985, 3.

111. "Baptist Pastors Write to President Ceausescu," *KNS* no. 182 (September 8, 1983): 12.

112. J. D. Douglas, ed., *Proclaim Christ Until He Comes: Calling the Whole Church to Take the Whole Gospel to the Whole World* (Minneapolis: World Wide Publications, 1990), 23–24.

113. Broun, 20.

114. Those who argued in favor of complete submission to the provisions of the law and to instructions received from the Inspector of Cults faced the practical problem of their inability to abide by their own principles. For instance, a pastor who pretended to obey the law, but failed to report a conversation to the secret police officer or the Inspector of Cults was caught in a major moral dilemma. Not a few of these 'obedient' pastors accepted gifts from abroad, entertained foreign guests, and received Bibles for distribution. Privately some of them admitted the existence of persecution, but officially they stated that churches enjoyed freedom.

115. Michael Bauman, "Jesus, Anarchy and Marx: The Theological and Political Contours of Ellulism," *Journal of the Evangelical Theological Society* 35, no. 2 (June 1992): 228.

116. Silviu Brucan, *The Wasted Generation: Memoirs of the Romanian Journey from Capitalism to Socialism and Back* (Boulder, Colo.: Westview Press, 1993), 160.

117. Denton Lotz, "Baptist Witness in Eastern Europe," *American Baptist*, July-Aug. 1976, 16. need to explain that this ref came from pope's chapter?Lotz estimated more than 200,000 Baptists in 1976. Pope, "Protestantism in Romania," 278, note no. 109.

Chapter Seventeen

Missions and Genocide in Rwanda

James Butare-Kiyovu

The 1994 Rwanda genocide was not a spontaneous epoch of
history, but rather a systematically planned and executed
catastrophe dating from colonial era until the post independence.
Do you then want to be counted and recognized on the annals of
history as a group that tried to distort facts and truths of the
Rwandan genocide? Distorting the facts of history should not be
the Western media's game. Truth is what should always triumph,
for if it doesn't, then what next?

Thomas Kagera
The New Times (Kigali)
March 28, 2006

Need for a Different Look at "History"

A Kinyarwanda Legend: Long before the colonial era and the
introduction of Christianity, Rwandans believed in one God, the
Creator *(Imana Rurema)*.

A Kinyarwanda legend says that God created three brothers: Gatwa,
Gahutu and Gatutsi. The prefix Ga- denotes a brotherly endearment.
The three brothers shared and still share everything in common: the
same language, the same culture, the same traditions, etc.

One day, God told the three brothers that he was going on a long
journey. He left a jug full of milk to each of the three brothers and
told them to keep their milk until his return.

After some time, Gatwa the youngest of the brothers started playing and ended up spilling his milk. Gahutu felt hungry and thirsty and decided to drink his milk. Gatutsi kept the milk.

When God returned he told the three brothers that because Gatutsi had obeyed him and kept the milk, he would be in charge of his younger brothers. God gave him cows that had produced the milk and that became the symbol of his stewardship and protection over his two brothers.

That legend (abridged for purposes of this paper) kept the three brothers living harmoniously together for centuries before the coming of the Germans, the first colonial masters to rule Rwanda. The legend can also be used to gain useful insights in the following complex systems that existed in pre-colonial Rwanda.

Kinship System – All Rwandans whether Hutu or Tutsi belong to various kinship groupings and lineages such as: abega, abasindi, abasinga, except for the Banyiginya, which was exclusive to the royal family.

Feudal System – In Rwanda there was a hereditary system of kings (abami), chiefs and sub-chiefs (abatware) who exercised the political and military administration of the country.

Ubuhake – This was a Master-Servant relationship that characterized the social system in pre-colonial Rwanda. It was based on the ownership of cattle and land. If you were a rich landowner with many cows, you would afford to have many servants *(abagaragu)*. Under the "ubuhake" feudal system the master did not "own" the servant in the same way a master owned a slave in countries that practiced slave trade and slavery. The relationship could be terminated, especially if the master failed to give the expected cow/cows and protection to the servant for the work accomplished. Apart from very few top aristocratic families, every Rwandan whether Tutsi, Hutu or Twa was answerable to someone else above him in this system of *ubuhake*.

Creation of the "Hima-Tutsi Empire" myth – When colonialists arrived in Rwanda, they were surprised to find a well-organized hierarchical leadership under a King (*Umwami*), which resembled in many ways the feudal Kingdoms in European countries. They started speculating that the Tutsis, especially the King and his chiefs *(abatware)* with whom they were in contact, could not be of the same origin as the people they ruled. They wrote their speculations in books, claiming among other things that Hutus were Bantu while Tutsis were Hamitic. They speculated that the Tutsis had come from somewhere north, probably from Ethiopia or Egypt herding their cattle along the river Nile. Their theory appeared to them all the more plausible because they found similar kingdoms in the Great Lakes Region, notably the Hima/Huma in Uganda and Burundi who seemed to have the same morphological features and also seemed to share the same customs and traditions.

The Indirect Rule Policy – The Germans who ruled Rwanda before they lost the First World War and the Belgians who replaced them decided to practice the so called *Indirect Rule Policy* whereby the traditional feudal system under the King and his chiefs was allowed to run side by side with the colonial system. The Tutsis, especially those in the higher ranks of the feudal system, had more access to the colonial education and to the colonial jobs. That colonial advantage considerably widened the gap, which already existed because of the inherent inequality in any feudal system.

Revival vs. inch-deep Christianity – A vast number of people in Rwanda (about 50% of the population) became and still consider their selves Roman Catholic. During the colonial times and until very recently most Roman Catholics were not known to read the Bible for themselves. Unfortunately the words the catholic priests recited (mostly on Sundays in Latin) could not be fully understood by the large majority of the attendants. As a result, there is a great need for Christian growth in Rwanda beyond the inch-deep understanding of the Scriptures. At the same time there was growth and revival amongst some Rwandan Protestants denominations (about 30% of the population) that read the Bible and/or listen to someone reading the Bible in their own mother tongue, Kinyarwanda.

Bad leadership – The educated Tutsis who had cohabited with the Belgian masters during the colonial era were the same ones who started agitating for independence. This happened in the late 1950's, when Congo and Burundi were also looking for independence. In 1956 the ruling Tutsi council sent a document to the UN asking for political autonomy. Belgium, which is roughly the same size as Rwanda, was not ready to hand over power and riches from her colonies without a fight. As far as Rwanda is concerned, there was an about-turn in the Belgian politics. In retaliation, the Belgian administration decided to support a few educated Hutus and helped them to revolt against the monarchy. In 1957, that group of educated Hutus around Gregoire Kayibanda published "The Hutu Manifesto" which called for the abolition of Tutsi privileges.

In 1959 after the death of King Mutara, a succession of events in Rwanda led to thousands of Tutsis being killed by Hutus while others became refugees especially in the neighboring countries of Uganda, Burundi, Congo and Tanzania. Tutsis who stayed in Rwanda became second-class citizens in their country and constantly faced physical and psychological harassments.

Distorted History – After the first attempt of genocide against the Tutsis and their exile in the 1960's the leadership in Rwanda started teaching a distorted history in order to justify their discrimination against the Tutsis. "The Hima-Tutsi Empire" speculations first made by colonialists were now taught in schools as historical facts. In my opinion such speculations were most unfortunate, but I don't believe in any way that they constituted a conscious "systematic planning of genocide" at the time.

Every time the regime faced some obstacle the Tutsis were used as a scarecrow to eliminate them. The Tutsis were vilified and referred to as *inzoka* snakes and/or *inyenzi* cockroaches. Since killing a snake or a cockroach is normal and expected, those who killed Tutsis got away with it. Many Hutus, after independence, developed a mentality of impunity as far as killing or mistreating a Tutsi was concerned. The euphemism for killing a Tutsi was referred to as *gukora* meaning "doing useful work."

The Cold-War factor – It would be difficult to justify the claim that Westerners (including missionaries) who lived and had embassies and projects in Rwanda did not know what was happening. One reason which may explain their silence, or in some cases their open support to the Hutu extremist regimes, is the cold war factor. The first President of Rwanda Gregoire Kayibanda was a former Roman Catholic seminarian who kept strong ties with the Catholic Church and with the Belgian Government.

The second President of Rwanda Juvenal Habyarimana was also considered a very devout Catholic and a friend of the West. Both had full protection from the West because they claimed to stand against communism. Western countries therefore ignored or turned a blind eye to the gross injustices and killings that were happening in Rwanda. That was also true with other countries such as Zaire (now the Democratic Republic of Congo) that were not aligned to the Soviet Union and communism. When the cold war period ended and the West started withdrawing the unconditional support, most of those regimes collapsed one after the other.

The Refugee factor – For over thirty years, Rwandans (mainly Tutsis) lived in exile, the vast majority of them in refugee camps. Both the first Republic of President Kayibanda and the second Republic of Habyarimana refused to do anything about settling the refugee issue. Their argument was that Rwanda is a small country and therefore refugees had to remain where they were. In the 1960's when the refugees made desperate and poorly organized attacks into Rwanda, the Tutsis inside the country were killed or persecuted. In the late 1970 when a younger generation of Rwandans formed a political organization that later became the Rwandans Patriotic Front (RPF) the regime in Rwanda still refused to have anything to do with them, totally convinced that they could not be a threat.

Genocide

Picture in your mind two women: one woman with a raised machete chasing another woman carrying a baby on her back. Let your mind focus for a moment on the two women and then briefly shift to a group of UN soldiers who are intently watching the chase. The UN soldiers are heavily armed. They have armored personnel carriers (APCs), which are labeled UN in big white letters. Then go back to the two women. The one with the machete has considerably gained ground on the one fleeing with her baby. Then, a ghastly thing happens. The woman with the baby has fallen down and the other woman is repeatedly cutting up the mother and the baby with the machete. Go back to the UN soldiers. They look horrified but none has moved.

During the Rwandan genocide, which took place from April to July 1994, I was still the RPF (Rwandese Patriotic Front) representative and my office was strategically placed in Brussels, Belgium. I had been part of the RPF and Government of Rwanda Joint Mission to UN in New York that had led to the UN Security Council Resolution 872. According to the resolution, the UN peacekeepers in Rwanda were not supposed to take sides. But how if the UN soldiers had decided to shoot in the air? Probably the woman with a baby could have escaped. Probably the genocide would not have taken place.

There was also the shocking news of the killing of ten Belgian peacekeepers along with Ms. Agathe Uwilingiyimana, the Prime Minister, they were charged to protect. I remember being summoned to the Belgian Ministry of Foreign Affairs. The message to the RPF organization was short and final. The remaining Belgian peacekeepers were pulling out of Rwanda.

Within days, the French Government and other Western governments started evacuating their nationals. We in RPF felt angry and scandalized that the UN Security Council could continue to sit in the company of the Rwandan ambassador and for weeks resist using the term "genocide" when the massacres were claiming thousands and thousands of mainly Tutsi people everyday. If that was not genocide, then what was it?

In an article commemorating ten years after the genocide, Sir Edward Clay, then High Commissioner to Uganda and non-resident Ambassador to Rwanda recalls: "It was not until the massacres of 1994 were well advanced that I and others even began to speak of genocide. Some had warned us in advance that this was planned.

Failing to recognize the validity of those warnings was at least a failure of information and of understanding and analysis."

The UN Security Council persisted with their flawed analysis of the situation and decided to reduce the UNAMIR (United Nations Assistance Mission in Rwanda) comprising at the time of 2,500 soldiers under the command of Canadian Major General Romeo Dallaire to only 450 personnel The violence that followed was unprecedented in the history of Rwanda and in the history of the world. One million people, mainly Tutsis, were brutally killed in a matter of a hundred days.

The Rwandan genocide did not result from a spontaneous outburst of anger because of President Habyarimana's death, as some people think. It was a very well prepared and very well executed genocide. And the powers that be did not fail to stop it for lack of information. The RPF office in Brussels, among others, sent out to the media, embassies in Brussels, ministries, international organizations, NGO's, political parties, church leaders, and others, numerous press releases warning of the systematic preparations of the genocide and the training and arming of the Interahamwe militia.

My office also distributed evidence of systematic propaganda by Hutu extremists who were using the hate radio RTLM and hate magazines. It was particularly shocking to read the "Hutu ten commandments" in one of the more virulent extremist publications called "Kangura." It was clear that a few evil people were playing on the ignorance of the Rwandan mostly illiterate population. Their strategy was to make them think that there was some Biblical justification for their extermination plans and they succeeded.

What Lessons Can Missions Learn from the Rwandan Genocide?

All religious missions in Rwanda at the time of genocide responded to the call of their governments for immediate evacuation, just like the rest of their fellow international community. Tutsi co-workers in Churches, hospitals and other mission projects were shocked to be abandoned when it was clear they faced certain death. But is it reasonable to expect any help from missions in such a situation? What can missions do when the UN and governments fail?

Hugh McCullum (1994:75) recorded in his book subtitled: *The Rwanda Tragedy and the Churches,* a testimony from a Rwandan pastor which shows the weaknesses of the Rwandan Church [and if I may suggest the weaknesses of the missions too] during the post independence rule to the time of genocide (1962 to 1994).

The pastor lamented:

> Why did the message of the gospel not   reach the people who were baptized? What did we lose? We lost our lives. We lost our credibility. We are ashamed. We are weak. But, most of all, we lost our prophetic mission. *We could not go to the President and tell him the truth because we became sycophants to the authorities.*
>
> We have had killings here since 1959. *No one condemned them.* During the First Republic, they killed slowly, slowly, but *no one from the churches spoke out. No one spoke on behalf of those killed.* During the Second Republic there were more killings and more people were tortured and raped and disappeared; and *we did not speak out because we were afraid, and because we were comfortable.*
>
> Now there has to be a new start, a new way. We must accept that Jesus' mission to us to preach the gospel means that we must be ready to protect the sheep, the flock - even if it means we must risk our lives - to lay down our lives for our sisters and brothers. *The Bible does not know Hutu and Tutsi, neither should we* [my emphasis in italics].

The international community has recognized its failure. For example, during a visit to Africa in 1998, President Clinton apologized to the people of Rwanda. He said: "All over the world there were people like me sitting in offices who did not fully appreciate the depth and the speed with which you were being engulfed by this unimaginable terror."

The United Nations has also recognized its failure and has designated April 7 (day when the massacres started) as the International Day of Reflection on the Genocide in Rwanda. The UN has also established an International Criminal Tribunal on Rwanda, based in Arusha, Tanzania and all countries are expected to search for and prosecute those accused of genocide.

What Attitude Should Missions Take?

On February 19, 2003 Elizaphan Ntakirutimana, a senior Pastor with the Seventh-Day Adventist Church in Mugonero, was convicted of aiding and abetting in genocide. His son Gerard Ntakirutimana, a medical doctor, was convicted of genocide and crimes against humanity. Both had found refuge and were living peacefully in USA before being extradited to Arusha.

Two Benedictine nuns, Consolate Mukangango and Julienne Mukabutera, who used to run the convent in Sovu, collaborated with the killers by providing them with the petrol that set the building on fire where 500 Tutsi were hiding. A Brussels court has sentenced them to fifteen and twelve years respectively.

Other religious people have been arrested and are still awaiting trial Many others are known to be still at large. It is a very sad situation to see former colleagues being pursued for genocide related crimes. However, it is also a sobering reminder that denominational Churches and missions in the West should make sure that they are not playing host to innocent looking associates who may have taken part in crimes against humanity.

An Approach That Will Make a Difference

Some people argue that Africa's poverty increases the competition for what resources there are within the country and this may have been one of the factors that caused the Rwandan genocide. It is a fact that most of the militia was unemployed youth who were promised money, jobs or land and property that belonged to the Tutsis. There was also evidence that most of them killed under the influence of alcohol and other drug substances provided by the organizers.

Others argue that ignorance was at the root of the problems in Rwanda. For example, it was ignorance that caused hatred that led millions of illiterate and semi illiterate Rwandans to believe in the distortions that were made by highly intelligent but evil extremists concerning the Hutu Ten Commandments.

Disease is another major problem that has taken over and has caused more deaths than the violence in the Great Lakes Region of Africa. First it was thousands of Hutu refugees who perished because of cholera and other diseases in refugee camps. Today, four million people have died of diseases in Congo alone because of the ongoing conflicts in the Great Lakes Region of Africa. There are also thousands and thousands of victims of rape during the conflicts who are now carrying the deadly AIDS disease.

In conclusion, I would like to refer to the Institutional Mission for WCIU (William Carey International University), which is to prepare men and women to discover and address the roots of human problems around the world.

My attempt in this paper has been to suggest some historical, cultural and socio-political issues that are at the root of the Rwandan Genocide. I believe this is in line with the educational philosophy and approach that WCIU would like to promote through its International Development courses at Masters and PhD level. For now, there are five MA students in Rwanda who will begin this course by July 2006. There are also two PhD associates and two MA students in Uganda who are in the pipeline. Part of their study will be to mentor and disciple others on the job using what they will be learning. This approach holds the key to the future of missions and NGO's that may wish to properly address the roots of violence and other problems around the world.

Legend:
1. A non-historical or unverifiable story handed down by tradition from earlier times and popularly accepted as historical
2. The body of stories of this kind, especially as they relate to a particular people or group or clan.

Bibliography

Arusha, Mary Kimani. "Nahimana Led Anti – Tutsi Committee, Expert Witness Says" *Internews*. (2002).

Butare-Kiyovu, James. "Ethnic Factor in the World Today: Rwanda's Genocide." (2004). (Unpublished).

Clay, Edward. "Time to Remember Rwanda Genocide." *The Nation (Nairobi), (*2005).

Jabweli, Okello. "No Plot for Hima, Tutsi Empire – Museveni." *New Vision*, (2002).

McCullum, Hugh. *The Angels Have Left Us: The Rwandese Tragedy and the Churches.* Geneva: World Council of Churches, 2005.

"A collection of modules on: Scripture Use; Literacy; Community Development and Peacemaking." (2002). The curriculum is currently being translated from English into Kinyarwanda. (Unpublished).

"The 'Hutu Ten Commandments' as published in Kangura, No. 6 (December 1990)." http://www.trumanwebdesign.com/~catalina/commandments.htm

"Why U.S. Didn't Stop Kigali Genocide." *The East African.* (2002).

"What Clinton Knew About Rwanda Genocide." *The East African.* (2004).

"What Next? Do You Profit from Distorting Rwanda Issues." *The New Times (Kigali).* (2006).

Chapter Eighteen

Missions in the Context of Violence
in the Middle East

Tony Maalouf

On November 21, 2002, a young missionary named Bonnie Witherall laid down her life for Christ in Lebanon, and succumbed to death at the murderous hands of an unknown Muslim extremist. She was serving the Lord in Sidon by practicing her nursing skills in a pre-natal clinic that ministered to needy and poor women, most of them belonging to the nearby Palestinian refugee camp of Ain el-Helweh.[1] A local Muslim publication denounced Bonnie's work and the Christian ministry she was helping as a "Zionist movement." They accused the Christian workers there of teaching Palestinian children to "forgive the Jews" and "leave them Jerusalem and the land they stole from them." A local Imam accused those involved in the Christian ministry among children as taking advantage of their poverty to make them "change religion!" Sadly, the murderer was not identified and the judicial case was forgotten.

A few months later, in the city of Tripoli in northern Lebanon, a young Jordanian convert from the majority religion lost his life while trying to dismantle a bomb deposited at the door of a European missionary family. Jameel was a vibrant and enthusiastic young Christian that the present writer had the privilege of having as a student at a local Baptist seminary. Following that murder, comments were heard accusing the missionary family of having political and Zionist agendas. As in the case of Bonnie, justice did not take place.

In the month of March, 2004, four American Christian workers from the Southern Baptist International Mission Board were killed in northern Iraq in a drive-by shooting in the city of Mosul. They were involved in humanitarian relief projects. Their death was one of many tragic expressions of anti-American and anti-western sentiments among Muslim extremists in Iraq that claimed the lives of hundreds of Westerners and Iraqis as well.

We may add to those episodes hundreds of cases of religious persecution that converts from Islam face on a daily basis in their communities. It is interesting to note at this point that Jewish Messianic believers face a similar maltreatment mostly at the hands of Orthodox Jews. According to ASSIST News Service, the police not only turn a blind eye, but even side with the persecutors. Until now, a Jew who put his trust in the Messiah jeopardizes his right to the Israeli citizenship according to the Law of Return.

This unfortunate opposition to the Gospel in the Middle East should not deter us from attempting to fulfill the Great Commission in that part of the World. If anything, it should create in us a greater commitment to pray for the lost there, and a bigger burden to share "the Gospel of Peace" in that hostile environment shredded by hatred and animosity. However, while missionaries and Christian workers should be ready to lay down their lives for the Gospel of Christ, one may need to stop and analyze some of the elements standing behind the rejection of the Gospel message in the Arab and Muslim context. By doing that, we will hopefully help improve the effectiveness of the Christian testimony.

Questions to Consider

When considering the topic of missions in the context of violence in the Middle East, one can't help but ask several questions. Is it possible that the opposition associated with the presentation of the Gospel in the Middle East is partly due to factors that are non-theological in nature? Is it possible that cultural antagonism stands behind some of the suffering in missions in the Middle East today? If so, do these elements diminish in any way the redemptive value of the missionary sacrifice for the Gospel in the Middle East? Is there anything the church should do to promote further contextualization of the message and its platform making it more adapted to the culture of the Middle East? Are there instances in Scriptures, especially in the Book of Acts, where Christians had to pay a heavy price for a misunderstood Gospel? If there is, may it be that suffering and martyrdom are the price that Christian workers have to pay to strip the Christian testimony from the cultural and political baggage and present a pure Gospel message as the only hope for the lost regardless of social settings? Would the blood of the martyrs that died for cultural, political and religious reasons become "the seed of the church" in the Middle East today?

It is not the attempt of this paper to do an in-depth analysis of missions in the context of suffering in the Middle East. It is its aim however to raise questions and stir up thinking in order to create a platform for a constructive and helpful discussion of the subject. Hence, the focus would be on the socio-political aspects of religious persecution.

The Middle East and the Church

The Middle East has always been a controversial region on the terrestrial globe. It stood at the crossroad of world civilizations; it produced and nurtured the world's three monotheistic religions; and it is recently yielding the most crucial world events, events that will very likely shape the history of mankind until its consummation. [2] Christianity started in the Middle East and spread from there to the rest of the world, and since two centuries it is attempting to reclaim that part of the world for Christ, thus going full circle.

Yet three major challenges face the church today in its missionary efforts in the Middle East. Religiously, Islam poses the greatest obstacle before the spread of Christianity. Following its rise in the seventh century A.D., this monotheistic religious reform out of Arabia significantly affected the Christian faith in the region where it was born. Having spread quickly into the Fertile Crescent area and North Africa, Islam caused a great demise of Christianity in the respective regions of its expansion. Under the Islamic Caliphate, Christians (as well as Jews) quickly became a minority, given the underprivileged social status as the *dhimmi* people. This categorization allowed them to be protected as "people of the book" paying double taxation as long as they did not choose to convert to Islam. The militant aspect of Islamic expansion, together with the traditionalism of Christianity contributed to the intimidation of Christians and the loss of the Great Commission burden in the Middle East.

Any presentation of the Gospel today in a Muslim context has to cope with the sensitivity and complexity of the religious setting there. Thus, it requires a full understanding of Islamic belief and practices, as well as the Muslim mindset. It should also attempt to offer Christian answers to various challenges raised within that system of belief.

Culturally, long centuries of world history witnessed the East-West polarization of human societies. Christianity gradually became associated with the West, while Islam was considered an eastern religion. Western societies moved toward individualism and liberalism at the level of thinking, politics, and human social behavior. This led to licentious lifestyles and an overt expression of sexual immorality, which is still undercover in societies revolving around of the honor-shame principle.[3] On the other hand, Middle Eastern societies maintained a strict and conservative social outlook and adherence to community social life and family values. Western liberal forms of thinking are coveted in the Middle East, yet they are not allowed to deeply challenge conservative social traditions. In a society where religion is considered a community choice and an affair of the state, western moral degradation reflected negatively on the Christian profile in the mind of the Muslim. Rejection of the Gospel became associated with rejection of the so-called western Christian societies. There is much to tear down in the mind of a Muslim in order to communicate biblical Christianity to him or her. Similarly, when doing missions in the Middle East, it is essential to bridge the cultural gap if we desire to avoid planting churches that will float as western cultural islands in an eastern cultural sea.

Politically, since the inception of the modern state of Israel, western biases and blind pro-Israeli stances have formed a major obstacle before western missionary efforts. Evangelicalism has become gradually associated with western politics in the region, which aim at maintaining Israel's supremacy in an Arab context. It is of essential importance to strip the Gospel message from the Zionist political stigma and present it as a pure message of salvation to the lost. Many Evangelical leaders in the West inadvertently make the current State of Israel an additional stumbling block before the Gospel of Christ through their indiscriminate political support of the Hebrew Nation. Thus, they jeopardize the preaching of the message among Arabs, and deceive the unbelieving Jews who should look to Christ as the only basis for claiming the Abrahamic covenantal blessings. While we need to be respectful of the right of all peoples—the Jews no exception—to live in dignity and security, the injustices committed in the land cannot be overlooked by Christians without jeopardizing the moral outlook of the God we serve. Therefore, it is a must that we restore the exclusivity of the Cross of Calvary in our presentation of the Gospel, as well as in the mind of the Middle Eastern audience.

Missions and the Religious Challenge

Tension between Christianity and Islam is continuously on the rise. The events of September 11, 2001, and the consequent war against terrorism have greatly affected the Muslim profile in the mind of people in the West. The average Muslim struggling to lead a normal life like the rest of humanity is sacrificed on the altar of militant Jihadists.

The western missionary in a Muslim context in the Middle East faces harder time now trying to ease the cultural/religious tension. Comments made on high levels of Christian leadership in the West attacking Islam, Muhammad, and Muslims have reverberated strongly in the Middle East and made frontline news. After aggressive statements made in the U.S. against Islam in 2002, the Dean of the Baptist Seminary in Lebanon affirmed that for three years the school "was not allowed to admit any students from outside Lebanon." They lost the opportunity of training for more than "100 students from all across the Middle East and North Africa." Those could have become "church and community leaders that would have played a substantial role in transforming their societies."

While we do not advocate political correctness, as opposed to uncompromising truth, it should be admitted that some statements lack depth and objective scholarship. On the other hand, uncalculated declarations force the Middle Eastern Evangelical believer and the western missionary to bear their consequences and fight a battle they did not choose in timing or framework.

On another scale, a missionary to the Middle East is faced with the challenge of finding a common ground, a bridge to build upon in order to introduce the Muslim to Christ. Often, this bridge is found on the level of the human and religious experience. When addressing the Athenians, Paul said to them, "God made from one blood every nation of mankind to live on all the face of the earth, having determined their appointed times and the boundaries of their habitation, *that they would seek God*, if perhaps they might grope for Him and find Him, though He is not far from each one of us" (Acts 17:26-27). Many Christians have recently asked the question, do Christians and Muslims seek the same God? Someone's answer to that question affects the amount of integration he or she is ready to make in a Muslim culture. It may also determine the amount of opposition a missionary is going to bear for the sake of maintaining the exclusivity of the Christian God. Though most Christians hold to the exclusivity of Christ when comparing their system of belief with Islam, many do believe that we are looking toward the same direction, talking about the same Creator. The present writer believes that Christians need not deny Muslims their monotheistic faith and the seeking after the God of Abraham, which they affirm. Jesus did not do that to the Samaritan woman, but he pointed out her ignorance of the essence of God saying, "you worship whom you do not know, but we worship whom we know" (John 4:22). The object of faith of the three monotheistic religions is the God of Abraham. Yet, only in Christ can we have full knowledge of Him; thus only in Christ can we worship God as He truly is.

Now how much religious contextualization should we make in a Muslim setting? A Christian worker serving Christ among Muslims in the Middle East related to the writer how opposition to his ministry was significantly reduced when he presented himself as a Muslim follower of Issa the Messiah. When asked about the possibility of deception in presenting himself this way, he affirmed that at all he discusses and studies with them is the Bible. He is also known among them as a follower of Jesus/Issa. He rarely associates with the Arab Christian church or the Western Christian church. He is the closest to an insider a western worker can be. He is vocal about his faith and in that sense, may be categorized as a C-5 worker. Is that type of integration essential in order to reduce opposition and preach a theologically understood clear Gospel?

Missions and the Cultural Challenge

Missionary efforts of the Evangelicals in the nineteenth century led to the starting of many churches. Yet, most of the churches started adopted a western style of worship, including hymns, tunes, and musical instruments. While public speaking is a longstanding practiced skill among Arabs, Christian preaching style, delivery and attire in the Middle East church have been heavily influenced by the West. In an era of intense globalization (Americanization) of culture, western culture is perceived as aggressively attempting to modify, and even replace the local culture. Rejection of western culture with its emphasis on individualism and moral laxity may have been behind some of the violence the church is facing in the Middle East. What are some of the ways to divorce the Gospel from its cultural western baggage? Are missionaries preaching an American Gospel or a Middle Eastern one? The first Jewish converts to Christianity held their meetings in the Synagogue. Should Muslim converts attempt to stay in the Mosque? Should Muslim converts pray five times a day, and present themselves as culturally Muslims by fasting Ramadan and sacrificing the *Adha*? If they should not do that while hiding their faith, can they do it while sharing their faith in Christ? Should Muslim converts call themselves Christians with all the cultural baggage that may be associated with the term or can they choose another term that describes their belonging to Jesus, like "Followers of *Issa*?" The answer to this and many similar ones may determine the amount of cultural suffering versus suffering for the pure Gospel.

Missions and the Political Challenge

While in Jordan in January of 2006, the present writer was surprised at seeing a statement by Pat Robertson making headline news in secular Arabic newspapers. The TV preacher was presented as a major representative of American Evangelicals. Commenting on Ariel Sharon's pull out of Gaza strip, Robertson believed that the prime minister's stroke condition was caused by God because he dared to "divide God's land" as it is stated in the book of Joel. He went on to affirm that God will set himself against any prime minister in Israel who takes a similar course to comply with UN resolutions! Even though Pat Robertson later apologized to Sharon's son, the local damage was made and, as usual, Evangelicals and missionaries in the Middle East have had to deal with repercussions of that and similar statements.

While the writer was serving as a full-time faculty at JETS in Amman, Jordan, the minister of foreign affairs in the country related to the founder of the seminary a common rumor, seriously entertained among people in authority. The school was accused of helping in the rebuilding of the Jewish Temple in Jerusalem! While this may sound funny, it shows that the secret police have done their homework in the age of the internet. They must have traced all the ramifications of Dispensationalist doctrine common among several Evangelical workers at the seminary in Amman. Having explored the history of that doctrine and some of the main vocal advocates, their conclusion was not way off the mark! Yet it was not what the school wanted to be known for.

On an episode of 60 Minutes aired not long ago on CBS, the "Bible Belt in America" was presented by Rev. Falwell as "Israel's only safety belt right now."[4] The same program portrayed the zeal of a large number of Evangelical Christians for political Israel today. At the same time, Yossi Alfer, who served twelve years in Israel's intelligence agency, the Mossad, described the unrealistic stand of Christian Zionists as "leading us into a scenario of out-and-out disaster."[5]

Though Christians are free to hold any position toward Israel, they should realize that Israel today is not the theocratic nation of the Old

Testament. It is true that God may not have exhausted all the promises made to Israel, particularly the spiritual ones. Yet, God is declaring his righteousness today among the nations through the church formed of both Jewish and Gentile believers in Christ. Advice from a church historian at Dallas Seminary for those working in the Middle East was, "do not sacrifice Soteriology and Christology on the alter of Eschatology." He explained it by saying, "do not let your stand on end-time events jeopardize the primacy of sharing the Gospel message."

When the disciples asked Jesus before His ascension saying, is it now that you will return the kingdom to Israel, he replied to them, "It is not for you to know times or seasons, which the Father hath set within His own authority. But ye shall receive power, when the Holy Spirit is come upon you, and ye shall be my witnesses both in Jerusalem, and in all Judaea and Samaria, and unto the uttermost part of the earth" (Acts 1:7, 8). Jesus prioritized the Gospel mandate over any possible political program in God's decree. If only we could catch the heartbeat of Christ!

Finally, I will conclude this brain-storming paper concerning missions in the context of violence in the Middle East with three quick remarks. *Religiously* speaking, there is no way to completely avoid suffering. That area of the world has always been controversial. Rising religious fanaticism will only increase that. Having three competing monotheistic faiths in it will keep it that way for a while. Yet, it is our prayer that God's supernatural vindication of the Gospel in the Middle East will increase today as in the days of Acts. This has already started in the moving of the Holy Spirit through dreams and visions and supernatural healings among the various children of Abraham.

Culturally speaking, the church should do whatever it takes to present the Gospel free of social baggage. It is not wrong to experiment with various aspects of contextualization and subject their outcome to scrutiny inspired from Scriptures. In an effort to evangelize the lost, Paul became everything to everyone. The next few years will demonstrate the application for the Middle Eastern context.

Politically speaking, when considering the Arab-Israeli conflict, Evangelical leaders should know that through Abraham, both Jews and Arabs were blessed. The present conflict in the Middle East "reveals a crisis in interpretation of history and theology. When the Lord called Abraham, whom both sides claim to be their physical ancestor, to go to the Promised Land, the Patriarch sojourned in the land of Palestine as a foreigner, becoming a blessing to his neighbors, because his heart was set on the heavenly city engineered by God (Heb. 11:8–10). Since the Abrahamic promises are appropriated by faith in Christ only (Gal. 3:6–9; Eph. 3:6), this should create among Christians a desperate burden to refrain from political agendas and invest in the spiritual awakening predicted among both the Arabs and Jews. The same God who predicted a shining of Messiah's glory over a faithful remnant of the Jews (Isa. 60:1–3) foreordained the drawing of the faithful Arab remnant to the glory of salvation light (60:5–7). God's visitation of Jerusalem in messianic times cannot be separated from his visitation of his people among the Arabian tribes of Midian and Sheba (60:6) or the Christian worship of Ishmael's children (60:7). Removing unwarranted biases against Arabs, which neither the Bible nor history sustains, would play a healing role in the Middle East conflict. It would also create a better attitude for dialogue between the antagonists. Meanwhile, prioritizing the redemptive mandate over the political agenda harmonizes well with the heartbeat of Christ in the Middle East equation (Acts 1:7–8). Eventually, only the impartation of the Gospel can bring lasting peace among these Abrahamic cousins and in this privileged geographical area of the world."[6]

Notes

1. Bonnie's surviving husband, Gary, tells their story in a moving book published recently that is highly recommended by this writer as a modern missionary biography. See Gary Witherall and Elizabeth Cody

Newenhuyse, *Total Abandon* (Carole Stream, IL: Tyndale House Publishers, 2005).

2. For a great discussion of Middle Eastern history during the Christian Era, see Bernard Lewis, *The Middle East: A Brief History of the last 2,000 years* (New York: Touchstone, 1995).

3. A very helpful book on Islamic mindset in general, and the culture of the Middle East in particular is that of Margaret K. Nydell, *Understanding Arabs: A Guide for Westerners*, third edition (Yarmouth, MN: Intercultural Press, 2002).

4. http://www.cbsnews.com/stories/2002/10/03/60minutes/main524268.shtml.

5. Ibid.

6. See Tony Maalouf, Arabs in the Shadow of Israel: The Unfolding of God's Prophetic Plan for Ishmael's Line (Grand Rapids: Kregel, 2003), 223-24.

Chapter Nineteen

Missions in the Context of Interethnic Violence

D.M. Kinoti

The balkanization of the world has accelerated after the cold war with the rise of ethnic identification and nationalist movements. Additionally, immigration and globalization has led to international cities with immense numbers of multiethnic communities that are struggling to co-exist with each other as witnessed across the world through interethnic protests, riots and even violent conflicts (e.g. in Kaduna-Nigeria, Los Angeles, and Paris). These realities, irrespective of their causes, have become a common phenomenon in the last quarter century—and are bound to endure in the twenty-first century—with the rise in ethno-religious infractions across the world.

The study and work on ethnicity has traditionally been undertaken by anthropologists and has primarily focused on non-western and pre-industrial societies. However, current trends of a smaller interconnected global village would challenge this perspective. In addition, the church's involvement is imperative in considering the rising sense of ethnic identity—and the attendant violence along ethnic lines—in order to develop appropriate means of engagement. To do this, there ought to be a proper understanding of the anthropological and socio-psychological perspectives of ethnic identification and violence. This study is an attempt to encourage that understanding and seeks to shed some light on what ethnicity is, how it has been exploited towards inter-group conflicts, and what the church can do about it.

Working for peaceful co-existence among ethnic groups is both part of the biblical mandate of the church and a prerogative of responsible human-community belonging. It is part of the Biblical message to take the gospel to the world (Matt. 28:19–20; Acts 1:8) and a fitting rallying call for the evangelical church, to 'take the full gospel to the whole world" as articulated by the monumental 1974 Lausanne Covenant. Finally, it fits well within the focuses of this conference, of Justice, Purpose and Action. Interethnic peacemaking has to be driven by our convictions that every human being (and therefore people group) is created in God's image and so deserves to live and thrive to their full potential without the hampering injustices of sin and violence, local or global. It is therefore our duty to encourage the growth within the church of a holistic missional attitude (which includes justice); that arises from our call to love God and His people (purpose), and one that energizes us into active engagement (action), for the Kingdom of God.

The New Ethnic Realities

Historically, interethnic conflicts were more common in rural pre-industrial communities of Africa, Asia, Latin America and parts of Eastern Europe. Studies focused on these areas and rarely at the west, unless for obvious interracial confrontations (e.g. between the White and Black Americans). However, in the last two decades, one can clearly talk of equally tragic conflicts in industrialized nations among ethnic groups. Inter-group (ethnic) tensions exist today in many more parts of the world than was the case a century ago (including France, Britain and United States and other places) revealing need for work towards building cultures of peace as part of the mission of the church. This is due to increased immigration and globalization that has helped bring different people groups together, especially in the major cities across the world.

An example of this dynamic is reflected in Los Angeles, one of the world's most diverse cities and a prototype of the world in the new century. According to the 2000 US Census, Los Angeles is home to people from over 140 countries, who speak at least 224 different languages making it the city with one of the largest and most diverse populations of any municipality in the world. It hosts some of the biggest and most urbane ethnic enclaves like Chinatown, Koreatown, Little Armenia, Little Saigon, Thai Town, Historic Filipinotown, and Little Ethiopia. Los Angeles is also home to the fastest growing Hispanic and Asian American populations as well as the largest populations of Armenians, Cambodians, Filipinos, Guatemalans, Israelis, Koreans, Salvadorans, Thais, Vietnamese, Mexicans, and Hungarians outside of their respective countries. It is also home to the largest populations of Japanese and Iranians living in the U.S., and has one of the largest Native American populations in the country. There are more than fifty foreign-language newspapers published in Los Angeles and more than ninety-six languages spoken by the more than half a million non-white children in the Los Angeles Unified school district.[1]

Together with this, interethnic differences and conflicts have become part the problems facing this populous city. Los Angeles has had a restive interethnic population leading to the 1943, 1965, and 1992 riots.[2] Ethnic based gangs[3] form part of the difficulties the city has to deal with especially in poor neighborhoods. Increasing tensions in high schools arising from students of different ethnic groups are becoming a common problem. These are not estimated to reduce as the population of immigrant communities increase.

These figures and realities of Los Angeles will be replicated in the next fifty years across the globe, as globalization and immigration moves people across the world. One can already see this growing trend in most major cities of the world (e.g. London, Paris, New York, Singapore, Moscow etc), much of which was not the case fifty years ago.

These dynamics and other global churnings (e.g. the ongoing war on terror, the shifting of the center of Christianity to the southern United States and global poverty among others), all challenge our past perspectives and call us the church to re-evaluate its mission efforts. It is obvious that many perspectives (and methods) that served us well in the last century may be shorthanded to deal with these new dynamics. Relocation and engagement might be closer than was in the past, but also cultural tensions brought about by proximity of diversities are going to require new processes of missionary work.

Also, what is in the ethnic identity that makes these efforts difficult as well as necessary? That is where we turn next, to explore the phenomenon of ethnic identity and its linkages to violence.

Ethnic Identity

For the purpose of this study, an ethnic group refers to a people group, small or large, "united by a common culture (including language, music, food, dress, customs, and practices), racial similarity, common religion, and belief, in common history and ancestry and who exhibit a strong psychological sentiment of belonging to the group."[4] Ethnic identity is not a fixed entity, but is the resultant kinship and cultural relations, and the national characteristics that identify members of a particular group of people. In this respect, ethnicity engenders territorial space, language, tribal affiliation, religious faith, or cultural and traditional origins and backgrounds. Although sometimes used to represent race, ethnicity delineates a person's historical and past origins not the same way as race does. Ethnicity is defined more by the biological and morphological differences between human beings including skin color, hair types, and other outward appearances.[5]

Ethnicity is an important and necessary dynamic of the human community. Scholars recognize the fundamental and universal reality of social life as determined by human communities, especially the ethnic group. It is through the ethnic group that kinship and solidarity, two important ingredients of society's formation and expression are established and transmitted across generations. Second to the family, it is through the ethnic group that the accumulated group lores and heritage are preserved and transmitted to subsequent generations. Also, needs of interpersonal affection, affiliation, and trust are learned and nurtured first within the family but also through the community/group. The ethnic group therefore forms the basis for loyalty because it provides both the identity and ability to mediate the needs and interests of the group with those of the supra structures (e.g. nation state). It also offers the assurances for the maintenance of the particular group's uniqueness even in a process of change. In this respect, the group has a personality, the identity upon which it can articulate its being and needs.[6]

Group identity defines the basis for coexistence with others. It articulates understandings of mutuality and enmity between the group and the Other(s). In this dynamic process of selfhood, a community's conscious articulation of its identity reveals areas of co-dependence with others that assures their survival as well as that of the Other. A more positive relation between groups is towards a peaceful co-existence other than violence. However, in conflict situations, violence may appeal to the group due in part to their self-interest while acknowledging the right for Others to life, at least for the purpose of fulfilling their needs.[7] Coexistence allows for the creation of mutual arrangements between the groups that facilitate cooperation towards specific goals (e.g. trade), whereas difficulties in finding a particular position of mutuality and or intense competition can lead to breakdown in relations and even violence.

Another aspect of ethnic identity important exploring in this study is ethnocentrism. Ethnocentrism, a term coined by William Graham Sumner (1906), is the viewpoint that one's ethnic group is better than another and against which all other groups are judged. Sumner notes that ethnocentrism is the view of things in which,

> One's group is the center of everything, and all others are scaled and rated with reference to it. Folkways correspond to it to cover both the inner and the outer relation. Each group nourishes its own pride and vanity, boasts its superiority, exalts its own divinities, and looks with contempt on outsiders. Each group thinks its own folkways the right ones, and if it observes that other groups have other folkways, these excite its scorn. Opprobrious epithets are derived from these differences.[8]

Ethnocentrism forms the root to some societal ills including nepotism, tribalism, and racism. These isms can be the basis upon which other violent societal forces entrench their destructive influences like discrimination based on heritage and systems of racism, including apartheid, colonialism and violence. These encourage disparaging treatment and exploitation or the denial of privileges to outright decimation based on ethnic identity.

Clearly, recognition of ethnic (and other) differences does not necessarily amount to ethnocentristic relations. However, this is possible when these feelings are exploited to gain power or privilege over the "Other". Additionally, although ethnocentric feelings are prevalent among individuals and or groups, it is only where these are fanned, that their ubiquitous nature stands in the way of trust relationships. Group identity in itself is benign. It is indeed necessary as the basis for altruism and other positive social exchanges. Not all identity consciousness generates conflict, rather, as Weiner (1998) asserts, conflict results from "narcissistic identity whose affirmation, pursuit and defense form an integral part of the essence of nationalism".[9] Nationalism, which is the sentimental loyalty to the ethnic group, plays an important role because it provides the group an avenue for self-articulation, and a platform to agitate for their important needs within an impersonal superstructure. However, when this loyalty becomes politically motivated, and statist ideals take center stage, desire for national self-determination—the right to sovereign statehood—emerges.

Ethnic distinctions have always been part of humanity. Community life, especially in pre-industrial societies, is organized into kinship, ethnic, and tribal systems while industrial societies increasingly are stratified into economic classes. In the past, ethnicity has not been regarded in social studies as a significant source of instability and social change.[10] This in part has been due to the assumption that the overarching hegemony gives structure to the represented divisions. However, with the increasing spread of interethnic tensions, studies are shifting towards considerations of the place of ethnicity in conflicts.

Interethnic Conflicts

An intrastate (internal) conflict can be of two major types, civil or inter-group. A civil war is an armed insurrection aimed against an organized government. A civil war differs from an interethnic war primarily because of its organization, that it is rebel based and against an organized government army or police. Greed, power, and grievance directed toward a government, form the main motivations for most civil wars. Any of these types of conflicts can either be tractable (i.e. short term) or intractable (long-term) in nature.[11]

Most categorization of wars avoided the term 'ethnic conflict' until recently due to the connotation of ethnicity as primitive and pre-modern. Value neutral language was employed (e.g. civil strife), which in most cases masked the realities of these conflicts, that they pitted ethnic groups against each other, or that they had certain characteristics towards identity.[12] An interethnic conflict has come to mean cleavages between groups based on differentiations in ethnic identities. The animosity is directed against another group, presumed to be different and may be for different causes. Ethnic conflict is a usually about "political, social, cultural or territorial issues between two or more ethnic communities."[13] The groups may or may not have outside support from the central government or otherwise. However, this distinction is complicated in situations where the government favors a particular ethnic group against another.

Researchers of the working group on the causes of war of the University of Hamburg counted, for the period between 1945 and 2000, more than 194 wars. Ninety percent of these occurred in developing countries. According to the Uppsala Conflict Data Project[14] there were fifty-eight armed conflicts in the world, from 1989 to 2002, a fourteen-year period. Ethnic related conflicts constituted a considerable number of these, with the following regional distribution: Africa (19), America (5), Asia (17), Europe (8), and Middle East (9). In addition, the 2004 yearbook of the Stockholm International Peace Research Institute (SIPRI 2004), records nineteen major armed conflicts in eighteen locations worldwide for the year 2003. This was the lowest number for the post-cold war period with the exception of 1997, when eighteen such conflicts were registered. Only two of the nineteen conflicts were interstate (international) in nature: the conflict in Iraq and the long-standing conflict between India and Pakistan over Kashmir. The rest were primarily intrastate conflicts. Four of the nineteen conflicts were in Africa and eight in Asia. Currently, there are about 115 ongoing-armed conflicts in the world.[15]

Ferron and Lattin (2003) note that since 1945, about 16.2 million people have died in about 122 internal conflicts spread across seventy-three countries compared with 3.3 million deaths in twenty-five conventional interstate wars. As part of their research, they found out that the number of civil conflicts has increased over time because they break out faster than they end. On average, 2.3 wars have begun annually, while 1.7 conflicts have been resolved each year. Additionally, internal conflicts last six years on average and bring about widespread refugee dislocation and economic devastation, as seen in Afghanistan, Somalia, and Lebanon. However, despite their prevalence and harm, more studies have focused on interstate (international) other than intrastate (internal) conflicts.

Related to both civil and interethnic conflicts are the heinous acts of genocide, defined as any act directed at the killing or decimation, in part or whole of a particular group of people, ethnic, national, racial, or religious.[16] Genocide is a crime that is part of the broader category of the international law under crimes against humanity, as defined by the Charter of the International Military Tribunal (also referred to as the Nürnberg Charter).[17]

These statistics point to a definite increase over the years in the number of interethnic conflicts in the world, not to mention the abounding racial tensions in the cities. Recent studies of notable situations include Ethiopia, Bosnia, Georgia (Abkhazia), Indonesia (East Timor), Lebanon, Rwanda, Russia (Chechnya), and Northern Ireland.[18] These and the ongoing city-neighborhood studies are shedding light into the needs that plague our world.

Causes of Interethnic Conflicts

It is clear that violence is learned, and not at all a biological characteristic. In 1986, UNESCO commissioned a study to determine whether conflict was biological, hence, primordially determined. The study group published the Seville Statement on violence that contributed a profound impetus to the movement towards redefining the causes for war and violence. The study sought to dispel the myth that war is intrinsic to human nature and challenge inaction based on inconclusive evolutionary science that promoted violent instincts, heritage, dominance, and claims of the "violent brain" theory as justification for war and violence. The resulting widely distributed document argued that warfare is a product of culture. It also clarified that although there may be biological causes to violent behavior, these are not determinative; on the contrary, the learning is within a human community.[19]

Interethnic conflicts are a tremendous threat to society especially due to the seeds of hatred that they sow, which might lead to other related conflicts. Apart from this, most violent people target the weak (e.g. unarmed women and children) and anyone identified with the other community, young or old. The great cruelty of ethnic conflict is that everyone is automatically labeled a combatant—by the identity they possess—even if they are not involved in the conflict. Entrenched hatred among the groups fuels the desire to decimate the other, leading to escalation.

Identity as a Cause for Conflict?

Does ethnicity or ethnic identification lead to conflicts? When do people result to their ethnic identities and for what benefits? These are important questions as we seek to understand the relations between ethnicity and conflicts. Not all people seek ethnic alliances and not all ethnic groups are involved in some form of animosity with their neighbors. Although we can distinguish persons with common nationality, religion, race, or some other ethnic characteristic (say in a census), those categories do not necessarily constitute a cohesive group, one that acts to defend what their members would consider common interests. Our interest in this part is how ethnic identity contributes to conflict.[20]

It is necessary to reflect on the place of identity in respect to inter-group conflicts due in part to the compelling hold the sense of belonging has on most people, but also, as indicated earlier, because of the growing number of inter-ethnic conflicts. Social psychology has sought to define group "as two or more people that are socially or psychologically interdependent: for the satisfaction of needs, attainment of goals or consensual validation of attitudes and values."[21] This interaction leads to cooperative social interaction and influence on each other. The individual develops loyalty to a group with which s/he identifies, usually by birth. Group norms and structure, most of which are developed instinctively, mediate the process of interaction with possibilities for cohesion. The benefits derived from the cohesion strengthen the attraction and further interdependence of the members. Other strengthening bonds include direct or indirect property ownership (e.g. land) by the members of the group. However, group-belongingness has a deeper, affective basis, that of psychological and familial attachment that distinguishes them from others. This is what is referred to as social identity, which is that "part of the individuals' self-concept which derives from their knowledge of their membership of a social group (or groups) together with the value and emotional significance attached to that membership."[22]

It is important to note that, most ethnic groups, most of the time, pursue their interests peacefully within the established economic and political channels. However, groups turn to conflict to achieve their goals or depending on the situation, in defense against attacks by another group. This often results in violence. Some of the causes of inter-ethnic conflicts include competition for scarce resources, ideological differences, fear of each other, and ancient hatreds. A particular conflict may result from one, or a combination, of these. Therefore, in themselves, ethnic groups do not necessarily result to hatred and violence with others, unless there are other mitigating factors including politics, religion, and competition for resources. That is where we turn next, to consider the role of these three in interethnic conflicts.

The Principle of Multi-Causality

Most conflicts are mixed-motive situations in which involved parties are both cooperative and competitive. Although there are discernable global causal factors, inter-group conflicts differ in terms of their origin and magnitude. There are, however, similarities in the reasons advanced by the parties for the origins and perpetuation of certain wars. Some are explicit (e.g. resources or boundary issues), while others are salient (e.g. identity or symbolic issues). Conflicts are, therefore, a result of a multiplicity of causes and rarely sparked off by one aspect. It is important to underscore that not all multi-ethnic, or multi-religious societies, experience violence. Even situations of economic or political change and resource scarcity do not necessarily degrade into violence.

The politicization of ethnic identity and cultural identification as a means to access resources (materials, power, status, etc) is the main cause of interethnic conflicts. Legitimating identity politics weakens integration and may instigate violence along cultural lines, especially where there are no adequate means of redress for those who perceive discrimination. These do not act in isolation, but in conjunction with others, and particular to the situation. A 'trigger' event (e.g. killing of an ethnic group member by the police) exacerbates certain situations to violence. Ethnically diverse communities that contain more than one of these causes are more likely to deteriorate into full-blown conflict faster in the case of a trigger event. It is therefore more appropriate to discuss the phenomenon of multi-causality—the idea that there are several causes acting together at different times towards violence.

It is clear from the literature available—both theoretical and case studies—that the causes of ethnic conflicts are not easy to discern in distinct categories. This might be due in part to the insidious nature of conflict, that it usually is loaded with more baggage than is easy to decipher. It is also because different causes act together at different times to exacerbate an incident making it difficult to determine the particular cause. In most cases, the issues at stake—including who stands to lose what—and the duration of the tension determine possibilities of resolution. Additionally, no two wars are the same due in part to the differences in the parties involved, and the issues and the methods employed in carrying out the conflict, among other differences.

In this respect, Crawford (2000) proposes the need to evaluate the effects of economics and social-political changes on a community's social contracts, in relation to the sustenance of peace. She argues that the maintenance of social contracts in any situation is through cultural institutions, which ensure the allocation of political and economic power. The observation and strengthening of these structures help maintain mutual non-competitive relations within, and between, groups. On the other hand, "cultural conflict escalates into violence when these institutions are weakened, disrupted, or transformed in ways that undermine the commitment to uphold these contracts or repress dissent." Her theory is that any forces that either interrupt or destroy these traditionally set processes, also upset the commitment to their maintenance and propagation hence creating an imbalance of power within the community, and can lead to conflict within that group or with others. Further, Crawford argues that historically, several global dynamics have had this unsettling effect in the world but the current economic globalization trend has done so in an unprecedented way. She contends that,

> Although there are many forces which undermine that commitment, globalization and economic liberalization are two of the most important current culprits. When the forces of globalization and the impersonal market have usurped control from domestic institutions and when those institutions can no longer credibly enforce agreements that ensured peaceful competition among politically relevant cultural groups, or when they can no longer enforce culturally discriminating policies, violence may be the only alternative course for political entrepreneurs making nonnegotiable resource demands on behalf of distinct cultural groups.[23]

Most of these societies are ideally in transition, not fully market economies and no longer traditional. The ambivalence created by such processes has its effects on established social structures. A dynamic economic and political change not only affects the overarching social structures but also social relations. Additionally, the embrace of the "outside" models of culture leads to unsettling established structures in ways that are not contingent with the familiarity of the local social orders.

Religious beliefs may not be a primary contributor to the conflict, but can be an added layer of contradiction in an already explosive situation. The fact that there are societies where communities espousing different beliefs live harmoniously side-by-side, support this position. Different beliefs, although distinct from each other, do not by themselves, lead to conflict. Their application and abuse spur disharmony. Adherents may be sincere and with no ulterior motives for hatred towards another when accessing certain beliefs. However, the differences can be fanned. This is especially the case in situations where religious association preceded the conflict. Religious convictions actually help members of a group identify with a super-ordinate goal in which case differences between them and other people are cast aside. Hence, irrespective of the other differences, religion becomes a basis for unity.[24]

Politicization of religious movements or the religious beliefs is part of the mix that causes interethnic conflict. This is possible, given the emotional attachments that are part of any religious belief system. In other related situations, the transformation of religious beliefs into the dominant political systems leads to the disfranchisement of the non-adherents, and can result into conflicts. In modern day terms, there are few democratic societies with ethno-religious and political tensions as pronounced as in the case of India. India has allowed, under its constitution, protection of religious rights. It has also allowed formation of political parties along religious lines such that overtly religious language and symbols are part of the political interpretation of the national life. This has not been without great unease between the different religious communities, as successive governments seek to establish their identity and enhance certain policies, some of which favor their religious convictions. Examples include the immediate former governments of Bharatiya Janata Party (BJP), a primarily Hindu party, which tried to cast India as a Hindu democracy. The party was inspired into power due in part to revivalist Muslim and Christian involvements in government. Hardgrave asserts, "Since the early 1980s, the rise of Muslim fundamentalism in India has spurred a heightened Hindu consciousness and led Hindu nationalists to project India's eighty-three percent Hindu majority as threatened."[25] This has resulted in numerous run-ins that have killed thousands of people on both sides, and caused untold suffering to others.

At the heart of most ethnic conflicts is deep discontent arising from historical actual or perceived political, social, and economic realities.

In the case of Africa, prevalence of war "is not due to the ethno-linguistic fragmentation of its countries, but rather to high levels of poverty, failed political institutions, and economic dependence on natural resources."[26] This is true of other continents where many wars, including struggles for ethno-national self-determination, are fought to change the power-property status quo. Ultimately, conflicts are about grievances, resolvable or not. Each side advances certain claims that they consider strong enough for which to fight. These may be genuine or false, but one's convictions count most in determining engagement. Hence, at the heart of every conflict is the process of enemy versus victim creation. The process might start with competing, to disagreement, to demonization of the other, and later to declaring of enmity. In spite of the causes, if this process is curtailed, the chances of a conflict are enormously reduced. Conflict is easy where fear, hatred, and distancing of them become entrenched. However, as the Secretary General of the United Nations notes, "fear of the 'other' is so widespread and ferocious that we may be tempted to think of it as an immutable attribute of the human animal. But people are not hard-wired for prejudice. In some cases, hatred is taught. In others, people are manipulated into it, by leaders who exploit fear, ignorance or feelings of weakness."[27]

Finally, it is important to note that although one can easily delineate possible causes of conflict in academic discourse, in actual conflict situations these are less discernable in clear categories. Additionally, these causes feed on each other as well as encourage the entrenchment of deeper justifications for engagements. Efforts for transformation (or resolution) of particular situations of conflict therefore need to engage the holistic picture, rather than the obvious. Strong ethnic/religious identification among mass supporters of violence is often an outcome of war rather than a precondition or cause. However, once violence emerges, individuals have to pick sides and often retreat to basic ethnic and religious groups as a means of protecting their physical, cultural, and economic security. In this way, the cycle is repeated, of choice and identity leading to the conclusion that wars may be caused by differing identities, but also wars "harden" identities.

Building Peace as Part of the Gospel

A monumental survey by University of California, Los Angeles carried out in 2001 interviewed an adult multiethnic sample of 866 respondents from Los Angeles County on race relations. This study found out that over sixty percent of the population believed that the Church was a more trustworthy institution—up against schools, governments, or businesses—to deal with interethnic conflicts and encourage understanding among groups (see Appendix A).[28] This is a profound sense of trust that people have on the church—even though most churches are divided along ethnic lines and are often not involved in issues of peacemaking. It is also unsettling to see the amount of effort the church has put into this, given this high expectation by the community. Is it a lack of understanding of the need, or avoidance, on the part of the church, or misplaced expectations by the people?

The foundational message of the Christian Gospel is love. God is love (I John 4:8, 16) and in His love he seeks to redeem a lost world through his son Jesus Christ (John 1:12, 3:16; Gal. 3:13–14). Jesus calls his disciples to love God as well as exercise love among themselves and toward others (Matt. 22: 37, Mark 9:50, John 13:33–35). Additionally, the disciples have a task to reconcile the world with God and with others (Matt. 28:18-20, I Cor. 5:17–21).

Spurred by this understanding, evangelical mission agencies have been about the conversion and discipleship of persons across the world. The preaching of the Gospel has been directed towards unshackling the chains of sin and setting persons free to their full potential as children of God. However, this has tended to focus more on personal transformation, the salvation of the individual, and less on the transformation of structures of power that lead to broken relationships. This is especially true in the engagement of peace, justice, and violence. There is a salient hope that the individual person will engage others in love and pursue peace. This against a divided community, lack of adequate training and historical non-engagement, does not help the situation.

The people's expectations are not misplaced, seeing they live in divided societies, and other institutions of trust either have disappointed them or have little capacity for such efforts. They also know the above mission of the church, and see it as the main hope against hatred and injustice. With this, the Church cannot avoid involvement, as these are its members, or its targeted mission field. The Lausanne committee on world evangelization captured this through their missional covenant in 1974 by asserting the need for the church to be involved in socia l responsibility.[29] They described the need to do so as part of the holistic Christian duty that recognizes social involvement as part of the mission of the Church. However, the translation of this commitment into realistic involvement has been slow at best. Part of it has been both theological and practical in nature. Hence, describing what constitutes holistic mission is still debatable. Also, there is fear that the church's involvement in these programs will lead to a loss of focus on the essentials, soul winning.

These theological differences and practice seep deeper into issues of peace, justice, and love for enemies, which are key ingredients to healthy coexistence between peoples, and which are strong New Testament teachings. Indeed, in many contexts the church cannot claim to be either indifferent to violence or a proponent for peace (e.g. Nazi Germany and current day war on terror). Hence, as Hays concludes, "On the question of violence, the church is deeply compromised and committed to nationalism, violence and idolatry"[30] This historical anomaly against the overwhelming evidence of Jesus' nonviolent teachings and ways, have compromised the position of the church as a player in peacemaking. This misnomer does not however abrogate scripture, which is rich in God desiring peace and righteousness for the world (Amos 3). It challenges those of us who follow Christ and His call, to explore our motives for involvement in the world, and how our actions and inactions continue to aid violence both locally and globally.

Undoubtedly, many churches are constituted along ethnic lines. Language and ethnic identity are two of the key identifiers for this phenomenon. This is true in both cities as well as rural communities across the world. Whether this is due to the mission methods of the church in the last century, or the affinity of similarity as espoused by the church growth movement, is debatable. What is clear is that this arrangement has not helped reduce animosity between ethnic groups, due in part to the alienation between groups.[31]

Even with this, the Church has the capacity to encourage the emergence of a new community based on love and concern for each other. If this capacity was harnessed, it can become energetically involved in the processes of peacebuilding, the ethos that engenders its character of love and testifies to the transformation by grace. This is a community with a more binding identity than a cultural one, not subject to the divisions along racial or ethnic lines. This is a community of God, a community of peace based on their faith in God. It is a strong tool to encourage nonviolence and the development of cultures of peace. This is clearly part of the Scriptures, and well within their means. The church has immense credibility within communities that many institutions do not have, and which, if adequately used, would immensely help towards peace.

It is instructive to note that when the church has stood up against violence and injustice, there has been positive change. Examples of this include engagements in the anti-slavery and civil rights movements. Both of these largely began with, and got their momentum from, the church.[32] Therefore, what is lacking in the Christian community is the faith to embrace the New Testament teachings as tenets by which to live. These tenets shape our lives towards active engagement rather than abstract and unachievable ideals. In his book *Just Peacemaking,* Glen Stassen (1992) explores the basis for active Christian engagement in nonviolence that goes beyond simplistic acceptance. He treats Jesus' teachings as high ideals, but evades true obedience. He argues that these teachings are meant to transform how we live our lives in relation to loving God and others. He also opposes passivity because it undermines the true meaning of Christ's intentions and instead proposes active initiatives aimed at encouraging justice and peace through nonviolent means.[33]

Hays (1996), also attacks this complacency born out of misplaced rationality and the often relied upon Christian tradition. He believes that the reliance on the just war theory, which has proven inadequate and broadly non-biblical, has led to the current support of violence and/or inaction among Christians. He categorically points out that the New Testament does not offer any justifications for Christians' involvement in war. Hence, it is not a question of a just or unjust war, but one of following scripture, which is clear towards nonviolence.[34]

Churches have a responsibility to encourage interethnic dialogue that is well-planned and multilayered. Traditionally, churches have focused on relationship building. However, this is only a first step towards building healthy and peaceful communities. Of necessity, it is to provide informed involvement on the institutional and global levels that include building empathy, advocacy, and positive reform of the structures of injustice and sin that lead to broken relationships. The church ought not to focus only at individual responsibility, although this is important, but also on institutional and governmental failures that brood dissatisfaction and encourage hatred. This calls their members to active involvement in cultures other than their own. Additionally, the church ought to explore creative means for exposing people to different cultures. By encouraging the building of positive relations between people across cultures, the church will help break down pervasive stereotypes that continue to feed the interethnic malaise.

Churches can be strong advocates to the governments and other policy bearing bodies to promote a culture of peace and understanding among people groups. This would include challenging these institutions to allocate more funds and efforts towards nonviolent studies and implementation across the world. The more these methods and the debunking of the culture of violence are actively pursued, the more likely these will be entrenched as a more positive way of life. The church, being a responsible member of society, cannot divorce itself from the issues facing its members and remain relevant. Hence, the church, out of necessity, must become a platform for engagement both locally and internationally.

The Church also would also be an agency for change by collaborating with individuals and organizations working in the areas of building peace. In recognition of the strengths of these other bodies, it allows the church to focus on its key competences (including evangelization). The church's input into these processes is crucial, since it introduces the faith element into the dialogue, which is ultimately important.

Conclusion

The ministry of peacebuilding has never been more needed and urgent in the world as it is today. Rising ethno-religious tensions are a common occurrence in the world over. With increased immigration, more communities that would not have had opportunities to be close to each other are finding themselves nested in the same neighborhoods. Additionally, whatever happens in one part of the world reverberates across the globe, because of the interconnectedness of the world today than half a century ago. No one society is unaffected. Given current global developments, these realities will be with us for a long time.

It is clear that the erroneous re-casting of the September 2001 attacks on USA and the follow-up wars in Afghanistan and Iraq into quasi-religious conflicts, have added to these tensions in ways that affect the church in many parts of the world. While our missional call remains the same, to make disciples among all people groups (Matt. 28:19), we have to reconstitute our methods and attitudes to be relevant. Doing this in the area of interethnic relations is clearly necessary. Many people see the church as a trustworthy player in this. Those of us in the church and those carrying out the call of Christ across the world ought to seize this opportunity.

Appendix A: Institutions That Help Reduce Ethnic Conflict

	White	Hispanic	Black
Most intergroup conflict is unnecessary (% "agree")	82%	88%	87%
% "Improve" relations between groups – % "worsen" relations:			
Churches	+67	+68	+63
Public schools	+40	+49	+24
Local government	+18	+39	+9
Private business	+18	+23	+1

Source: David O. Sears, "Assessment of Interracial/Interethnic Conflict in Los Angeles" (March 12, 2002). Center for Research in Society and Politics. Paper 1-2002. pdf. Available online at http://repositories.cdlib.org/crisp/1-2002. Accessed on Feb. 11, 2006

Notes

1. Discussions on the ethnic growth of Los Angeles and its impact is an ongoing discussion among many scholars including Marks, A. Mara., 2000, *Los Angeles at the 21ˢᵗ Century: An Assessment of Race and Human Relations*. The City of Los Angeles, official website available online at www.lacity.org, and the City of Los Angeles Human relations Commission, Available online at http://www.lacity.org/hra/pdf/ hrafin1.pdf. pg 18, Accessed Feb. 07, 2006; See also Gottlieb, Robert. 2005. *The Next Los Angeles: The struggle for a livable city*. University of California Press); William Fulton, Jennifer Wolch, Antonio Villaraigosa, Susan Weaver. (2003) *After Sprawl: Action Plans for Metropolitan Los Angeles*. CA: USC-Southern California Studies Center and Zena, Pearlstone, (1990) *Ethnic L.A.* Los Angeles: Hillcrest

Press. For complete figures on ethnic groups in Los Angeles and California, and the 2000 US Census website available online at http://quickfacts.census.gov/qfd/states/06/0644000.html.

2. These riots had different causes but all had an ethnic slant to them. For more information on the riots, see Almaguer, Tomas, 1994, *Racial Fault lines: The Historical Origins of White Supremacy in California.* Los Angeles: University of California Press, and Jiobu, Robert M. (1988). *Ethnicity and assimilation.* (Albany: State University of New York Press).

3. According to a research carried out by Alejadro Alfonso— (http://www.streetgangs.com/)—in 1996, there were over 150, 000gang members in Los Angeles, most within over 600 groups formed along ethnic lines. The main ones were along African-American, Hispanic and Asian gangs.

4. Taras & Ganguly, 1998: 9.

5. Ethnic identity and ethnicity are difficult concepts to define exhaustively. Different Social Scientists posit different distinctions for both. Some argue that the definition should not be based on overt features (i.e. observable traits of language, culture and common ancestry), rather ethnicity is a 'reference group that individuals may choose to invoke, ignore' depending on their situation. Others argue for a composite meaning, that includes the observable aspects and the subjective identification by the member. See Royce, Anya P., (1982) *Ethnic Identity: Strategies of Diversity,* (Bloomington, Indiana: Indiana University Press), pp. 20–28: Others argue that we need to look at the positive social functions that the identification performs (i.e. the achievement of a positive social identity in relation to an out group). See Tajfel, Henri (1978) *The Social Psychology of Minorities.* Minority Rights Group.

6. Royce, Anya P., (1982) *Ethnic Identity: Strategies of Diversity.* (Bloomington, Indiana: University of Indiana Press), pg. 2.

7. Weiner. 1998:15.

8. Sumner, 1906, pp. 12–13.

9. Weiner, Eugene (ed), *The Handbook of interethnic coexistence.* New York: The Continuum Publishing Co. 1998), pg. 65.

10. De Vos and Romanucci-Ross, 1995:12.

11. Wiberg and Scherrer (1999) use the Institute for Political Science, University of Hamburg, Arbeitsgemeinschaft Kriegsursachenforschung (AKUF) description.

12. Wiberg, Håkan, and Christian P. Scherrer. (eds) *Ethnicity and Intra-State Conflict.* (Aldershot, Hants, England: Brookfield Vt. USA, 1999). Pg 63.

13. Brown 1993: 5.

14. AKUF - Eriksson 2004:625-636.

15. A detailed and updated database for global occurrences of conflict is available from the Uppsala Conflict data Program website, http://www.pcr.uu.se/database/index.php, (Accessed January 20, 2006).

16. UN, *"Convention on the Prevention and Punishment of the Crime of Genocide"* OHCHR-UNOG Available online http://www.unhchr.ch/html/menu3/b/p_genoci.htm, [Accessed Feb. 05, 2006].

17. "Nürnberg trials" Encyclopedia Britannica from Encyclopedia Britannica Online. Available at <http://www.search.eb.com/eb/article?tocId=9056532>, [Accessed Jan 16, 2006].

18. In recent years, some people-groups have sought nationalistic self-hood, but also interethnic conflicts have received increased media coverage after the cold war. For discussions on the emergent phenomenon of ethnic conflicts and their spread, see Lake, David A. and Rothchild, Donald S. (eds.) *International spread of ethnic conflict: Fear, diffusion, and escalation.* Princeton, (N.J.: Princeton University Press. 1998), pp 3–32; Also Crawford, Beverly and Ronnie D. Lipschutz Ed. *The myth of ethnic conflict: Politics, Economics, and "Cultural" Violence.* (Berkeley: University of California Press. 1997). pp 3–42; Also Cairns and Roe, 2003.

19. Experts in various fields—Biology, medicine, psychology, sociology, chemists, etc—issued this 1986-draft statement drawn in the city of Seville, France after concerted studies and opinions. UNESCO adopted the Statement in 1989 and the findings have been published in journals around the world. The statement has received widespread support by many professional organizations including the American Psychological Association, which has encouraged research in this area. See the document posting at www.unesco.org/cpp/uk/declarations/seville.pdf [Accessed online Feb. 9, 06].

20. William Petersen, ed., *The Background to Ethnic Conflict* (Leiden: E. J. Brill, 1979). Pg 11.

21. See Turner's discussions in Tajfel, (1982) (ed.), *Social Identity and Intergroup Relations.* Pg 15.

22. Ibid pp 15ff. Social Psychology has devoted efforts to understand both the cognitive and social dimensions of the individual and their relationships with the group and other groups (see Weiner, The Handbook of Interethnic Coexistence). Models of personal identity

against social identification and cohesion abound. They try to delineate group influences from individual behavior and identity that is personally determined and or the socially conditioned. They also explore reasons for group formation, cognitive association and inter-group relations. Most agree that individuals have capacity for personal determination and cognitive action, but are also products of the group ethos and practices through the processes of socialization and attribution. See also Jocelyn Linneken and Lin Poyer (eds), *Cultural Identity In The Pacific*, (Honolulu, Hawaii: University of Hawaii Press, 1990).

23. Crawford, The myth of ethnic conflict, pg 6.
24. See Marty, M. E and Appleby, R. S. (eds), *Religion, Ethnicity and Self-identity*, (Hanover: New England, University Press of New England. 1997). Pp 53–88.
25. Hardgrave, Robert L., (1993) *India: Government & Politics in a Developing Nation.* (Harcourt Brace Jovanovich College Publishers) pg. 83.
26. Ibrahim A. Elbadawi and Nicholas Sambanis, 2000, "Why Are There So Many Civil Wars in Africa? Understanding and Preventing Violent Conflict" World Bank Working Paper.
27. Kofi Annan, Address to the United Nations Department of Public Information (DPI) seminar, "Confronting Islamophobia: Education for Tolerance and Understanding", New York, 7 December 2004 - UN Chronicle online edition, Available at http://www.un.org/Pubs/chronicle/2004/webArticles/112204_Conference.asp. [Accessed 12-Jan-06].
28. Sears, David O., "Assessment of Interracial/Interethnic Conflict in Los Angeles" (March 12, 2002). *Center for Research in Society and Politics.* Paper 1-2002. http://repositories.cdlib.org/crisp/1-2002. pdf. pg 12, figure 6. [Accessed Feb. 11, 2006].
29. It is monumental that this key Evangelical community chose to repent for their inaction towards their social responsibility. However, I would argue that little has changed in the engagement of the church in certain areas of their social responsibility, especially interethnic peace and conflict resolution. For the full document, see online at, http://www.lausanne.org/Brix?pageID=12891 [Accessed Feb 20, 2006].
30. Richard Hays, Moral Vision of the New Testament. pg 343.
31. The Church growth movement as espoused by many missiologists in the 1970s and 80s including Donald McGavran proposed that churches grow along homogenous communities (including status and ethnic groups). This thesis might be true when considering numerical other

than holistic discipleship growth. Additionally it complicates efforts to deal with relational issues including interethnic relations if we can only deal with people like us. For example, in most sub-Saharan Africa, denominations (and mission agencies), established along tribal lines as a way to avoid conflicts among themselves. However, these only served to amplify existing divisions among the tribal communities. Hence, certain communities became Methodist or Presbyterian, or other. This identity became synonymous with their tribal identity. Even though they may not fight for being a certain denomination, this added another layer entrenching other than erasing their divisions.

32. Other notable movements where the church has been actively involved include the Anti-Nuclear proliferation and the Jubilee /debt forgiveness movements.

33. Stassen, Glen, 1992. Just Peacemaking: Transforming Initiatives for Justice and Peace, Louisville KY: John Knox Press.

34. Richard Hays, 1996, Moral Vision of the New Testament, pg. 342.

Bibliography

Almaguer, Tomas, (1994), *Racial Fault lines: The Historical Origins of White Supremacy in California.* Los Angeles: University of California Press.

Augsburger, David, (1992). *Conflict Resolution Across Cultures: Pathways and Patterns.* Louisville, Kentucky: Westminster/John Knox Press.

Brown, Michael E. (ed), (1993) *Ethnic conflict and international Security.* Princeton: Princeton University Press.

Collier, Paul, (2001) *Implications of Ethnic Diversity.* Retrieved from www. http://econ.worldbank.org/wbsite/external/extdec/extresearch/extpr ograms/extconflict/0,,menupk:477968~pagepk:64210511~pipk:64 210513~thesitepk:477960,00.html (pdf document).

Crawford, Beverly and Ronnie D. Lipschutz Ed. (1997) *The myth of ethnic conflict: Politics, Economics, and "Cultural" Violence.* (Berkeley: University of California Press.

Fearon, James D. and David D. Laitin, "Ethnicity, Insurgency, and Civil War", *American Political Science Review vol.* 97, 1 (March 2003): 75-90.

Fulton, William, Jennifer Wolch, Antonio Villaraigosa, Susan Weaver. (2003) *After Sprawl: Action Plans for Metropolitan Los Angeles.* CA: USC-Southern California Studies Center.

Gilliam Jr., Franklin D., "The Politics of Cultural Diversity: Racial and Ethnic Mass Attitudes in California" (June 1, 1988). *Institute for Social Science Research. Volume IV. 1988-89 - Conference on Comparative Ethnicity: The Conference Papers, June 1988.* Paper 14. Retrieved on Feb. 22, 2006 from http://repositories.cdlib.org/ issr/volume4/14.

Gottlieb, Robert. (2005). *The Next Los Angeles: The Struggle for a Livable City.* CA: University of California Press.

Hardgrave, Robert L., (1993) *India: Government & Politics in a Developing Nation.* Harcourt Brace Jovanovich College Publishers.

Hays, Richard B., (1996), *The Moral Vision of the New Testament: a Contemporary Introduction to the New Testament Ethics*, New York, NY: HarperCollins Publishers.

Ibrahim A. Elbadawi and Nicholas Sambanis, (2000) "Why Are There So Many Civil Wars in Africa? Understanding and Preventing Violent Conflict" World Bank Working Paper.

Jiobu, Robert M. (1988). *Ethnicity and Assimilation.* Albany: State University of New York Press.

Lederach John P., (1997) *Building Peace: Sustainable Reconciliation in Divided Societies*, Washington DC: United States Institute of Peace Press.

————, (1998) *Preparing for Peace: Conflict Transformation Across Cultures.* New York, NY: Syracuse University Press.

Linneken, Jocelyn and Poyer, Lin (eds), (1990). *Cultural Identity in the Pacific*, Honolulu, Hawaii: University of Hawaii Press.

Lausanne Covenant (1974) available online at http://www.lausanne.org/Brix?pageID=12891. [Accessed on Feb. 20, 2006].

Marks, A. Mara., (2000) *Los Angeles at the 21ˢᵗ Century: An Assessment of Race and Human Relations.*

Marty, M. E and Appleby, R. S. (eds), (1997) *Religion, Ethnicity and Self-identity*, (Hanover: New England, University Press of New England.

Lake, David A. and Rothchild, Donald S. (eds.) (1998) *International spread of ethnic conflict: Fear, diffusion, and escalation.* Princeton, (N.J.: Princeton University Press.

NA. Conflict Dataset, Available online at the Uppsala Conflict data Program website, http://www.pcr.uu.se/database/index.php, [Accessed January 20, 2006].

NA. "Nürnberg trials" Encyclopedia Britannica from Encyclopedia Britannica Online. Available at <http://www.search.eb.com/eb/article?tocId=9056532>, [Accessed Feb. 16, 2006].

NA. UN, "*Convention on the Prevention and Punishment of the Crime of Genocide*" OHCHR-UNOG Available online http://www.unhchr.ch/html/menu3/b/p_genoci.htm, [Accessed Feb 05, 2006].

Petersen, William. (1979). *The Background of Ethnic Conflict*, International studies in Sociology and Social Anthropology ; v. 28;. Leiden: E.J. Brill.

Romanucci-Ross, Lola, and George A. De Vos. (1995). *Ethnic identity : creation, conflict, and accommodation*. 3rd ed. Walnut Creek, CA: AltaMira Press.

Royce, Anya P., (1982) *Ethnic Identity: Strategies of Diversity.* Bloomington, Indiana: Indiana University Press.

Sears, David O., "Assessment of Interracial/Interethnic Conflict in Los Angeles" (March 12, 2002). *Center for Research in Society and Politics.* Paper 1-2002. <http://repositories.cdlib.org/crisp/1-2002>.

Stassen, Glen, (1992). *Just Peacemaking: Transforming Initiatives for Justice and Peace*, Louisville KY: John Knox Press.

Sumner, W. G. (1906) *Folkways: A study of the sociological importance of usages, manners, customs, mores, and morals.* Boston: Ginn.

Tajfel, Henri (1978) *The Social Psychology of Minorities.* Minority Rights Group.

——, (1982) *Social Identity and Intergroup Relations.* Cambridge: UK, Cambridge University Press.

Taras, Raymond and Ganguly, Rajat. (1998) *Understanding Ethnic Conflict: The International Dimension.* New York: Longman Press.

The City of Los Angeles, official website available online at www.lacity.org

The 2000 US Census website available online at <http://quickfacts.census.gov>.

Weiner, Eugene (ed), (1998) *The Handbook of interethnic coexistence.* New York: The Continuum Publishing Co.

Wiberg, Håkan, and Christian P. Scherrer. (eds) *Ethnicity and Intra-State Conflict.* (Aldershot, Hants, England: Brookfield Vt. USA, 1999).

Zena, Pearlstone, (1990) Ethnic L.A. Los Angeles: Hillcrest Press.